John M. Wood

DESKTOP MAGIC

Electronic Publishing, Document Management, and Workgroups

A Solomon Press Book

VAN NOSTRAND REINHOLD
I(T)P™ A Division of International Thomson Publishing Inc.

New York • Albany • Bonn • Boston • Detroit • London • Madrid • Melbourne
Mexico City • Paris • San Francisco • Singapore • Tokyo • Toronto

Copyright © 1995 by Van Nostrand Reinhold
A division of International Thomson Publishing Inc.
ITP™ The ITP logo is a trademark under license

Printed in the United States of America

For more information, contact:

Van Nostrand Reinhold
115 Fifth Avenue
New York, NY 10003

International Thomson Publishing GmbH
Königawinterer Strasse 418
53227 Bonn
Germany

International Thomson Publishing Europe
Berkshire House 168–173
High Holborn
London WC1V 7AA
England

International Thomson Publishing Asia
221 Henderson Road #05–10
Henderson Building
Singapore 0315

Thomas Nelson Australia
102 Dodds Street
South Melbourne, 3205
Victoria, Australia

International Thomson Publishing Japan
Hirakawacho Kyowa Building, 3F
2-2-1 Hirakawacho
Chiyoda-ku, 102 Tokyo
Japan

Nelson Canada
1120 Birchmount Road
Scarborough, Ontario
Canada M1K 5G4

International Thomson Editores
Campos Eliseos 385, Piso 7
Col. Polenco
11560 Mexico D.F. Mexico

All rights reserved. No part of this work covered by the copyright hereon may be reproduced or used in any form or by any means—graphic, electronic, or mechanical, including photocopying, recording, taping, or information storage and retrieval systems—without the written permission of the publisher.

1 2 3 4 5 6 7 8 9 10 QUEFF 01 00 99 98 97 96 95 94

Library of Congress Cataloging-in-Publication Data

Wood, John M., 1945–
   Desktop magic: electronic publishing, document management, and work groups / John. M. Wood.
      p.   cm.
   "A Solomon Press book."
   Includes bibliographical references and index.
   ISBN 0-442-01772-3
   1. Desktop publishing—United States. 2. Records—United States—Management—Data processing. I. Title.
   Z253.5.W66 1994
   686.2'2544536—dc20
                                            94-36141
                                              CIP

COVER ILLUSTRATION CREDITS, left TO right
TOP   1. Silicon Graphics, Inc. 2. ©Kevin Lombardi, Wavefront Technologies, Inc.
         3. Compton's NewMedia, Inc.
         4. Adobe Systems, Incorporated
BOTTOM 5, 6, & 7. Adobe Systems, Incorporated
         8. Solomon Press

Text and cover design by Solomon Press staff

To Lori and Vanessa—keep on smiling

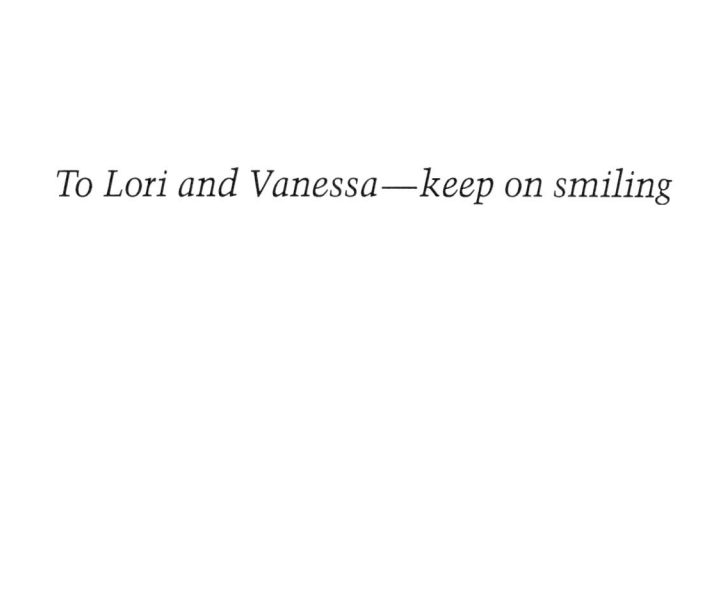

Preface

> Access to ideas makes all the difference.
> — *Arno Penzias*

*t*his book is about making knowledge accessible to individuals and workgroups through distributed computing, electronic publishing, and computer-assisted management of documents—critical repositories of information in most organizations. To get the most out of the documents we create and publish, whether for print or electronic distribution, we need ways of freeing information from the constraints of proprietary computer hardware and software technologies. We also need to envision how this information can best be channeled to our customers and other audiences such as collaborating groups within an organization.

New technologies can distribute knowledge, but technology alone will not help organizations recognize the need to share ideas and information. Why should organizations bother to share knowledge? One reason is increased competition. To bring products to market on time, to innovate, or to deliver services effectively depends more and more upon rapid access to information. Technology can help us organize information and efficiently distribute it within organizations, but only if we encourage new ways of sharing information and learning together.

After choosing the title *Desktop Magic* I worried that this catchy phrase could be misleading. I feared that readers would interpret the book's title to mean that point-and-click computing can solve all problems without prior thought and preparation. But I kept the title because magic is relevant to the experience of using computers even in conjunction with complex constructions such as documents. After all, by combining discoveries of modern quantum physics, silicon/crystal engineering, and graphic programming, we can now make a metaphorical reference to the controllable work space of a computer display screen as a desktop. It is a marvel that vendors of software products can mask the complications of computing with the aid of graphical user interfaces and window management systems. Users of computer systems should not be bothered with the complexity of operating them. Otherwise there would be no cost benefit to purchasing computers for workplace applications. But before we put computers to work in organizations, we need to examine existing processes and rethink ways of doing business. There is also a special challenge to computerizing documents; we need to cultivate the content inside them because it represents the knowledge of our businesses, our government services and legal systems, and our research. The paradox of desktop magic is what we must put technology back in the box until we are ready to use it. The magic doesn't work very well unless we review our process and objectives, learn and collaborate together, and abandon crude assumptions that substitute technology for human beings and their knowledge.

Much of what is said in this book applies not only to corporations and government organizations, but also to the academic world, commercial publishers, and individuals. As time goes by, the distance between users and makers of electronic documents from all walks of life grows smaller. The amazing growth and success of the Internet, a world wide collection of computers, can be attributed to many factors, but users are universally impressed with the wealth of information available on the network. Most of that information is stored in electronic documents that can be exchanged and explored within seconds. The Internet would not be possible without a common sense approach to interoperability in computer networks and the use of standards for exchanging and accessing electronic document information. New beginnings in communication and collaboration are helping us realize the potential and reusability of electronic document resources. This book tries to introduce some of the tools, standards, and approaches that make access to knowledge less difficult.

Acknowledgments

*t*his book would not have been possible without the generous support of many individuals.

I'll begin by thanking Sidney Solomon and Raymond Solomon of The Solomon Press for their imaginative book and cover design, wise and timely advice, and superb project direction. Without their guidance the book would never have seen the light of day. Krish Mandal, also of The Solomon Press, helped with editing, data conversion, and formatting. Kip Shaw of Pageworks performed wonders in page makeup and typesetting, using QuarkXPress. Many thanks to Mary Russell for her thoughtful and tenacious support in copyediting and indexing. Dianne Littwin of Van Nostrand Reinhold had enough faith in the project to support it from proposal phase to finished product. I applaud her for her patience and publishing know-how.

Special thanks to Chris Locke and Linda Turner of Avalanche Development Corporation, Warren Perry of Interleaf, Faye Merrideth and Bill Wengler of ArborText, Kent Summers and Paul Lamoureux of Electronic Book Technologies, Tom Mills of InterCAP, Linda Burman of SoftQuad, Greg Cornelison of Claris Corporation, Bob Wagner of Xerox, and Richard Gallagher of Swanson Analysis Systems.

I am also indebted to Michel Barbier and Michel Cabanel of Schlumberger Industries in Velizy, France, for entrusting me with responsibilities related to electronic publishing and document analysis. My gratitude also extends to colleagues at Loral Data Systems for their inspiration and exchange of ideas. Steve Frayer, Jon Wolf, and Linda Wicks provided assistance with illustrations.

Finally, I wish to salute my teachers for their dedication, my parents for their encouragement, and my wife and daughter for their understanding and support. I also apologize for overlooking the contribution of specific persons not mentioned in this acknowledgment.

— John Wood

Trademarks

Folio VIEWS is a registered trademark of Folio Corporation.

FrameMaker and FrameBuilder are trademarks of Frame Technology Corporation.

Worldview Press, Relational Document Manager, RDM, Intellecte, and Interleaf 5 and Interleaf 6 are trademarks of Interleaf Corporation.

Microsoft is a registered trademark and Microsoft Word, MS-DOS, Windows 3.1, and Windows NT are trademarks of Microsoft Corp.

UNIX and OPEN LOOK are registered trademarks of UNIX Systems Laboratories, Inc.

SPARC and Sun are trademarks of Sun Microsystems, Inc.

X Window System is a product of the Massachusetts Institute of Technology.

DynaText, DynaBase, and DynaTag are trademarks of Electronic Book Technologies.

FastTAG is a registered trademark and Proof Positive and SGML Hammer are trademarks of Avalanche Development Corporation.

SmartLeaf is a trademark of DataBase Publishing Software, Inc.

Open ODMS and Odesta Document Management Systems are trademarks of Odesta Corporation.

GUIDE is a registered trademark and GUIDEviewer is a trademark of InfoAccess, Inc.

WordPerfect is a registered trademark and Intellitag is a trademark of WordPerfect Corporation.

QMS and ColorScript are registered trademarks of QMS Inc.

Novell and Netware are registered trademarks of Novell Corporation.

Xerox is a registered trademark and Ethernet, XSoft, InConcert, Visual Recall, and Docutech Network Publisher are trademarks of Xerox Corporation.

PostScript and Acrobat are trademarks of Adobe Systems, Inc.

ADEPT Editor and Document Architect are trademarks of ArborText, Inc.

xii   Trademarks

GIF is a trademark of Compuserve.

Documentum and Workspace are trademarks of Documentum, Inc.

SoftQuad Author/Editor, SoftQuad Enabler, SoftQuad Rules Builder, SoftQuad Explorer, Soft-Quad Hot Metal Pro are trademarks of SoftQuad, Inc.

TOPIC is a registered trademark of Verity, Inc.

Saros and Saros Mezzanine are registered trademarks and Saros Document manager is a trademark of Saros Corporation.

Near and Far is a trademark of Microstar Corporation.

OPEN/workflow, OPEN/profound, and OPENimage are trademarks of Wang Laboratories, Inc.

BASISplus is a registered trademark and BASIS SGMLserver is a trademark of Information Dimensions, Inc.

OmniDesk is a registered trademark of Sigma Imaging Systems, Inc.

PageMaker is a registered trademark of Aldus Corporation.

Fulcrum is a registered trademark and Fulcrum Ful/Text is a trademark of Fulcrum Technologies Incorporated.

IconAuthor is a registered trademark of AimTech Corporation.

Kudo and Imspace Systems are registered trademarks and Image Browser is a trademark of Imspace Systems.

ActionWorkflow and ActionWorkflow Analyst are trademarks of Action Technologies, Inc.

Audre is a trademark of Audre, Inc.

CMS/Workflow is a trademark of Workgroup Technology Corporation.

Logos is a trademark of Logos Corporation.

AutoCAD is a registered trademark and Animator Pro is a trademark of Autodesk, Inc.

OmniMark is a registered trademark of Exoterica Corporation.

Lotus Notes is a registered trademark and SmartSuite is a trademark of Lotus Development Corporation.

QuarkXPress is a registered trademark of Quark, Inc.

Illustrator, MetaLink Author, and MetaLink Run time are trademarks of InterCAP Graphics Systems, Inc.

OLIAS is a trademark of HAL Software Systems, Inc.

Parlance Document Manager is a trademark of Xyvision, Inc.

IBM is a registered trademark of International Business Machines Corp.

CADleaf is a registered trademark of Carberry Technology.

Macintosh is a registered trademark of Apple Computer, Inc.

(Other brands and product names are trademarks or registered trademarks of their respective companies.)

Contents

Preface	vii
Acknowledgments	ix
Trademarks	xi
Introduction: Electronic Publishing is Everybody's Business	1
What Is Electronic Publishing?	2
Workgroup Versus Personal Publishing	3
1 Affordable Desktop Technology	7
From Individuals to Workgroups	9
Tools of the Trade	11
Solutions	35
2 From Groups to Standards	39
Workgroups: Avoiding the Pitfalls	40
What's In an Interface?	43
Document Interchange Standards	48
Putting It All Together	51

On-Line and Paper Distribution — **56**

3 Document Presentation Design—Format — **63**
Who Does the Presentation Design? — **64**
Where Does Content Fit In? — **67**
Objectives for Presentation and Information Design — **69**
Guidelines for Document Presentation Design — **72**
Presentation Design Variables — **74**
Style Sheets and Templates — **83**

4 Document Information Design—Content — **99**
Redefining Publishing — **99**
Project Briefs — **116**

5 Graphics for Electronic Publishers — **119**
Generating Graphics — **120**
Drawing and Paint Program Features — **122**
Graphic Source Material — **129**
Graphic Displays — **133**
Color Models — **137**
Reviewing Graphics On-Line — **138**
Visual Design — **138**
Interchanging Graphical Information — **139**
Postscript: Medium for Graphic Output — **144**
Graphic Information — **145**

6 Dynamic Data and Smart Documents — **151**
Integrating Information and Applications — **153**
Groupware to the Rescue — **157**
Using Databases and Documents Profitably — **158**

7 Interoperability and Electronic Publishing — **171**
Case History: From Information Search to Deadline — **172**
Connectivity Is Key — **174**

Local Area Networks: Ethernet and More	**175**
Telecommunications and Electronic Publishing	**177**
Communications Services and the Internet	**179**
Document Conversion Programs	**184**
Putting Digital Documents to Work	**190**

8 Multimedia and Electronic Reference Documents — **195**

Electronic Document Viewing	**196**
Content Object Organization and Synchronization	**210**
Document Delivery Mechanisms	**216**
Intellectual Property Rights	**221**

9 Reengineering the Document Process — **223**

Electronic Publishing: Catalyst for Process Change	**224**
Reengineering Documents	**225**
Document Reengineering Opportunities	**228**
Workflow and Accountability	**236**

10 Document Management — **241**

Why We Need Document Management	**241**
What It Is	**242**
Types of Document Management Systems	**246**
Major Document Management Functions	**253**
Document Management and Standards	**261**
Organizational Responsibility	**263**
Application Samples	**264**

11 Workgroup and Enterprise Solutions — **267**

Creating Group Involvement: Inviting Stakeholders	**267**
Analyzing Requirements	**268**
Tips for Planners	**275**
Evaluating Tools	**276**
Workgroup/Enterprise Publishing Products	**283**

12 Electronic Publishing is Changing Careers   **307**
    Opportunities   **308**
    Academic Publishing and Digital Libraries   **344**
    Putting Desktop Magic to Work for You   **350**

Bibliography   **353**

Glossary   **357**

Index   **365**

Introduction: Electronic Publishing is Everybody's Business

Corporations, government agencies, universities, libraries, news organizations, publishing houses, and individuals have a vital interest in the tools and techniques of electronic publishing. Until recently, being an informed manager, a productive employee, or knowledgeable anybody meant being schooled by paper documents. Paper suits our reading habits, but too much paper can make a nightmare out of finding information and managing changes to documents that sit in file cabinets or library shelves. Paradoxically, electronic publishing tools not only allow us to distribute and retrieve electronic documents for viewing on computers, but also help us create paper documents efficiently and in color. With proper planning, we can manage and distribute our documents to suit the exact purpose and audience.

This book describes electronic publishing technology, explains its uses, discusses its multifaceted operational environments, and underlines the importance of planning for its successful implementation. Designed as a practical guide for use by managers, career specialists, and generalists, it provides an understanding of the tools and the processes which are changing the way businesses, corporations, and governments produce paper and electronic documents. The reader can acquire knowledge about:

- Use of technology for workgroup publishing
- Use of multiple authoring systems for text, graphs, and mixed media
- How to access and adapt electronic information
- Electronic document interchange
- Use of desktop color and on-demand printers
- Document management
- Electronic document viewing, hypertext, and multimedia
- Career opportunities generated by electronic publishing

This is not a user guide to a specific publishing program, although there are ample illustrations of many different programs. The book emphasizes how electronic publishing ties powerful technologies together allowing us to communicate in exciting and novel ways. It shows how we can use electronic publishing to manage and reuse information as well as to present and distribute that information in a variety of forms. Important to all users, emerging standards affecting the evolution of electronic publishing are explained. Many case histories are offered from which readers may model effective publishing solutions. A glossary is included of technical terms that have become a part of the electronic publishing vocabulary.

In order to avoid introducing technology into the workplace in a haphazard way, emphasis has been placed on business processes related to the use of electronic publishing technologies and applications. Attention is given to methodologies and the models for using the technology. Much of the text is devoted to the planning and process analysis related to management and integration of electronic publishing.

WHAT IS ELECTRONIC PUBLISHING?

Electronic publishing has come to include two different formats for final product or presentation. One process creates paper documents, the other distributes information electronically for video display and related media documentation.

"Camera ready" or typeset quality paper documents may be produced by using a set of hardware and software tools that, taken together, automate document creation and assembly processes. This includes the entire spectrum of applications made possible by advances in digital electronics and the computer software that automates specific production tasks. Electronic publishing software integrates text and graphics material for output from laser printers, image setters, and other hard copy devices. Word processing and desktop publishing software are a part of the technologies involved in the preparation of printed documents.

Expanding the traditional meaning of the word "publishing," the second process is not associated with traditional print technology but with the distribution and display of electronic documents. Hypertext is an example of one technology involved in the explosion of electronic document and multimedia publishing. Hypertext allows users to link such elements as words, paragraphs, sections, or "chunks" of text information. Hypermedia extends this nonsequential linking to images, audio, and film in a mixed media presentation. Paperless publishing includes: electronic books, such as encyclopedias delivered on Compact Disk Read-Only Memory (CD-ROM); digital libraries, accessible by high speed telecommunications links, allowing readers to access books, newsletters, reports, or multimedia collections and view them from a video display; interactive electronic technical documents, allowing technicians to repair equipment by following procedures and diagrams that "interact" with a technician's queries; and paperless factories, allowing assembly workers to fabricate and assemble products by reading work instructions from video displays and by viewing drawings electronically.

Electronic publishing is more than the automation of presentation technologies: one for paper pages and one for video terminal display. As the drama of electronic publishing unfolds, it is the information contained within documents that is demanding center stage. There are ways to automate, retrieve, reuse, and update information within documents whether or not intended for paper or electronic publishing distribution. Structure and content oriented electronic publishing technologies include: authoring systems based upon standards such as Standard Generalized Markup Language (SGML), database publishing, document databases, and full text indexing and control features of document management systems. In order to use content based electronic publishing, special attention must be given to the generation, identification, and structuring of information contained within documents.

WORKGROUP VERSUS PERSONAL PUBLISHING

Electronic publishing includes two commonly used systems: personal publishing and workgroup publishing. The difference between these two is as much a matter of approach and methodology as it is technology.

Workgroup electronic publishing is a multiuser system typically integrating different computers in a network. Workgroup publishing is not limited to paper presentation and does not rely on one computer platform or publishing program. By contrast, personal publishing refers to single user adaptation of electronic publishing. Personal publishing applications are usually small in scope (a newsletter, a leaflet) and the resources need not extend beyond one's desk or "desktop."

Workgroup electronic publishing involves at least several of many players. It necessitates routine communication of data between users, understanding the specialized functions users must perform, and standardization of user style and data control procedures. Workgroup publications may include very large documents, such as 1000 page aircraft maintenance manuals, but a sales brochure or newsletter may also qualify as an electronic publishing workgroup project, perhaps deriving some of its contents from a document database shared by many users.

Although electronic publishing technologies used by workgroup and personal publishers have much in common, multiuser systems require networking and information integration to be a high priority. Technology alone—computer platforms, application software programs, and peripheral devices—do not define the difference between personal and workgroup publishing. Instead it is the methodology employed in workgroup publishing that substantially differs from that used for personal publishing.

Open Information Magic

Increasingly, the user community is demanding electronic publishing systems that provide compatibility and portability among different computers. Some applications reside on Macintosh and IBM/Microsoft/Intel based personal computers (PCs) and the latest breed of power PCs jointly developed by IBM, Apple, and Motorola. Others use workstations made by Sun Microsystems, DEC, IBM, HP, or Silicon Graphics. So-called "open system" standards have helped users and vendors overcome barriers to interoperable computing. Significant efforts in document interchange standard development reduce the risk of unsuccessful document information sharing due to proprietary computer processes.

Emerging industry standards for electronic document interchange include Standard Generalized Markup Language (SGML), Computer Graphics Metafile (CGM), Open Document Architecture (ODA), and other standards adopted by the International Organization for Standardization (ISO), the Open Systems Foundation (OSF), and special interest forums that influence electronic publishing issues. De facto industry standards, such as PostScript, are also important in the realm of presentation design.

A variety of software applications are considered, such as document authoring and browsing tools from Interleaf, Frame Technology, ArborText, and SoftQuad. Methods are discussed for integrating popular desktop publishing formatting programs such as QuarkXPress with standard based publishing architectures. SoftQuad, a leading vendor of SGML products, has developed a product that converts SGML tagged data into QuarkXPress presentation design formats. Organizations can convert existing electronic document data to SGML with products such as FASTtag from Avalanche Development Company. Integration of various graphic, database, and document management programs are included for illustration as well as reference to multimedia and hypermedia products. Electronic document and text retrieval products from Verity and Fulcrum are intelligent indexing and search technologies that guide electronic publishers and users of electronic documents to critical information. SGML viewing products, such as DynaText from Electronic Book Technologies, OLIAS from Hal Software Systems, and Explorer from SoftQuad are considered. Numerous references are made to document management products from Interleaf, Documentum, XSoft, and others that workgroups use to find, secure, update, and distribute documents.

Since electronic publishing programs can now be linked to other applications such as spreadsheets, databases, and photo image editing software, vendors are making business partnerships with each other in order to integrate these processes across desktops and networks. The impact of this integration on the workplace is illustrated by interesting examples of collaborative vendor relationships. Aldus Corporation and Adobe Systems, Inc., have merged specifically to meet the challenges created by electronic publishing. There are also many new opportunities for users as well. Understanding how electronic publishing has affected professional careers, job descriptions, and business opportunities is a key theme of this book.

As more and more organizations introduce or expand electronic publishing facilities, they would do well to contemplate the words of the Renaissance motto: "Make haste slowly." The measure of efficiency for making publications should not only be how many publications can be produced within the shortest time possible but should extend to other criteria as well. Additional metrics for efficiency should specify how easily an audience can find information stored in electronic or printed documents. Quality tests can check whether redundant information found within separate documents is accurate and whether a system is in place to tell authors and other contributing parties about the status of that information. Document design efficiency assumes minimal human intervention in the document formatting process once an automated design has been set up. Most importantly, workgroups who have access to electronic publishing technologies should continuously reassess the process of making paper or electronic documents, communicate and solve problems found in the process, and be skeptical when it is said, "We have always done it this way."

CHAPTER 1

➤ *Electronic publishing functions*

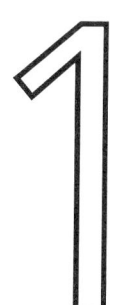

➤ *Who are the users?*

➤ *Hardware and software*

➤ *Up and running*

Affordable Desktop Technology

*a*dvances in computer technology in recent years have enabled new directions in electronic publishing. Affordable, high speed, desktop computers have allowed developers of electronic publishing programs to deliver feature rich products to a broad spectrum of users. Covering diverse applications, these product technologies automate functions in graphics, composition and page layout, multimedia, color printing and scanning, and electronic document viewing and distribution. The expansion of computer networks has also allowed workgroups to share in making documents interactively.

Electronic publishing is not only altering the ways individuals and groups prepare, distribute, or print documents, it is also reshaping the way we structure and access information. Individual documents can be seen as containers linked to much larger bases of information. Content based electronic publishing is helping us to understand that there is more to documents than their form, that the content of one document may be a subset of an organized electronic information base.

The rapid growth of computer systems on workplace desktops and the historical declines in the cost of the hardware platforms have allowed many more people to take advantage of the benefits of using electronic publishing. Some users find opportunity in the workplace to participate in electronic publishing workgroups. Other users may set up personal desktop publishing systems for business or private use.

Few professions have been left unaffected by the computer revolution. Whether in manufacturing, engineering, medicine, or scientific research, computer assisted technology has changed the way people work. Electronic publishing is no exception.

Much of the exacting manual work formerly required for typesetting, document layout, and text and graphics integration has been simplified. The automation of the manual processes associated with the preparation and format production of documents encompasses the first major function of electronic publishing: computer controlled creation, layout, and assembly of documents for print applications. Once a presentation design is complete, the computer based desktop publishing system takes over for the more mechanical routine tasks which can be automated.

The second major function of electronic publishing is the distribution of electronic documents for viewing from video display terminals (VDTs). Whether it is done for legal or medical reference documents, electronic text books, interactive technical manuals, computer-based training or other applications, this distribution combines a set of authoring, indexing, and display tools that allow recipients to view and interact with documents.

These first two functions deal with the format and appearance of documents. Other functions apply to document information design. The analysis of document structure and content and the use of computer assisted resources to encode document information through authoring and conversion processes is the application of information design. Organizations value information design because it improves communication processes and results in effective information access. To retrieve information from a printed work, we turn to a table of contents, an index, an abstract, a glossary, or a bibliography as points of departure. With computer documents, users often resort to the printed version of the document as a means of information search. This has made computer users dependent on paper and it is one reason skeptics have scoffed at the idea of a paperless office. The inability to find computer document information efficiently has also added to insecurity about the cost benefit of computer assisted technologies on professional desktops. But electronic information retrieval systems are changing that viewpoint. Special computer document retrieval software allows users to ask questions about such things as how many times a reference to an increase in prime interest rates appeared in a headline of a newspaper or periodical between January and June 1994. Other queries can be about specific aspects of an insurance policy, a safety procedure in a petrochemical plant, a diagnosis of patient's heart condition, or instructions for jet engine repair.

To retrieve document information efficiently, it is helpful to identify a document's structure and content. Specific sets of information can then be automatically retrieved, directed to a formatting template for display or print, or stored in a document database. Developments have enabled new ways of organizing information meant for print or electronic distribution. Structured content based editing systems, such as those that support the Standard Generalized Markup Language (SGML), separate the formatting, or presentation aspects related to containing the document, from the information held by the container. SGML also requires a neutral form for interchanging data. This means the data is not hardware or software dependent so that different computers and programs can retrieve and reuse it. Computer information used to create documents for print and electronic distribution can, if properly organized by implementing appropriate processes, standards, and technologies, be reused and redirected to create new documents.

If projects are planned properly, electronic prepress functions and electronic document distribution can be organized concurrently. The planning of document information design is called document analysis. It is a critical step in the development of a document management strategy. Document management systems facilitate workgroup access to sets of documents and the information stored in documents by combining the power of database technology, automatic indexing and text retrieval tools, and computer networks. With document management systems, electronic publishers can access and control archived documents as well as keep a publication project development on track. Workflow features of document management systems allow workgroups to create electronic procedures for document checkout, review, approval, and notification of distribution. The synchronization of document content allows document or database administrators to check the status of changes in source information (drawings, tables, text, or other objects) that may be used in one or more documents. For example, if an artist changes a drawing to be used in a proposal, a training guide, and a brochure, the change control feature broadcasts the status of that drawing to ensure the corrected drawing is targeted to each of the related documents. Document management systems enable computers to control processes related to creation and distribution of many documents dispersed over networks. A diagram of interrelated electronic publishing functions is shown in the Figure 1.1.

FROM INDIVIDUALS TO WORKGROUPS

Electronic publishing cannot be separated from the user groups it most closely serves. Computer assisted publishing for the newspaper, magazine, business, engineering, scientific, and governmental applications has steadily evolved and offers affordable systems for organizations whose primary mission is the making of publications or for those groups who produce documents in support of an overall enterprise.

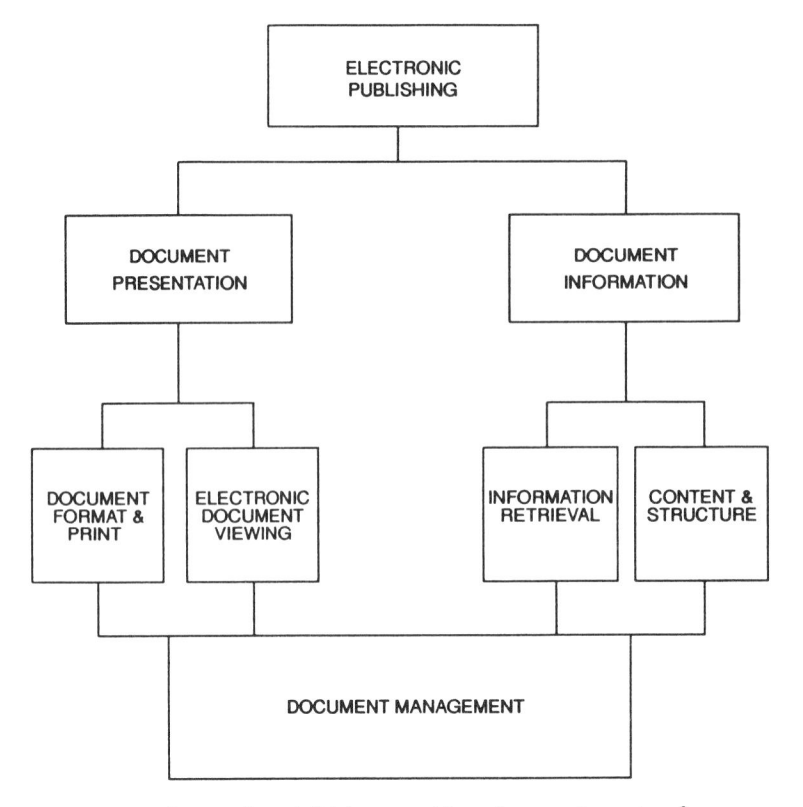

Figure 1.1. Electronic publishing combines two major sets of technologies: presentation or format technologies and information or content technologies. Document management is a set of computer assisted tools that helps control document libraries, workflow, presentation processes, and retrieval of information.

Within user groups there are subgroups responsible for different activities related to the generation and distribution of documents. For the sake of classification we give these subgroups a common name—workgroups. Workgroups involve many types of individuals who collaborate on projects leading to a publication and who are responsible for maintaining the information after publication. Workgroups include authors, subject matter experts, editors, graphic artists, management information specialists, marketing and business communicators, and production specialists who need to be able to find and reuse information electronically.

Although making documents is the primary business for users in periodical and broadcast journalism, typesetting houses, printing establishments, and some service bureaus, producing documents is a background or secondary business in many corporate, government, and small business organizations. The number of documents now produced in-house by organizations in the United States is estimated to be as large as one billion documents a day. Whether in manufacturing, insurance, engineering, law, business, or government, documents store critical information. The documents may be small publications such as brochures, advertisements, invitations, and reports, or larger documents such as business plans, proposals, manuals, specifications, contracts. Instead of relying exclusively on outside resources to produce and print documents, large organizations often choose to do the job "in-house."

Many organizations are still adjusting to the introduction of word processing, What-You-See Is-What-You-Get (WYSIWYG) desktop publishing technology, and the laser printer. Although user communities have employed word processing and computer assisted composition tools to speed up the production of documents, it has often been difficult to find, integrate, reuse, and update information in documents.

Novel approaches to the automation and management of documents require a fresh appraisal. We focus our discussion on workgroup publishing solutions, although many chapters address topics also important to personal publishers who want to learn more about issues related to connectivity, standards for interchange, and new ways of accessing and distributing information.

To profile populations of document producers and consumers, an analysis is made of the information used within documents and the structures used to organize that information. The particular information needs of the pharmaceutical, aviation, defense, and telecommunication industries are examples of population profiles. A primary aim of this work is to show how electronic publishing can be used more effectively by a cross section of workgroups from diverse industries or professions, who share a common interest in new technologies.

TOOLS OF THE TRADE

There are many technologies and tools that make electronic publishing possible. The marriage of special software tools to selected hardware devices creates a basis or platform for electronic publishing users. Compatibility between hardware and software tools, including existing computerized resources, needs careful attention. Planners and system analysts must anticipate future requirements and growth needs and always test the configuration prior to purchase. Additional questions to be answered are:

- ► How big are the documents to be created?
- ► What specific hardware is required to support electronic publishing software?

- Will electronic interchange and distribution be needed?
- What are the requirements for graphic and other nontext forms (photos or video, for instance)?
- Is the proposed equipment compatible with existing equipment?
- What are the information retrieval requirements?
- How will the document information be reused?

Hardware Devices

Electronic publishing hardware consists of computer controlled devices that process, store, print, or electronically display, documents. The equipment includes a desktop computer, video display terminal, keyboard, mouse, scanner, laser printer, and disk and tape drives. Generic devices such as Compact Disk–Read Only Memory (CD-ROM) that store electronic documents for distribution have acquired special significance for electronic publishers for delivering an electronic document or retrieving multimedia documents from other publishers.Hardware is in a state of evolution and as the prices have fallen in recent years, the technology becomes more affordable for users. Figure 1.2 shows a sample hardware configuration.

Personal Computers

Personal computers have always had a significant presence on workplace desktops. Personal computers are versatile, portable and, by reputation, competitively priced. Not surprisingly, desktop publishing owes a large part of its success to the meteoric rise of the personal computer. As the performance capabilities of personal computer systems have evolved and networking between personal computer workstations have become more common, the personal computer platform has earned respect as a powerful workgroup tool. Personal computer performance is measured in terms of the computer's processing capabilities such as central processing unit speed, memory and disk storage capacities, spare slot availability, and communication options. These criteria also apply to Macintosh and workstation computers, the most significant performance features relating to CPU speed and memory capacity.

Central processing unit (CPU). The CPU is the core microprocessor in the computer. It processes massive sets of instructions at blinding speeds and it controls the operations of the computer. The leading suppliers of CPUs for the PC, Macintosh, and workstation computers are Intel and Motorola.

A critical feature of a microprocessor is the speed with which it obtains, decodes, and executes instructions. The time the CPU takes to fetch new instructions is called a "clock rate" and it is measured in megahertz (MHz). High performance CPUs have ratings between 33 and 64 MHz. Another measure of CPU speed is "throughput," which is the number of instructions passing through the computer per second. PCs, MACs and workstations are rated according to how many million instructions per second (MIPS) can be throughput.

Memory capacity. Computers use internal memory chips to store and recall data and sets of instructions or programs that the CPU executes. Several types of memory devices are used. Read only memories and programmable read only memories serve the purpose of storing programs that are permanent (that is, they cannot be altered). Random access memory (RAM) is a read/write type of device that allows the information stored in the device to be changed. The capacity of RAM used in desktop computer configurations is critical to the efficiency of applications such as electronic publishing. The size of memory devices is measured in

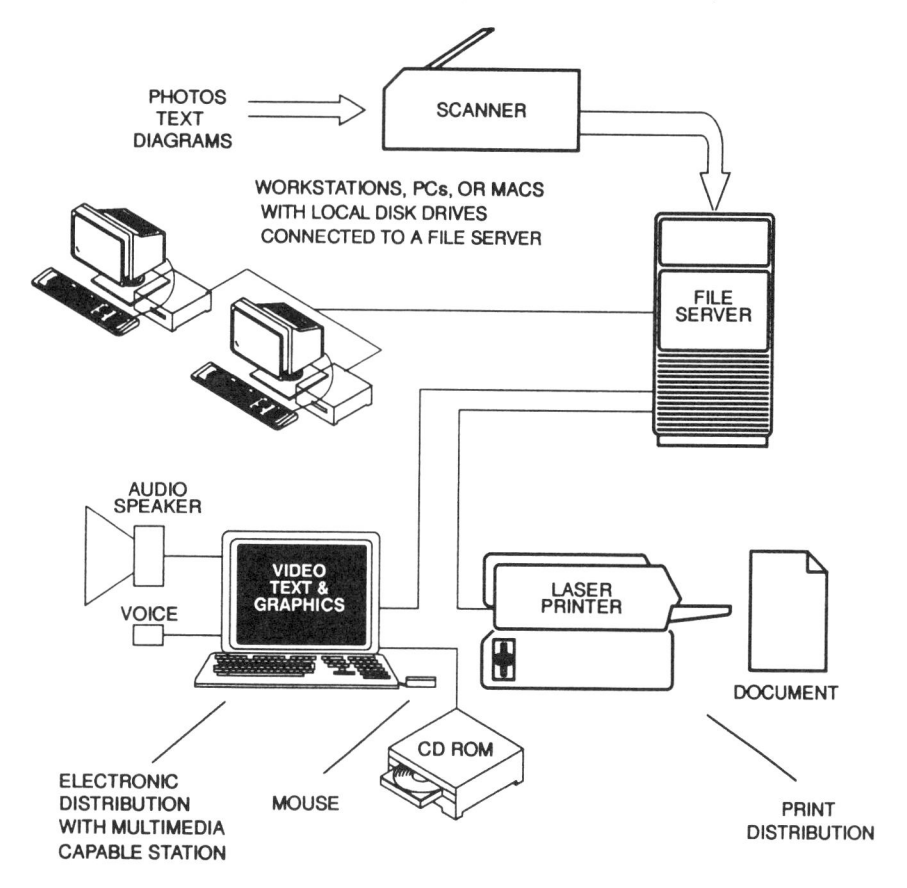

Figure 1.2. Simplified example of an electronic publishing system showing a sample hardware configuration.

bytes (a byte is 8 bits of information); desktop computers are configured with n megabytes of RAM where n is a number typically between 1 and 64. Electronic publishers increasingly need more RAM to manipulate complex files such as a 2 megabyte color illustration, or a 3 megabyte document made up of combined text and drawings. PCs and other desktop computers allow room for adding RAM. This feature of expanding RAM capacity is an important consideration in the selection of desktop computers. A megabyte of RAM can be purchased for under 100 dollars. If desktop users want to manipulate large documents and work with feature rich graphic programs they need between 8 and 32 megabytes of RAM memory to be comfortable with the configuration. Choosing a computer with the capability of expanding RAM capacity is critical.

Personal computers compete with workstations in terms of processing speeds, disk transfer rates, memory capacities, bus bandwidth, and throughput. The enhancement of PC capabilities is important in developing publishing system software because it means challenging programs requiring a lot of computing power are possible. The so-called power PCs from IBM and Apple are changing the concept of the PC as it has been known for a decade. Power PCs are adopting a different architecture and placing more emphasis upon computing between differing computers and operating systems. One limitation of the traditional PC is the default operating system software, MS-DOS, because it is not a multitasking system. Chicago and MS-NT Windows (the latest operating systems for personal computers from Microsoft) give PC users and product developers a tool for making the PC handle more tasks at the same time. Communications technology in PCs is one nonstandard variable of paramount importance for workgroups. Workstations come with standard communications interfaces such as Ethernet; PCs do not (although Novell's Netware, among other offerings, provides connectivity solutions for PC workgroups).

Macintosh Computers and Electronic Publishing

The Apple Macintosh computer and the Apple LaserWriter printer have such importance in the development of desktop and electronic publishing that it is impossible to leave them out in a discussion of developments in the field. From the easy-to-use features to the wealth of applications that run on it, the Macintosh helped pioneer a desktop revolution.

By implementing a design idea dreamt up at Xerox Parc research, the Macintosh became synonymous with a "point and shoot" graphical user interface. It was the first computer to allow users to manipulate applications with graphic icons instead of computer commands, making it very user friendly from the start. Such ease of manipulation and access minimizes the user's need to learn more complicated operating system interfaces. The Macintosh operating system (called the

System) does not require inexperienced users to memorize dozens of computer commands as a prerequisite to proficient manipulation and management of files. With the development of world class publishing applications on the Mac, a loyal following of users has been established. Apple has now launched the successor to the Mac in the Power PC. It uses the same evolving operating system as the Mac but opens up the architecture to allow for other operating systems including Microsoft Windows. Most importantly, it increases the processing speeds, disk storage and RAM expandability, and a variety of multimedia ready options. Prices for desktop Apple Power PC platforms range from 1500 to 7000 dollars.

Workstations

A workstation is a multiuser or standalone computer designed to attract users and developers of advanced computer applications. Unlike PCs and Macs workstations were not designed for a consumer market. A workstation is a system designed with integrated networking, and a multiuser and multitask operating system (for example, UNIX, VMS, OS2). Because of built-in communications capabilities, workstations are ideal workgroup tools. When workstations are attached to a network, they are clients of a file server configured for access to large disk drives, databases, and network connectivity. A file server is a machine that provides a variety of services to a client such as access to specialized electronic publishing software programs.

Computer workstations from their inception were conceived as tools for complex graphic and similar computing intensive applications. Individual workstations feature high performance microprocessors, high speed central processing units, expandable memory capacities and disk drives, and built-in network communication subsystems. Once found exclusively in engineering and scientific laboratories, workstations are now commonly used in finance, telecommunications, and electronic publishing. Leading workstation vendors include: Sun Microsystems, NeXT Computer, Silicon Graphics, DEC, IBM, Hewlett Packard, and Data General. Figure 1.3 shows a sample workstation configuration.

The choice between the use of a personal computer or workstation for electronic publishing depends upon specific requirements such as the number of users on the publishing system, the rate of learning for trainees, and the choices among application programs that may be available on different platforms.

Client/Server Computing

The workstation relationship to the file server is referred to as a client/server connection. Client/server computing architectures allow workstation users to share application programs, a database, or disk storage space. This sharing creates what has become known as a distributed work environment. For example, file

Figure 1.3. The Silicon Graphics Indy workstation, a leading edge multimedia ready platform, can handle motion picture video without addition of special hardware. It comes with a small digital camera mounted on top of the monitor for use in video conferencing sessions. (Courtesy of Silicon Graphics, Inc.)

servers, loaded with the appropriate publishing system software, allow workgroups to share network licenses and collaborate on a variety of client workstations. This use of shared intelligence helps people working in a group environment achieve optimal solutions for collaborative projects. Publishing applications such as books, proposals, and complex technical manuals may be efficiently distributed by workstations connected to a file server. Once only the province of workstations, client/server architectures now include personal computers and Macintosh stations using special software packages and networking tools.

But what about the host computer? The host computer has traditionally been the primary, or central computer, in a multielement system; it is the system that issues commands, has access to important data, and has versatile processing capabilities. Host computers are the mainstays of data processing and are still used by large corporations, government, and industry for accounting, taxes, payroll, management information, and other typically centralized computing functions. With the increased processing capabilities of desktop computers, however, the role of the host computer in many organizations is changing. Some companies have adapted host computers to the role of a file server or specialized data bank.

To enter data into the electronic publishing system and manipulate it, users typically employ a combination of a keyboard, a mouse, and a scanner. Disk and tape drives are used to store data. To output data, users revert to printers or distribute their data electronically via a network, CD-ROM, or other storage media.

Input Devices

Keyboard. Although we are witnessing the arrival of such advanced techniques as intelligent character scanning, palmtop stylus computing, and voice recognition systems, a large proportion of information input to computers is still generated by keyboard. It plays an important role as the mainstay for data manipulation and text editing. With the cursor the user controls the interaction of the keyboard with computer display, a symbol (such as an arrow) indicating the current position of interaction with information on the screen.

Some common keyboard conventions include:

> ➤ Alphabetic Keys. These keys include the letters of the alphabet, punctuation mark keys, and text formatting keys such as <return> <spacebar> and <tab>
>
> ➤ Numeric Keys. These keys include the numbers 0 through 9 at the top of the keyboard, at the side, or both
>
> ➤ Navigational Keys. Arrow keys are used to move the cursor sideward (left or right) or upward-downward
>
> ➤ Modifier Keys. These keys can be used together with other keys to create special results. The keyboard shift key is normally used in conjunction with letter keys to create capital letters. It is also used in many programs as a combinational key to create other commands
>
> ➤ Function Keys. Labeled with F1, F2, etc., these keys are used in many word processing and electronic publishing programs to execute certain commands such as to make a string of text into bold type or to print a file

Word processing programs usually assign special keys to perform such special publishing functions as italicizing a string of words or placing revision bars in the margins to indicate changes in paragraphs. Some publishing programs allow users to modify the keyboard for the purposes of performing functions important to users.

A word of caution. Excessive use of a computer keyboard without attention to methods for prevention of wrist injury can be a health hazard. Repetitive motion injuries such as Carpal Tunnel Syndrome can afflict workers who continuously use the keyboard. New designs based on ergonomic research have led to safer boards such as that shown in Figure 1.4. (Ergonomics is a science that considers human physiology and behavior.)

Mouse. A common hardware device used for human interaction with the computer is the mouse. It is a positioning device used to initiate actions, to select items from menus, and to assist in the creation of graphics, page layout, and a variety of other functions. Figure 1.5 is a picture of an ergonomically designed mouse.

Scanners. A scanner is a device that turns visual information into digital data in an appropriate form for processing by a computer. Hard copy source material such as photos, drawings, and text pages are input to the scanner that in turn creates bitmapped files. A bitmapped file contains an array of bits that define the image captured. Some scanners can capture color photos and images as well as black and white material. Scanner editing software is used for modification and enhancement of scanned images or for optical character recognition of text scanned into the system.

Storage Devices

Storage devices are critical in electronic publishing applications. These devices include hard and floppy disks, tape drives, videodisks, and CD-ROM.

Figure 1.4. Computer keyboard with ergonomic design that uses a split V-shaped naturally contoured slope for support of wrists and hands, to minimize injury as a result of excessive use. (Courtesy of Marquardt Switches Inc.)

Figure 1.5. MouseMan is an ergonomically designed mouse with finger grooves, sensitive buttons for easier clicking, and contoured curves and slopes to fit the hand. (Courtesy of Logitech).

Disk drives. Three types of disks are relevant to this discussion: so-called floppy disks, hard disks, and CD-ROM. Floppy disks are available in sizes of 5¼ inches and 3½ inches to the side. Floppy disks have several uses in desktop computer configurations. First, the floppy disk is a conventional means by which software application programs are loaded into a computer. Second, floppy disks are used for archival storage of files and for backup of existing files. These disks are portable and therefore provide a means of exchanging document files in the absence of computer to computer communications.

Permanent, or hard disk, subsystems are used to store user created files, directories, operating system programs and application programs. The storage capacity of the hard disk is extremely important for publishing applications. System planners and administrators must configure sufficient disk space to avoid disk saturation and maintain a healthy margin of available space for new data. Off the shelf PCs are configured with 80 to 550 million bytes of hard disk space. Sufficient storage space is needed for system programs and application programs as well as the document files created by publishing applications.

CD-ROM, compact disk-read only memory, has the capacity of storing enormous quantities of data, for example, 600 million bytes of data on a single 12 centimeter (4.7 inch platter). This 600 megabytes is the equivalent of 200,000 typed pages single spaced. CD-ROM disks plug into compact disk drives. For electronic publishers, CD-ROM technology offers a vehicle for electronic document deliveries.

At the present time, CD-ROM reproduce drives are not expensive (they are priced between 150 and 400 dollars). CD recording devices, referred to as CD-Rs, are now available for less than 10,000 dollars. See Figure 1.6. As CD-Rs become price

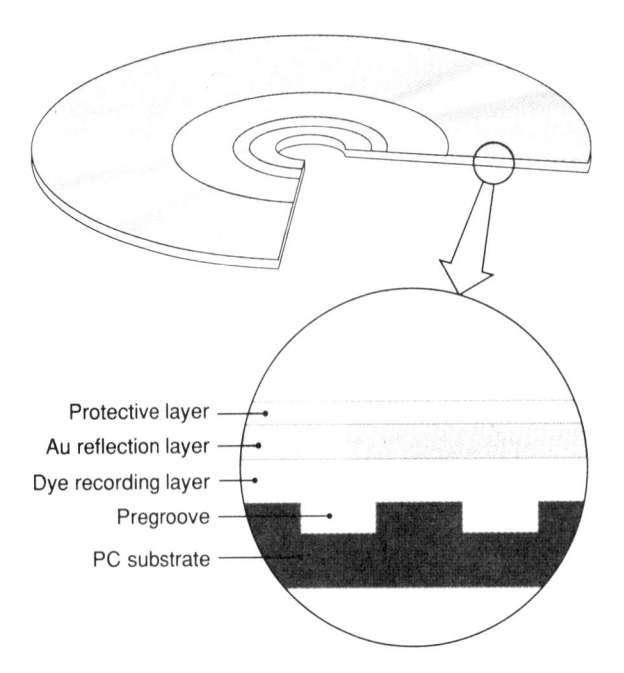

Figure 1.6. CD-R media is comprised of four layers: a top protective layer, a gold (Au) reflection layer, the dye recording layer, and PC substrate. A laser in the CD-R heats the bottom three layers. In the process, the recording layer fuses and is impressed as the substrate layer expands. (Courtesy of Phillips Consumer Electronics.)

competitive, more users will purchase them to record and deliver electronic documents or multimedia collections. Currently, many electronic publishers use service bureaus to record the material they develop onto CD-ROM. Electronic document collections can also be delivered on other magnetic media such as tape, or telecommunicated to recipient computers via networking devices.

CD-ROMs are an example of optical disk technologies. Optical disks can store data as microscopic pits on the disk surface. One advantage of optical disk storage is that light is used to read and write information and no mechanical contact is required. In addition to CD-ROM, there are two other optical disk technologies which are write once/read many (WORM) and erasable optical drives. WORM devices are useful for storing and archiving large quantities of data. Double-sided WORM platters can store 650 Mbytes per side of a platter.

Erasable optical drives have great potential for data storage because of high storage capacity (300 Mbytes per side of disk) and read/write capabilities. The disk cartridge has the advantage of being removable but compared to conventional hard drives its access times are twice to three times slower. Erasable optical drives are relatively expensive (3,000 to 5,000 dollars) and disk cartridges cost over 100 dollars. As the price of these devices declines and the disk access time improves, the erasable optical drive should become a staple of system configurations.

Tape drives. Electronic publishing systems contain data that users can not afford to lose. Computer backups to magnetic tape or other storage media are practical and necessary. Tapes can hold large quantities of data. Compact tape cassette drives can be mounted inside a computer base or external to the unit. A variety of software programs enable users to backup their data or file it for archival storage. Tapes are also a valuable and inexpensive means of recording electronic documents for electronic media delivery.

Videodisk. Another media used for storage of sound, text, still pictures, and full motion video is the videodisk, typically rated for a ten year life time. Since videodisks can be used in computer controlled random searches, they can be used to deliver multimedia productions.

Computer Displays

Displays are used in electronic publishing to create and produce documents and to view and retrieve information from electronically distributed documents. Computer display configurations are comprised of a monitor, a video memory storage device, and software programs that control the display. Most video display terminals in use are cathode ray tube (CRT) monitors, although in popular laptop computer models other types of displays such as liquid crystal, gas plasma, and active light emitting transistors are used.

Both monochrome and color CRTs use a raster scanning technique to display images on the screen. The raster is a set of horizontal lines of pixels or picture elements. (Pixels are tiny dots that collectively make up the display.) A matrix of pixels represents the image on the display screen. The matrix is stored in video memory located on a special display board or the computer motherboard. Each pixel on the monitor is included in this display map. (Refer to Chapter 5 for details). A pixel is represented by a binary number that varies with the type of display system. An eight bit per pixel monitor can display 256 colors or shades of gray.

The display image in video memory is scanned sequentially by a video controller. The binary numbers stored in video memory represent the state of a pixel with respect to its present color or gray scale content. These numbers are applied to digital to analog converter circuits that produce a voltage proportional to each number. The voltages are used by an electronic gun situated toward the back of CRTs which emits an electron stream toward a phosphor coated video display screen. Since the light output of the phosphors on the screen dissipates rapidly, the electron beam which typically refreshes the phosphor at a rate of 60 times a second or higher helps avoid the problem of flicker. For monochrome displays a single color phosphor is used on the screen. Most color display monitors use three different phosphors that glow red, green, and blue when an electron beam excites them. The dots are tiny and the light emanating from the dots appears to the viewer as a mixture of these colors. Close approximation of true color requires 24 bits per pixel, allowing for 16,777,216 colors.

Features of computer displays important to electronic publishers include screen resolution and size. A 13 inch color monitor that is 640 pixels wide by 480 pixels high has a resolution of 72 dots per inch (dpi). A 19 inch monitor that is 1,024 by 768 pixels offers the same 72 dpi resolution. This resolution is suitable to support 24-bit color display. The size of a monitor can be critical in electronic publishing. To display an entire 8 1/2- by 11-inch page on the screen, may require a 19 or 21 inch monitor.

Communications and Networks

All desktop computers can exist in a standalone mode or have some connections to other computers via a network or telecommunication options. Increasingly, PCs are being tied to local area networks (LANs) and, in turn, these LANs can be interconnected to wide area networks (WANs) extending the range of communications capabilities of the desktop. For example, with an Ethernet card installed in the PC, MAC, or workstation and appropriate software running to link computers for the transfer of data, the desktop computer becomes a powerful collaborative device for transferring documents. Telecommunication options include use of a modem either internally mounted in an available computer backplane slot, or externally connected to the computer for sending and receiving data over telephone lines. The only drawback to modems is the data transfer speed. It may take hours for a lengthy document to be transferred over a 2400 baud modem connection.

Computer networks and telecommunication devices permit an orderly transmission and reception of information, allowing workgroups to collaborate on electronic publishing projects efficiently. Subgroups can work on their special part of the project (research, analysis, design, writing, editing, illustrating, reviewing and so forth) while another workgroup prepares for production. Using document management technologies, workgroups can determine the status of projects in progress, search for information across several computers and networks, and control the process of production and electronic distribution.

Local Area Networks (LANs) are becoming more prevalent in the work place as distributed desktop computing becomes more popular. Common LAN types include Ethernet and Token Ring. Ethernet based LANs operate at a transfer rate of up to 10 million bits per second.

Electronic publishing workgroups can also interactively collaborate on projects over a wide geographical distribution via Wide Area Networks (WANs). The Internet, for example, is world wide network linking computer systems. Users can share information over the Internet, participate in discussion groups, and have access to vast electronic libraries. The Internet is the most notable example of what is popularly referred to as the electronic superhighway. Meanwhile public telephone companies, among others, are promoting a technology called Asynchronous Transfer Mode (ATM) that will simplify data communication services through implementations of a standard model known as Broadband Integrated Services Digital Network (B-ISDN). Public B-ISDN networks support the exchange of multimedia information such as films, music, electronic books on demand.

Hardcopy Output Devices

Laser printer. Without the laser printer the desktop publishing phenomenon would never have happened. The laser printer provides typeset "camera ready" quality output at an affordable price. The laser printer creates a picture of a page in its memory. A laser beam in the printer then scans across a rotating, positively charged drum. The part of the drum struck by the laser beam loses its charge. A negatively charged, powdered toner is attracted to the positive section of the drum and is printed onto a sheet of paper attached to it.

Laser printers can print pages of various proportions and at various speeds. Most low end laser printers output only "A size" pages (8½ by 11 inches) only. The average speed of such low end printers is 8 to 12 pages per minute. Some laser printers can print "B size" pages (11 by 17 inches). Very high speed laser printers, sometimes called demand printers, can print over 100 pages per minute. The printer speed varies with the density of the information on a formatted printed page.

Demand printer. On-demand printers are useful for high volume printing applications. This device is connected to computer desktops via a local area network. It can be used to make multiple copies of electronically stored documents at high speeds. Especially useful in office environments that need timely output of reports, proposals, manuals, product catalogs, business records, legal documents, and other publications, demand printers produce 300 to 600 dots per inch quality for each document printed. The Kodak LionHeart Document Management System is a 92 page per minute printer that allows for automatic collating and binding among other features. The Xerox DocuTech Network Publisher is a high volume (125 pages per minute) and high quality laser printer.

Demand printers permit last minute changes to the document without risk of missing the delivery deadline. Demand printers keep detailed records of all jobs processed and the management software allows for queuing and prioritizing of print demands.

Color printers and copiers. Desktop color printers use a variety of techniques including dot matrix, ink jet, thermal transfer, dye sublimation, and digital proof printing. Color copiers are available to make short runs of copies made from masters that may have been printed desktop from color printers as shown in

Figure 1.7. Effective use of color can significantly enhance the quality of documents and presentations.

The quality of desktop color printing depends upon other components that the electronic publishing system uses to prepare and process the text and graphics sent to the printer. These include the color monitors and graphic display hardware that control the resolution and quality of color imaging. Other factors influencing the quality and effectiveness of color output are the color scanners and the color scanning software employed to modify and enhance color photos scanned into the system.

Image Setters. It is not uncommon for many desktop publishers to create their work on a desktop publishing system and then take their PostScript output to a service bureau for pre-press production. Image setters provide high-resolution quality output on photo-paper or film. Image setters are often referred to as photographic printers. Many desktop publishers who cannot afford such a device use their laser printers for low grade proofs of their work and go outside for prepress work.

Multimedia

Many devices contribute to the creation of a multimedia collection for electronic delivery. The scanner, for example, can be used to capture still photos; CD-ROM drives can playback encyclopedic multimedia programs from commercially available disks; computer networks can deliver information (film, music, animation, electronic newsletters, and books) from a variety of sources; computer monitors can display the information on desktops. Two special interfaces are men-

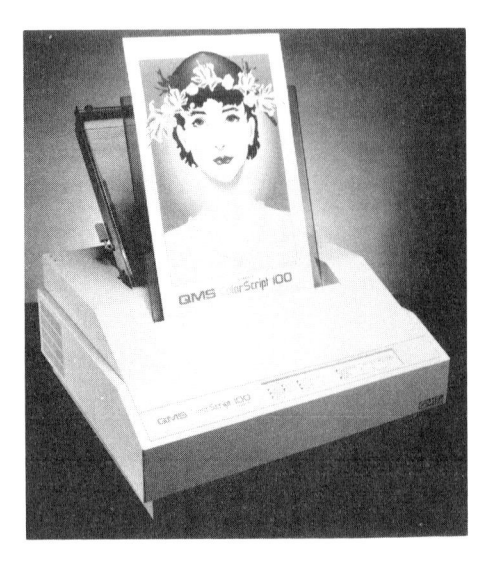

Figure 1.7. The QMSR ColorScriptR printer. (Courtesy of QMS, Inc.)

tioned here for the benefit of users interested in creating multimedia collections using audio or video material.

Audio. To integrate sound or music into a multimedia project has obvious benefits whether for a sales presentation, a kiosk at a trade show, an interactive training project, or essay in musical theory. The sound used in multimedia productions includes speech, music, sound effects, and pre-recorded sound from a disk or tape. To integrate music from a source, several components are required. Some of the components are conventional audio devices used in our homes: cassette players, compact disk players, microphones, and speakers. These devices can become part of a multimedia environment when they are connected to a computer audio board that encodes an audio source input signal, stores the information on disk and reconverts it to audible sound upon a computer playback request. The audio board in the computer converts analog or waveform sound into digital information. Once the information is digitally encoded, it can be stored and processed by a variety of computer programs. To hear the sound again, the digital sound is reconverted to analog data on the sound board and output through speakers.

Another special computer audio standard, the Musical Instrument Digital Interface (MIDI), connects a computer and electronic musical instrumentation. The MIDI was developed to connect electronic musical instruments, synthesizers, and controllers to computers. The standard has gained widespread acceptance and the MIDI interface is a standard feature of most sound boards. The MIDI is a serial computer interface with a transfer rate of 31,250 bits per second (bps). A typical configuration involves the connection of an electronic keyboard to a synthesizer. The message carried along the cable digitally encodes the information captured by key depression or release.

Since the combination of sounds made from a synthesizer's MIDI interface can be stored on disk, these preset sounds can then be reselected, recombined on the synthesizer, and edited. In short, it enables the creation of musical voice and/or instrument combinations. The computer issues a command to its MIDI adapter that combines the selected sounds from the disks and routes them to speakers.

Motion video interfaces. A computer requires a video adapter board or circuitry to accept a motion picture video analog input signal. These adapters receive either a National Television Standard Committee (NTSC) or PAL signal for display on the computer screen. Some video boards can convert analog video reproduced from a VCR to a digital representation that can be modified by the computer to be displayed in a window. The computer in turn can command the modified video frames to be output to a VCR tape operating in record mode. A full motion video card can acquire, process, and compress multiple video frames and store them. This video equipment used in conjunction with animation, graphics, and other multimedia software that accommodates the sequencing of time based information provides a powerful tool set for creative publishers. The Silicon Graphics Indy workstation (5000 dollars) and the Macintosh Centris AV (2500 dollars) are ready off the shelf to accept motion video.

Software Tools

The computers and peripheral devices that we have just described would not operate as an electronic publishing system without computer software. Software programs that control both the normal operations of the computer (called the Operating System) and other programs that automate specific functions or tasks (called Application Programs) are essential to electronic publishing system performance.

Operating System

The operating system is a set of programs which organizes files, executes commands, and manages the flow, storage, transfer, and retrieval of data. The most widely known operating systems are Microsoft Corporation's Disk Operating System (MS-DOS) familiar to users of personal computers, the UNIX operating system used on major workstations, and the MAC operating system (called the System) developed by Apple.

Operating systems provide a base for organizing the system. System files control the processes that wake the system up at power-on time and direct the flow of information from one moment to the next. Operating systems allow users to manage files, diagnose and solve problems, find information, and keep the system secure. Operating systems have become more user friendly with the development of Graphical User Interface (GUI) and windowing systems that use visual menus and graphic icons to run applications and manage files.

Programming: the Object Connection

Without programs, computers are dumb machines, designed with basic instruction sets which by themselves will not accomplish complex automation. Computers need instructions to carry out various tasks and solve problems. Application programs are the instruction sets required to perform complex algorithms. High level programming languages can be used to write programs that are independent of the brand of computer. These high level languages are removed from the machine level instruction set which is unique to a proprietary machine. Examples of higher level languages are FORTRAN, PASCAL, C and C++.

Many publishing programs available in the marketplace use C language. The C language is flexible enough to allow programmers access to the computer at a lower level but also to perform general purpose functions of a standardized higher level language. Just as natural languages have grammar and syntax, so do high level program languages. The C language (like many high level languages uses a compiler) a program that translates statements into a form the computer understands.

Object-oriented programming, with a high level language such as C++ or LISP, provides greater integration and appending of processes, tasks, and discrete elements. Most advanced programs have gravitated to object-oriented programming for the flexibility and the control of documents or parts of documents. Object-oriented programming works with three key concepts: objects can pass messages to each other; objects can inherit the properties of other objects; and object programming ties data and the processes working with that data. More electronic publishing programs are using object-oriented programming techniques, because of the added power and flexibility to manipulate data.

Application Programs

From accounting to aerospace, from computer-aided manufacturing to computer-aided publishing, application programs help users solve problems. Application software includes all the programs that allow users to create, scan, assemble, interchange, search, print, view, compound, deliver, and manage documents. No one program performs all of these functions. Some vendors sell one specific application program. Some sell sets of programs and establish partnerships with other vendors to offer complementary computer-assisted publishing solutions.

There are hundreds of electronic publishing related application programs available. Core electronic publishing programs combine several programs into one bundle such as text formatting, graphics, table and equation editing. Other programs are intended for one specific function such as a utility software thatprints special PostScript fonts not available in a standard word processing package. By classifying these programs into groups, we can understand how they relate to each other.

Authoring and editing tools. Authoring tools can be divided into two broad groups: those that aid in the formatting and presentation of information and those that are used in the organizing and structuring of documents. The formatting programs are used to create documents with a variety of text composition, page layout, and graphics capabilities. Some of the desktop publishing tools combine several editors: text, graphics, equations, and tables, for example, into one bundled package.

Authoring tools include:

- ➤ Text editors and word processors
- ➤ WYSIWYG page layout and composition tools
- ➤ Structure and content based SGML authoring and editing systems
- ➤ Multimedia authoring packages

Word processors and text editors. These programs enable data entry and formatting of text with features that vary depending on a specific need. Traditional text editors have been available on mainframe computers for many years with elaborate formatting capabilities evolving over time. Most of these programs, however, require explicit markup commands to enable the formatting of text.

Word processing tools were the forerunners of desktop publishing packages. Commonly distributed on user desktops throughout an organization, advanced word processing tools such as Microsoft Word, WordPerfect, MacWrite, and AmiPro offer a range of capabilities for the creation, assembly, and printing of text formatted documents. These word processors have evolved to allow the incorporation of graphics within a document imported from another graphics editor or created from a graphics editor within the system.

Desktop publishing page layout and formatting software. Aided by WYSYWYG display technology, users can lay out pages and documents for required typographical elements for output to a hard copy device such as a laser printer. The page layout capabilities of most desktop programs setup the required numbers of columns, the position of headers and footers, pagination, margin control, widow and orphan control, and a variety of other features. Text editors within the desktop

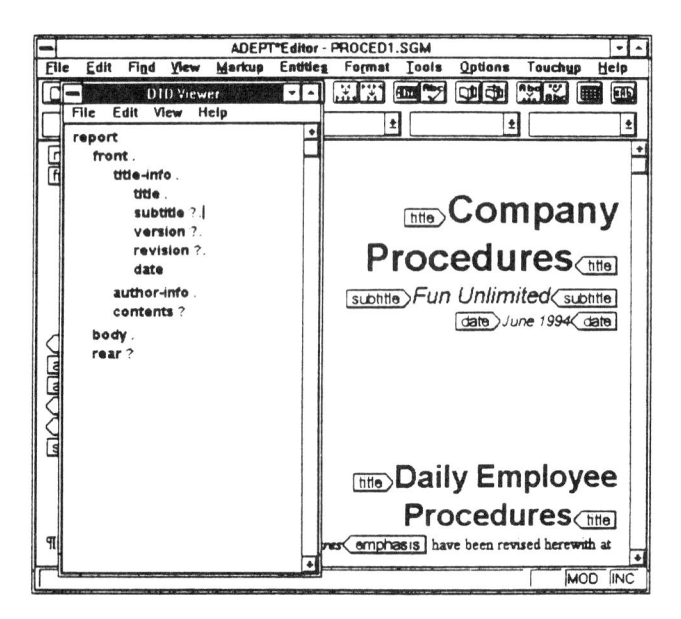

Figure 1.8. An example of one SGML authoring tool by ArborText, a leader in developing user friendly SGML authoring. (Courtesy of ArborText, Inc.)

programs control composition features such as word and letter spacing, hyphenation, and font selection.

Structured SGML authoring tools. SGML authoring tools allow writers to structure and author documents according to rules established in a document type definition (DTD). SGML authoring products are not used to format documents but to encode information in a neutral way so that the data can be exchanged among differing computers and reused for multiple outputs (electronic document and hypertext viewing, print, database storage and retrieval). Contemporary SGML authoring tools are used to encode information within a preordained structure and content design. See Figure 1.8. These authoring systems minimize the need to memorize all of the syntax and markup coding conventions required by a DTD.

Multimedia/hypermedia authoring tools. Multimedia authoring systems are used to organize the collection of information (text, graphics, sound, video, and other content) for multimedia presentations. The authoring tools typically include software necessary to accommodate the sequencing of time based information (audio, animation, and video sequences, for example). See Figure 1.9. Some of these systems also provide the presentation style manager for collections of multimedia information. Word processors, SGML authoring tools, and graphic editors may also be used to create source material for multimedia collections.

Hypertext and hypermedia technologies allow the nonsequential linking of related text or, in the case of hypermedia, text, graphics, video, and other information to be displayed for electronic viewing. The material linked together may

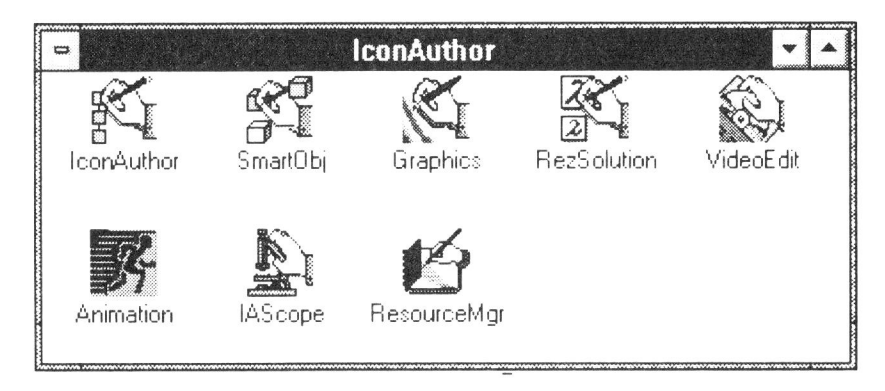

Figure 1.9. This authoring tool is a top level icon interface to mulitimedia—IconAuthor. Authors can build mixed media collections (video, animation, graphics, audio, and text) and also create their own icons to organize media collections so that audience can interact with the presentation. (Courtesy of AimTech Corporation.)

consist of text and other information such as graphics, film, animation, photographs. Some multimedia authoring programs have built-in iconographic flow chart, hypercard, or storyboarding techniques to aid in the creation of training, sales presentations, or other multimedia applications.

Hypertext and hypermedia allow readers to navigate from one point of a document to another, or even between documents and with appropriate technology, simultaneously displaying on the computer screen portions of related information from separate chapters or sources. The electronic information can also be a mix of various media such as text, graphics, animation, audio, and film. Hypertext and hypermedia collections are sometimes called Electronic Reference Documents (ERDs).

Equation editors. Both word processing and desktop publishing systems provide equation editing capability. Equation editors offer formatting and typesetting of mathematical expressions. Some, such as the FrameMaker evaluating tool, allow users to evaluate algebraic expressions.

Table generating software. Automatic table generators allow for the setup and format of columns, rows, table headings and other required table properties such as rule lines for columns. Table generating software accounts for the flow of tables to multiple pages and adjusts the elements to the page flow, including table titles and stubs. See Figure 1.10.

Graphic editing programs. Used for the interactive creation and editing of computer graphics, graphic editing programs include:

- Illustration tools
- Paint programs
- Computer-aided design (CAD) tools
- Free hand drawing programs

Many graphics editors support color options and some operate independently of text editors. In other publishing programs (Interleaf, FrameMaker, PageMaker, WordPerfect and PageMaker, for example), the graphics editor coexists with text editor for ease in merging text and graphics. See Figure 1.11.

Document conversion programs. Conversion software or document interchange software allows documents to be transferred from one system to a different program with minimum loss of document formatting or information. Some conversion programs retain the formatting characteristics of text composition while others attempt to translate graphic pictures. Translating proprietary file formats made by one vendor into a format acceptable for import into another editing program is the purpose of file format conversion programs. Automatic conversion of proprietary text formats into neutral interchange SGML can be done by special translation programs as well.

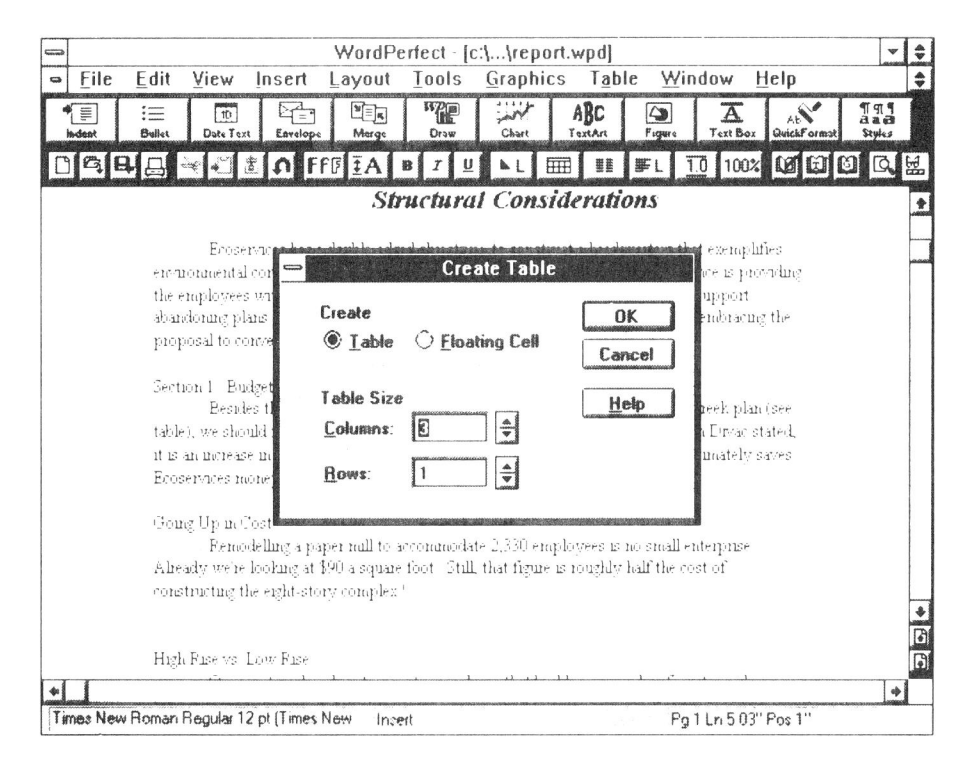

Figure 1.10. Automatic table generator interface from WordPerfect v.6.0 for Windows illustrating options for setup and formatting. (1991–93 WordPerfect Corporation. All rights reserved. Used with permission.)

Graphic file format conversion programs translate or convert a proprietary vendor format into a format acceptable for import or export by another program. Graphic converters translate two types of formats: vector and bitmap. A vector drawing is produced by a mathematical representation of a graphic line or curve. A bitmapped drawing is defined by an array of bits. Typical vector formats used for conversion of proprietary formats include Computer Graphics Metafile (CGM) and Hewlett Packard Graphics Language (HPGL). Encapsulated PostScript (EPS) and Tag Image File Format (TIFF) are examples of bitmap formats.

Text file format translation programs convert text files from one format to another to make a file format compatible with an application program running on an exporting or importing system. A popular text conversion file format is the Rich Text Format (RTF) from Microsoft. The RTF file format preserves the format or appearance of the document from one platform to another. Other translator software includes SGML conversion software that converts proprietary file formatted documents into documents tagged according to a predefined set of structural

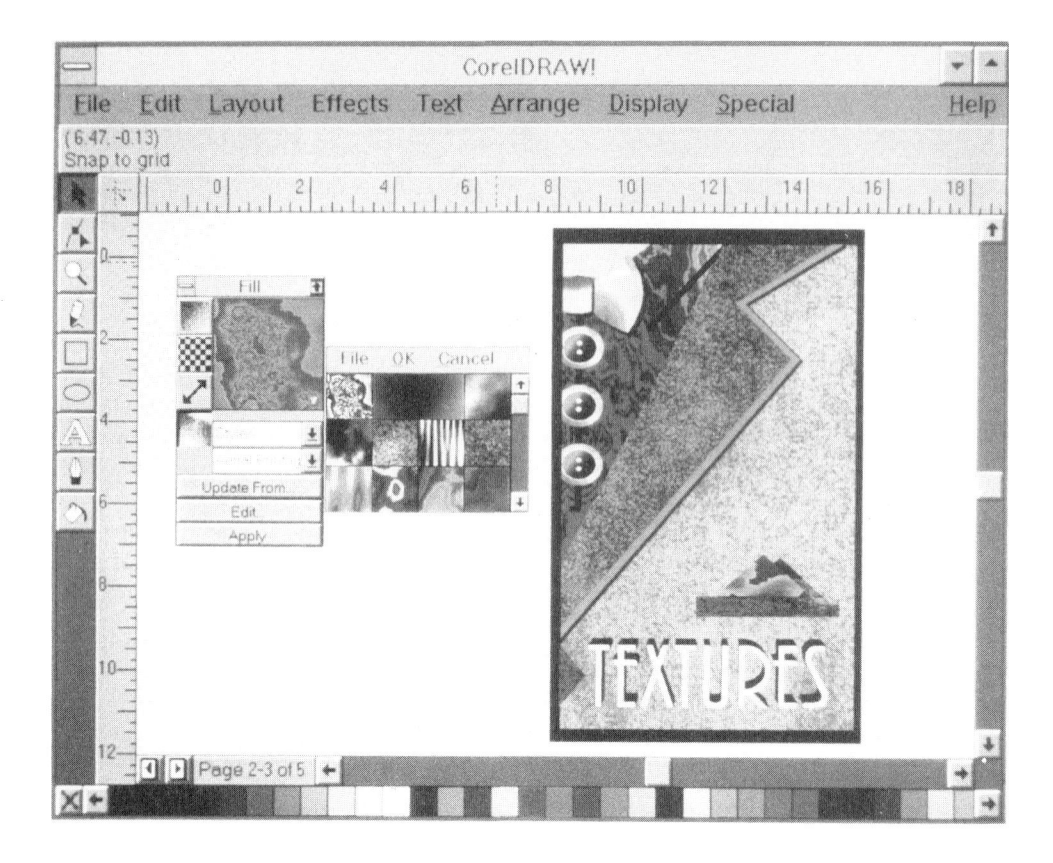

Figure 1.11. Sample from CorelDRAW! graphic editing program which provides extensive tools for creating and modifying drawings in color and grayscale. (Courtesy of Corel Corp.)

coding rules. SGML encoding does not preseve document formatting information. FastTAG from Avalanche Development Company is an example of a product used for SGML conversion.

Database publishing. Database publishing provides for the automatic generation and assembly of document information. There are two types of database publishing. The first is a report generator that builds documents (financial reports, product catalogs, or phone directories) by loading fixed length records from databases. The database publishing software assists in the assembly and formatting of information funneled into documents by linking to the template and style sheet features of existing word processing or desktop publishing programs or by offering its own formatting capability. The programs are not database programs but interfaces to existing databases. They help extract information from a database and direct the data to a document formatting program.

A second type of database publishing is evolving, and is more ambitious in scope. It involves the retrieval of variable length information including text and non-text objects (graphic images, for example) from a database. The rise in popularity of SGML has spawned interest in document database applications because SGML encodes document information according to a pre-defined model. Special programs can be used to extract subsets of the encoded information to assemble documents. Document formatting for page or screen presentation uses programs that decode tags identifying information structure and content, and present the data according to a visual presentation model or template.

Document image processing. Document image processing makes digital versions of paper documents and other graphical source information (for example, photographs, color slides, and illustrations). Combining the use of optical scanning, character recognition, image processing software, and display technologies, document image processing is altering office automation objectives. By digitizing documents that once occupied file cabinets and drawers, document imaging tools are helping government agencies, insurance companies, and other organizations reduce dependency on paper. Document image management subsystems (Figure 1.12) are used for archive and retrieval of document sets stored on a variety of media including optical storage systems. The management of document imaging files has been enhanced by the use of document indexing and retrieval programs that enable rapid search and access of information stored in an electronic document repository.

Scan image and photo edit software. Scan image editing software is divided into several types. Intelligent character and optical character recognition software enable the computer to generate text that has been scanned. The text can be manipulated after the intelligent character recognition software has made the translation. Graphic scanning software allows for pixel edit of the bitmapped graphic. Other scanning software modifies color images or photos that have been scanned into the system. See Figure 1.13.

Electronic viewing programs. These programs offer a means of viewing collections of electronic documents. It is the nonlinear aspects of electronic documents that makes the technology at once attractive and disconcerting when compared with conventional paper document presentation. Many electronic document viewers and browsers support hypertext links to nonsequential information in an electronic document collection. See Figure 1.14. The reader can browse through a document or many documents for specific information related to a topic, keywords, or other information search criteria. Viewing technologies can be either page oriented or not. Page-oriented viewers capture pages directly from documents pre-formatted for print. Non-page viewers abandon the printed page as the paradigm for viewing information. Stressing the need for grouping sets of infor-

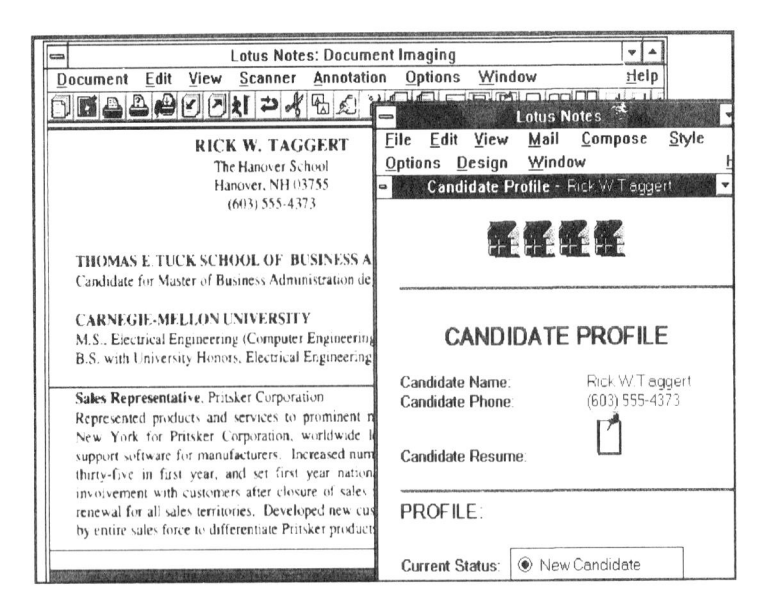

Figure 1.12. A document image management system using Lotus Notes: Document Imaging. This software works together with image editing tools from Kodak. With the help of Lotus Notes, workgroups can readily access specific documents that have been scanned into the system. They can readily share, annotate and distribute paperless documents, contracts, customer letters, diagrams, or reports. (Courtesy of Lotus Development Corp.)

mation chunks, including SGML structure and content tagged collections, some programs underline the need for information design to establish a rich environment for electronic presentation.

Text retrieval programs. Text retrieval software enables searches across a large body of documents and information based upon keywords, structures, or Boolean expressions. A key feature of text retrieval programs is the ability to generate an index of information automatically from a set of documents. A text retrieval system can be used in conjunction with an electronic viewing or browsing system so that readers can use icons and menus to look for information. See Figure 1.15.

Page description languages. A Page Description Language (PDL) is a graphics package used to assist developers of applications for publishing, printing, and page layout, and to free them from learning all the machine-dependent processes of printing devices. A page description language works with an interpreter resident in a device such as a printer. The most popular page description language available is the PostScript language designed by Adobe. There are thou-

Figure 1.13. Scan image edit of photo with user interface tools available to modify the image. (Courtesy of Mentalix Corporation.)

sands of application programs that incorporate PostScript for purposes of page layout, font management, and printing. PostScript can be used as a screen description language as well as for printing devices. Other important page description languages include Hewlett Packard's Page Control Language (PCL) and the Xerox Interpress language.

Multilingual document translation software. Documents can be translated into foreign languages by using multilingual document translation software. For corporations who sell products internationally, creating documents in several languages can be a serious requirement. The challenge of computer integrated translation has been met by Logos Corporation and Brink International who also provide direct links to the some of the major word processing and desktop publishing tools. This makes it possible for a document created in one language to retain some of the formatting characteristics of the original language after translation.

SOLUTIONS

Given the range of capabilities presented by specific electronic publishing programs, system planners need to be mindful of the objectives of the system and how different software programs and work processes can be deployed efficiently.

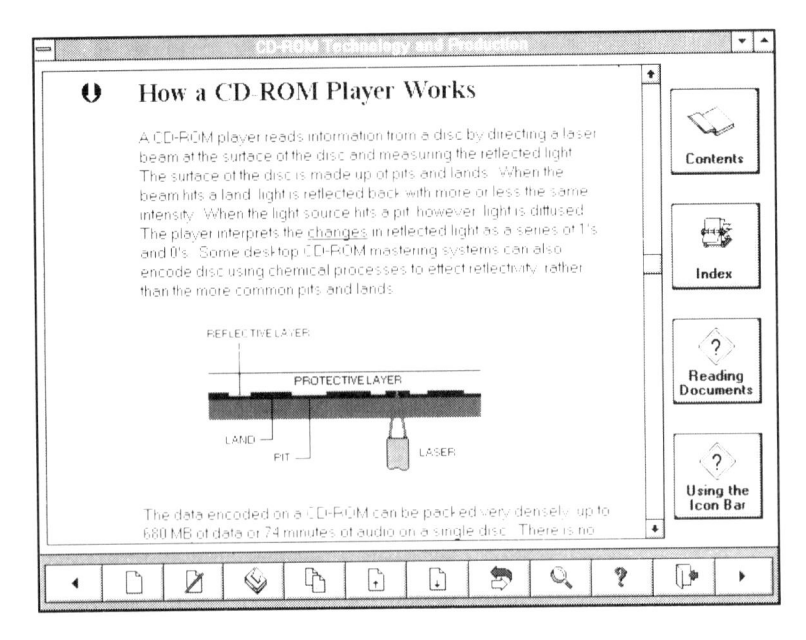

Figure 1.14. Sample of an electronic document viewing program. Authors construct documents including hypertext links with the Guide authoring tool from InfoAccess. The Guide Viewer allows readers to point and click and navigate through an established document information base. (Courtesy of InfoAccess, Inc.)

Many books devoted to a specific word processing or desktop publishing program provide step by step guidelines of one program's ability to format and print documents. These are valuable guides to the use of specific tools. But there is more to integrating an electronic publishing system than learning how to use a single vendor's package.

Many critical processes may be streamlined by applying electronic publishing technology. An index or table of contents can be generated automatically. Page layout can be executed with the help of a video display terminal and laser printer. Illustrations can be drawn efficiently with a variety of drawing and graphic design tools. Templates or publication style and page layout models can be electronically stored and instantaneously retrieved for use with various projects. Electronic data stored from other systems may be imported for use in a project. Publication groups can perform many required document development and production tasks concurrently from desktops in a network. But instead of just helping to quicken the production of paper documents, electronic publishing is changing the way producers and consumers of documents access information. Document retrieval and

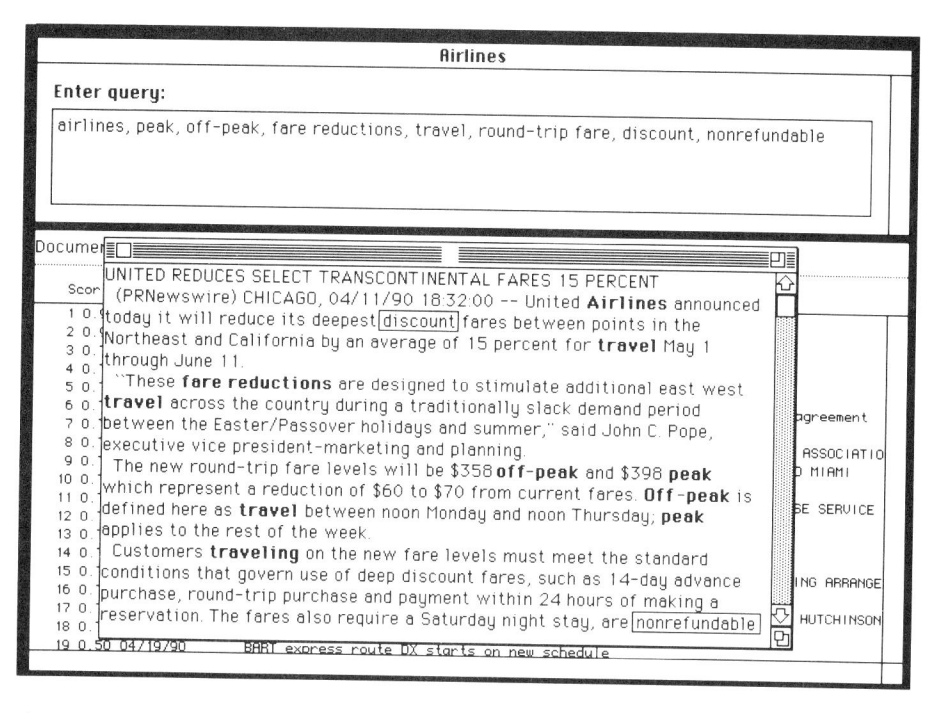

Figure 1.15. Sample of a text search that begins with a user query for key words and concepts. The system automatically marks and displays the words that match the user defined query. (Courtesy of Verity, Inc.)

indexing and document management and distribution systems are part of a new content paradigm in electronic publishing.

What Is a Document, after All?

A document is not always what it seems. We are accustomed to thinking about documents in paper molds but this represents only one electronic publishing function. In the broader sense of electronic publishing, a document is an intelligent structure that can be combined with other sets of information for electronic delivery, for information retrieval, and also for printing pages. Companies are beginning to understand what electronic documents can do to be more productive. We need to rethink our objectives and the methods we use to create and process documents with computers.

CHAPTER 2

➤ *Workgroups and more*

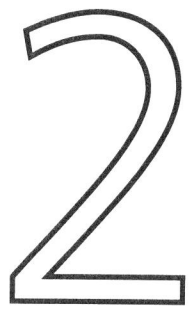

➤ *Open standards*

➤ *A matter of substance*

➤ *A paperless world?*

From Groups to Standards

*t*o better understand the function and use of electronic publishing, we must first examine its gradual evolution through four interrelated stages. The first is the move from individual to workgroup publishing. The second is the confluence of open information standards for publishing and the simplification of computer use through graphical user interface and window management systems. The third development is the appearance of document management technologies that support information integration, document search and retrieval, image management, and workflow. The fourth is the use of digital graphics and formatting technologies that provide on-line as well as paper-document distribution from the desktop. This chapter examines the interrelation of these four factors. See Figure 2.1.

The diagram links developments that appear isolated, but their coincidence gives new meaning to publishing system usage. The linkage suggests that channeling workgroup collaboration, supported by industry norms of desktop access and interoperability standards, enables efficient reuse of information for on-line or paper distribution and database storage.

This analysis points to some critical issues:

➤ User and workgroup responsibilities
➤ Authoring and editing with icon interfaces
➤ Windows for multidocument processing and presentation
➤ Standards for document interchange

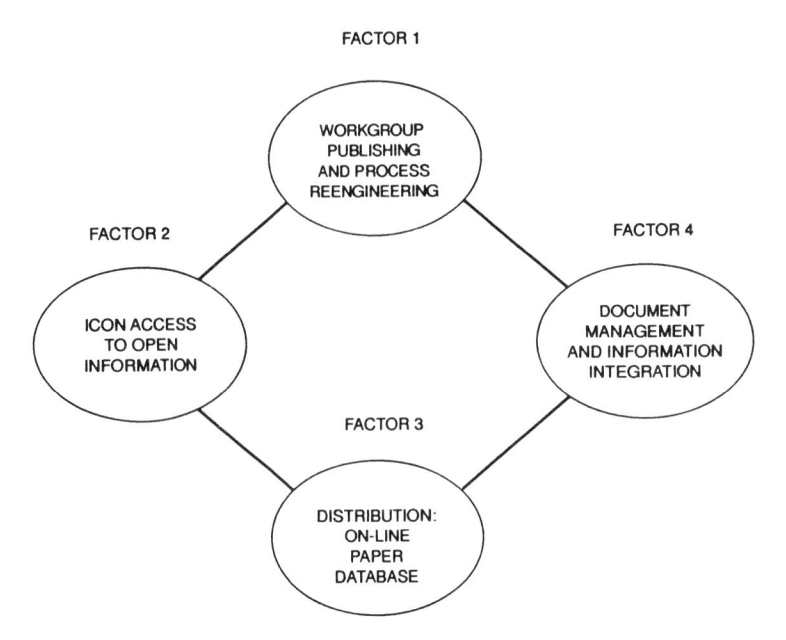

```
                    FACTOR 1

              ┌─────────────┐
              │  WORKGROUP  │
              │ PUBLISHING  │
              │ AND PROCESS │
              │REENGINEERING│
              └─────────────┘
FACTOR 2                          FACTOR 4

┌──────────┐                    ┌──────────┐
│ICON ACCESS│                   │ DOCUMENT │
│  TO OPEN  │                   │MANAGEMENT│
│INFORMATION│                   │AND INFORMATION│
└──────────┘                    │INTEGRATION│
                                 └──────────┘
                  FACTOR 3

              ┌─────────────┐
              │DISTRIBUTION:│
              │   ON-LINE   │
              │    PAPER    │
              │  DATABASE   │
              └─────────────┘
```

Figure 2.1. Four interrelated factors which have shaped the development of electronic publishing.

- Planning a document management strategy
- The role of graphics and document imaging in electronic publishing
- Using document databases
- On-line document distribution

WORKGROUPS: AVOIDING THE PITFALLS

The growth of computer networks used in conjunction with electronic publishing systems has brought workgroups to the fore which requires a different approach to creating, revising, and distributing documents. Much commentary on desktop publishing focuses on how to learn the use of a specific system and how to "come up to speed" on design and layout of pages for prepress printing or on-line presentation. Little attention is given to requirements and responsibilities for workgroup collaboration necessitated by the introduction of networks, client server computing, and multilayer publishing applications. Part of the problem is that the technology transfer to user desktops has occurred without sufficient understanding of how such technology affects the methodologies, work practices, and cognitive processes of professionals who become "end users."

Effects of Technology Transfer

Proponents of technology improvements in the workplace are quick to predict first level effects of introducing technology, most notably, productivity improvement. Less attention is paid to second level effects of introducing the technology, namely the influence it has upon people and their work habits which may, in fact, cause counter productive effects.

Examples of such counter productivity are easy to find. Much can be learned from a large corporation in the aerospace industry which designs and manufactures tape recorders and high speed electronic communication devices. The corporation bought a computer-aided publishing system on the premise that it would decrease the time necessary to produce documents of all descriptions. Several months went by and a study, performed to measure productivity gains, showed mixed results. For projects involving the creation of new documents, the study (based upon performance against project budgets) showed some significant productivity improvements had been achieved. In cases where gains were not achieved, however, some interesting lessons were learned.

One lesson learned was that successful projects often involved small groups, combining authors and production personnel. Project planning and preparation of the individuals to work as a team had been underlined in each successful case. Team members had preliminary exposure to the technology in evaluation settings. By contrast sample projects that did not flourish showed secondary effect hazards because the definition of processes by which authors, editors, and other participants worked together had not been adequately thought through, and projects that required many authors working from different groups were problematic. Similar secondary effects occurred on projects involving groups who were not clear on whose role it was to perform various tasks. Whether or not writers should create a drawing for a document or whether that should be the exclusive province of illustrators was never clearly defined. Illustrators who now created drawings more efficiently than before had difficulty retrieving earlier versions of the same drawings because insufficient attention had been given to planning an efficient library and drawing index system. Consequently, many drawings had to be done over.

In addition to process problems, there were secondary effects on a technical level. Projects involving large scale data conversion were complicated by proprietary format and compatibility issues. Upon closer examination, it was found that this technical difficulty was exacerbated by certain counterproductive decisions. Exorbitant amounts of time were spent reformatting documents that had already been formatted and disagreements over correct style and similar issues served to increase the time spent on tasks which did not take time before the technology was installed.

Planning to accommodate for second level effects is critical. System planners should recognize the conflicting demands of being, at once, a user and a professional. Individuals attempting to fulfill the requisites of a job as an author, editor, researcher, illustrator, or designer, are at the same time learning the tools for expanding their individual skills. The challenge for system planners, analysts, managers, and human resource specialists is to distinguish between the professional and technical view of individuals as users.

A sticky area is the multiplicity of authoring tools. These tools include text editors, word processors, WYSIWYG publishing programs, graphics programs, spreadsheets, hypertools, and multimedia authoring. All too frequently these tools are purchased without a clear definition of how the author uses the tool or how information gets from the author's desktop to another. Often, those tools are seen as personal assets to achieve immediate ends without concern for the need to share the information in its electronic form.

Authoring tools produce digital information which can be integrated and shared as a resource. Networking tools require users to develop a mindset of collaboration. This deviates from a "personalized" desktop model where the user is perceived as working in isolation.

A Shift in Focus

As network and collaborative publishing technologies have matured, there has been a shift in user focus from the individual to workgroup models. This shift is by no means universal and may be offset by the lack of support or failure to implement the model in some part of the organization. There are often cultural obstacles when electronic workgroups extend beyond the immediate boundaries of traditional departments, creating problems ranging from simple misunderstandings about objectives to intraorganizational disputes about control.

Many companies introduced electronic publishing while adopting the personalized desktop as the model of the publishing system. This view of the user as a detached entity was derived from cultural bias and technology limitations concerning desktop capabilities. Some of the factors conditioning the individualistic user model include:

- First generation desktop technologies did not sufficiently address workgroup processes and document management
- Earlier technological limitations of processing speeds, memory capacities, and network integration prevented effective integration of tools
- Preoccupation with desktop publishing as a formatting tool obscured the importance of electronic information sharing and access
- Fragmented organizations failed to see electronic documents as parts of a chain of information for distribution of knowledge

To reap full benefits from electronic publishing tools, companies and individuals must focus their attention to process engineering, that is, the design of a process by which documents are created, shared, processed, and managed. Document process engineering empowers workgroups to discuss ways to solve process problems, eliminate inefficiency, and increase productivity.

Experience has shown that the following factors enhance cultural acceptance of workgroup connectivity:

> ➤ Focus upon a business process and customer requirements
> ➤ Increased deployment of local and wide area networks
> ➤ Lower cost for distributed workstations and file servers
> ➤ Applications involving groupware and group decision support systems
> ➤ Management acceptance of quality team involvement and other developments such as process engineering
> ➤ Technical developments in document management that allow for workflow cycle management of group projects

Effective workgroup publishing requires a well-defined process. Advocates of process reengineering remind us that the process needs to be continuously examined and improved. This applies to minigroups who work together, as well as to the large workgroup or to the team when the concept expands into joining multiple workgroups from different organizational departments.

WHAT'S IN AN INTERFACE?

Collaborative publishing for workgroups received a boost with the development of graphical user interfaces. By simplifying most aspects of human interaction with computers direct manipulation and iconic interfaces permit publishing workgroups to perform an array of tasks involved in authoring, communicating, managing, formatting, and distributing documents.

A Graphical User Interface (GUI) is the industry term for pictorial tools displayed on video terminals which help users interact with application programs and computer operating functions. Most word processing, desktop publishing, and other authoring systems feature graphical interfaces to allow users interactive manipulation of operations such as creating text, graphics, and tables.

Publishing applications were among the first to benefit from the introduction of windows and graphical user interfaces. The development of these same interface conventions has also opened up opportunities for delivery by producers of interactive multimedia and electronic documents. Interacting with electronic books or articles via graphical interfaces is crucial to the success of electronic document viewing and multimedia.

There are three main styles of user interfaces all of which are widely used in publishing applications. These include direct manipulation, iconic, and What You See Is What You Get (WYSIWYG) user interfaces. Direct manipulation interfaces are such that the objects and relations to be operated on have a visual representation. An example of a direct manipulation interface in action is the drag and drop technique of many GUIs. The user points at a picture of a file and then moves or drags it across the display screen to drop it in a visual representation of a directory or trash can. The second type of user interface style are iconic interfaces. An icon is a small picture representation of an action or an object. Sample icons are shown in Figure 2.2. Icon pictures, sometimes combined with words, are used to represent an object, property or action. Icon interfaces help users recognize and remember how to perform operational tasks.

Another style of user interface is WYSIWYG. Popularized in many desktop publishing programs, the WYSIWYG interface has enabled many users of text and graphics applications to visualize what they are creating on the screen. WYSIWYG composition systems use proprietary file formats to encode the information they process into formatted pages of documents. As a result, the electronic document data and format cannot be easily interchanged.

Many older generation word processing packages had no GUI at all. In those cases users had to rely upon memorizing keyboard coding conventions mapped by the specific word processing program. Now popular word processing programs such as WordPerfect and Microsoft Word for Windows provide graphic interfaces that make liberal use of icons and other graphic devices that help hide the complexity of computer program operations.

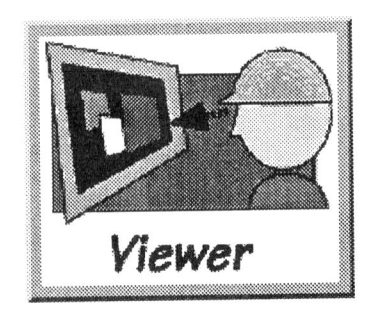

Figure 2.2. Sample icons used for graphics application programs. (Courtesy of Carberry Technology.)

Windows: An Eye Opener

Windows are rectangular frames on video display terminals that serve as a work area for various tasks and applications. (By default, a window is a rectangular subset of a bitmapped screen. See Figure 2.3.) When it appears on the screen, a window may be sized incrementally up to full screen or minimized to icon shape. As appropriate, windows may be tiled, layered one upon another, or moved from one position to another on the display terminal. User interface differences in window conventions between Motif, Open Look, MS-Windows, and Macintosh windowing systems are more a matter of degree than kind. Workgroups must decide upon suitable windowing tools to meet collaborative goals. It is also possible to have different window systems running within the same workstation.

Windows are controlled by a window management system. The window management system has two parts: a window manager and a window system. Users interact with a window manager when they create, size, move, and open windows. The window manager determines the look and feel of the user interface. The window system includes the functional programs that cause the windows to be created, sized, moved, and so on.

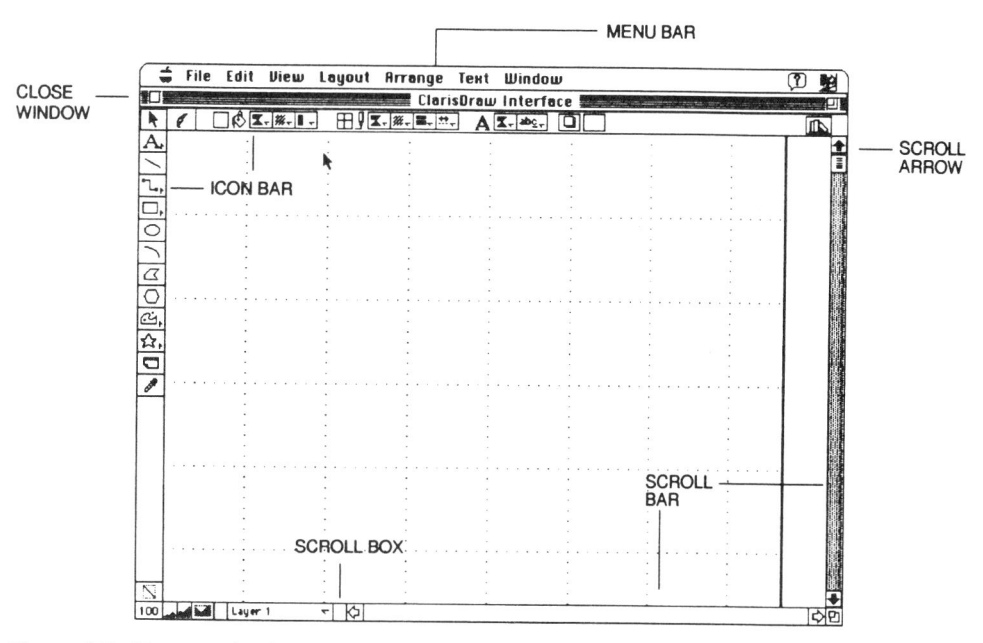

Figure 2.3. The standard Macintosh window interface. Some menu bar categories and icon selections are application independent. (Courtesy of Claris, Inc.).

For electronic publishing, windows add flexibility to the setup, creation, and management of documents, allowing users to perform many operations or tasks concurrently. With windows, users of some composition systems can open several chapters of a book, copy from one to another and perform edits rapidly. Each open chapter of the book may occupy a window or similarly, the windows may fill up with several pages of the same chapter so that an author, editor, or illustrator can examine how changes in one part of a document affect another part. Users can run different applications at the same time.

Open Look and Motif are graphical user interface implementations of the X Window system. Originally developed at the Massachusetts Institute of Technology, the X Window system is used in many Unix operating workstation platforms. The window managers for Open Look or Motif running on top of X control the form and look of the window. Other window managers control Microsoft Windows for PCs and the Macintosh windowing system. The Motif graphical interface has gained widespread acceptance. Motif has the backing of the Open Systems Foundation (OSF), a consortium that includes IBM, Digital Equipment, and Hewlett Packard. Open Look, developed by AT&T, has been adopted by Sun Microsystems.

Conventional user interface features of windowing systems include menu bars, scroll bars, and user or client work areas. The menu bar is a horizontal bar that appears near the top of the window. It identifies menu categories for user selection. When the user selects one of these categories with a control pointer, a pull down menu appears with submenu selections. A scroll box or slider is a small square or rectangular marker that indicates to the user the relative position of the information in the work area. By moving a scroll box with a control pointer, for example, the user can scroll through pages of a document or change the relative position of a drawing.

Interactive Roadmaps: Context Sensitive Menus

A menu is a visual guide to selection of user options. From initiating the setup of a scanner to launching a keyword search, users manipulate popup, pulldown and pullout menus and dialog boxes with the help of a window management system and the application software that makes use of it.

While each vendor develops unique menu items, the menu structure across vendor platforms exhibits many common elements. For publishing applications these menus can control document creation, editing, printing, viewing, and distribution. Context sensitive menus are particularly important to application developers and users because they can immediately clarify the choices available to a user of a program depending on the location (or context) of the cursor or pointer within a window.

For example, a context sensitive dialog box is a menu that serves to guide the user toward decisions often associated with delimiting an intiated process. Dialog boxes remind users of the consequences of a command action. They may deter user action, or seek user okay on an action. For this reason dialog boxes may have cancel buttons allowing users to exit from a situation before executing a procedure. Typical actions prompted by dialog boxes are—apply, retry, start, stop, reset, cancel, or close. See Figure 2.4. Buttons are graphical controls that work in a window frame by pointing to them and clicking with a mouse. Buttons are a great advantage to electronic publishing applications. For example, WordPerfect version 6.0 for Windows provides buttons for a variety of actions that could in the past be initiated only by the use of control keys. The user can customize each button for a particular application. A default button set includes actions for closing, opening, printing, cutting, pasting, font control, and spell checking.

Menus help electronic publishers perform a variety of operations from setting page layout and numbering, drawing and editing and image manipulation to document display, electronic distribution and printing. See Figure 2.5.

A popup menu literally "pops up" on the screen when the user depresses a mouse button. Popup menus, like dialog boxes, and pull down menus, have the value added feature of being context sensitive so that options available on the menu are dynamically related to the state of processes active within the program and the position of user interaction.

A cascading menu illustrates some of the dynamic qualities of graphic menus. Cascading menus are formed in tiers usually to the right of the parent menu. Cas-

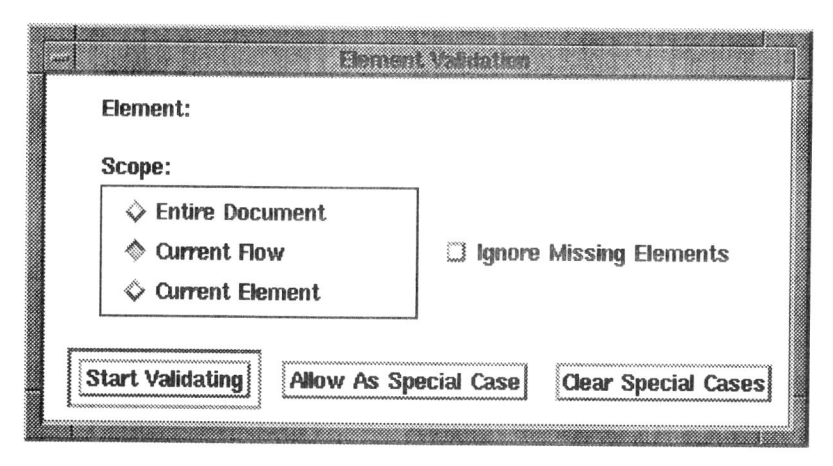

Figure 2.4. User menu dialog box illustrates purpose of context sensitive feedback decision guidance. (Courtesy of Frame Technology Corporation.)

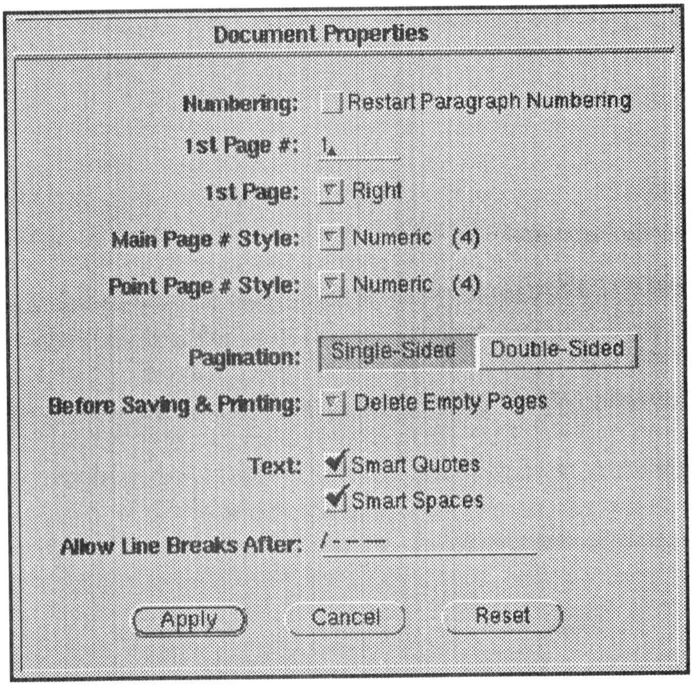

Figure 2.5. Using FrameMaker setup menus to aid paragraph numbering and sequencing, pagination, and numbering style. (Courtesy of Frame Technology Corporation.)

cading menus are submenus that provide more options and submenu selections. The user becomes aware of a cascading menu by an arrow pointing normally in a rightward direction.

DOCUMENT INTERCHANGE STANDARDS

Graphical user interface and window technology have made electronic publishing more accessible to workgroups. But direct manipulation of icons and buttons does not guarantee access to data that is formatted in proprietary document files. The computer markup used to format a document can make document interchange difficult. If diverse word processing and publishing programs are being used within an organization, the disparate file formats used can actually handicap the interchange of documents and information.

Ideally, text, pictures, and other source information available in electronic form should be interchangeable. In reality, document interchange is not simple.

Since there are literally hundreds of word processors, text editors, and graphic editors in use, there are severe limits to the exchange of proprietary file formats (that is, these formats are native to the developer/vendor of the product). The adoption of "open" standards by many organizations and vendors allows document interchange according to neutral ground rules.

Format Codes and File Formats

Formatted text refers to text that has been arranged by word processing or desktop publishing systems so that paragraphs, indents, positions of titles, columns, lists behave according to computer instructions. Markup codes make the format features of the program work. The format codes tell the system what space to use between subheadings and the text above and below, what font to use for section headings and body text, what page margins to apply, and other numerous format instructions. To export or import such text from one system to another requires special translator or conversion programs. Many publishing systems provide translators so that export and import conversion protocols can be applied to files from diverse programs.

Formatted text or graphics imported into the publishing systems can be converted by intermediate translators, but translators are not always reliable as a means for electronic document interchange. Figure 2.6 shows a menu for importing and converting a Microsoft Word file to an Interleaf document. The problem with translators is that there are never quite enough of them and a new version of a publishing program may cause the translator on someone's desktop to become outdated.

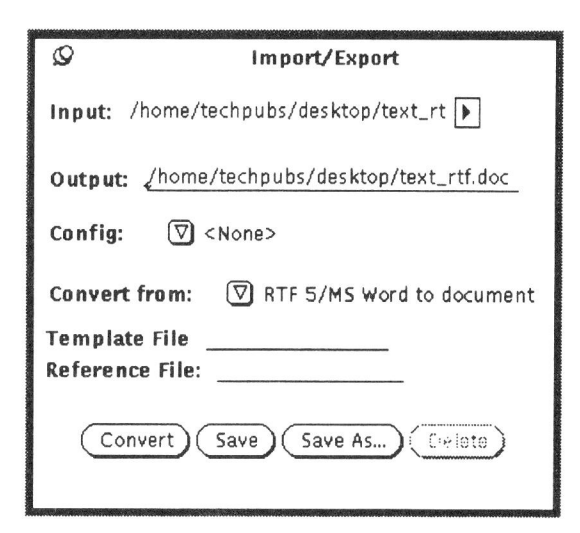

Figure 2.6. File format conversion menu sample from Interleaf 5 for Open Look. In this case an MS-Word document in rich text format (RTF) is being converted to an Interleaf document.

ASCII—A Common Denominator

Unformatted text is a text source that is stripped of its control format. The base standard for unformatted text is the American National Standard Code for Information Interchange (ASCII, pronounced "askee"). ASCII is the default for exchange of unformatted text between computers. Most publishing systems provide for converting formatted ASCII documents into plain ASCII. The baseline ASCII standard (ANSI X3.4-1977) defines a numeric equivalent for every letter (upper and lower case) as well as other control characters such as FF (Form Feed), CR (Carriage Return) and ESC (Escape).

Each character and letter of the alphabet is represented by a binary 8 bit code. In ASCII, the first bit of each 8 bit string is a zero and the next seven bits represent the actual character—either a one or a zero. The number of possible combinations of ones and zeros is 2 to the 7th power or 128. The standard ASCII code, therefore, defines 128 characters. As an example, when one types c at the keyboard, the computer registers the keystroke in the form of 7 binary digits (1000011).

The International Organization for Standardization (ISO) Standard 646 International Reference Version (IRV) provides a list of characters for electronic manuscript preparation. The ISO 646 standard includes ASCII characters, some diacritics, and math symbols. Users of SGML authoring systems who want to unambiguously represent special characters including diacritics and special symbols such as a bullet or an em dash can use the entity reference symbols defined in ISO 8879-1986 for ENTITIES Publishing and the ENTITIES Diacritical Marks. The entity reference for a bullet is &bul; and for a lower case e with an acute accent is é.

The value of ASCII and the ISO standards that have added solutions to familiar characters found in publications is that they allow users of different hardware and software products to share information electronically. Because software vendors have created formatting codes that are proprietary (cannot be recognized by another publishing program) users rely on standards such as ASCII to exchange data. Plain ASCII, however, does not give extra clues to senders or receivers about the data structures or how it relates to similar data, or how the data should be processed.

Neutral Interchange Text Standard: SGML

ASCII is a baseline neutral standard for data interchange. Although indispensable, plain ASCII is dumb because it does not identify the information content or form of a document. Other standards have been developed that allow for the neutral interchange of document data as well as an identification of the information within it. ISO has promulgated SGML as a neutral standard for data interchange. SGML is a meta language which provides several key features including:

> A means of describing the content and architecture of documents
> A neutral technique for transferring data between diverse proprietary systems and applications
> A method of mapping multiple inputs to a standard output

SGML employs generic markup which is descriptive rather than specific and does not tell the computer how to process the information. Specific markup, on the other hand, encodes information regarding the form of a document (layout, fonts, leading, margins, and other format considerations).

SGML has three distinct parts that make conforming documents work. The first part is the document declaration which outlines the syntax for describing a document. The declaration may choose to follow the ISO 8879 standard or modify it to meet specific documentation requirements. The second part is the document-type definition or (DTD) which defines the structure and content of information for a family of documents. The making of a DTD is an evolutionary process involving document analysis, information requirements definition and the specification of document elements and attributes which are repeated, unique, or varied. The third part of SGML is the document instance. The document instance is the application of the DTD to a given document. The document instance is a marked up document containing tagged text, tables, and equations. Graphical objects are not included in the document instance proper, but SGML provides syntax conventions for figure references that specify the location where the graphic object is to appear and where the object is stored. (Chapter 4 examines the role of DTDs and document instances in greater detail).

One of the most significant benefits of using SGML is that it preserves the value of data over time as technology and platforms evolve and change. SGML separates document structure and content from processor-dependent formatting technologies. Once document data is encoded in SGML, it can be reused for multiple forms of presentation.

PUTTING IT ALL TOGETHER

There are several layers of automated integration in electronic publishing. The first layer is the set of tools that help organize the format and automatically sequence the information, for example, layout control, pagination, table of contents and front matter generation, index generation, and so forth. The collective set of editors for text, graphics, tables, charts, equations, and print drivers, are essentially aids in document formatting assembly.

The second layer of electronic publishing integration involves interfaces to application programs that store information the documents will ultimately contain. This type of desktop information integration allows workgroup publishers to automate multifunction tasks. Information integration, a powerful but little understood aspect of electronic publishing, establishes automated interfaces to applications concurrently running on computers with electronic publishing tools. Examples of such interfaces include: databases, spreadsheets, drawing packages, document management workflow integration, or custom designed document file format translation. Using the computing power of tools designed for functions such as calculating, organizing, drawing, or communicating data, the information source generated by such tools residing on desktops can be wedded to the formatting, printing, and electronic distribution capabilities of electronic publishing. Executed properly, document assembly is automated by intermediate formatting templates or style sheets, that is, document information from a data source is automatically fed into a document while the assembly and sequencing process of the document is handled by the template. Although the applications benefiting from this integration vary, the principal high level processes are similar.

Financial Reports—A Dynamic Example

To illustrate the automatic integration of data using the case of financial reports, we assume the report which contains many pages of financial information is published periodically. The essential layout does not change drastically over time but the financial data does. This financial data resides in a database which is maintained by departmental accountants. The database record automatically formats the data into rows, cells, and columns. Using an electronic publishing system, the final report is generated by a publication group. Since the format of the report has already been designed, the main task of the publication group is to integrate the updated financial information, print a master from a laser printer, and take the master to reproductive services for printing, assembly, and distribution of copies. Similar applications exist for the integration of a publishing program and a spreadsheet tool.

There are alternative ways to integrate the information into a document. One inefficient alternative is to rekey and reformat the data into tables in the document, since this duplicates an effort already expended to enter the data and risks creating errors in the process of rekeying. Other alternative methods include the scanning of the data into a document or reformatting a comma-delimited ASCII file. Reformatting a comma delimited file (where the data in cells, rows, and columns in the table are separated by commas in the ASCII file) represents an increase in efficiency, but still requires additional time and effort.

Another alternative is made possible by a special linkage that simultaneously updates the values in the financial table as well as the financial report. As the values of the spreadsheet are entered, an intermediate program allows the same values to be updated in the report minimizing the risk of error in entering the values. Some vendors refer to such updates as hot links.

Fidelity Investments uses a similar linkage technique to publish financial mutual fund reports to participating subscribers. These statements, sent periodically to subscribers as required by the Securities and Exchange Commission, are formatted and printed in a simple and attractive layout. Critical information within the statement is contained in tables that present a summary of financial performance over a period. By using effective process integration techniques and electronic publishing technologies from Interleaf, Fidelity can reduce the chance of rekeying errors in the financial reports, because the data in the financial statement is updated automatically from data updated in the database. Figure 2.7 is a sample from the Fidelity Magellan Fund semiannual report.

Document Management

Until recently, organizations have ignored the magnitude of information stockpiled in documents. The increase of electronic documents produced on word processors, text editors, scanners, and distributed desktop systems has only exacerbated the problem. A new set of technologies has emerged that address the broad based concern for the information contained within documents.

Traditional Management Information Systems (MIS) departments within companies that use large centralized computer systems manage only 5 to 10 percent of the information within the organization. Typical information managed by MIS groups include financial accounting, procurement data, and bills of material databases. The largest percentage of information within an organization, however, is contained within documents such as business plans, proposals, reports, manuals, specifications, training literature, and marketing bulletins, all of which provide information important to an enterprise. When organizations use an ad hoc approach to controlling documents, an opportunity is missed not only for productivity savings but for becoming more competitive.

Document management systems are now gaining much attention as tools which enable organizations to create electronic document libraries, search for information across network databases, identify information changes in different versions of documents, provide secure document access, and manage workflow processes in the creation, assembling, and production of documents. See Figure 2.8.

Document management systems include an assortment of tools such as intelligent scanning and document image management, document database systems, text indexing and retrieval systems, and native SGML products that enable access to reusable elements across documents. Documents, including SGML encoded

Financial Statements

Statement of Assets and Liabilities

Amounts in thousands (except per-share amounts)   March 31, 1994

Assets

Investment in securities, at value (including repurchase agreements of $784,775) (cost $29,708,139) (Notes 1 and 2) – See accompanying schedule		$ 33,198,290
Short foreign currency contracts (Note 2)		
Contracts held, at value	$ (531,716)	
Receivable for contracts held	517,000	(14,716)
Cash		1
Receivable for investments sold		1,409,916
Receivable for fund shares sold		326,738
Dividends receivable		40,519
Interest receivable		36,441
Other receivables		6,667
Total assets		35,003,856

Liabilities

Payable for investments purchased	1,458,144	
Payable for fund shares redeemed	396,546	
Accrued management fee	21,808	
Other payables and accrued expenses	7,892	
Total liabilities		1,884,390
Net Assets		$ 33,119,466
Net Assets consist of (Note 1):		
Paid in capital		$ 28,265,640
Undistributed net investment income		94,879
Accumulated undistributed net realized gain (loss) on investments		1,283,512
Net unrealized appreciation (depreciation) on:		
Investment securities		3,490,151
Foreign currency contracts		(14,716)
Net Assets, for 475,054 shares outstanding		$ 33,119,466
Net Asset Value and redemption price per share ($33,119,466 ÷ 475,054 shares)		$69.72
Maximum offering price per share (100/97.00 of $69.72)		$71.88

The accompanying notes are an integral part of the financial statements.

Annual Report   46

Figure 2.7. Sample page from the financial statements of Fidelity Investments Fidelity Magellan Fund which is updated using automated systems to integrate changes. (Courtesy of Fidelity Investments.)

data, can be stored directly in a document database. Document management systems used should suit the requirements and philosophy of an organization.

Document management tools are helping organizations find and deliver information. By using these tools, electronic publishers can expedite the workflow of documents through cycles of review, editing, and production. Workflow tools typically operate over local area networks. A worker is sent a copy of an electronic document and asked to take some action such as perform a review of the document by a certain date. Part of the workflow system may give the reviewer a chance to make comments on the electronic document without actually changing the original. Once the task is completed, the document can be dispatched to the author for action against the comments. Document workflow systems take advantage of electronic document distribution and electronic mail tools. Delivery and presentation tools are an essential part of the technology used to work efficiently without paper.

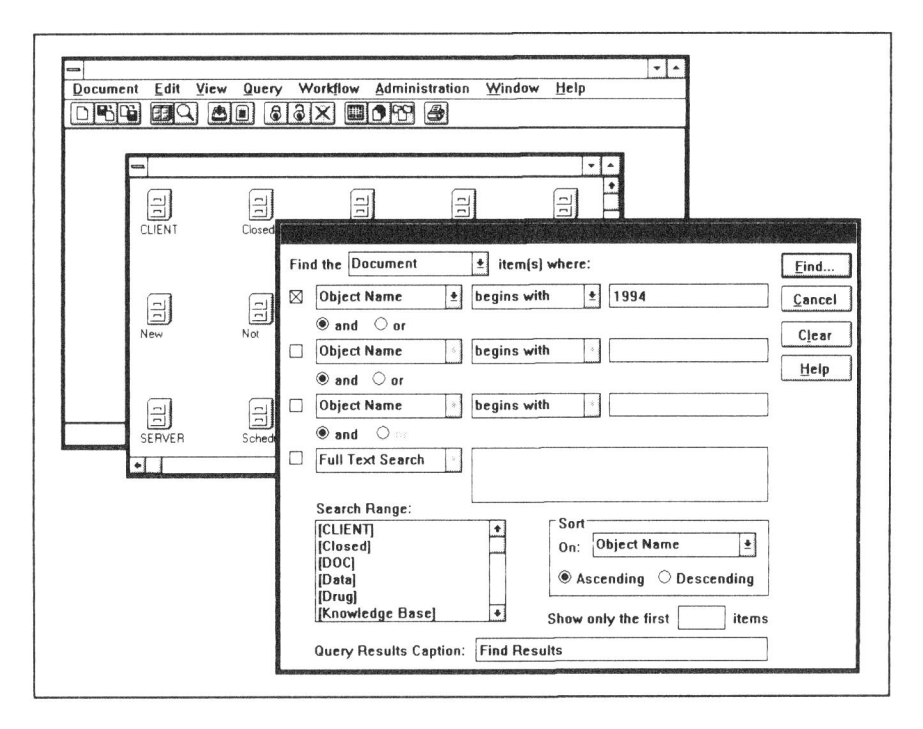

Figure 2.8 The powerful functions of an enterprise document management system include document library control, workflow control, document search and retrieval, and document status and change control. This screen shot shows the initiation of a search for document objects. (Courtesy of Documentum, Inc.)

ON-LINE AND PAPER DISTRIBUTION

Electronic publishing technology has evolved to a state where it is possible to distribute large volumes of information for print or for viewing via a video display terminal. The possibility of delivering electronic or printed matter to audiences is what electronic publishing is all about. A critical technical development in the evolution of paperless publishing is the capacity to store large volumes of information on optical media. The availability of CD-ROM and on-line viewing software has made possible the storage of documents as well as the viewing and distributing them possible at affordable prices.

Applications benefiting from the use of electronic document viewing and distribution include:

- Medical reference works and images
- Manufacturing
- Training
- Electronic libraries
- Interactive technical manuals
- Multimedia presentations

Instead of the time honored principle of rhetorical sequential organization of information, paperless publishing invites audiences to browse and search for information either sequentially or nonsequentially. Roles have altered for all participants in the process from authors to publishers to reader/viewers. Now audiences can participate or interact with the process in many different ways. Since the information presented is not bound by normal page sequencing, the information presented on the screen does not have the relationship to a physical printed page that we have known.

Education and training projects are growth areas for interactive hypermedia publishing. The Perseus Project is an excellent example. In this case the technology is applied to benefit the humanities. Scholars from Harvard, Yale, and other universities have teamed together to recreate bilingual (Greek and English) editions of Greek classics interspersed with still color photos, illustrations, maps, and motion video. The book is a reference work that can be used by scholars and students alike. The team working on this project views it as a major breakthrough for research efforts by future scholars.

The Perseus database includes a rich assortment of information stored on CD-ROM. The project allows access to multidisciplinary information that scholars would normally have to travel widely to collect and never hope to find bound together in printed collections. The cost of printing a high volume of still color photos is prohibitive. Viewers of the Perseus database can see multiple color photo views of historical artifacts such as Greek vases. The imagery of poets, dancers, and singers on these urns helps students and scholars of classic literature understand more about the significance of the texts that they study. Such photographs are displayed in windows on the screen, while other windows may display literary texts as well as commentary from other scholars. Figure 2.9 is a screen from the Perseus hypermedia database.

An interactive electronic technical manual (IETM) is a practical model for an application of electronic document viewing and distribution. An effective use of IETM technology is the delivery of maintenance on-line documentation to benefit testing, fault isolation, repair, and parts ordering for complex equipment and machinery. The manual is for the technician whose job depends upon having accurate and complete information to perform critical tasks in diagnosing and correcting problems promptly and efficiently. Working with paper is often a hindrance

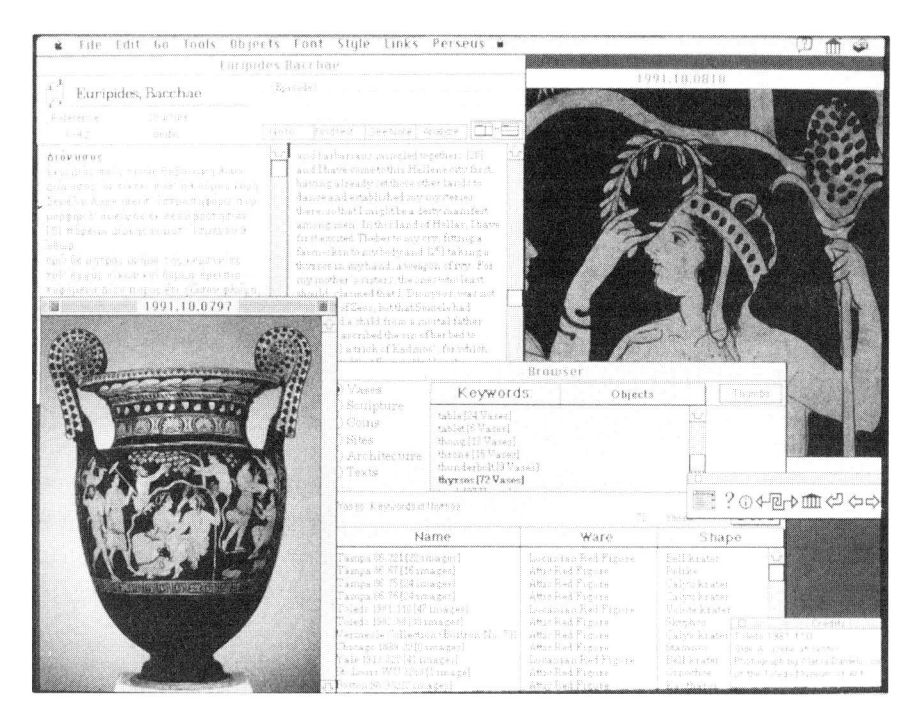

Figure 2.9. Perseus interface sample showing the range of information available to students and researchers available on a single screen. (Courtesy of Maria Daniels, Perseus Project.)

because the bulk of the technical documentation (sometimes multivolumes) makes searching for information awkward and difficult. Rather than page by page information, IETM technology makes it possible to branch across several key pages for simultaneous viewing of correlated information. The Department of Defense through its Computer Aided Acquisition and Logistics program, has encouraged subcontractors to deliver IETMs for use.

Figure 2.10 is an example of an IETM showing displays within Motif windows of information concerning the operation of a Boeing Model 767 Aircraft. The viewer of this document can select from a table of contents listed on the left hand side of the main window. When the user selects a topic (in this case, Ground Pneumatic), the text and graphics related to the subject are instantly retrieved. When the user desires to zoom in on a graphic detail to get a closer view of part of the instrument panel, the zone selected immediately pops up in an auxiliary window. This IETM was developed with a product called DynaText from Electronic Book Technologies (EBT). It is one of various viewing technologies available, but a main product discriminating feature is its conformity with SGML. DynaText accepts SGML input and automatically builds full text retrieval index based upon standard SGML. A style sheet editor is available to define presentation format.

Advances in Scanning and Laser Printing Technologies

The impressive growth of technologies supporting electronic presentation and delivery has been equalled by the development of numerous digital hard copy devices. Once upon a time, desktop publishers had only to think about the deployment of 8 to 20 page per minute, 300 dot per inch, laser printers. Now everything from high speed demand printers to thermal color printers are accessible and affordable.

There are several factors to consider when evaluating which hard copy devices to add to an electronic publishing system. Companies can selectively make investments in the quality of hard copy outputs and also consider how copies of documents are made. Some tradeoff issues to consider involve the use of high speed demand laser printers that collate and even bind documents instead of high speed copiers. If managed properly, desktop color devices (scanners, image setters, and printers) can reduce the cost of outside printing services, since limited quantities of color reproduction can be controlled with digital devices.

Desktop Color Scanners

Scanners can be used not only for color in print related projects but also in electronically distributed documents. Scanners range in cost from inexpensive flatbed models to high end rotary drum scanners. The quality of inexpensive

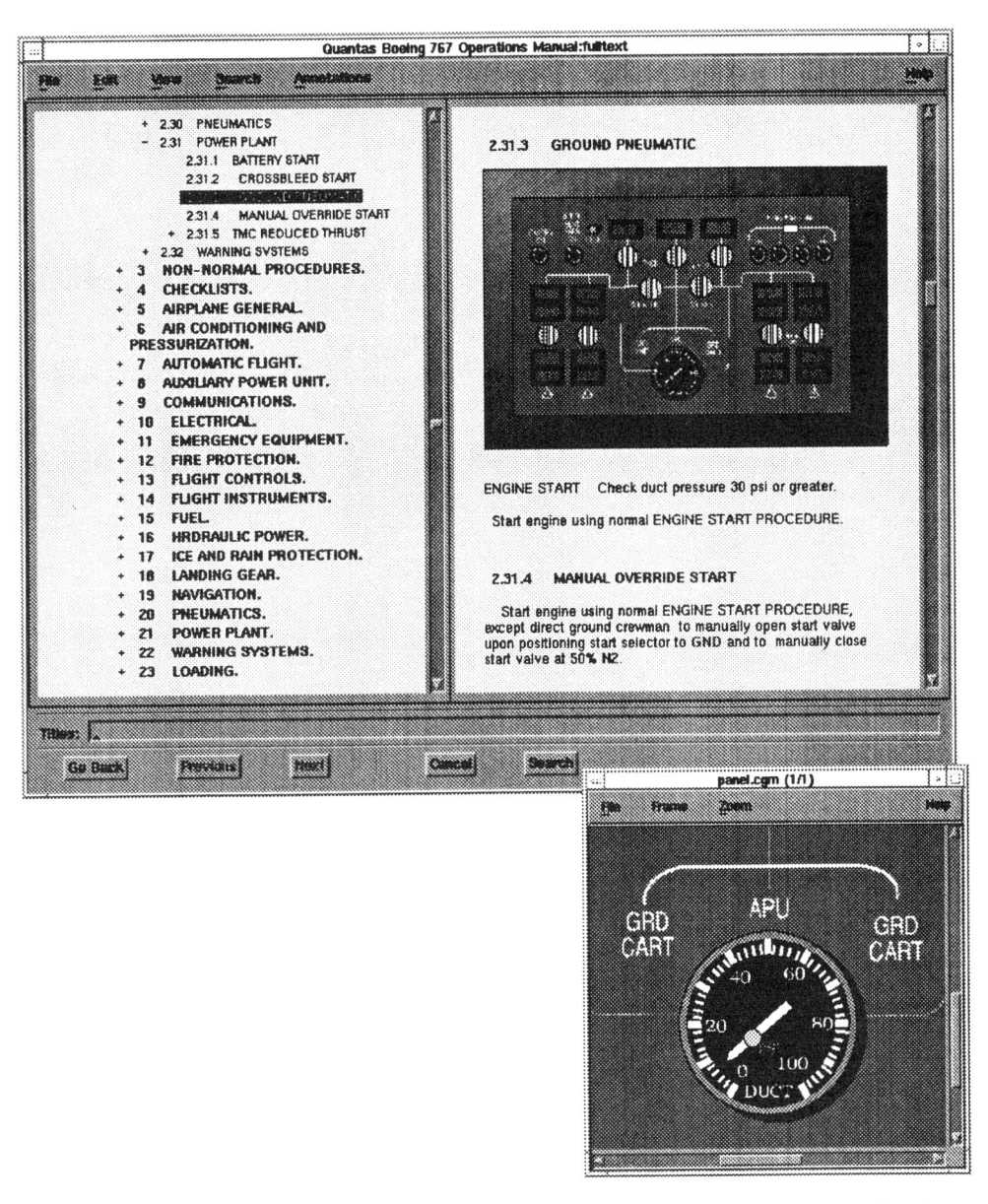

Figure 2.10. A sample from an Interactive Electronic Technical Manual (IETM) application that offers access to needed information with the point and click of a mouse instead of searching through paper volumes. The user can zoom in on graphics, browse through topics, or access information that is dynamically linked. (Courtesy of Electronic Book Technologies.)

scanner equipment has improved dramatically. Desktop color scanning of color prints and slides has improved as well as photo image processing because the reduced cost for high speed microprocessor and memory devices has allowed an increase in the amount of information sampled. This creates much higher rate of accuracy in capturing and editing digital color. Enhanced photo imaging software has contributed to the increased quality of desktop production. Similar advances in color printing technologies allow output of high quality prints from affordable desktop devices. Obtaining good results with color still requires knowledge and skill. Properly used, color not only improves document appearance but also can increase understanding of the information in documents.

Desktop and Demand Printers

Desktop printers are no longer limited to low resolution 300 dots per inch (dpi) models. There are now 2400 dot per inch desktop printers available for under 7000 dollars which not long ago was the price of a 300 dpi printer. Desktop printers currently sell for from one-tenth to one-half that price depending upon specific features. As the cost of the hardcopy devices goes down, the performance capabili-

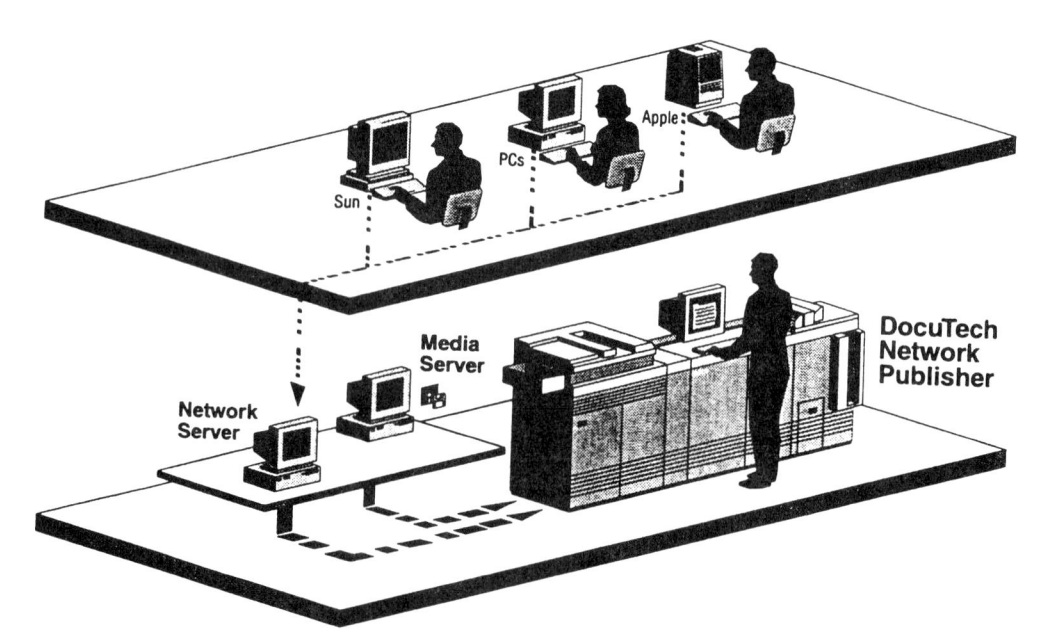

Figure 2.11. High-speed DocuTech Network Publisher showing network connectivity of demand printer to user stations—PCs, Macs, and Sun workstations. (Courtesy of Xerox Corp.)

ties of this hardware advance. Because of this attractive cost-performance ratio, priority should be given to maximizing the efficiencies and quality of the output expected from an investment. This also means that organizations should control paper waste, which is costly, and concentrate upon managing hard copy resources based upon critical needs.

One way of managing print resources within organizations is to explore the use of demand printers. They provide high speed, medium to high resolution, quality documents with many additional features including collating and binding. Many demand printers can be accessed by workgroups over a network. By shifting focus away from paper consumption to demand production, organizations can better manage the flow of paper output. Demand printers can help reduce storage of paper documents. By using electronic document review, edit, and signoff procedures, organizations can also eliminate need to over produce intermediate paper documents. Demand printers use internal technology similar to production printers except they are connected to a network.

CHAPTER 3

➤ *Separating format and content*

➤ *Measuring effective design*

➤ *Automation for print design*

➤ *Electronic presentation design*

➤ *Design for information access*

Document Presentation Design—Format

*d*ocument presentation design determines the appearance and style of documents. Computer assisted design automates document format and layout, font manipulation, and style management for print or electronic document viewing. (Document presentation design is distinguished from document information design, a subject treated in Chapter 4).

A review of presentation design is indispensable for personal and workgroup electronic publishers because in the final analysis good design results in effective communication. There are many models showing how to incorporate design criteria into an automated scheme on a desktop. Word processing, desktop publishing, and electronic document presentation systems offer models, default templates, and style sheets so that documents can be created without intensive training.

While we agree that effective design improves communication, there is no consensus on what users need to know about design. Users in organizations with access to word processors, desktop publishing, multimedia authoring, and graphic tools may have no training or background in graphic arts; however, as users of electronic document composition programs they participate in the designing of electronic documents.

Understandably, there is a need to offer style guidelines for users with limited backgrounds in design. This eliminates time consuming and counterproductive misuse of a tool acquired for its productivity savings. Some companies are learning there is no substitute for a professional designer with adequate expertise in electronic publishing techniques and practices. But with or without such help, there are other concerns about document information enveloped in files created by document formatting tools. Because the file formats used by word processing and desktop publishing software are proprietary, document information can be difficult to retrieve, display, and reuse. The problem seems trivial for personal publishers who know where all the information is, how to get it, and reuse it; but for medium to large organizations impeding access to information can be costly. Generally speaking, there are three major problems related to design and workgroup electronic publishing:

➤ Excessive preoccupation with format by authors and editors can be counterproductive

➤ Using proprietary word processing and desktop publishing file formats can make data less reusable

➤ Creating document presentation designs on an arbitrary basis can stifle effective communication

To make intelligent choices concerning the role of design in electronic publishing, some key issues need to be addressed including the evolving role of WYSIWYG (What You See Is What You Get), responsibilities for design, and metrics for design effectiveness.

WHO DOES THE PRESENTATION DESIGN?

WYSIWYG Displays

The development of WYSIWYG displays has changed the field of design and typography forever. The ability to see composed pages on the screen and the immediate effects of issuing text and graphic formatting commands has had an enormous effect on document production in the workplace. WYSIWYG makes use of a bitmapped screen to approximate the appearance of a page output from a laser printer. Figure 3.1 is an example of WYSIWYG document as it appears on a video display terminal.

The distribution of WYSIWYG to many desktops in the workplace has been accompanied by growth of direct user manipulation of page layout, automated text composition, graphic editing, and multimedia authoring tools. WYSIWYG is a suitable point of departure for discussions of how publishing technology affects both the process of making documents by workgroups and the responsibilities of

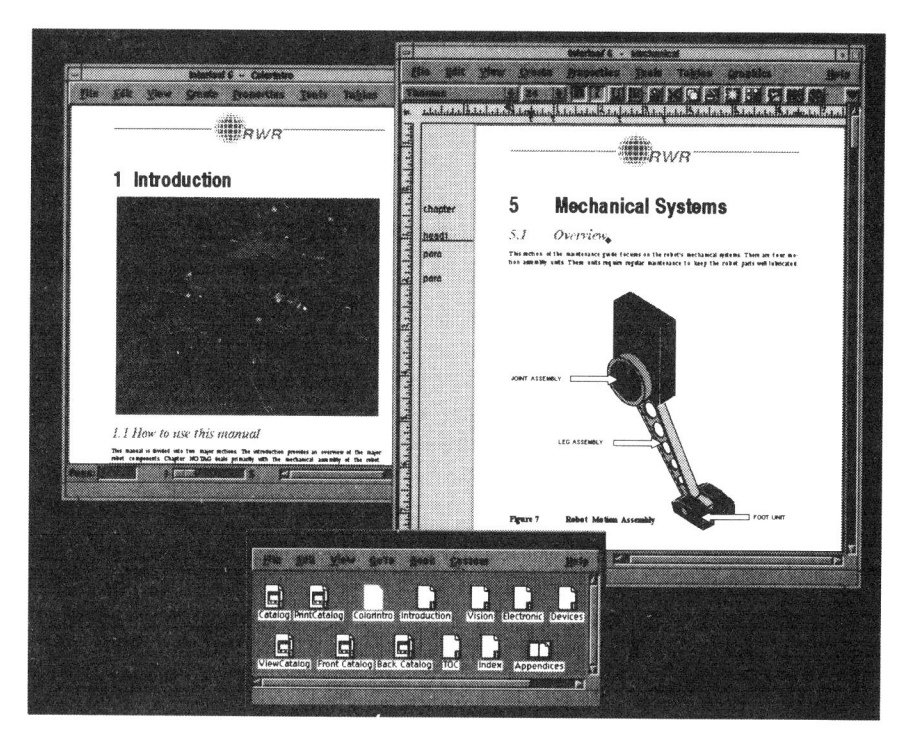

Figure 3.1. WYSIWYG display for interactive document creation and editing using the Interleaf 6 for Motif. (Courtesy of Interleaf, Inc.)

users creating and implementing a design. The process reduces the steps used in document production such as the automation of page layout and composition. WYSIWYG allows users to view the effects of specific commands such as the cutting and pasting of graphics and text, global changes in font size, and automatic adjustments in page margins. With the spread of WYSIWYG and windows technology to the desktop, more and more users become de facto contributors to expanded workgroup publishing process.

WYSIWYG and desktop publishing software has shortened the production cycle of documents within many organizations. Users of different tools, however, may assume roles not necessarily congruent with their job classification. For example, it is not clear that all document authors should be spending time with document formatting process. The following case studies address aspects of the design dilemma for workgroup publishers. Who should generate document designs that become templates on a desktop presentation system? Graphic artists? Any user?

A Cost Quality Tradeoff—Case Studies

A corporation invested in an electronic publishing system to reduce the costs and save time in producing proposals, manuals, and reports. The technology was placed in the hands of writers, artists, and production editors. In time, desktop publishing, word processors, and graphic packages sprouted up on desktops of people whose roles had little to do with formatting and producing documents. The more these individuals used the technology, the more some of them presumed that their design ideas, if not perfect, were worthy to publish. Little, if any, regard had been paid to design standards.

Within this corporation, proposals sent to prospective customers were part of the lifeblood of the business. Following the production of a 400 page proposal, a senior official complained that the production group had unnecessarily changed the appearance of several drawings he had done with his desktop drawing package. The graphic artist who made the changes pointed out that the original drawings were inconsistent with other drawings in the proposal. The official objected that the re-make of his illustrations was contrary to the purpose of acquiring his desktop graphics editor in the first place, which was to increase efficiency in the "process" and save money. He could not accept the argument that if 30 different authors made diagrams with no regard for design criteria there might be a problem in preserving a consistent graphic standard throughout the proposal. The artist argued from the position of quality; the senior official defended the bottom line.

In a related corporate case, a word processing specialist who now had access to desktop WYSIWYG technology assumed that she was a document designer because she felt it was now part of her role as production operator of a system to integrate text and graphic elements in publishable documents. Because she sometimes worked as an implementer of style templates she thought it qualified her for the role of designer. She had virtually no graphic arts training, but since the technology was at her disposal she claimed her stake within the publishing process.

In both of these cases the traditional production-related responsibilities for executing a design were not properly understood by all participants. These anomalies are symptomatic of *haphazard automation.* The problem is magnified because traditional publishing groups within organizations are not the only ones with access to the technology. To integrate a workgroup publishing solution within an enterprise requires a cohesive plan and attention to the shifting capabilities of the technology.

Personal or Group Publishing?

Investment in computer technology should always be preceded by a thorough examination of how it is going to affect work processes and whom it is going to affect. Most organizations have a limited understanding of what work processes will be changed by the computer technology.

Word processing and desktop publishing technology have often been brought into organizations and deployed as if individual desktops were personal publishing facilities. The personal desktop publishing model, where each individual assumes expertise for aspects of a project, including formatting chores, is not a viable paradigm for in-house or commercial publishing. When office cells operate as fragmented publishing centers, they undermine the practical objectives of increasing productivity. Gains in productivity become offset by the cost of sustaining personalized desktop publishing technology, by failure to capitalize upon goals of enterprise-wide information sharing and by failure to standardize design procedures. Whereas the personal desktop publishing model implies that an individual will try to do as many functions within a desktop as possible according to personal preference, the workgroup model encourages a collaborative process tailored to the requirements of an organization. The personal publishing model inevitably can cause duplication of design effort within an organization and quite possibly impede the reuse of critical information.

WHERE DOES CONTENT FIT IN?

The role of information design is often neglected in planning the use of computer-assisted publishing. This is in part because much of the original publicity surrounding the desktop publishing revolution focused upon document presentation and layout capabilities. Since attention was given to page layout and formatting, document information analysis took a back seat to document appearance. Consequently, many word processing and desktop publishing users are not accustomed to:

➤ Distinguishing information and presentation design objectives
➤ Authoring and editing with a structure–content based tool as opposed to a formatting tool

Accessing and adapting information from electronic documents can be difficult and the problem can be exacerbated by the proliferation of information distributed on computer desktops.

Separating Document Format From Structure and Content

Some publishing systems deliberately separate document format from document content and structure. ArborText, SoftQuad, Interleaf, Datalogics, and XSoft (Xerox), among others, offer Standard Generalized Markup Language (SGML) authoring systems. Others including Lotus, Microsoft, and WordPerfect have introduced SGML based authoring tools. SGML makes use of generic or descriptive markup. Generic markup does not require a computer to format the information but it identifies the information in a logical structure denoted by markup code (commonly called a tag). Thus the markup for a logical structure known as a paragraph could be identified by the tag <p>. This does not tell the computer how to process the paragraph in terms of its format characteristics. It allows users to access information denoted by the tag <p> regardless of what computer platform it resides upon or what publishing tool is used to process all paragraphs even across many different documents.

Most authoring tools (word processors and desktop publishing page layout programs) encode the information as it will appear visually on printed page. SGML markup is *format neutral*. It adheres to a declared model of structure and content defined in a Document Type Definition (DTD). Word processing and desktop publishing systems provide an implicit sense of document structure through visual layout of elements on a page. Type styles (sizes, and weights), text indentation and alignment, and various forms of spacing and positioning create a complex of style parameters.

SGML authoring tools are editing systems that automate and enforce the structure which all documents have. Books, for example, contain front matter, a body that breaks down into chapters, sections, and other sub-elements; and end matter. Because SGML markup is descriptive, it can specify document content and structure. Since the markup is also generic, it can be processed on various computers. Definition of format is omitted from the markup.

In the past SGML authoring tools have been considered as user unfriendly. More and more SGML authoring tools, however, feature graphical user interfaces to guide an authoring session. The SoftQuad Author/Editor system, for example, allows users to visualize the document element structure and SGML markup while creating the document. Figure 3.2 shows a tutorial sample of an SGML authoring tool user-interface. Easy to use tools like SoftQuad's Author/Editor provide access to a structure and content template for a document, so that authors do not need to remember complex syntax and coding. What the author sees on the screen is not the composed document but the markup. The system dynamically responds to use of structural elements by providing feedback on the validity of element usage in any given context.

The reasons for detaching the structure and content from presentation format is that the data is easier to interchange and the unformatted data can be reused for a variety of applications (print and CD-ROM, for example). If we separate document presentation and information design, automated computer assisted formatting processes enable efficient production of *either electronic or print documents.* There are different automated solutions to accommodate formatting of vendor neutral SGML encoded information. We will examine some of these at the conclu-

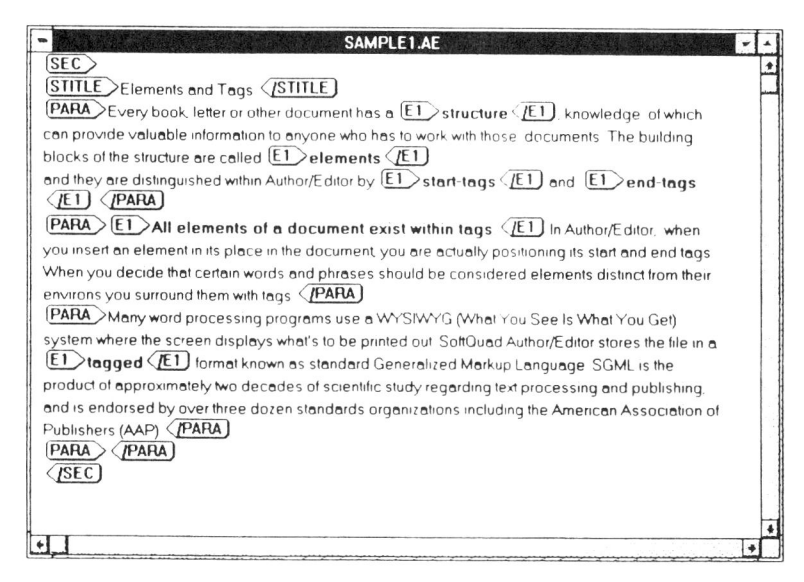

Figure 3.2. SGML authoring is made simpler by user friendly SGML interface. The user can see the structural markup and enter data within the appropriate boundaries. (Courtesy of SoftQuad Inc.)

sion of this chapter after we review the factors that must be addressed before submitting a design to the automated templating process.

Figure 3.3 shows a variation of document structure and format with Frame-Buildert, a product from Frame Technology that allows authors to structure and validate document information. Although FrameBuilder is not an SGML system, it supports the concept by defining a document's structural elements to enhance information reusability. FrameBuilder departs from the SGML authoring approach because it does not entirely segment the tools needed to provide conformity from the tools used for interactive WYSIWYG formatting. It also includes graphics directly in the document whereas SGML authoring tools make external entity references to pictures and illustrations that are to be inserted.

OBJECTIVES FOR PRESENTATION AND INFORMATION DESIGN

Information design requires a logical breakdown of documents into structural and content elements within families of documents. Similarly, presentation design specifies document format and layout elements specified of the information design. Workgroups should coordinate parallel analysis of document information

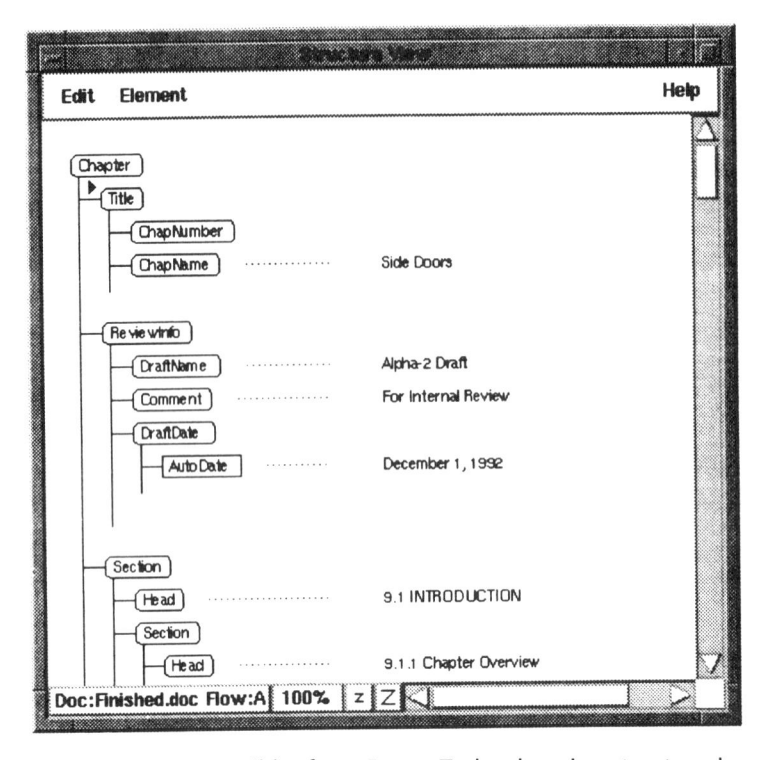

Figure 3.3. FrameBuilder from Frame Technology is a structured SGML friendly authoring system that does not strictly adhere to SGML authoring rules. FrameBuilder supports the concept of authoring according to a structure but unlike native SGML authoring systems, it allows for the definition of style and formatting of elements as well as manipulation of graphics within the file structure of the authoring system. (Courtesy of Frame Technology Corporation).

and presentation design. Table 3.1 summarizes the distinct objectives of the two group efforts.

The presentation design is concerned with the appearance and format of the information. Some of the questions to be raised by the designer include:

> ➤ Is the format presentation for one document only or for a family of documents?
> ➤ Is the document meant for electronic as well as paper presentation?
> ➤ How will the document be packaged? How will it be *printed* and *bound*? How many copies will be printed?

Table 3.1. Guidelines for document presentation and information design guidelines for workgroups

Document Presentation Design	Document Information Design
Research the typographic requirements	Analyze document content and structure
Prepare design	define document elements
Develop design model	Examine data conversion requirements
Create prototype	Determine if public DTD can be used
Test results	Create new DTD if necessary
Create master template of page format	Provide DTD usage samples

➤ What formatting and style management tools will be available?
➤ What is the quantity of diagrams, photos, and other graphic material?
➤ What are the costs for electronic document design?
➤ What types of viewing stations does the audience have?
➤ How can the design make the information easier to find?
➤ What are the special needs of the audience?

The information design is concerned with structure and content of the documents independent of presentation. The information design team must ask:

➤ What source data exists? Is it accessible electronically?
➤ Is the information stored in a proprietary format?
➤ Does the document model break down into a logical hierarchy? How valid is the structure of subheads and sub-subheads, for example?
➤ Will the information change over time and will those changes have to be documented and controlled?
➤ Will this publication be the unique container for the information or will the data be used in other documents?
➤ Will the information be presented at different levels for different audiences, for example, beginning, middle, and advanced level?

The designers should know budget constraints, the capabilities of available human and technical resources, and schedule requirements. Presentation and information design should be planned in parallel. The information designers define a structure for information so that it can be accessed, adapted, and reused. The presentation designers assess the requirements of publications, specifying the layout and composition for a document or families of documents. If the project calls for a unique design, a similar planning process is followed except no special attention is given to the reusability of the design, whether for print or electronic display.

We will cover the process of document information design in Chapter 4. The remainder of this chapter is devoted to presentation design practices.

GUIDELINES FOR DOCUMENT PRESENTATION DESIGN

The presentation design process can be broken down into stages that start with the project's conceptualization and lead to its testing and fine tuning. The first step is to grasp the document's objective. Good design enlivens the content of documents and makes them readable and attractive. Design planning must also account for designs that will be repeated for the life of a family of documents (reports, manuals, guidelines). This concept definition applies to electronically presented documents as well as print oriented documents.

During the research phase, designers investigate requirements and collect data that will help make a design. The research might include a survey of the audience, a formal study of audience requirements, or a comparison with sample documents of the same genre.

The audience influences the design in obvious and not so obvious ways. Large type with fanciful illustrations may be suitable for children books but unacceptable for another audience. The size of type used on the video display terminal for electronic document viewing also depends on the anticipated distance of the viewer from the video terminal. Sometimes understanding the audience requirements demands considerable probing. Presentation designers should identify the specific needs of the audience population. Some of the requirements may be delineated in reference material; other times surveys may be conducted. The research should include sufficient data to enable the designer to begin a series of design models.

Development

During the development phase the presentation designers make a design model (paper or electronic presentation) that can be evaluated for its effectiveness. Techniques to be used include storyboarding, and flow charting. Storyboarding allows workgroups to share and visualize ideas and design sketches on boards or pieces of paper that can be displayed (in a sequential manner) on a wall for comment by the design team. The team encourages feedback and mutual support. Storyboarding is a technique that works with on-line multimedia as well as paper document projects. It can be used with the design of proposals, newsletters, reports, books, and multimedia presentations.

Flow charting is a valuable technique for visualizing design alternatives. Multimedia developers use flow charting to determine how an audience will interact with collections of information. For example, in order to visualize how hypertext branches from one set of information to another, a flow diagram can show how specific relationships will be presented.

The prototype phase is the initial design mockup which can be presented as a set of sample pages for book length works, a dummy brochure or newsletter for smaller document designs, or a full blown draft document if a preexisting design from an electronic library can be modified to suit the available information. For on-line electronic documents, the prototype may consist of a table of contents, a hierarchy diagram, and a style guide to default values of elements in a structural model such as a document type definition.

The prototype should be accompanied by a set of design specifications. The specifications can be used to begin the process of building a template for a print document or automated setup of an electronic viewing style guide and hypertext navigation model. The prototype specifies and demonstrates the most complete a set of design features possible.

The test methodology measures the effectiveness of the design. One method is to solicit expert opinion. Another is to quantify "defects" according to quality related criteria such as consistency and completeness and whether the document complies with certain industry or government related specifications. Mini surveys can be conducted within an audience population that may resemble the document's target audience. The surveys should solicit feedback on how the design of paper or electronic documents helps the reader learn, do, or research something. With the feedback from such tests, designers can modify their models.

Measuring the Effectiveness of Presentation Design

Measuring and quantifying the effectiveness of document design can be done through the conduct of surveys and interviews, formal analysis of documents with reference to standard criteria, and less formal peer feedback analysis. What are some of the criteria that can be measured? One of the main criteria is the ease of finding information inside a document. Another set of criteria gauges the document's usability, especially if the document's purpose is to help an audience perform practical tasks or learn something. Criteria may focus on quality in text design for example, readability of text, or comprehensibility of graphic design such as illustrations. Collecting sufficient sample data to establish a profile requires gathering data on a spectrum of document types.

Design specialists have to articulate and help identify the cost benefit of design for documentation. There are several ways this can be achieved. One way is to argue that good design gives companies a competitive advantage, as many times a document sent to a customer represents the first impression of a company. Effective design always improves the quality of the communication. By demonstrating there are cost effective alternatives in design quality, the design team can suggest strategies that reduce costs through choice of design options.

If the resources of a company do not permit the employment of a professional designer, it may mean having to train existing staff to create designs. Nonexpert designers can look to models, books, and other sources for assistance. Where possible, soliciting feedback from expert designers helps to keep the design effort on track and add credibility to the process. Design specialists should become well versed in the capabilities of the equipment, so that they better understand the limits and features of a system and to identify special needs. If designers are not provided with adequate tools to perform the task at hand it is just one of the problem solving variables they confront.

PRESENTATION DESIGN VARIABLES

Presentation design must be viewed as a set of variables dealing with the form and presentation of printed and electronic documents. The vocabulary of design has specialized meaning to students of layout, composition and typography. Document design has also been extended to include electronic document and multimedia presentation. Although the specific execution of commands that produce different kinds of type, spacing, and control vary from one system to another, the concepts related to graphic arts design and practice are independent of the vendor products.

Assuming the designer has successfully thought through and planned the design with a specified format, an electronic publishing system makes the process consistent. For example, page or window setup involves the precise application of preselected measurements for all elements—margins, headings, subheadings, fonts—the set of specifications that make up a page or display window presentation. A graphic artist or production specialist has responsibility for molding a given manuscript to the design formula. The designer, editor, and production person use a special vocabulary or markup to specify the typographical requirements of page and document layout. Many of the terms used in specification markup refer to measurements such as points, picas, leading, kerning, margins, gutters, and font size. Typefaces and similar information are specified.

Variables for Electronic Document Design

Creating designs for on-line documents is a challenge because they are viewed and read from a video display monitor with the added possibility of mixing other media (film and audio, for example) in the presentation. Designs for conventional printed material are inextricably linked to the medium of paper. From a designer's perspective, a critical difference is that the sequencing of information is not the same. The nonsequential structure of hypertext documents, for example, requires special flexibility in design where the page is no longer the unit of presentation.

Electronic books, reports, and multimedia presentations no longer have to conform to paging conventions as we know them from printed literature. Chunks of information can be organized into collections of variable length text structures with links to other graphics or video, for instance. Electronic document viewing and delivery engines now support the use of SGML encoded information. Other multimedia systems use a variety of techniques (such as cards) for authoring and viewing the information. Some document browsers use serial paging mechanisms while blending nonserial hyperlinking techniques. Since a variety of methodologies have been adopted, the development of electronic documents for viewer interaction continues to offer challenges. Factors to be considered in the on-line design process include:

- How is display formatting controlled?
- What level of interactivity between the reader/viewer and the information is supported?
- Is color used in the presentation?
- What navigational tools are available for text searches or indexing?
- What other tools will aid in finding and adapting information?
- What objects can be displayed? Text only? Text and graphics? Other media?

Providing users on-line access to the information is important. The designer should anticipate the media to be used by end users. How will they access this information? How will viewers focus upon the information presented? Research and requirements analysis are critical. Attention must be given to details of size and placement of information inside windows including the ability to support inline graphics.

Time is one of the most significant design variables in multimedia or hypermedia presentations. Designers familiar with the nuances of two-dimensional space must become attuned to sequencing time based information (video, audio, and animation). The synchronization, duration, and linkage of specific information must be planned and edited. Multimedia designers coordinate digitization of video clips, animation sequences, and audio, as well as the synchronization these elements. On-line or multimedia presentation requires coordination between the design team and technical support groups. Technical support includes any requirements for the writing of programs or scripts to integrate content elements or automate other features of the presentation.

Interactive Display and Dialog

The display screen and windows provide the spatial framework for viewer interaction. The tools include icons and buttons and user interface elements. The designer should strive for simplicity and consistency in repeated elements such as locations of titles and navigation controls. Keeping the user interface as uncluttered as possible is essential for effective on-line design. The designer needs to know a good deal about the types and quantity of information content that will be accessed via the display system. Will the information be limited to small chunks of text or encyclopedic volumes of text with mixed objects? In any case, the designer must research the possibilities and requirements before committing to any plan. The designer must also consider how the viewer will dialog with the system. For example, will hyperlink buttons be used to guide viewers to interrelated information? Such buttons or other icons are normally embedded with elements in a document (a table of contents item or illustration for example) which may be accessed. Sometimes a table of contents or index list can appear within one panel of a window such that when the user clicks on a topic the information linked to the topic immediately appears in another display panel. Figure 3.4 is an example of a presentation from an electronic textbook where topics can be selected directly from a dynamic table of contents. The establishment of a consistent graphical alphabet of icons, symbols, and other devices used for interaction with the system is also essential.

One of the main variables designers must contend with are the constraints imposed by the authoring and viewing programs available to them. As electronic document browsing programs evolve and add automated design features, they make the task of the designer somewhat easier. These features include prebuilt templates that designers can modify to suit specific needs. Many companies delivering electronic documents to their customers are also using the technology in-house for a variety of applications. Designers collaborating with authors and editors, for example, can actually use the technology to reengineer the publishing process by using electronic document viewing for edit, review, and approval cycles.

Accessing and Adapting Information

Effective on-line design results in easy information access and adaptability. Critical to finding information is the method employed for navigation through an information base. The user or viewer needs a clear and logical map to the information facilitated by the design. Since electronic document viewing conventions are

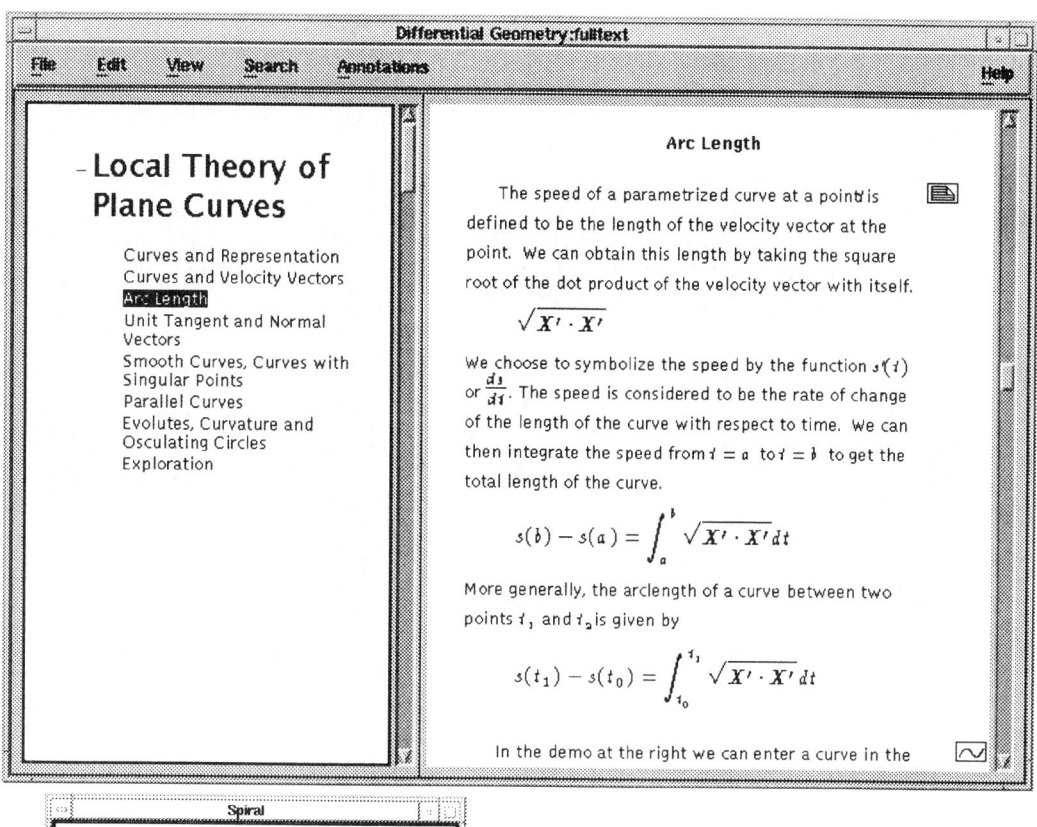

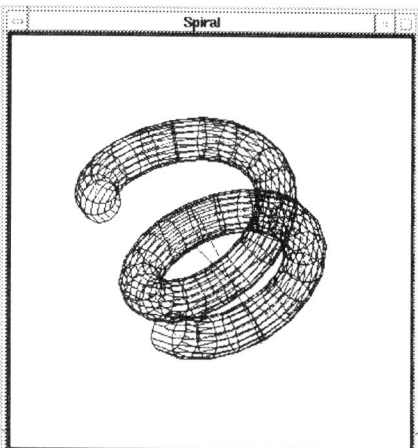

Figure 3.4. A design for access to information must consider how viewers are going to select topics of interest. In this case, the selection of the highlighted topic of arc length on the left, brings the viewer directly to the information shown at right. (Courtesy of Electronic Book Technologies).

still new, it is important not to overwhelm an audience that may feel uncertain exploring on-line documents. Users do not want to get lost and be unable to return to the spot where they began their navigation. The ground rules for interacting must be built into the design. Designers should discourage overdevelopment of links that confuse an audience. Every effort should be made to let users find the information they need.

Just as readers of printed documents are able to underline information or dog-ear pages, users of on-line documentation systems need to annotate documents delivered electronically. Facilities for note making are common among authoring and viewing products. Notes can be used by document readers for reference. Bookmarks help users navigate to key points of information quickly.

Some electronic document authoring and viewing systems continue to add special features for adapting information. FolioViews from Folio, Inc., for example, provides a method of indexing information in real time so that collaborators always know where new information is. Shared electronic documents can become living documents. The idea of the living document is important whether we are distributing the document to workgroup partners or other customers. Folio documents reside in Infobases and users can highlight parts of documents in the Infobase just as readers use a highlighting pen to mark paper based documents.

Many electronic publishing viewing systems allow for annotations to be attached to documents like sticky notes. A note that appears within its own window can become a record attached to a document for personal reference or workgroup reference. Notes can be effectively used to give feedback to other players on a project. Writers, designers, and editors can use the annotation features of browser tools to communicate specific ideas about a document while it is in development. Electronic notes can serve as an electronic storyboard process. Figure 3.5 illustrates a publication editing cycle in which an electronic document is routed from editor to author with an editorial note attached.

Electronic Document Style

One of the advantages of SGML is that the format of the information appearing on the display screen is not rigidly dependent upon the authoring system used in the creation of the information. Figure 3.6 shows an example of the DynaText electronic book publishing system from Electronic Book Technologies manages style presentation. Designers can map SGML structural elements to style sheet format tags. The style definitions determine font type, size, color, visibility, and the like. Style selections are made from menu options and are typically created for the set of elements defined in the document type definition. Dynamic style features can also be used such as the conditional visibility of elements. Other companies offering document viewing based upon SGML validated data include Interleaf, InfoAccess, and SoftQuad.

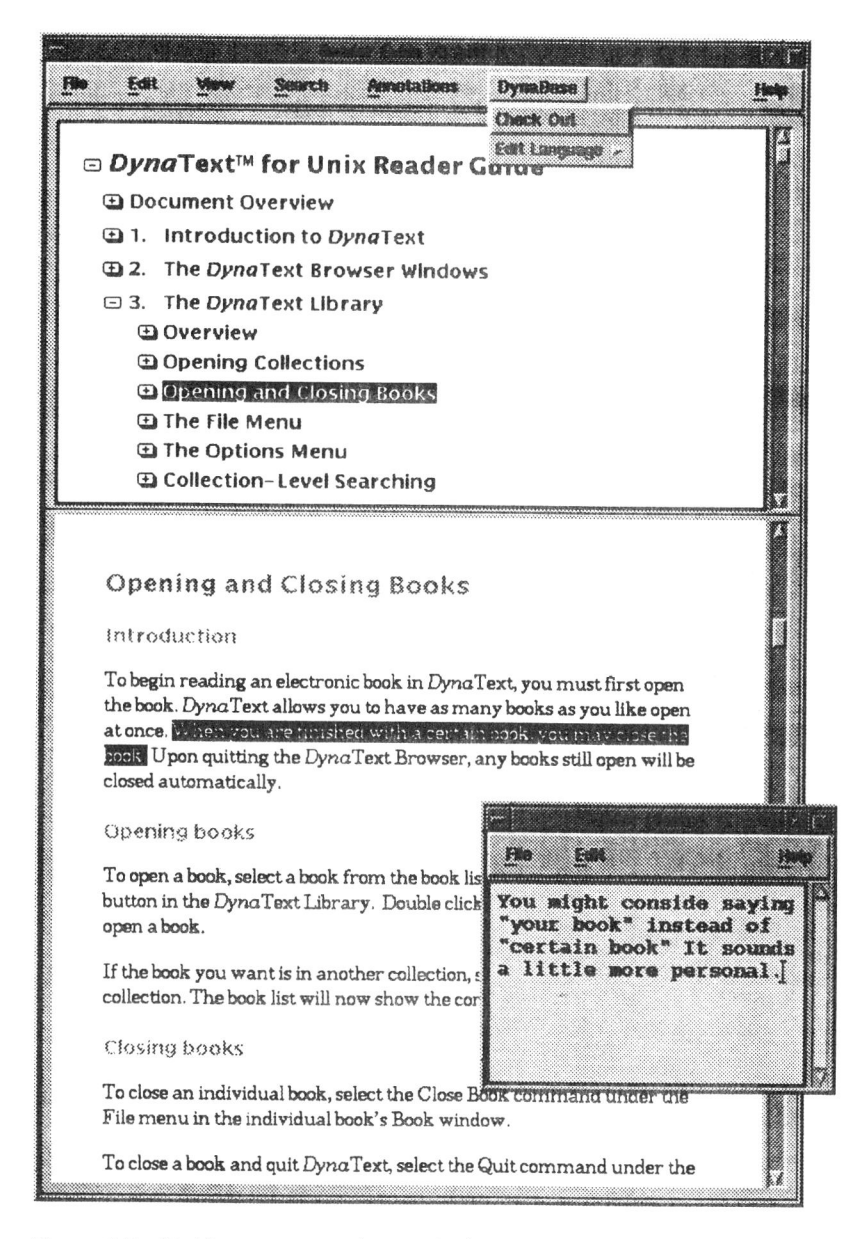

Figure 3.5. Making notes to electronic documents is an important asset to electronic publishing for both document producers and consumers. In this diagram a document reviewer attaches a note to a document using the annotation feature of DynaText, an electronic book publishing system. The author makes a correction using a native SGML editor. Another product, DynaBase, can keep track of document updates. Using annotations is one example of how designers and editors can use electronic publishing tools in a collaborative setting. (Courtesy of Electronic Book Technologies.)

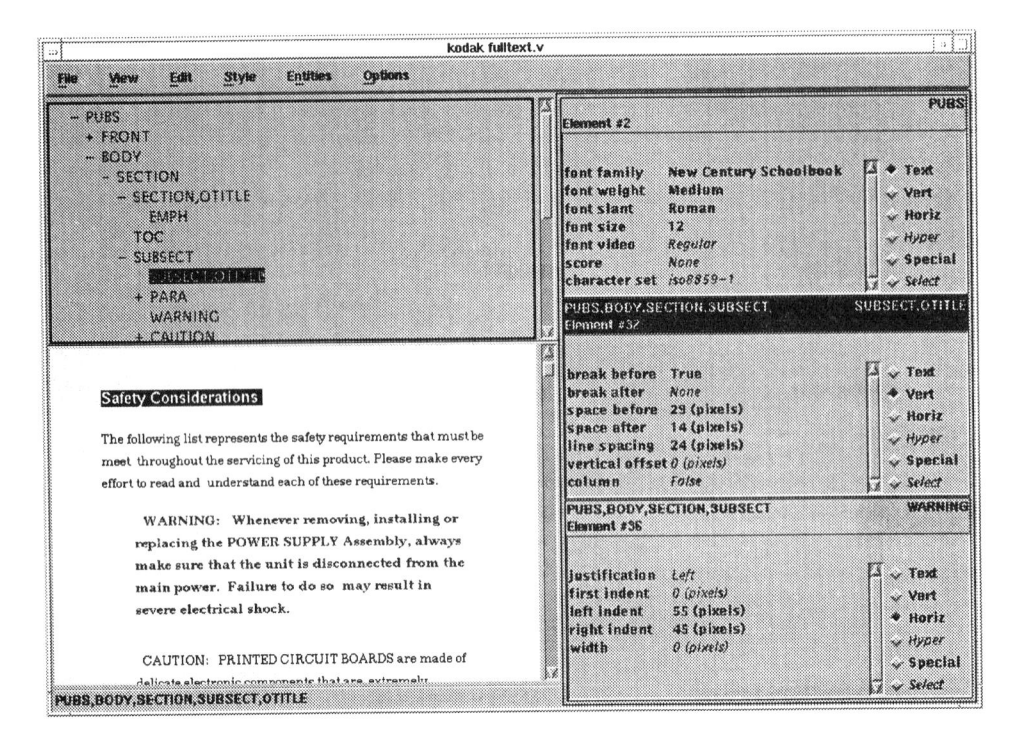

Figure 3.6. The format of an electronic document or book is managed by a style manager. The Interactive Style Sheet Editor (InStEd) from EBT provides immediate access to style definitions. In this case the DynaText Browser view is updated automatically as the style sheet (shown at right) is updated. (Courtesy of Electronic Book Technologies).

Some document viewing systems take the original document, primarily designed for print, and provide software that drives the display for viewing. In these cases the design of the document is relatively fixed. Some systems integrate text indexing and retrieval tools to add intelligent search capability to the viewing experience. If the display system is based on PostScript (such as Adobe's Acrobat), the document viewing styles can be enhanced, by scaling the type sizes, or creating thumbnail views of multiple pages on the screen at one time.

There are a few critical design tips for on-line presentation, such as that the type size should not be too small. Many other design tips counsel avoidance of gimmicky and inappropriate designs. There is a temptation to overdo special effects in the design of electronic documents. Long after the novelty of special effects wears off users may still need to access the substance of documents. Much of what applies as design criteria for electronic documents applies to paper documents. Designers should strive for simplicity, economy, and usability, as there are not many definitive style standards to follow. One standard is a military specification (MIL-M-87268) covering style and format rules for interactive electronic technical manuals. Although it is meant for specialized applications, this does provide some practical advice on the implementation of consistent user interaction with the electronic document.

Page Design Variables

Developing the right formula for page layout is a step by step art process. Some designers work from models such as grids to help flesh out the page design. The design of a page and the package that envelops pages must have consistency of expression. The page size, or physical trim size, of the published work is a major consideration determined by several criteria including:

- Size of manuscript
- Cost of paper
- Cost of printing options
- Type of binding required

Once the page size has been selected and the designer has reviewed specific structure and content requirements with the document analysis group, a rough layout of pages for the document can proceed.

Using Grids

Page layout can be done using a grid to divide the available page space into manageable units. The grid measures the page horizontally and vertically so that columns, illustrations, and photographs can be placed on each page. Space for margins and between lines, words, columns, characters, and figures each requires a judicious decision.

The outline grid is used to begin the orientation of all elements that will appear on the page. The designer makes similar grid sketches for all parts of the document (title page, cover, table of contents, table and illustration grids and so forth).

Figure 3.7 shows instructions for the setup of the page. The designer specifies the details of page layout and typography for each element. The desktop publishing operator can implement the page setup for a document in a straightforward manner.

The master page information in PageMaker includes text and graphic elements that will be repeated throughout the document. This includes running heads, column layout, rule lines, and page folios. It serves the purpose of maintaining document and design consistency. Any item that is controlled within the Master Page is repeated for every page, unless specifically deleted.

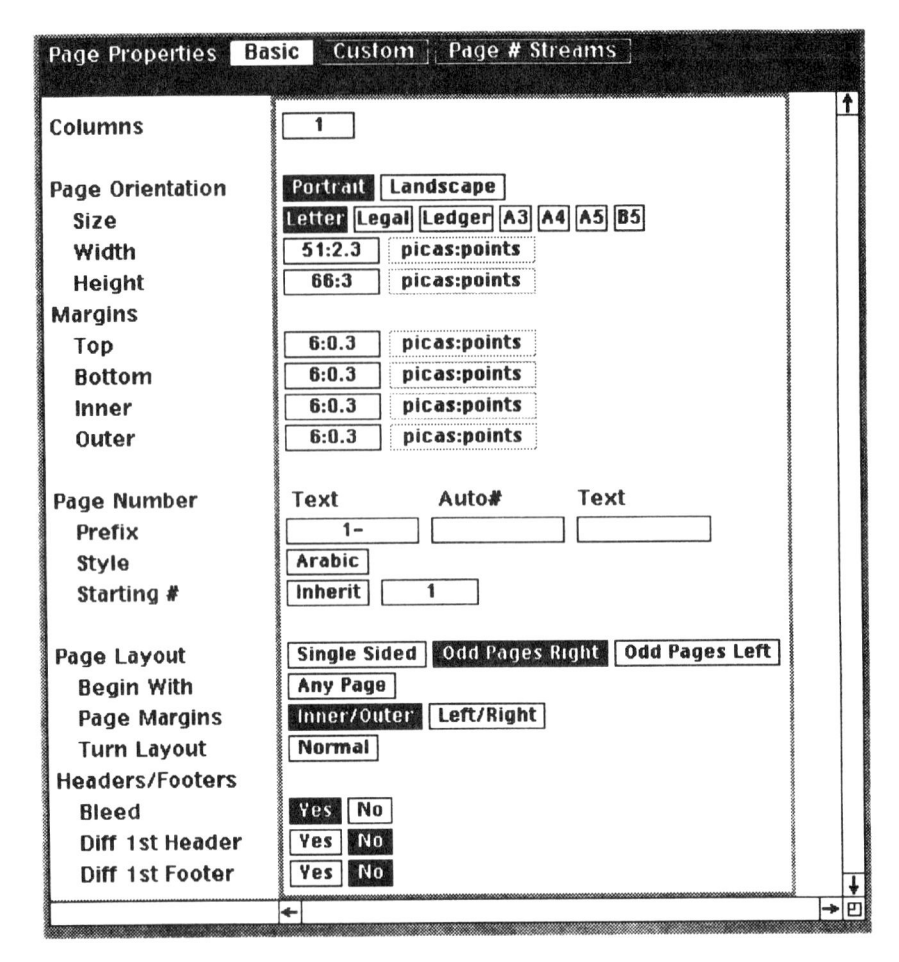

Figure 3.7. Setup of a document page using Interleaf 5.

Columns and Column Widths

Before specifying column width, the interrelation of type size and column width should be determined. For single column formats the recommended number of characters per line should within the 60 to 90 range, and for multiple column formats the number of characters should not be less than 30 per line. Line length and type size are factors in readability. Multiple columns, for example, work well in newspaper formats, because with small type (7 or 8 point) the human eye fatigues more easily as the number of characters increases and the line length exceeds a certain limit.

A page layout is made in columns: single, double, or multiple. An electronic publishing formatting system controls column creation so that the sizing of a column and gutter width, the use of symmetry and asymmetry, alignment, vertical justification, the placement of illustrations, are all computer controlled.

The choice of a single, double or multiple column format depends upon the type of document, audience requirements, and other conventions. Double column formats may expose columns of equal width or, for special layout effect, the columns may be of unequal width where the column of broader width might be used as the main text and the narrower column is used for explanatory emphasis.

The subject of symmetrical design versus asymmetrical design and the issue of text alignment refers to a design layout that is centered or off-centered. Whether to use one or the other depends on the type of document and the effect to be made by the publication. Asymmetrical use of margins may be helpful if a single column fully justified format is selected. Full justification is used for most books. Asymmetry may work less well if the same single column is ragged right.

The placement of illustrations is important in multiple column formats. The column width of an illustration can be placed in a single column format or within the single column itself. Due consideration must be given for what works best in regard to the layout of illustrations within the column.

Figure 3.8 shows a column choice menu for body and master pages from FrameMaker. The default for column setup in FrameMaker is single column. In FrameMaker, the Master Page controls the layout of columns in documents. Body pages inherit the definition of the columns. All single sided documents in FrameMaker have a master page called right and all double sided documents have left and right master pages. Master Page columns used for a layout are referred to as tagged text columns with a flow tag such as flow tag A in Figure 3.8.

STYLE SHEETS AND TEMPLATES

Style sheets and templates are predefined style and composition elements for a specific document type. Desktop publishing systems store layouts so that stylistic rules of publication become system controlled. A template ensures consistency throughout a document. The system remembers the specifications for body text, headings, and all related elements for documents such as books, magazines and journals, proposals, or reports. Although there is some variation from system to system, a template concerns the totality of document layout and assembly. A style sheet, adjoined to a template, defines the specific typography of elements such as headings, body text, and lists.

Desktop publishing systems typically use default units for composition such as a paragraph. When a new file or document is created, the user can begin to

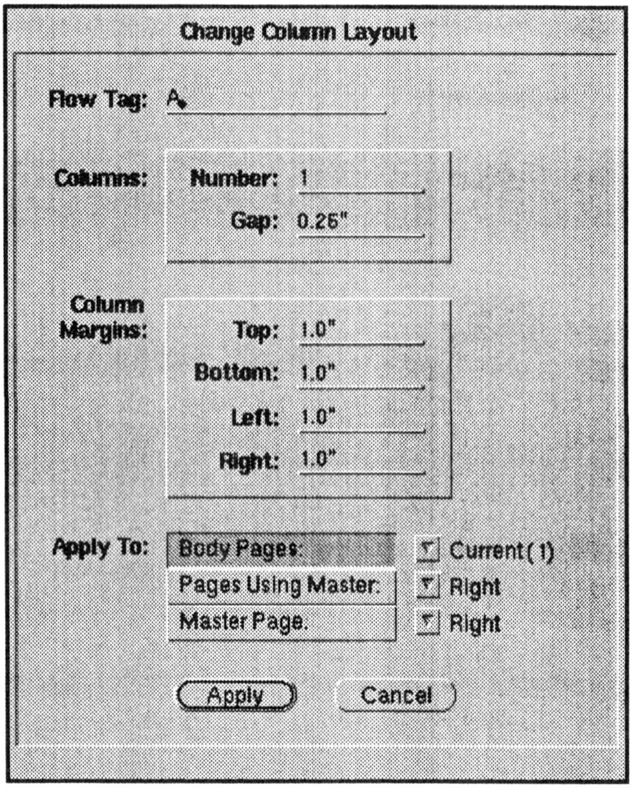

Figure 3.8. Setup of text flow for column in FrameMaker. (Courtesy of Frame Technology Corporation).

compose paragraphs that contain default parameters. Figure 3.9 shows the setup of the default paragraph composition unit from Interleaf 5. Once the user has defined the desired behavior of the paragraph, all paragraphs named para can be made to inherit the setup of para. By changing the name para to another name such as title, the composition properties of the title will be defined. Thus, the user can specify the characteristics of all the format objects that make up a document. This is how a style sheet or template is created with most desktop composition systems.

Other systems such as FrameMaker, Mircrosoft Word, PageMaker, and Corel Ventura use similar techniques. The user sets up the characteristics of style elements based on a default unit such as a paragraph. This building block is then copied and variations are added to make a new style for a heading, a list, or other structural units that will become the basis of the document text elements. When a set of units has been established, the basis of a style sheet or template has been formed.

PageMaker offers default styles to help build a style sheet. Each formatting unit is called a style. The default styles define typographical characteristics for body text, heads, subheads, and so forth. The styles are viewed and redefined with a style palette. Style sheets are combined with page layouts to form templates. Saving a prebuilt template as a customized template is shown in Figure 3.10.

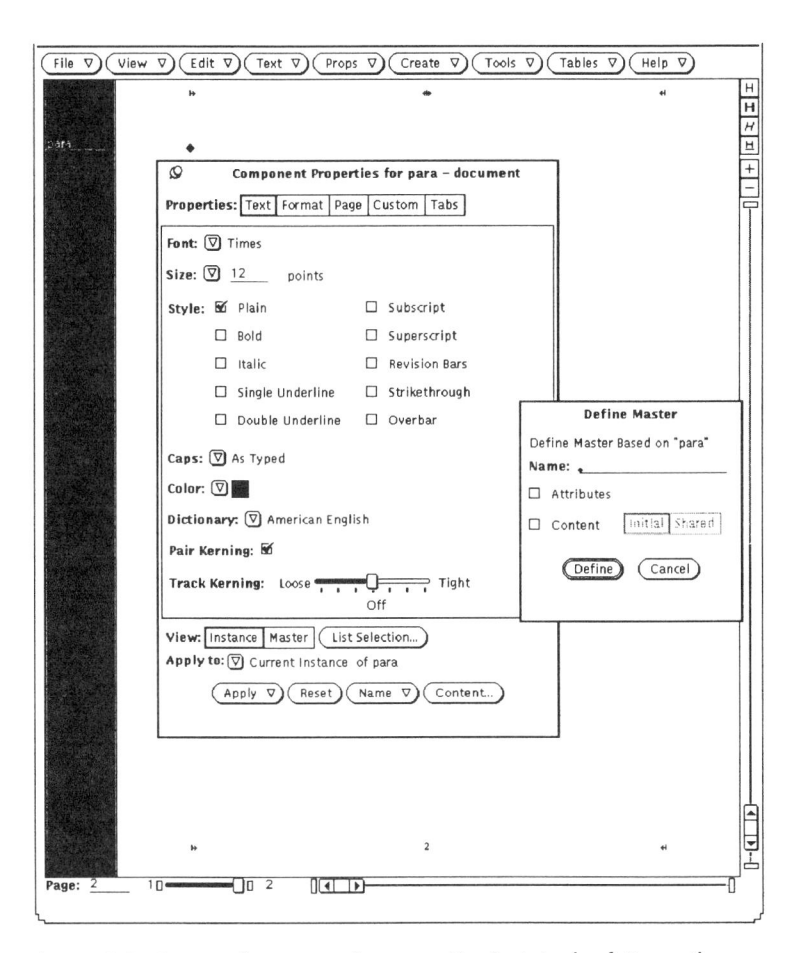

Figure 3.9. Setup of paragraph properties in Interleaf. From the default paragraph (called para in the default Interleaf document) the user defines the format of the paragraph: line spacing, alignment, margins for indents and above and below spacing, of paragraphs. A related menu allows users to define the properties of the paragraph text for its typographical characteristics: font, size of type, use of bold or italic, and other effects such as kerning control.

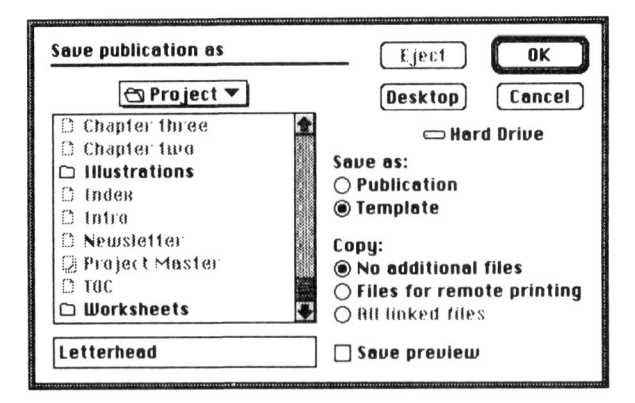

Figure 3.10. PageMaker offers a variety of prebuilt document templates. Users can load these templates, modify them, and then store a revised template file by using the save as template feature as shown in the screen shot above. (Courtesy of Aldus Corp.)

Letter Spacing and Word Spacing

In desktop publishing and typesetting the width of each letter varies with its character. The letter I occupies less horizontal space than the letter M. (In the old typewriter world, all the letters are the same width. In so-called pica machines there are 10 characters per inch, and in elite there are 12 characters per inch.) When there is little or no difference in the space between characters and words, the text presentation is unreadable, as shown in the following example:

Staytunedfornews.Thepresidentspokeinformallytoreporteronthewhitehouse lawn.Hedidnotseemdistrubedaboutquestionsconcerningtheforthcoming election.

If the space between words exceeds the space between lines, the text can hinder reader comprehension.

Stay   tuned   for   the   news.
The   president   spoke   informally   to   reporters

Horizontal control of letter space is achieved by kerning and tracking, Tracking refers to the relative looseness or tightness of space between characters and kerning is the technique of making characters, especially irregular characters, fit together. Designers of electronic fonts have created letters with an elegant fit by kerning pairs. Programs provide fine control of type through kerning and tracking.

The space between words should be fixed within a line to allow the eye to assimilate information with ease. The objective is to harmonize letter spacing and word spacing for readability. (When margin justification without hyphenation is selected, the user must watch for so-called "rivers" or "lakes," that is, excessive spacing between words within a line or grouped in several lines.) Word spacing and letter spacing are set up in most desktop publishing systems via menus. Figure 3.11 shows the setup of word and letter spacing characteristics in Interleaf. Also shown in the menu is the setup for automatic hyphenation for the paragraph being defined.

Alignment and Justification

Sometimes the word spacing used is affected by how the text is aligned. Text is normally justified flush left; the first character of type of each line is thereby

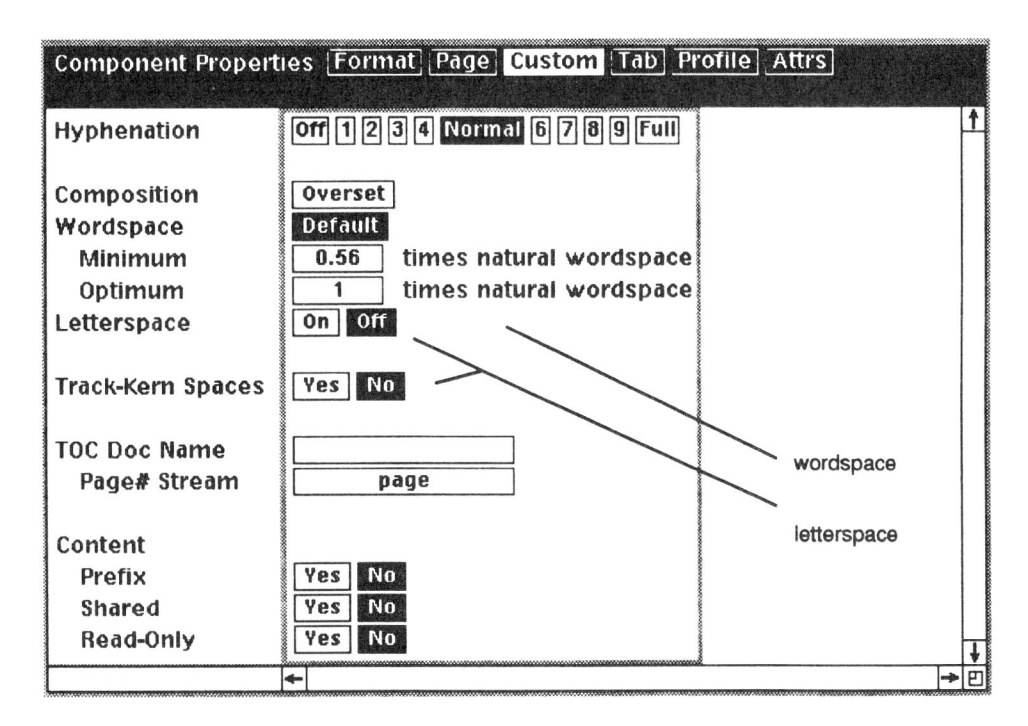

Figure 3.11. Word spacing and letter spacing setup in Interleaf 5.

aligned. The ends of these same lines on the right side may be either justified or "ragged right." The argument for left justification is persuasive. It is easier to read text that is flush left because it is easier for the eye to follow. The decision to use ragged right or right justified margin is a matter of esthetics and suitability. The two styles of alignment are as follows:

> We are living in an age of indecision and we are uneasy about the future. The events that have shaped our lives will not always guide us to abandon our Hamlet complex. (Flush left, ragged right)

> We are living in an age of indecision and we are uneasy about the future. The events that have shaped our lives will not always guide us to abandon our Hamlet complex. (Left and right justified)

Vertical Space (Leading)

Line spacing, or leading, is defined as the distance between the baseline of one line of text to the top of the line beneath it. The expression 10/12 Bodoni (called "10 on 12") means that a 10 point font is being used with a distance of 12 points from one baseline to the next. In the days when print shops used cast type, lead was used below the typeface letters to create the space as in the example here, with two points of leading. The conventional measure of the length of a line of type is in picas, one pica being equal to twelve points, and six picas equal to one inch. Line spacing, referred to as leading, is measured in points.

> Communication regarding the progress of children in their studies is very important. Parents need to know how their sons and daughters are doing on a periodic basis. Unfortunately, fruitful communication can only occur if teachers and parents communicate honestly and accurately. (10/13, 3 point leading)

> Communication regarding the progress of children in their studies is very important. Parents need to know how their sons and daughters are doing on a periodic basis. Unfortunately, fruitful communication can only occur if teachers and parents communicate honestly and accurately. (10/11, 1 point leading)

Paragraph Spacing

The space between paragraphs should be uniform to make the paragraphs stand as units and to create an attractive appearance. Desktop publishing systems require the user to program the space above and below a paragraph with a value that will be added for each successive paragraph.

In book work it is customary to have no extra space between paragraphs but spacing above and below subheads is important to program. Usually there should be more space above a subhead than below.

Automatic Front Matter Generation

One key features of word processing and desktop publishing systems is the ability to automatically generate the table of contents, listing headings with the page number locating that heading upon user command. Figure 3.12 shows the setup of automatic retrieval of a table of contents from FrameMaker. Users can also setup an automatic number sequence that will insert section or subhead numbers when a subhead is created. If a subheading is deleted, the numbering sequence of the remaining subheadings readjusts without user intervention. Similarly, numbering of diagrams and tables and textual references to tables and diagrams can be sequenced in an automatic mode. Even more important is the automatic generating of indexes. Software is available that generates a complete list of all the words used in the manuscript, and this list can be used by a skilled indexer to determine which words should be included in the final index, and which

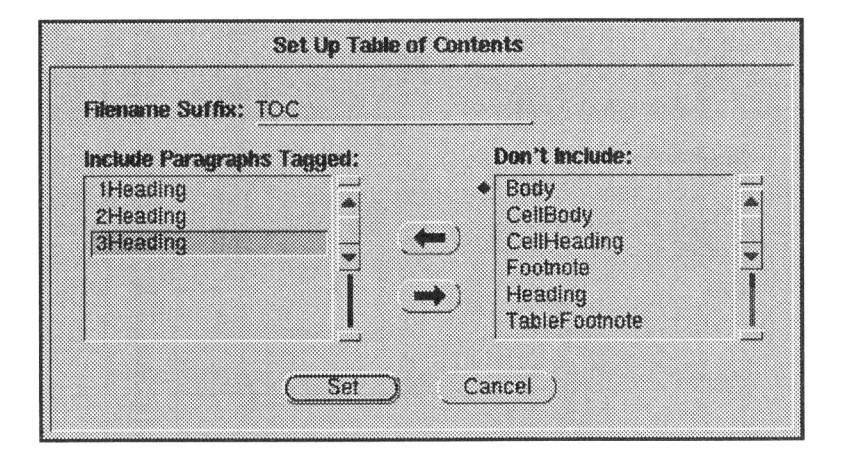

Figure 3.12. Automatic table of content generation is enabled after the user sets up a particular document to list all occurrences of subheadings or other objects to be included as desired. When the document is completed, the system will automatically retrieve those objects setup such as all level 1, 2, and 3 subheadings with title and page number. Similar lists of tables and illustrations can be generated after a similar set up procedure is completed. (Courtesy of Frame Technology Corporation.)

words need cross referencing. Also, many word processing programs allow you to flag the words that the author wants included in the index.

Selecting a Typeface and Font

As with all aspects of design and typography the typeface should be chosen not only to appeal to the reader's eye but to meet the intrinsic requirements of the document, that is, the economics of production and the constraints of layout for a publication. In a desktop publishing system, the typeface also depends upon what fonts can be supported by hardcopy laser printers, typesetters, and display. For electronically delivered documents, due consideration should be given to the size of type to be displayed on the screen and the typical distance of the viewer from the display.

A typeface, or type family, refers to the specific type design such as Times Roman, Helvetica, Bookman, and Palatino. In this family there can be differences in type, weight, and slant. A font is a the composite subselection of a type family, so that 12 point Helvetica bold is a font from the Helvetica typeface. Figure 3.13 shows examples from Adobe's Multiple Master font technology. Available in many desktop publishing programs, this technology employs two or more variations in a typeface to calculate intermediate variations in the typeface.

Most fonts used in electronic publishing are character outline or so-called scalable fonts. Outline fonts are graphical forms based upon precise mathematical models stored in the computer and interpreted by devices that display and print

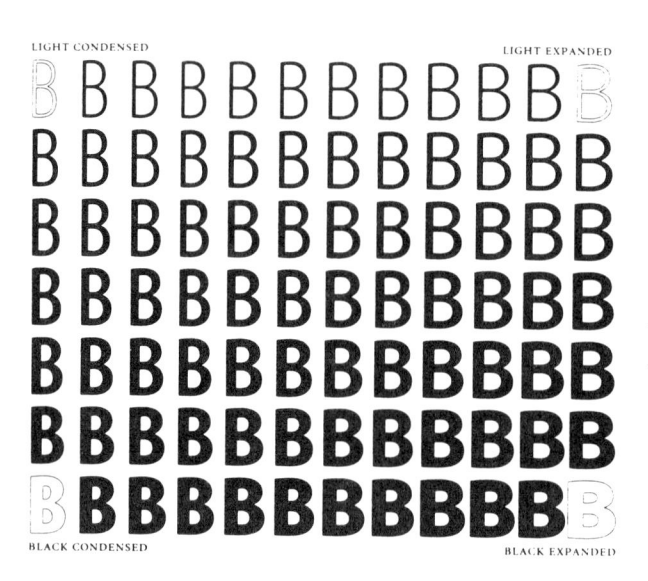

Figure 3.13. An example of an Adobe Multiple Master typeface showing a design matrix based upon a weight variable. The four corners depict the master designs. The fonts in between are instances made from the master designs. Users can select a weight by choosing a point on the design axis. (Courtesy of Adobe Systems, Inc.)

those letters. PostScript from Adobe is the most widely selected font for developers of electronic publishing programs and printing technology because PostScript fonts are independent and portable from application to application.

Special Automation for Long Documents and Books

Many desktop publishing systems provide special tools for the creation of long documents and books. Interleaf, for example, has a suite of powerful tools to integrate the formatting and composition of book length works. Some of the key features of Interleaf book automation are: the sequencing of chapters of variable length; editing for tables, charts, and illustrations; numbering of chapters, sections, and pages; generating tables of contents and indexes, and using special master templates, called catalogs, to provide consistent book format.

Tools such as those from Interleaf, Frame Technology, Quark, and Aldus are powerful aids for in-house publishing and are also used extensively in commercial publishing. Figure 3.14 shows a slice of the process of making a commercial book from the creation of design to camera ready production.

Automating Output: SGML to Formatted Pages and Screens

If the document presentation design and electronic presentation design have been logically separated in a development process how can the nonformatted information now be formatted for print or electronic display? There are several possible solutions.

Since many companies have already invested in word processing and desktop publishing tools which they cannot afford to abandon, they may be able to gradually introduce validated SGML files to a desktop formatting program via special translation programs. For example, the Enabler from SoftQuad allows structured SGML files to be formatted into QuarkXPress templates. Refer to Figure 3.15. SoftQuad also provides its Explorer document viewing program that accepts SGML encoded data for display. Another alternative is to use special conversion tools (from companies such as Avalanche) that translate formatted files into SGML. When the documents are converted, the SGML data is available for multiple reuses. The data can be sent to formatting templates from originating system or be used for other purposes such as on-line document viewing.

Style standards such as the Formatting Output Specification Instance (FOSI) are used by ArborText and Datalogics, for example, to support formatting of SGML tagged data. Datalogics has developed a system (DL Composer) by which the SGML structured text content is automatically output according to a format specification. It automates the assembly and publication of a print or electronic document

THE SOLOMON PRESS PUBLISHERS

98-12 66th Ave., Suite 2, Rego Park, New York 11374
718-830-9112

SPECIFICATIONS
for the volume of four plays by
JOSHUA GOLDSTEIN

Page size	6-1/8" × 9-1/4"
Type area	24 × 45 picas overall
Head margin	5/8"
Gutter margin	7/8"
Basic type for "speeches"	10 pt. Stone Serif on 12.5. *Speaker's name:* 9 pt. Frutiger caps, flush left followed by one em space. *Speech:* 10 pt. Stone Serif, carryovers indent one em. *Stage directions within speech:* Stone Serif italics in parens.
Spacing	Allow half line space after each "speech."
Stage directions not within speech	9 pt. Frutiger on 11, flush left, 10 pt. left indent, one line above and below.
Running head	*Verso:* title of play, centered, set in Frutiger ital. U/lc *Recto:* Act/Scene, centered, set in 9 pt. Frutiger U/lc
Folio	In head, flush outside type area, set in 9 pt. Frutiger ital.
Name of speaker	Always in caps, as in manuscript
Major stage directions	*Such as LIGHTS, SILENCE, EXITS:* set flush right, with no punctuation; one line space above and below, set in 9 pt. Frutiger ital. caps.

Figure 3.14. Steps in the development of making a printed book for commercial publishing can be quite complex. These steps include the making of sample pages based upon a set of design specifications, using a desktop system for typesetting and prepress work, and the integration of elements for camera ready production. Above: The design specs as approved by the publisher. Right: Sample coded input for use with the QuarkXPress program. Overleaf: The final pages, shown at 80 percent of original size. (Courtesy Pageworks, Delhi, New York.)

```
@ct.play:MARTIN NIGHT
@ct.num:<IOKt0z30f"StoneSerif">Act<\!f>
<IOKt30z40f"Frutiger-Black">ONE
@rul.top:
@sta.1:<*p(0,0,0,8,0,0,g,"U.S. English")z24>A<z9> bedroom
suburb outside of New York City. The den of the
<*p(0,0,0,11,0,0,g,"U.S. English")>Grove home. Evening. Time:
the mid-<\h>sixties. A door to the bedrooms, and another to
the outside. <I>The Roundman,<I> a boy of fifteen, stands on a
scale (with a height bar) in the middle of the room. He wears
a shirt with broad horizontal stripes that accentuate his
considerable, but not unusual, adolescent chubbiness. His crew
cut is beginning to grow <\h>out.
@rul.bot:
@dia:<Kt10z9.5f"Frutiger-Roman">The
Roundman<\!f><\!f><Kt0z10f"StoneSerif">It's no <\h>use.
@sta.3:[He gets off the scale and goes over to the pull-<\h>up
bar. He struggles without being able to do even one chin-
<\h>up.]
@dia:<Kt10z9.5f"Frutiger-Roman">The
Roundman<\!f><\!f><Kt0z10f"StoneSerif">It's no <\h>use.
@sta.3:[He runs back to the scale and weighs himself once
again, hoping that somehow he had misread his weight before.
He jiggles the weights on the scale, trying to force a good
result.]
@dia:<Kt10z9.5f"Frutiger-Roman">The
Roundman<\!f><\!f><IKt0z10f"StoneSerif">(out of
breath)<I><\!f>It's just no <\h>use.
@sta.3:[He gets off the scale.]
@dia:<Kt10z9.5f"Frutiger-Roman">The
Roundman<\!f><\!f><Kt0z10f"StoneSerif">In a few minutes Dad
will be home, and I will still be five feet nine and one
quarter, two hundred and eight pounds in my socks. Or five feet
nine and three quarters, two hundred and eleven pounds in my
<\h>shoes.
@sta.3:[<I>The Roundman<I> grabs his pectorals.]
```

Figure 3.14 *(continued).*

MARTIN NIGHT

Act ONE

A bedroom suburb outside of New York City. The den of the Grove home. Evening. Time: the mid-sixties. A door to the bedrooms, and another to the outside. The Roundman, *a boy of fifteen, stands on a scale (with a height bar) in the middle of the room. He wears a shirt with broad horizontal stripes that accentuate his considerable, but not unusual, adolescent chubbiness. His crew cut is beginning to grow out.*

THE ROUNDMAN   It's no use.

[He gets off the scale and goes over to the pull-up bar. He struggles without being able to do even one chin-up.]

THE ROUNDMAN   It's no use.

[He runs back to the scale and weighs himself once again, hoping that somehow he had misread his weight before. He jiggles the weights on the scale, trying to force a good result.]

THE ROUNDMAN   *(out of breath)*   It's just no use.

[He gets off the scale.]

THE ROUNDMAN   In a few minutes Dad will be home, and I will still be five feet nine and one quarter, two hundred and eight pounds in my socks. Or five feet nine and three quarters, two hundred and eleven pounds in my shoes.

[*The Roundman* grabs his pectorals.]

19

Figure 3.14 *(continued)*.

64   Martin Night

BILLY   You didn't make anything happen. Now go finish packing.

THE ROUNDMAN   I won't have to go military academy?

BILLY   Of course not.

[*The Roundman* exits.]

BILLY   *(to audience)* Towards the end of July, a lieutenant I was dating and who had, of course, thrown me in Lake Mékinac, took me for a sail to the far end of the lake to show me what he said was a strange boys' camp. I'll never forget it. We came around a little point of land. And there, near the shore, we saw the oddest sight. The "campers", who were mostly young men, were standing in the water with their pants rolled up to their knees, talking in strange accents and gesturing vigorously. I was fascinated. So, the next day I made some inquiries. I learned that these young men were German Jewish refugees who had escaped to England in thirty-nine and from there had been deported to Canada and placed in internment camps, out of fear that as German nationals they might be spies. With the war over, some Jewish philanthropies had arranged a holiday for them. Right there on Lake Mékinac! I couldn't believe it. I asked if I might visit. You see, I wanted to get close to what I thought of as real life.

[*The Roundman* enters with a suitcase. Though *The Roundman* can hear *Billy*, *Billy* cannot hear *The Roundman*.]

BILLY   *(to audience)* The camp director was thrilled that Billy Huntington wanted to come and when I arrived I was treated like visiting royalty. A reporter from the society section covered my tour and snapped photographs of me handing a check to the director.

THE ROUNDMAN   *(to audience)* I wish you could see those pictures. Mom was really beautiful.

BILLY   *(to audience)* But I wanted to do more and a few days later I returned to offer my services—although I didn't have any idea what I would do. "Just spend time with the

Figure 3.14 *(continued)*.

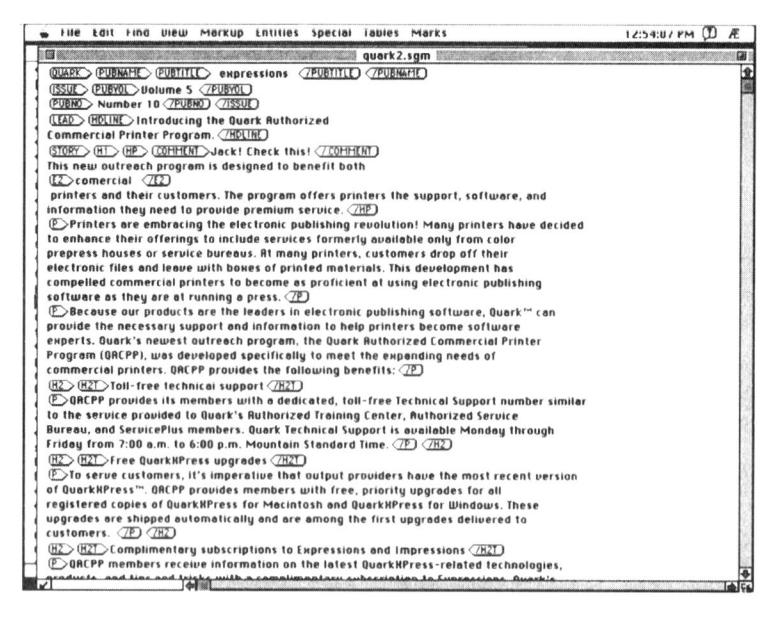

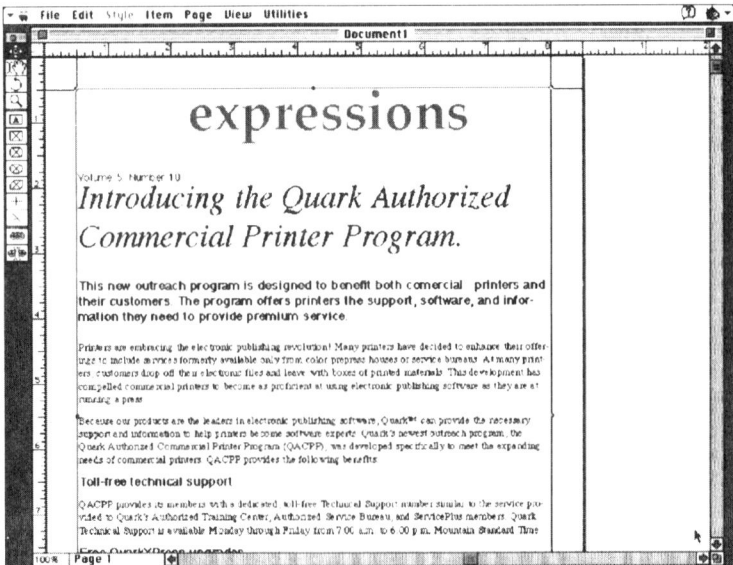

Figure 3.15. The Enabler product from SoftQuad allows for the automatic conversion of nonformatted SGML data into a QuarkXPress formatted document. Shown in the top window is the unformatted SGML document created with SoftQuad's Author/Editor. In the lower window, the same SGML encoded information is automatically formatted in Quark XPress via the Enabler software. The format neutral SGML information can be reused and output to an electronic document display program. (Courtesy of SoftQuad Inc.)

from SGML tagged data. The DL Composer operates as a batch process meaning that a command file is used to execute a background process with minimum operator interaction. The process translates the SGML encoded data directly into a formatted document. ArborText is another leading supplier of SGML authoring tools which uses FOSIs as a means of formatting documents. Interleaf, by contrast, has developed an SGML authoring system which also has a very feature-rich composition and document assembly tool set. Interleaf provides vehicles to output SGML encoded data to its own proprietary desktop composition system for print applications and to its WorldView Press electronic document viewing system.

CHAPTER

4

➤ *Document structure*

➤ *Reusing information*

➤ *Business risks*

➤ *Generic markup*

➤ *Workflow design*

Document Information Design — Content

Computer controlled processes for electronically delivered documents and printed documents are not mutually exclusive. Effective results depend upon the predictable reuse of electronic information.

Once document producers pursue electronically delivered as well as printed documents, one of the fundamental decisions is how to handle a shared information base used for different types of document distribution. Most organizations use word processing and desktop publishing systems to format information on pages. Many electronic delivery and display technologies abandon the page as the unit of document organization. Other systems use it as the simplest model for both electronic and print presentation.

REDEFINING PUBLISHING

What are some alternatives for managing document information while offering multiple forms of presentation? One is to offer display versions of the paper document. There are a variety of imaging and distribution systems that allow video viewers to read raster versions of pages from the electronic document as they were organized for a printed page. This solves one problem with a one-to-one correspondence between the information in the print version and the electronic version. The viewer, however, cannot readily take advantage of intelligent access to information within electronic documents, including hypertext links between nonsequential document details because document imaging systems create graphic images, not machine readable text.

Another method is to use a page description language (PDL) version of the document for display. Unlike raster image versions of documents, the PDL document files capture a document's text, so these files can be attached to navigational tools and high powered text retrieval and indexing engines. Nonsequential navigation is possible such as the approach taken by Interleaf's WorldView and Adobe's Acrobat electronic viewing products. Users can create separate templates with one for the electronic presentation and another for the printed presentation.

One can also use different authoring tools and information bases for electronic document delivery and print distributed information. The disadvantage of this approach is that it may be necessary to maintain two distinct document databases: one for electronic document delivery and one for hardcopy documents. A final alternative is to create data in a reusable, neutral format that allows it to be deployed for various presentation forms. This approach has been adopted by organizations that use SGML based document systems. The advantage of this alternative is that the information can be managed in one place, while subsets of the data can be distributed for print or electronic media.

Not all document developers and publishers face identical requirements, so solutions vary from case to case. Some office computing workgroups are nonprofit centers within a business or government organization that deal with large sets of information and long documents such as 500 page proposals or technical manuals. Still others produce thousands of relatively small documents and distribute multiple sets of documents across computer desktops within their organization. Many are publishers of magazines, newsletters, and books for profit in legal, medical, scholarly, or commercial book publishing. Whatever the differences, however, all publishers who want to deliver not only electronic documents, but also to maintain a viable capability in print applications have to choose between using separate databases, or a single information base. Deciding how to achieve goals with different approaches and sets of tools requires some understanding of organizational commitments and financial resources, the goals and expectations of clients, customers, and partners, and the methods and tools that can be used to produce documents.

Analyzing the Needs

A primary step in any publication's development is to determine its purpose. This includes a clarification of audience needs and objectives, the selected topic or topics to be addressed, and the distribution medium best suited to the audience. The method of document distribution alone does not guarantee insulation from information overload. In addition to the normal goals of persuading, informing or entertaining, document producers need to redouble efforts at facilitating fast and efficient access to document contents. Long library searches are undesirable in today's just in time information environment.

Electronic documents can help audiences find data on assorted topics in a nonlinear fashion. Collaborators from different departments in a company who want concurrent access to information relating to the development of a product, for example, can query documents that form a collective electronic knowledge base. Electronic document distribution is being used in many information intensive industries to reduce dependence on paper documents. Electronic documents are easier to maintain and update than printed documents. By distributing electronic documents to customers, publishers and organizations not only help their clients reduce paper waste but also contribute to their productivity and efficiency in delivery of services. Finally, electronic documents can incorporate mixed media elements (film, sound, and animation) that are not feasible in other publications.

As collaborators assess the purpose of individual documents in the context of a delivery medium, they need to reexamine the conceptual framework for authoring, merging, and reusing computer generated information. This is not an academic exercise, but a prerequisite to learning how computers help us create multipurpose uses of document information. During a transition period, many publishers will find this to be the key to maintaining multiple distribution capabilities. It will also help communicators understand the goals in document information access.

Business Strategy and Risk Analysis

Measuring and controlling costs related to document development and distribution is a business requirement. Finding a way to provide both electronic and paper delivery services while maintaining reasonable control of costs is a difficult challenge. Managers and planners of electronic as well as printed books, documents, and articles routinely justify their investment in technology and their budget for labor and material expenses. Making the transition to electronically delivered documents while continuing to produce printed documents requires more than a balance sheet; it presupposes a plan and a vision of how electronic publishing will transform our work and our products for the better.

While reviewing criteria for distributing documents in print or electronic form, planners should consider questions such as:

> ➤ Is the customer base satisfied with print delivery?
> ➤ Where does the information originate? From one author? multiple authors? from an existing source of computer information?
> ➤ Will this information be reused for other audiences in the organization?

- Is the customer an advocate of electronic information delivery?
- How large is the information base to be delivered?
- What are the current material and printing costs?
- Will customers continue to demand print versions of the electronically delivered documents?
- How will production schedules be affected by a transition to electronic document delivery?
- Are internal groups within an organization dependent upon the document information to do their job?
- Will electronic publishing enhance the competitive position of the business?

The answers will give planners some basis for thinking through the relative worth of electronic document delivery before oversimplifying bottom line costs. Planners also need to understand how changes to workgroup operations will affect productivity. The plan may call for a gradual shift in methodology, but this will vary from case to case.

Transforming a publishing environment to support nonprint as well as print presentations is not always easy. One way of initiating change is to experiment with a manageable project as a pilot before transforming all processes at one time. This may be less disruptive to existing organizational objectives.

The pilot program may also help establish baseline metrics for cost analyses. Although the material costs for on-line documentation can be cheaper than printed documents, the overall costs of development are not always apparent. A potential cost benefit that will require a special cost metric is the creation of an organizational information service infrastructure no longer depending upon paper distribution. Many organizations as different as aerospace companies and insurance providers are claiming savings in millions of dollars due to a change in internal document practices from print to electronic presentation. With electronic document delivery the time recovered in information search may more than offset the cost of production.

The traditional unit cost measurement for printed work is the page. The cost of the page is determined by labor time and material costs associated with all phases of the project, from conception to production. While new costs associated with electronic document delivery such as distribution of specific media (CD-ROM, for instance), and the purchase of tools related to viewing technology are measurable, a significant factor in the calculation of electronic presentation is cost avoidance. Collaborating authors can avoid duplicating effort, by doing the research and writing once but applying it to different presentation forms. Costs regained in doing business differently become a significant metric. Design costs for print and electronic presentation can be controlled by insisting upon the use of standard templates and output specifications for both electronic and print presentation.

Adopting A Document Structure

Adopting a structured approach to authoring documents will help make the transition from paper to electronic document distribution. What does document structure mean in reference to computer controlled authoring and distribution systems? Structure is the organizational breakdown of a document into its constituent elements. These elements include familiar units of document structure such as sections, paragraphs, and headings. Many word processing and desktop publishing systems give visual feedback of structure to an author by using different forms of indentation, font size, and page layout. The visual approach to structure, however, depends upon a particular proprietary editing system and upon the printed page as a visual frame of reference.

Making computers and authors understand document structure opens barriers to document information. Authors can work with the computer's knowledge of structure to advantage. Once computers learn document structure, information can be accessed. There are various approaches to document structure but the most widely accepted is SGML. This standard encourages a systematic breakdown of structure and content through the Document Type Definition (DTD). SGML uses a method of generic coding with tags to identify elements that have been declared in a DTD. For example, if we have declared an element for footnotes by a generic tag in documents, we can search for all occurrences of footnotes in the document. Through DTDs designed for Braille users, document structure is helping the visually impaired get access to information efficiently.

A structured approach to authoring can help teams of authors and editors collaborate. By conforming to a structural model of the DTD, the group can follow guidelines that help maintain a consistent approach to categorizing information resulting in efficient management.

Document structure and corresponding markup of information elements for different media—on-line delivery system, CD-ROM, database, or print application—makes the SGML approach a multipurpose resource for reusing information.

Although there are many obvious differences in the content, size, and types of publications, there are generic structures that can be used for several classes of documents (books and articles, for example). These models may help groups get started with certain types of projects. Public DTDs include the Rainbow DTD from Electronic Book Technologies (EBT), the ISO 12083:1993 DTDs for books, articles, and serials supported by the American Publisher's Association, and public DTDs such as the United States Department of Defense Mil Std 28001 are available. These public DTDs define a generic structural model for a document type. The ISO 12083:1993 creates a generic model for a structure of a book. Such models are very useful for document interchange among authors, publishers, and editors. Organizations can in fact create their own DTDs to satisfy the specific document needs within their own environment. Creating and modifying DTDs has become much simpler with products such as Near & Far from Microstar. This graphical tool allows users to create DTDs and drag and drop between different DTDs with a point and click interface.

What's in a Document?

Before creating a DTD, a group goes through a preliminary stage of analyzing and specifying structural needs. Known as document analysis, it is process of breaking down the structure and content requirements. See Figure 4.1. The docu-

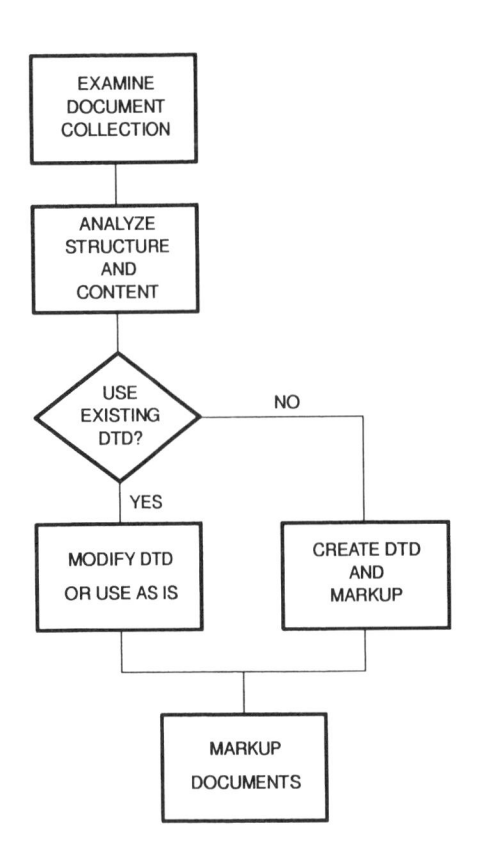

Figure 4.1. Document analysis is a decision making process. A critical decision is whether to use an existing document type definition (DTD) or create a new one. Public DTDs can be used such as the book or article models as defined by ISO 12083:1993, for example or the analysis team can create its own DTD. The DTD will define the structural and content elements of the document.

ments in question may be a book, an article for a popular news magazine, a scholarly journal, or a hypermedia publication. The structure provides a frame for content and is not to be confused with a document's presentation form.

Specifying document structure can be done in several steps leading to the draft of a DTD. A familiar place to start is to create an outline or table of contents to identify the levels of topics in a hierarchy. (SGML approaches information as a hierarchy of elements.) Models of documents in an existing class can be examined structurally.

Next a tree structure of a typical document can be sketched to determine what the document elements are, what elements are required and which are optional. See Figure 4.2. A set of elements for a book chapter might include chapter, chapter title, chapter number, section headings and paragraphs. To describe the hierarchy of elements in a chapter we define what is called the content model of the element, "chapter." The content model of a paragraph which has no sub elements is PCDATA (parsed character data). The PCDATA default is ASCII. Any special character types are defined as entities. In addition to specifying document elements, the document structure chart can be used to identify the element attributes. In SGML attributes give additional information about the elements they describe. such as the security level of a document. Another use of the document structure chart is to anticipate the uses of document structure for forms of presentation.

Document analysis requires the teamwork of many individuals including authors, subject matter specialists, graphic artists, editors, and document production specialists. They can define the document elements to be encoded in generic tags or identifiers of that structure. These tags identify the convention for an element name, that is, a chapter as <ch>. Angle brackets are used to enclose the tag, <ch>, which then appears at the beginning of the chapter. If end tags are used, the tag </ch> comes at the close of the chapter.

It is a challenge for authors to use structured methods. Some applications and user requirements do not warrant a structured approach such as advertising copy that is heavily layout intensive. For other applications the structured approach frees authors from concerns over appearance. Authors will get used to the transition because a growing number of tools provide structured authoring. There are also display tools that accept SGML encoded elements and provide an electronic presentation interface. Authors will need training on the purposefulness of using a structured approach but that training will go a long way toward building a new infrastructure to support both electronic and print applications.

The reuse of information within publications should be anticipated, for example, the encoding information for reuse to a CD-ROM or a print document. Document information with value over a period of time is referred to as legacy data. For many organizations their legacy data serves as a knowledge asset. A single

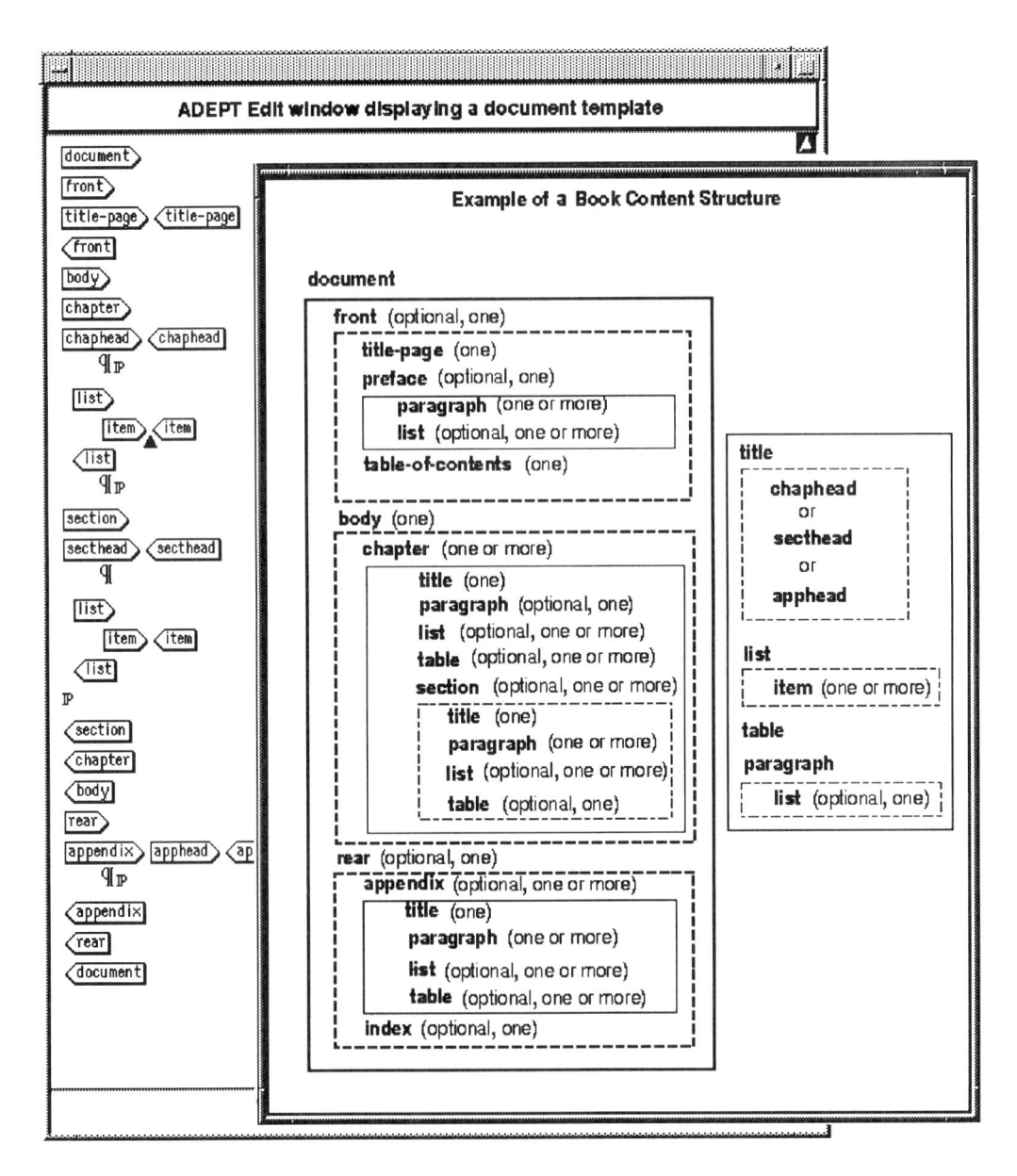

Figure 4.2. Creating a document type definition begins with a structure tree indicating a hierarchy of document elements and subelements, in this case a book. Using tools such as the Adept-Editor from ArborText makes it easier to visualize the structure of a complex document. Users can see at a glance which elements are optional or required as well as those that can be repeated more than once. (Courtesy of ArborText, Inc.)

source of information, designed for efficient reuse, may furnish data for computer based training, hardcopy proposals, interactive repair manuals, marketing feature descriptions, and quality test requirements.

What Information Is Reusable?

By using structured and content based approaches to documents, authors and other collaborators add value to the data. A structured markup scheme such as SGML allows workgroups to control detailed document information in the same way that databases provide strict control of records that contain phone numbers, names, and addresses. If access to this information needs to be restricted, SGML attributes can be used to manage security levels of access to sensitive data.

The effective reuse of document information depends upon organizational goals and understanding of information life cycles. Will the information used in certain documents be repeated in others? How many different groups may need to share and use this data? What kinds of documents share similar information? Organizations depend on document data for competitive and strategic reasons. Computers change and evolve more rapidly than data that sometimes needs conserving. The life cycle of an airplane is relatively long and the information needed to support its longevity may outlive various computers and computer programs that house and manipulate the information. This is one reason that the aviation industry has embraced SGML. An organizational knowledge base that consists of SGML encoded information becomes readily accessible to end users no matter what computer they are using. This is a powerful asset to businesses, publishers, libraries, and government organizations.

Other criteria are important to reusable information including data accuracy, easy use across computer platforms and programs, and adaptability for many presentation forms. If the data is worth conserving, it pays to revisit the information model being used to mold it.

Document analysis is not only a breakdown of document structure but it also specifies document content. The process of analyzing content as well as structure adds texture to information design. SGML can be used to construct an information base by employing content tags as well as explicit structural tags. A generic tag such as <chapter> for chapter denotes the element chapter within a document hierarchy. Tags such as <warning> or <safety> tell us something specific about the content of the information associated with the tags. The data encoded by content tags, whether it relates to safety hazards or sailboats, is accessible not only in one document but in all the document instances that conform to the DTD requiring those elements. The organization that created the documents as well as any other organization or publisher that requires this information will identify and access the tag. Organizations are increasingly using content based elements as a database of information. By nesting or embedding content based markup within the document stream, the information can be extracted upon user query.

One added benefit of using SGML based document information design is that the data will be pre-conditioned by a set of rules so that computer indexing and searching tools will have a greater range of pattern matching possibilities to exploit in response to a document query. Allowing multiple audiences to access information more readily is a direct return on the investment in design. These audiences include customers and clients outside the organization but also internal organization customers. Text retrieval from an SGML knowledge base can be a powerful asset for any organization. Elements having special significance within offices and other workplaces can be translated into computerized SGML information. The crucial stage of the translation is in the document coding process, otherwise known as document markup.

Electronic Manuscript Markup

Markup is information put into the document to make it easier for the computer to interpret. Markup can be neutral or proprietary. Most users of word processing, desktop publishing, and typesetting tools mark up a document according to a proprietary coding scheme that controls the format or appearance. SGML tags are generic identifiers of the document's structure and content, they are vendor neutral, and therefore generally understood by computers.

SGML markup delimits content for easy handling by a computer, and uses a set of generic coding tags that have been identified in the document type definition. Authors and editors may be able to use a public domain document type definitions such as ISO 12083: 1993 DTDs for books and articles. These DTDs have special appeal to authors, editors and publishers who want to get started using SGML but do not have the time to develop their own DTDs. Workgroups can develop their own DTDs based upon their own specific document publishing and information design requirements. Authors need an SGML authoring tool to enter the markup into the manuscript. Other text editing tools can be used to enter the markup when the author has a thorough understanding of SGML and the requirements of a given DTD.

Authors using SGML tools are insulated from the details of the SGML syntax conventions. They do not have to remember the syntax of generic tags, because they are visible on the screen. If a DTD element for a title requires a beginning tag <title> and an ending tag </title>, SGML authoring tools help writers insert the tags automatically, show them and hide them upon computer command, and provide context sensitive support as to whether an element can be used where authors indicate. Authoring tools also validate the conformity of the markup by parsing the SGML used. An SGML parser program ensures that a document instance complies with the document type definition. Refer to Figure 4.3.

SGML authoring systems provide the markup of complex structural objects such as lists, tables, and equations as well as such comparatively simple objects as paragraphs. Although SGML is primarily a standard for text markup, it accommodates the reference to figures and illustrations as well. The DTD can declare an element <figure> and use an entity reference as a place holder for a graphical object that is stored outside the document. The actual graphics are stored in other files or directories in specific file formats.

If the document data is not in SGML, it can be converted by using conversion tools such as FastTag from Avalanche Development Company or other SGML conversion products. A public DTD created by Electronic Book Technologies (EBT) called Rainbow was designed to help companies who use proprietary word processing and desktop publishing programs convert to a basic SGML format. This markup can then be transformed into other markup required by specific industry DTDs.

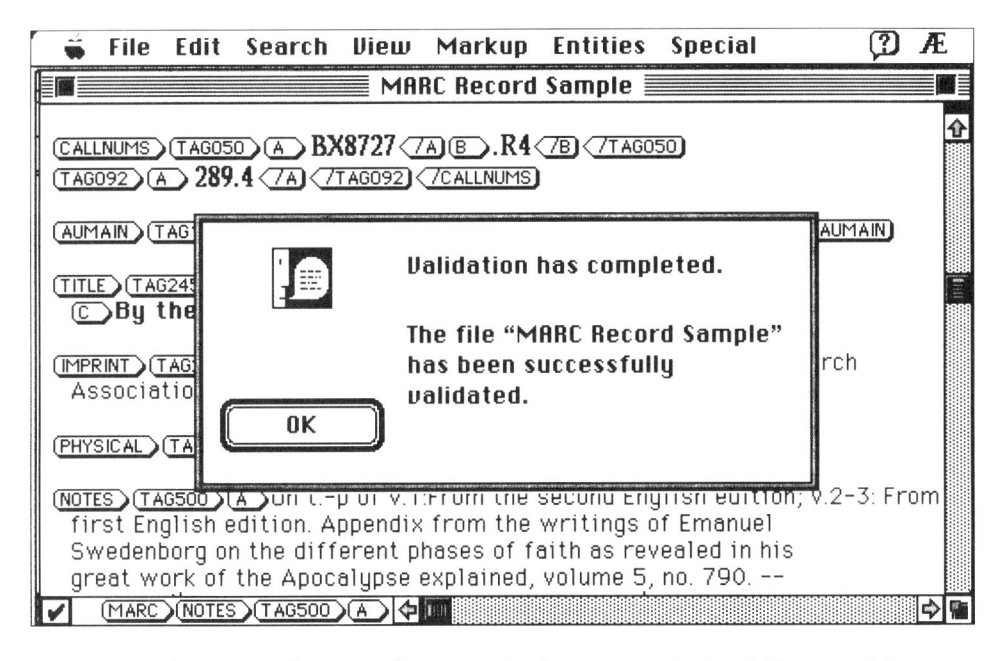

Figure 4.3. An important feature of SGML authoring systems is the ability to validate whether the document markup conforms to the rules of a document type definition as well as SGML rules. Using a program called a parser, SGML authoring tools allow writers and edtiors to validate their documents. This screen shot shows the culmination of a successful validation using the Author/Editor program from SoftQuad, Inc. (Courtesy of SoftQuad, Inc.)

DynaTagt from EBT converts proprietary word processing formats into SGML tags contained in a DTD. Once proprietary formats have been converted into SGML, the encoded data can be used directly by EBT's DynaText electronic book viewing product. See Figure 4.4.

All DTDs do not use the same markup. They can and do use different markup schemes. For example, one DTD may provide a generic tag for a paragraph as <p> while another may use <para> as its tag. Special SGML transformation tools convert the information markup from one DTD to another. OmniMark, a programming scripting tool from Exoterica Corporation, can be used to help in SGML

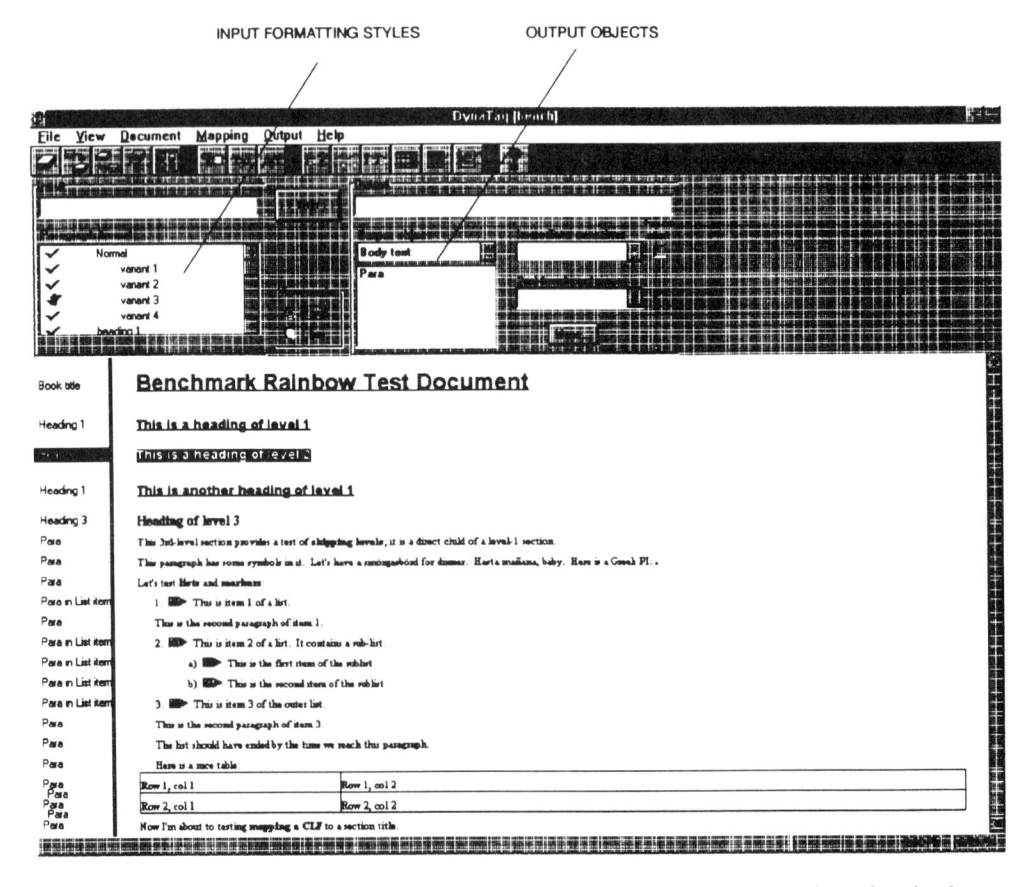

Figure 4.4. A user interface screen shot of DynaTag from Electronic Book Technologies. The product converts word processing proprietary formats into SGML tags conforming to a given document type definition. Shown in the upper left is the input formatting style names from the word processing formatting program. These style tags are then mapped into SGML structure tags for output shown in the panels on the right side of the screen. (Courtesy of Electronic Book Technologies, Inc.)

transformations as well as other SGML conversion and validation processes. SGML Hammer from Avalanche is another tool that can be used to transform SGML data from one DTD to another.

It is not practical here to discuss all aspects of SGML markup and syntax. Entities and attributes, however, deserve special mention. Attributes provide additional information about an element and how it is to be processed. Attributes can identify references in the text to figures, tables, footnotes, or other information. For example, the syntax for an attribute reference to a figure may appear as: <fig id = plane>. An entity reference defines an object that will be included in the manuscript as it is being processed. Entities can include items as characters that are not on a keyboard, a file representing another chapter or section, a figure, or other information. A marked up document is referred to as a document instance. See Figure 4.5.

Information Brokers

No two observers of the content and structure of documents will view the breakdown of documents in exactly the same way. Information design is collaborative and not an individual process. Potential team candidates are authors, database specialists, and members of other workgroups whose work may be affected by the information design. One advantage of using SGML as an information design tool is its flexibility, allowing many different ways of viewing documents. SGML supports a variety of document type definitions that suit a class of documents, focusing on content or structural elements or a hybrid of both approaches.

In effect, the design team plays the role of information broker. Some highly successful DTDs have occurred when workgroups representing document developers, document end users, and subject matter specialists have participated in discussions and industry forums to define mutual information needs. For example, collaborating groups from the auto industry have used a content modeling approach to establish guidelines for Environmental Protection Agency (EPA) mandated J2008 vehicle emission service information requirements. The task force includes officials, automotive engineers, service technicians, as well as SGML analysts. They have thought through a data model for a car with defined information categories related to emission controls for participating manufacturers. The model became the basis for developing a draft DTD. It established automotive service information categories related to emission controls such as "engine" and "electronic controls." The task force adopted a content oriented approach in organizing information about cars and emission services. Although car makers could not agree completely on definitions of all categories, they could agree to associate service information with various categories. The task force members became brokers of information in the process, resolving problems through compromise.

```
<book>
<front>
<titlegrp>
<title>Desktop Magic</title>
<subtitle>Electronic Publishing Document Management and Workgroups</subtitle>
</titlegrp>
.
.
.
<chapter>
<chapterno> 4</chapterno>
<chapti>Document Information Design</Chapti>
<list> <item> Document structure</item>
<item> Reusing information</item>
<item> Business risks </item>
<item> Generic markup</item>
<item> Workflow design</item>
</list>
 <p> Computer controlled processes for electronically deliv-
ered documents and printed documents are not mutually ex-
clusive. Effective results depend upon the predictable reuse of
electronic information. </p>
 <p> Once document producers pursue electronically deliv-
ered as well as printed documents, one of the fundamental de-
cisions is how to handle a shared information base used for
different types of document distribution...</p>
.
.
.
<subsect>REDEFINING PUBLISHING</subsect>
<subsect1>Weighing Delivery Alternatives</subsect1>
.
.
.
</chapter>
.
.
.
</book>
```

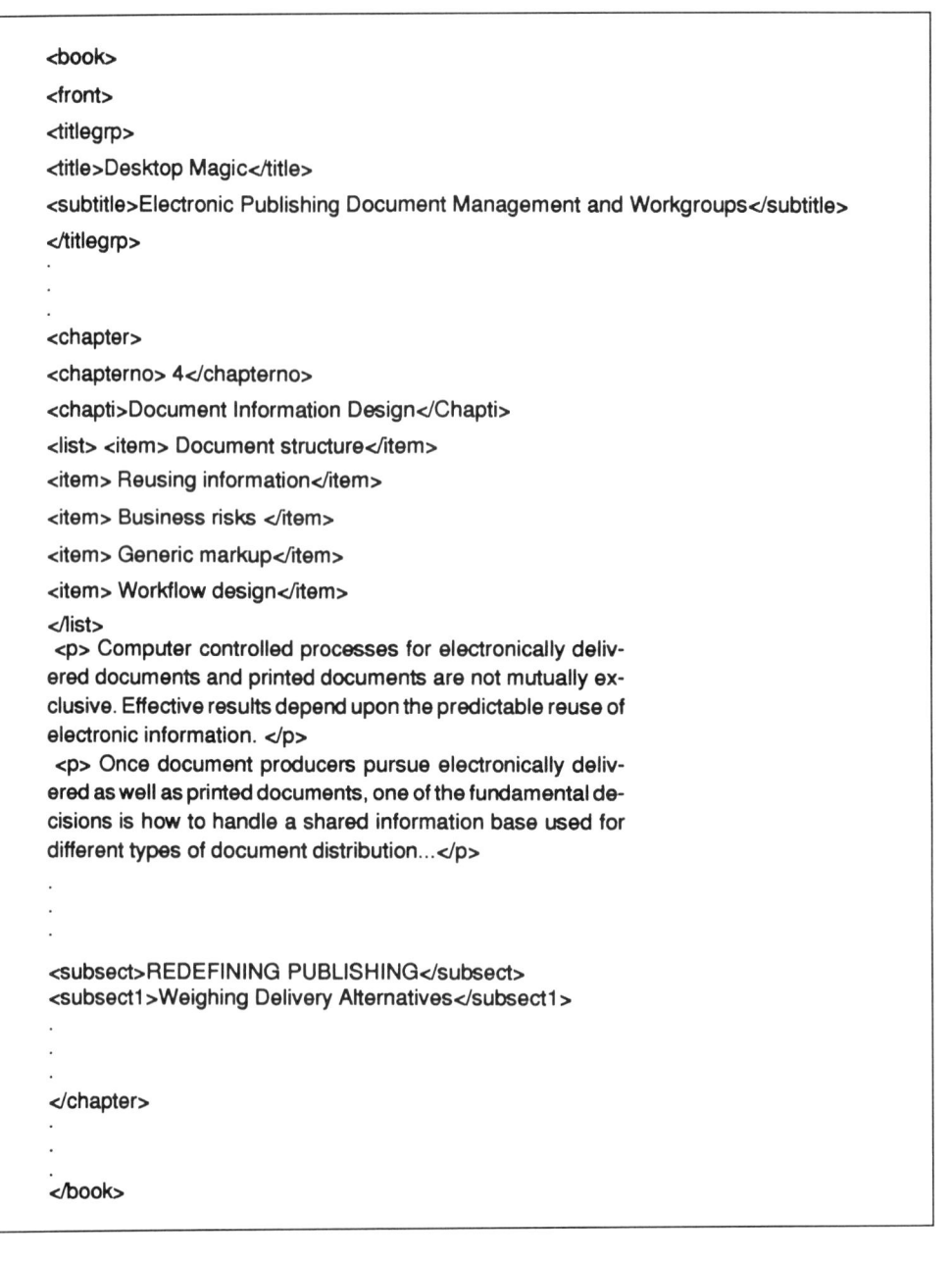

Figure 4.5. A sample specimen from this book marked up according to ISO12083:1993 Book DTD. A representative sample of the markup has been used to show, for example, that a chapter in this instance has certain required elements including a chapter number and title.

Although the J2008 task force collaboration represented a large scale effort among multiple car makers and government members, small scale workgroup collaborations can be effective in the information design process. The participants could be editors and clerical staff of a newspaper or magazine trying to streamline information exchange; office workers seeking efficient access to corporate legal, financial, or product data; or government workers in need of a structured information resource for their documents. Putting stakeholders together (end users, document analysts, authors, and other players) is critical to information design. It can be decided whether to follow a document definition that is content or structure oriented or some combination of both.

How can we assign a value to document information design? Product development, especially for information intensive projects, helps illustrate the need to design information in connection with group project goals. Product engineering, manufacturing, service, and marketing information can be represented as a family tree, a structural hierarchy that breaks down into sub categories or branches of information. (For example, product model branches may divide into the parts, features, and service subbranches and leaves that makeup the tree). Document analysts may help define classes of documents and the structural properties to which the product information belongs. Other subject matter experts and authors may advise upon specific information areas that benefit product developers, support personnel, and customers. A suitable DTD can then be developed from an existing model or from scratch. The long term cost benefit of building an information model that will support products through their life cycle can be a powerful justification for document information design.

Computer Setup Meets Workflow

Comprehensive setup of an electronic publishing system entails the transfer of specific knowledge to computers. It includes the downloading of instructions to a computer (typically via graphical interfaces) to automate the formal presentation, structure, content, and distribution of documents.

Computers follow instructions given to them. Various electronic publishing programs store these instructions so that the creation, composition, and distribution of documents behave in a predictable fashion. The setup of an integrated electronic publishing system applies a group's knowledge of information and presentation design. In conjunction with the setup, workgroups should analyze requirements and design a workflow scheme that accommodates information and presentation design processes. Workflow represents the work steps to complete tasks and subtasks related to documents from inception to distribution.

Computer setups of electronic publishing tools inevitably affect workgroups and the flow of work among workgroup members. The impact the automation has on current work processes should be thought through as well as the flow of work among team members. There are many variables to consider. Among them are the stability and composition of the workgroup itself. The team may be fluid or permanent. The team may include writers, editors, designers, illustrators, photographers, document analysts, subject matter specialists, and many others. Another variable includes the tool set available to the team. From authoring tools such as SGML editors and traditional word processors, to page layout and composition programs, data conversion products, graphic editors, database and display software—the list of tools is formidable. The machine setup of these tools must make sense in relation to the flow of work among group members, and the business processes that the work directly or indirectly supports.

Using a model such as that presented in Figure 4.6 will have practical consequences for the work to be performed by group members. Authors and editors, for example, will need to focus on information design, not presentation design. The presentation for paper or on-line documents can be done by graphic artists, designers, typesetting specialists with the aid of computer programmers familiar with design presentation needs.

The introduction of a workflow scheme is not merely a technical decision. It has business consequences and may require workers to adopt different approaches to tools they are using. Many groups already using word processing and desktop publishing tools resist changing to this type of workflow model not because the technology is difficult or unattractive, but because they do not want to change work practices. Using SGML frees writers and editors to concentrate on the logic of document structure and content. In turn, presentation specialists can concentrate on computerized presentation design.

Workflow actuates a business process. Document workflow can intersect with other business processes as well as being a process by itself. For example, the creation of a technical document for product maintenance has a workflow all its own but the use of this document and its information is integrated with other business processes as it relates to service policy and contracts, training, and field support. The information workflow shares boundaries with several other business information domains.

Every organization has unique workflow requirements so that in addition to modeling information and presentation design, workgroups should consider a workflow design model. Computerized workflow and document management systems are now available to help automate workflow processes.

Computerized workflow systems can route documents from one desktop to another to expedite review and signoff and they can help track the sequence of work steps to keep a project on an efficient schedule. Such systems remind reviewers and authors of pending tasks and can deliver to the desktop the work to be

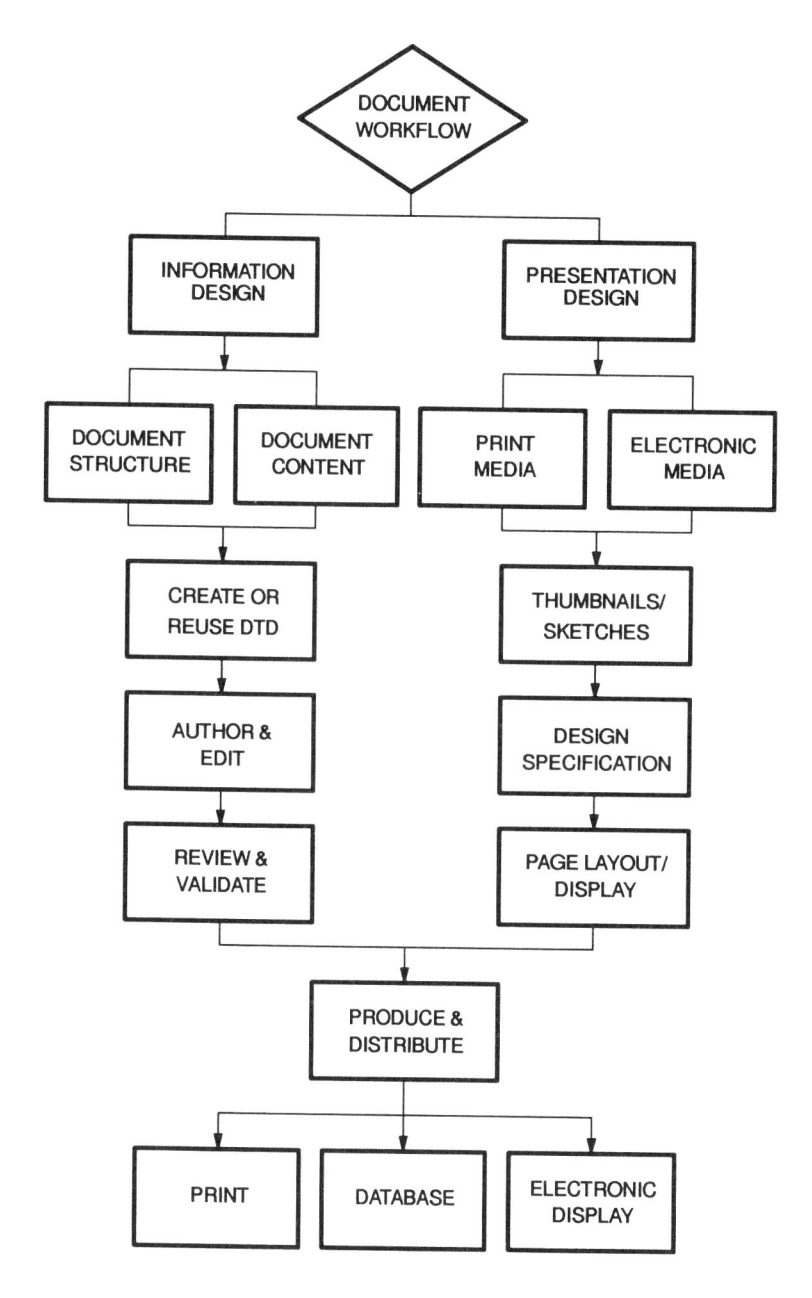

Figure 4.6. Generic publication workflow model separating information and presentation design processes with the objective of supporting multiple types of document distribution in an open publishing environment.

done. Collaborating groups can formulate a workable pilot or design model to test before a technology is purchased and implemented. Thinking through business processes and how documents and document information fit those processes are critical prerequisites in workflow design. The design architects need to be conscious of the information and presentation designs in order to build a system that uses the expertise, computer technology, and information effectively in an organization.

PROJECT BRIEFS

A startup publishing company is applying information design concepts in publishing automation to business advantage. Led by its entrepreneurial founder, the company has adopted a business plan based upon innovative publishing and information services. The company concentrates on vertical markets in medical and physical fitness books and also publishes two newletters—one to fitness buffs that is available in print and electronic form and another for health professionals. It frequently publishes hardcopy and electronic (CD-ROM) books, and works with authors to cultivate different distribution media as a key part of its market strategy. As a secondary business, a core consulting group advises other companies about applying technologies and methodologies toward publishing solutions.

Vertical markets have given the company a jump start in publishing medical references and medical textbooks as well as an array of popular health, fitness, and sports books. It has successfully published a suite of medical reference and textbooks on a range of topics from pediatric medicine to clinical diagnostic works. Technical document information in health care and physical fitness has been adapted for a variety of expert, student, and lay audiences who want to know about everything from diagnosing a child's fever to the effects of jogging on the females over forty. The company enthusiastically supports multilevel readership for students, physicians, and lay people and believes that information design is essential to cost effective distribution of documents in various presentation forms. Three main factors have played a dominant part in shaping the vision and direction the company has taken.

First, the company has established a viable market for both printed and electronic publishing delivery. It has a relatively small fourteen person, permanent staff comprised of two designers, two document analysts, two marketing specialists, two editors, two writers, one programmer, two clerical support, an office manager, and its CEO. To compensate for the small staff, the company has established a network of subcontractor resources for supporting services including printers and software houses that press multiple CD-ROM copies. The company has the financial backing of a small group of physicians and health care specialists who also serve as technical consultants on many proposed titles.

Second, the company, from the outset, perceived information reuse as a bridge to multiple markets. As part of its business plan, a means was developed for organizing one information source to many uses for tiers of audiences. It realized, for example, that much information of use to health professionals is also of interest to the general public. Diverse sub-audiences (families, the elderly, and young professionals, for example) share certain information needs but have special interests as well. By applying consistent information design principles to its base, the company can aim at several levels of audience through its publications. This efficient use of resources translates into company profits and growth.

Third, the company made a decision that its documents would be stored in an open neutral format. It selected SGML as the best available solution because it offers a workable means of reusing the information in a variety of print and nonprint applications. It preserves valuable information with minimum risk of obsolescence as technology evolves. The company's document analysts and editors work directly with authors and encourage them to use SGML authoring tools. The company established a set of DTDs modeled upon ISO 12083:1993. Authors have been supplied with a fully documented DTD and have been given appropriate coaching and training if they were SGML novices. The company provides authors with videotapes and other material to help them learn SGML. Because the company has a special agreement with a provided of SGML authoring tools, it can help authors acquire an authoring tool as a discount, or rent appropriate tools to authors as part of a contractual agreement.

Principal company planners have developed a generic workflow model paradigm for information design and development. By definition the model presupposes a group effort. The model incorporates the roles of permanent staff members as well as authors under contract and subcontractors. A subset of the workflow process deals with the information design sequence for handling prospective book proposals. Many of those steps intersect with processes that are in motion from the inception to completion of the project.

Step 1. Solicitation and review of book proposal. This included a brief writeup with outline. During this discussion the idea for having a print and an on-line book occurs. The collaborative group begins by planning the document with a definition of its audience and market potential. Oftentimes the reviewer will request further information and clarification of project goals.

Step 2. Market Analysis. A review team studies each proposal and makes a preliminary recommendation. The group can recommend peer review of proposal by specialists in the field. Reviewer and market specialists try to assess market potential of book.

Step 3. Feasibility Analysis. The feasibility step determines investment risk. The development cost must be kept within threshold level to make reasonable return on investment. Feasibility includes analysis of potential of book as a print and/or on-line project.

Step 4. Information Model. The company has developed a generic set of DTDs. Before deciding on how the project under consideration should be developed, document analysts determine whether the project lends itself to adaptation to existing DTDs or whether a new DTD will be needed. To meet the challenges of creating on-line documents and paper documents the document analysts carefully review with each author the special markup requirements of attributes and entities to indicate the multiple paths for use of the information.

Step 5. Presentation Design. The company embraces a workflow model that keeps information and presentation design on separate tracks. Sample pages for a printed book are developed by a staff designer along with a detailed set of typography specifications for book elements. The designer (or graphics arts specialist) selects the appropriate elements to match the requirements of the publication. Presentation design requirements for CD-ROM electronic books are also modeled and a staff designer drafts a set of specifications in consultation with the programmer analyst who has special knowledge of user interfaces.

The staff presentation designers work with a variety of tools. Layout and typesetting tools include Quark XPress and PageMaker desktop publishing products for print design and composition. SGML to Quark conversion interfaces are used to optimize efficiency in pre-press page layout and typesetting. The designer for the hardcopy book worked on preparation of sample pages for the book. Another designer also collaborated with specialist worked electronic versions, using the DynaText electronic press and viewing product from Electronic Book Technologies and their Interactive Style Editor for on-line presentation.

Step 6. Final printing and production is done at selected printers for print book production and a software company for CD-ROM press production. A value added feature of the production workflow is that the printers can reuse a PostScript output of the Quark and PageMaker programs. The software house responsible for CD-ROM production is familiar with the requirements of recording interactive media.

The startup publishing company believes that electronic publishing will continue to redefine lines of demarcation between publishing and information services. It recognizes that publishing tools can be used to enable the production of documents from a document database and as a content provider, it is preparing for the delivery of information over wide area networks. The company is conscious of many hurdles in legal copyright disputes for information and it is following developments in that field carefully. But they never want to lose what they believe is a competitive advantage: a methodology for reusing document information for multipurpose publishing.

CHAPTER

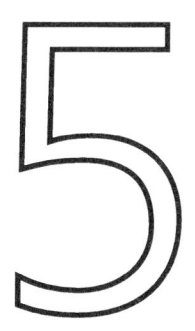

5

➤ *Making and manipulating pictures*

➤ *Raster image and display systems*

➤ *Color processing*

➤ *Graphic conversion and interchange*

➤ *Intelligent graphics*

Graphics for Electronic Publishers

Computer graphics is integral to any discussion of electronic publishing from the manipulation of font and display technologies, to page layout and the use of page description languages, or the graphical interface that helps us manipulate a drawing program. In this chapter we are concerned with the creation, manipulation, and exchange of graphic information that appears in electronic or printed documents. Versions of drawings included for electronically delivered documents have different attributes than printed versions of drawings. An electronic drawing can be a 3D image. Another electronic picture may have hyperlink buttons connecting related drawings or explanatory text. A grayscale printed version of a drawing can be derived from an electronic color version used in a multimedia display. Electronic documents can also contain graphics in motion (animation and video), a subject we shall touch upon in Chapter 8. Presently, our discussion is restricted to the creation, manipulation, and exchange of still pictures.

As we create more and better images we need to remember that these pictures can be used in one or more documents and represent part of a chain of information. The picture created in a Computer Aided Design (CAD) drawing that renders an object to be manufactured may also be used in a printed brochure advertising the product, or in an electronic maintenance manual showing how to repair the object. Graphic images can be purposefully interchanged and reused.

120   *Graphics for Electronic Publishers*

GENERATING GRAPHICS

Drawings are used for many different purposes. Drawings created for architectural plans, business presentations, advertising and studio design, or technical illustration are examples of graphic software that can be used by studio artists, illustrators, technical drafting personnel, marketing and sales analysts for specific objectives.

Some graphic programs are part of the overall publishing package. Interleaf, FrameMaker, and PageMaker are examples of programs with page layout and text editing capabilities including graphics and image editing software as well. Other graphics programs, such as CorelDRAW, Adobe Illustrator, and ClarisDraw, are independent of any text editing or page layout program. Most graphic programs provide access to primitive elements for the creation of rectangles, squares, arcs, ovals, circles and lines. Some programs include a library of symbols that can be used for rapid and efficient creation of drawings. General utility tools common to graphics software packages include features for scaling and sizing, zoom-in techniques, and grids for rectangular or isometric guides to a drawing.

Raster versus Vector Graphics Programs

There are two basic graphic programs used to make still drawings. One is the vector type. The other is the bitmapped or raster image.

A bitmapped image is an array of dots or pixels. Examples of bitmapped images are scanned images and drawings made with popular computer "paint" programs such as Paintbrush and Macpaint. Scanned image editing programs that allow for modification of digitized photographs, line drawings or other source material are also examples of bitmapped graphics programs. One problem with a bitmapped

Figure 5.1. The jagged edges on raster image of a sans serif L are more visible when magnified.

drawing is a phenomenon called aliasing, that is, when the jagged appearance of some bitmapped lines and curves (comprised of tiny dots and pixels) are visible especially if the image is magnified. Figure 5.1 is a rasterized character (in this case, the letter L) that shows its jagged edges when magnified. Vendors of bitmapped programs use antialiasing algorithms to mitigate the jagged effect.

Many graphics programs, such as the widely used paint programs, are bitmapped based systems which generate two dimensional images. Bitmapped image systems also edit scanned photographs or line drawings. Continuous tone raster images use color, shading and richly textured shapes. Halftones made from photographs are raster graphic images enhanced by computer imaging techniques.

With vector or object based drawing systems, the basic difference from pixel graphic systems is the method of storing information—the picture—in the computer's memory. In a vector system the drawing is not stored as a set of pixel values but as a list of vectors or lines. This list may also segment the illustration into layers.

A vector is a small line represented in some format by a program that describes the operation position or coordinates of the line. A line, for example, is stored in a computer's memory as coordinate positions represented by a starting point, a stopping point, and a particular style. The user of a graphics program, whether it is an integral portion of an electronic publishing program or an independent graphics program, selects from a menu or toolbox primitives furnished for the creation of lines, circles, arcs, rectangles, ellipses and so forth.

The fundamental unit of vector based system is a line. A line is a graphic primitive commonly called a vector, which is normally defined or encoded by four numbers or Cartesian coordinates as shown in Figure 5.2.

A drawing can be made up of a combination or set of vectors. More advanced vector graphics programs are sometimes referred to as object drawing systems

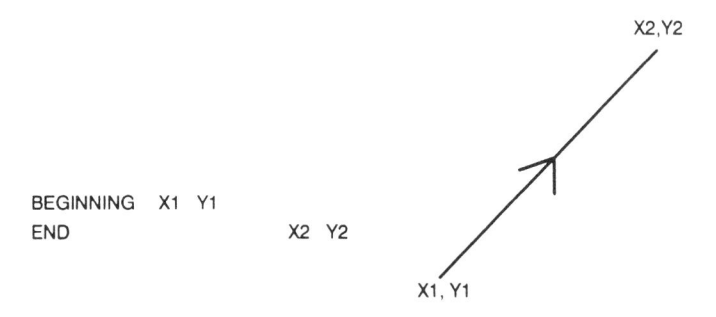

BEGINNING X1 Y1
END   X2 Y2

Figure 5.2. Sample vector encoding showing the Cartesian coordinates used in the vector drawing.

which include three dimensional models. Although the vector is based upon a precise mathematical construct, the display on a computer display terminal (CRT) may appear jagged, because CRT terminals are raster devices. When printed from a high resolution PostScript laser printer, a vector drawing results in a high quality impression.

DRAWING AND PAINT PROGRAM FEATURES

Whether the program is a drawing based vector program, a raster program, or some hybrid of both programs, there are many common features such as the use of primitives to create drawings and the manipulation of editing and utility commands for the efficient execution of a drawing.

Graphic Primitives

The basic geometric elements used in graphic editing systems are called primitives; the user works with primitives to create a drawing. Primitives include lines, rectangles, circles, arcs, and curves. The geometric forms used to create graphic line art, studio design, architectural presentations, and CAD drawings are based upon primitives.

Creating pictures with a computer is made easier with the point and click selection of graphic primitives to begin a drawing. These graphical user interfaces feature icons in shapes that indicate a primitive form to be selected or editing operation to be performed by the user. Sample primitives, toolboxes, and tear off palettes from ClarisDraw are depicted in Figure 5.3.

One difference between the behavior of primitives in vector based programs and bitmapped raster programs should be noted. The primitives in vector based systems are scalable but not divisible. When we select a vector primitive rectangle, for example, the primitive cannot be broken down into four lines. Two or more vector primitives or vectored objects can, however, be layered one upon another. This is not the case with a bitmap only system. The objects cannot be layered one upon another without distorting the shape of the image.

Special primitives that are available in some drawing programs include Bezier curves. These curves are named after Pierre Bezier, the French mathematician who created the mathematical models for such curves while analyzing possible uses of sheet metal. Adobe PostScript character outline fonts are built from bezier curves.

Object libraries can be made of vector symbols. These symbols can be user generated or delivered "off the shelf" by the graphics vendor. The symbol library can be used for efficient execution of drawings. A mechanical engineer may need symbols that include solid geometrical designs for modeling product designs, while

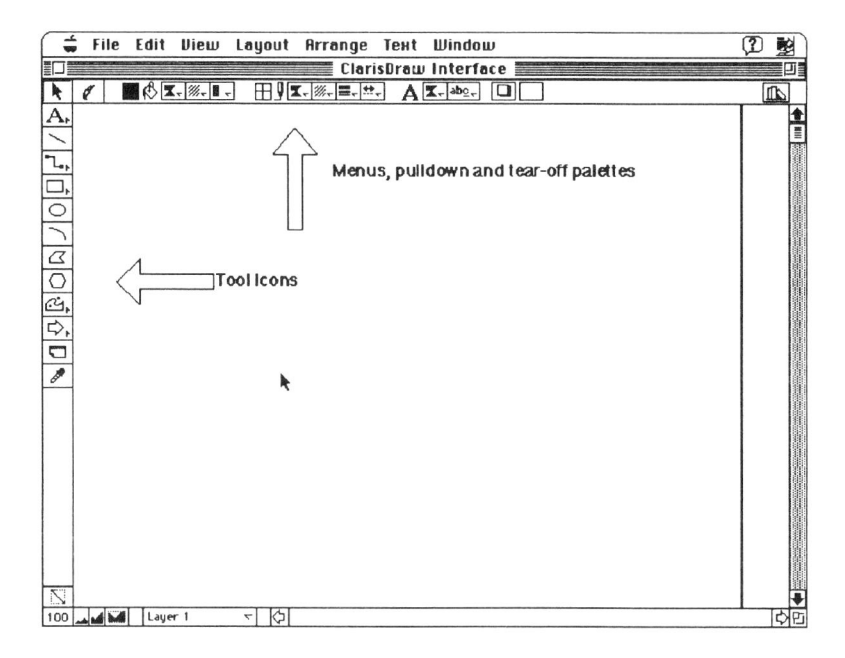

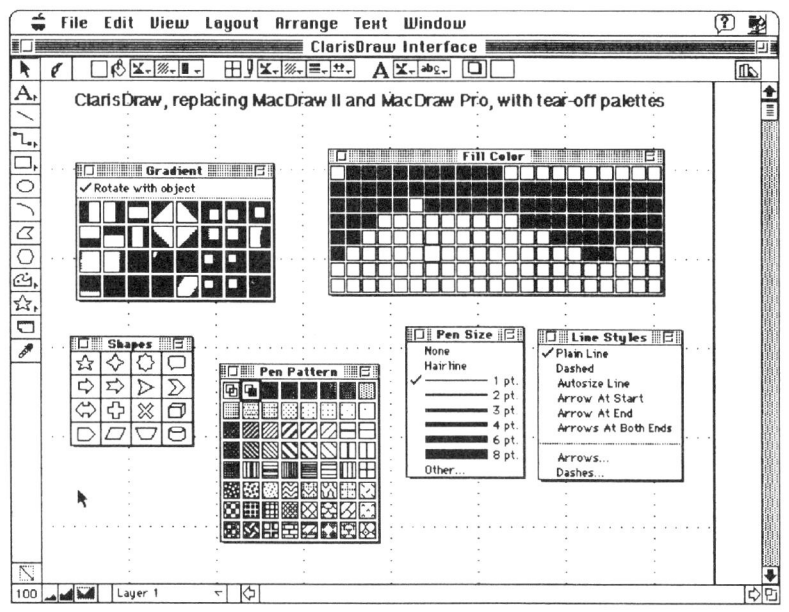

Figure 5.3. A sample of toolboxes, palettes, and icons available with ClarisDraw. Along with menus and dialog boxes, the user applies these tools in creating a drawing by pointing and clicking with a mouse. (Courtesy of Claris Corporation.)

an architectural draftsman may use a library of floor plan symbols to flesh out office building design presentations. A set of lines or geometric shapes may be grouped together as a single object. Creating custom symbol libraries makes the use of computer graphics more efficient. Interleaf uses the concept of Named Graphic Object (NGO) that permits a specific graphic to be added to a user menu. Users can then directly select this object (for example, a staircase or set of walls for drawings of buildings) directly from a menu.

Using a Graphics Grid

Most graphics systems provide a grid for the control of lines in the composition of a graph. Grids depict even sections of an art area like the squares on graph paper. Most graphic subsystems allow a two dimensional rectangular grid with x and y coordinates, while others provide an additional, three dimensional isometric grid with x, y, and z coordinates. The "snap to" or aligning feature of a grid allows for accurate spacing and delineation of lines or objects.

Modifying Graphic Images

Being able to modify graphic pictures is a critical part of a graphic editing system. The procedure for editing a graphic object is to select it and then apply some command such as cut, copy, move, size, or other actions made available via dialog boxes, pull down menus, and icons.

Sizing the Graphic Objects

Graphic editing packages allow for sizing and scaling of all or part of the objects within the graphic image area. Sizing commands sometimes provide for percentage enlargements or reductions. In many drawing programs, an individual object is manipulated by handles that appear at the corners of the object.

Changing Line Widths

Variations in line widths can be used for emphasis, contrast, or special effects. Line thickness for shapes with text can either support or intrude upon the meaning of the text. From a purely formalistic viewpoint, different thickness in lines is used for formal contrast reasons or to create differences in tone, rhythm, and movement. A variation of line widths and line styles can be selected as shown in Figure 5.4.

Cut, Paste, Copy

Other common utility commands available for editing are cut, copy, and paste. These commands help in the creation and editing process. The cut, copy, and paste commands are also used to place graphic objects created with an external program

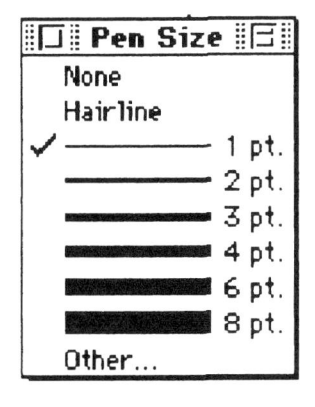

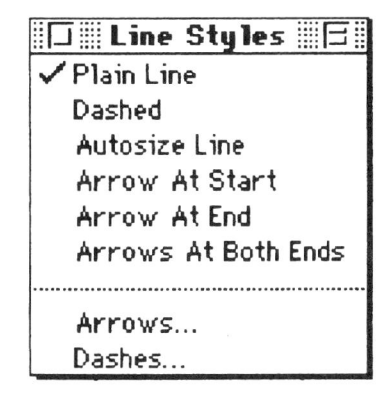

Figure 5.4. Sample menu to select line width variations and line styles from ClarisDraw. (Courtesy of Claris Corporation)

directly into a formatted document if the system allows. In Figure 5.5 a drawing created with the AutoCAD design and drafting system is copied and pasted into a Microsoft Word for Windows document. Many word processing and desktop publishing systems have their own graphic editing tools that allow for the direct creation and editing of graphics in a document.

Undo

Most graphic editing tools allow the user to undo or recover from a mistake. The undo function immediately reverses an operator error or unwanted effect. This can be indispensable, because a serious error in graphics composition can potentially ruin hours of work. The undo command typically appears as part of an edit menu.

Move, Rotate and Align

Aligning graphic objects and text within a graphic object is a basic requirement in drawing. Drawing programs feature alignment commands that select the objects to be aligned according to some spatial reference such as align left sides. Move commands allow for the vertical, horizontal, or diagonal repositioning of objects.

Rotation commands allow movement of an object in a clockwise or counterclockwise direction by a specific number of degrees or a user guided circular rotation. An object or text may be rotated to establish its proper relationship to other objects in a drawing, or to present a different view and perspective for the viewer.

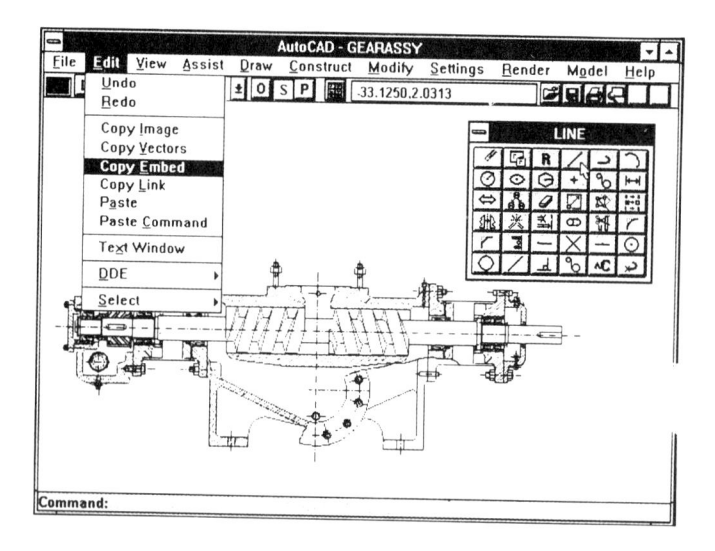

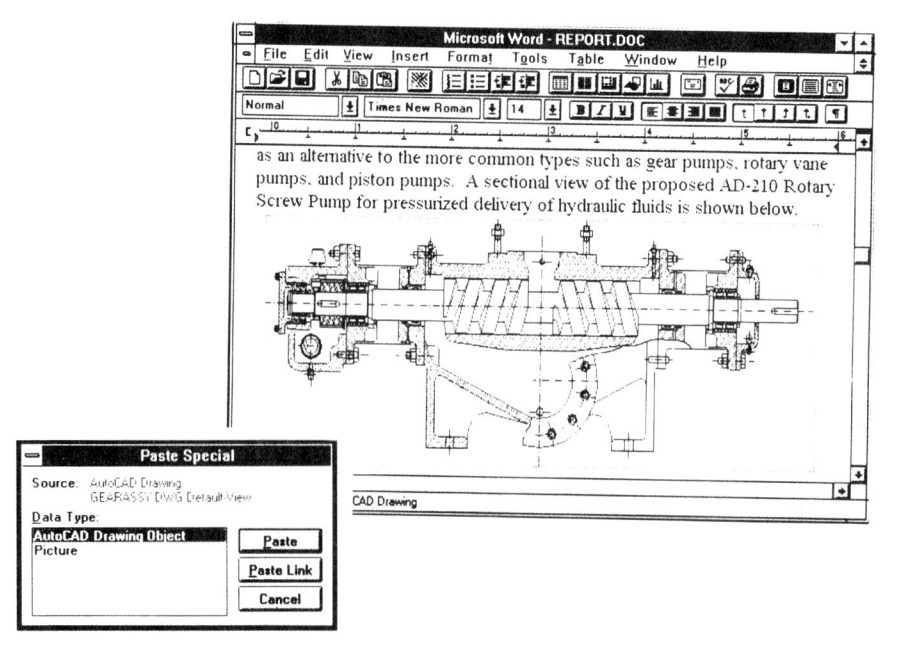

Figure 5.5. In this diagram an AutoCAD drawing of a gear assembly is copied and pasted into a Mircrosoft Word document. By using Microsoft's Object Linking and Embedding (OLE) technology, the AutoCAD drawing can be called up from within Microsoft Word, edited, and placed back into Microsoft Word with a few clicks of the mouse button. (Courtesy of AutoDesk, Inc.)

Zoom In Viewing For Close Up Editing

It is sometimes impossible to modify details required to make fine adjustments without the use of a "zoom in" or close up enlargement of an image. This function permits finer control of diagonal lines, curves, corners and adjoining lines. Figure 5.6 shows a "zoom in" sample where the corners of a line illustration of a connector are not smooth. By using a zoom technique the user can obtain finer control of details to correct the jagged lines.

Grouping

Drawing programs provide commands for grouping of objects. Grouping is a technique of combining two or more objects into a set. If a drawing with complex interconnections between lines has been created, grouping the set may serve several purposes. First, the grouped set can become a symbol to add to a symbol library. Second, the grouped set can be exploited with one command. The purpose of the grouping is to make the manipulation of the combined set useful and effective. Typically, a group command is a drop down or dialog menu selection.

Drawing programs usually include an ungroup command along with the group function. Ungrouping separates elements that have been previously grouped. This function is helpful when individual elements from a set of related objects need modification but we do not want to disturb the other elements in the group.

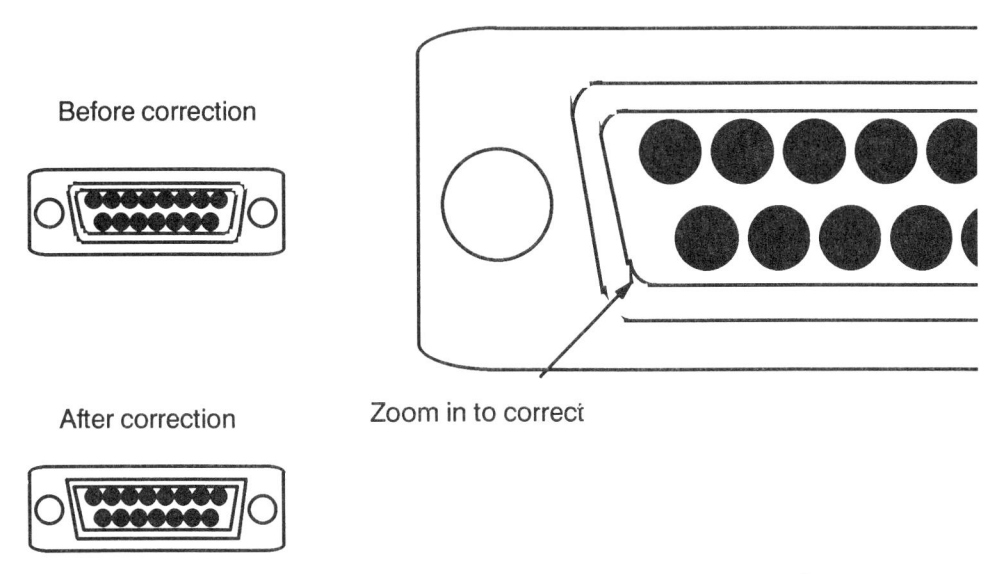

Before correction

After correction

Zoom in to correct

Figure 5.6. Zoom in technique for close up editing. One practical use of a zoom magnification is the fine tuning of an image especially in cases where the limited size of the monitor or the complexity of the layout would otherwise prevent precise editing.

Using Fill and Shade Patterns

Fill and shade patterns can serve various purposes. A pattern such as a hatched pattern can achieve a special effect by adding tone, texture, and contrast to pictures. Shading can be used for effective design as well. Most graphic packages offer an array of patterns that are intended "to fill" a geometric object. Figure 5.7 presents an example of a use of shade and texture creating the subtle illusion of solid surface in a mechanical illustration.

3D Construction

3D programs are becoming more available to electronic publishers. Drawing, CAD, and architecture programs are incorporating 3D as a standard feature. Interactive 3D programs typically furnish a set of icons that represent building blocks for

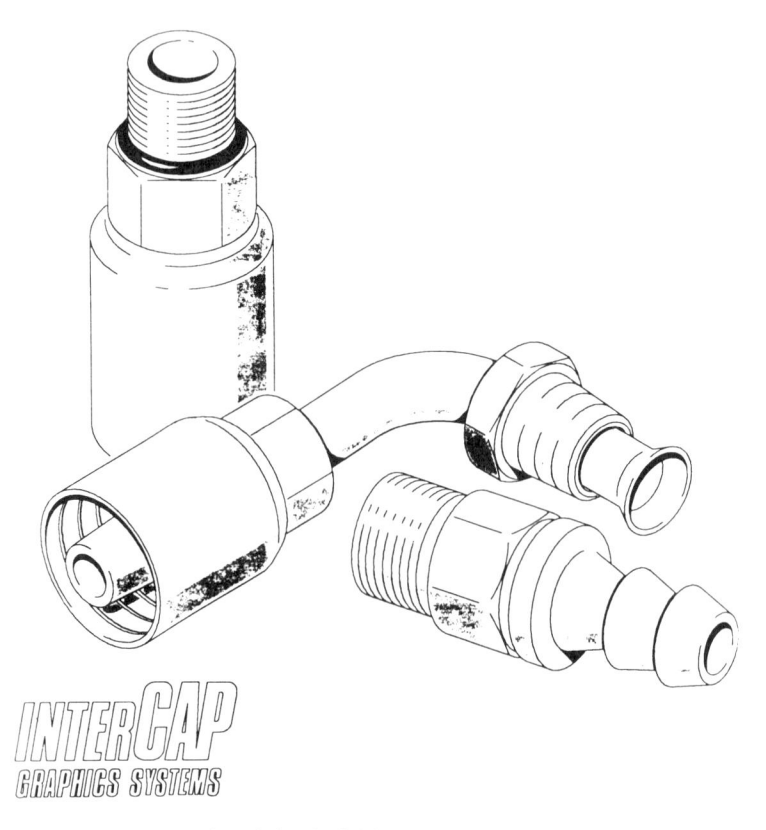

Figure 5.7. Example of shade fill for surface texture and solid. (Copyright InterCAP Graphic Systems, Inc. 1991.)

the user. The building blocks can be general purpose primitives (cubes, cylinders, spheres, parallelepipeds and so forth) or they may be application specific objects (doors, walls, windows, and gates, in an architecture program.) Most programs provide 3D grids that allow users to make judgments regarding spatial relationships between objects. As graphic technologies evolve, the demand for visual photographic realism increases. By refining capabilities in illumination and shading, for example, vendor software products can produce 3D display of 2D elements.

GRAPHIC SOURCE MATERIAL

The origins of graphic objects we use in documents may be from a variety of sources. These may include photos or drawings scanned into the system, images we capture from a computer terminal display screen, electronic clip art delivered on a CD-ROM, or computer drawings retrieved from an existing library.

Screen Capture

Screen capture is a technique used to select a portion of the video screen, store the captured image on disk as a file, or print the image. Screen capture or screen dump software utilities are sold by various companies. Some screen capture utilities are part of the software operating system utilities. The Snapshot screen capture facility shown in Figure 5.8 is a Sun Microsystems Operating System (OS) utility.

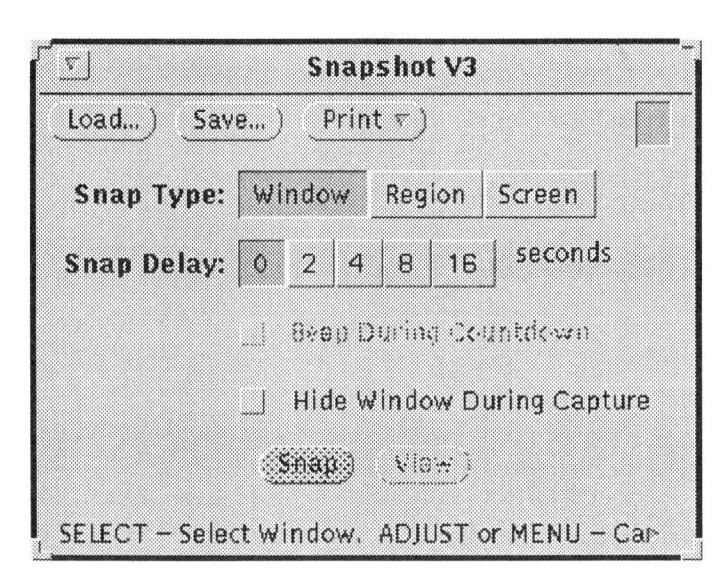

Figure 5.8. Screen capture with Snapshot tool from Sun Microsystems, Inc.

Clip Art

Clip art refers to the use of preexisting design images contained in a catalog or like resource. Traditionally, such art is used for readily available solutions to design application needs.

Figure 5.9 is a sample clip art application from Lotus Development Corporation's SmartPics product. There are many electronic clip art collections available on CD-ROM icluding Kodak color photo clip art. Just as graphic primitives may be combined to form a library of symbols, so can on-line clip art can be combined with other graphic material to create hybrid designs. The clip art images are available in a variety of graphic file formats that can be imported into many electronic publishing systems.

Legal Issues and Copyright

If we use clip art as source material for our publications we are responsible for obtaining permission from the holders of copyright for the images in order to reuse

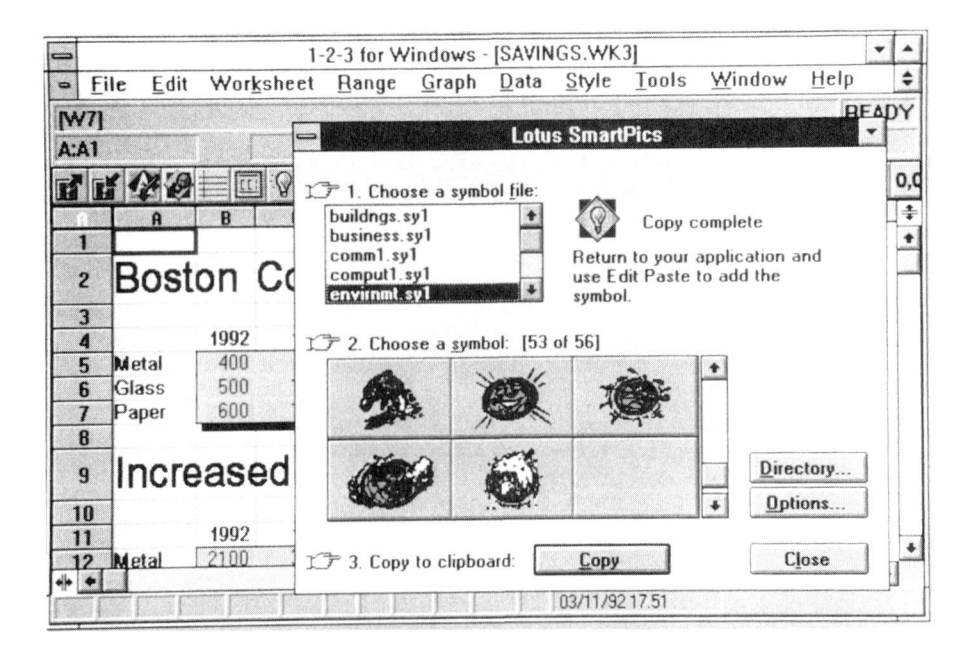

Figure 5.9. Clip art sample using SmartPics from Lotus Development Corporation. In this case the user copies an environmental symbol from a SmartPics symbol file and the system prompts the user to paste the symbol in a file from another application—Lotus 1-2-3 for Windows. (Courtesy of Lotus Development Corporation.)

them. (The same requirement applies to scanned images which we discuss next.) Some clip art is in the public domain, which means that one can reuse the pictures without penalty.

Scanned Images

Scanners can serve as a major resource for capturing paper drawings, images, as well as black and white or color photos into an electronic publishing system. Entire documents can also be scanned into a system. Scanners and the images they capture are converted into digital form so that computers can process the information contained in the images. The applied science of how computers process scanned information is called digital imaging.

Human visual perception is based upon the way light reflects off objects. White objects reflect light; black objects absorb light. Scanners use transducers called photoreceptors that output an electrical voltage proportional to the amount of light detected by the photoreceptor. The relative intensity of light reflected off input sources is converted from light energy (photons) into electronic voltages (electrons). A common photoreceptor that produces electrons from light energy photons is the charged-coupled devices (CCD). Other photoreceptors include liquid crystal displays.

The overall design of a scanner is similar to a photocopy machine but instead of printing the image to paper it is stored on computer disk. A typical desktop flatbed scanner has a rectangular glass plate onto which a drawing or photo is placed facedown to be scanned. Under the glass a scan head moves the length of the page by means of tiny rails. This illuminates the original input source and the intensity of the reflected light is measured by an array of photoreceptors which are lined in position. The image is moved by the scanner across the array of CCDs. As the image passes the scanning head, the photoreceptors produce a line of pixels to be stored in computer memory.

Most desktop scanners use a technique called reflective scanning. High ended scanners use transparent scanning technology with a rotating drum which results in a higher resolution image. Rotary drum scanners used in color specialty houses are very expensive but these devices are being adapted to desktop size and pocketbooks.

Computers represent, store, and process information as a set of digits or binary code. Binary means two states or bi-level. All data including drawings and photographs can be represented by combinations of ones or zeros, on or off conditions. To take a simple example, a black and white line drawing can be represented as a grid of picture elements or pixels, where one white pixel is represented as a zero and a black pixel as a one. In a slightly more complex system, each pixel may store two bits. This allows for definition of four colors or shades of gray (black, white, dark gray, and light gray). Most grayscale scanners provide for eight bit definition of a pixel. At one end of the scale eight zeros represent a white pixel and eight ones represent a black pixel. Grey scales in between the black and white can be represented as percentages of full scale black (light absorption) or zero scale white (light reflection), Table 5.1 is a list of grayscale values based upon an eight bit definition of grey scales up to 2 to the 8th power. Up to 256 values can be represented. Increasing the pixel depth allows for a greater representation of the image.

Color Imaging

A desktop color revolution is being launched by progressive techniques in pixel depth processing for digital color modeling. The principles behind gray scale sampling and imaging can be applied to color scanning and processing. If we can increase the sample size used for grayscale (256) to each of the three prime additive colors (red, green, and blue), we can multiply 256 times 256 times 256 for a total of 16,777, 216 colors. Scanners use two basic methods to accommodate the scan of three colors. In a three pass system sensors go over the original three different times (one pass per color). Another technique is to illumine each row successively with red, green, and blue lights.

Twenty-four bit color (8 bits each for red, green, and blue) offers sufficient pixel depth to enhance digital color imaging process techniques. Image editing software from companies such as Mentalix allow users to merge photographic images or other scanned information with amazing fidelity. The net effect of a color desktop system, however, does depend also on the processing and output devices used. These include digital color printers and image setters as well as the monitor and software used in the color editing process.

Resolution is measured in dots per inch (dpi). The higher the resolution, the greater the granularity of pixel information in the digital imaging process. The quality of the input scan depends upon the dynamic range of a scanner to capture

Table 5.1. Pixel Depth Grayscale

Bits per pixel	Shades of gray
1	$2^1 = 2$
2	$2^2 = 4$
3	$2^3 = 8$
4	$2^4 = 16$
5	$2^5 = 32$
6	$2^6 = 64$
7	$2^7 = 128$
8	$2^8 = 256$

the full range of colors and shades of gray. Files containing color images can become extremely large as one color photo can contain many bits of information. To calculate the size of color image files, the following formula can be used:

File size = Resolution(R)² × bits per pixel × 3(rgb) × size in square inches of input image.

For example, to estimate the file size of the image of 5 × 7 inch color photo with a scanner resolution equal to 300, multiply 300 by itself to obtain the total number of pixels or 90,000 pixels. If each pixel is represented by 8 bits, multiply 8 times each pixel (90,000) to get 720,000 bits. This bit count must be multiplied by 3, or 3 × 720,000 = 2,160,000 bits to account for the red, green, blue samples acquired in the color scanning process. The color photo in this case is 5 × 7 inches, or 35 square inches. Multiplying 35 × 2,160,000, gives us 75,600,000 bits, which can be converted into bytes, dividing by 8, to derive a file size of 9.45 Mbytes.

File Compression

As file sizes for graphics color and photographic images can be extremely large, file compression techniques are used to reduce the size of the files. Compression software uses algorithms that are generally divided into two types—lossless and lossy. Lossless compression means that when the image is decompressed (returned to the original) no information is lost. Lossy compression achieves a higher rate of compression because it eliminates information that does not contribute to the data content.

Since file compression helps utilize disk and memory capacity more efficiently, the purchase of file compression software is a wise investment. There are a variety of lossless utility programs on the market including PKZip and Stuffit where the compression ratio is 2:1. The Joint Photographic Experts Group (JPEG) standard for data compression provides file reduction to one tenth of the original size. JPEG uses a lossy compression algorithm called Discrete Cosine Transform which eliminates pixel information that contributes little to the quality of the overall image. Fractal Image Compression method is another lossy method based on a different mathematical algorithm than the JPEG standard.

GRAPHIC DISPLAYS

Computer displays cannot be overlooked in the discussion of graphics. In a common configuration, a picture is made by the computer on a cathode ray tube (CRT) by guiding an electron beam over the inner part of the tube. The beam energizes a phosphor coating on the screen and produces a glowing point. Each time the electron beam passes over a position a dot can be intensified and this is called raster scanning. Figure 5.10 presents a raster grid where each cell of the grid is a pixel (or picture element) and a horizontal line of pixels is a raster.

Computer monitors are rated by the number of pixels they show. The video display uses a coordinate system so that any point on the screen may be selected for representation. A standard starting point for the coordinate is the bottom left corner of the CRT screen. Resolution is measured in pixels, that is, the numbers of pixels in rows and columns and the higher resolution means the higher quality of the image. A low resolution monitor has no more than 640 by 350 pixels. Medium range monitors such as the IBM Visual Graphics Array support at least 640 by 480 pixels. High end monitors display 1,024 by 786 pixels, or better.

A raster display system consists of several key components including a frame buffer, a video controller, and the display monitor with its DAC converter. The frame buffer is a computer memory image of the display screen which stores a binary number for each pixel in the display. This number is used by a video controller to specify how each dot may be intensified. The DAC converts the digital value into a voltage level for each dot as the electron beam scans the screen.

A video display monitor is used to create and display drawings. Displays vary in size and price. Distributors of drawings for electronic viewing must anticipate the type of display equipment that a target audience is likely to own. There is a wide variance in the cost and quality of these displays.

Monochrome Video Displays

A raster CRT display makes pictures from tiny pixels. At its simplest level, a raster CRT provides a grid of pixels referred to as a bitplane. To manipulate each pixel in the grid in terms of its light intensity, we are constrained by the number of bits stored in memory per pixel. With a black and white display, one bit is used to represent one pixel. The possibilities are limited to two states—one is black the other is white. If the number of bits is increased to two, we can now represent 2×2, or four intensity levels for each pixel (black, dark gray, light gray, and white). The

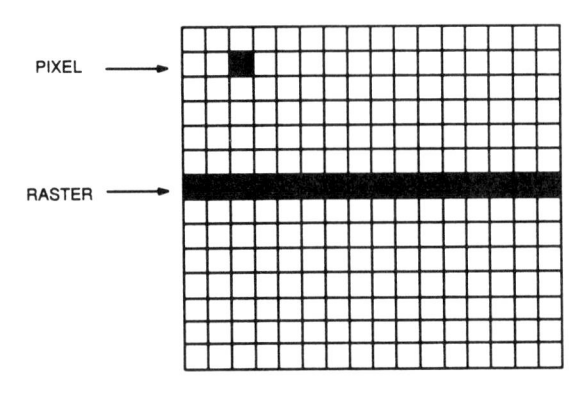

Figure 5.10. The entire picture on a raster display is made from a raster, a set of lines comprised of rows of pixels.

result is the variation in gray scale. If the CRT has phosphors that can be excited to greater degrees so that it can store 8 bits per pixel, it can offer 256 levels of gray. We have seen this variation before with respect to another raster device, the scanner.

Color Video Displays

The industry standard color model for display monitors, the Red Green Blue (RGB) standard, specifies the colormap specific to a color display. The colormap in computer memory is thus made up of an array of red, green, and blue values. With color display technology, a pixel comprises red, green, and blue phosphors that are acted upon by separate electron beams. The relative intensity of these distinct colors tricks human perception into seeing a single color. Most color displays use a scanning beams to excite pixels, although some flat panel color displays use direct addressing. Figure 5.11 is a diagram of the use of electron guns to excite red, green, and blue phosphors on a CRT display.

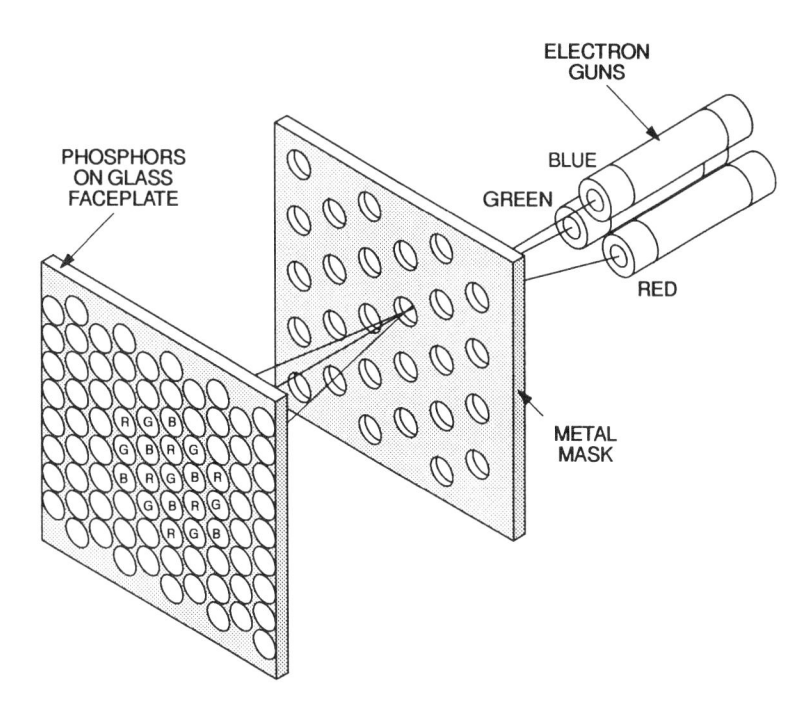

Figure 5.11. Use of electron guns to excite red, green, blue color display with RGB phosphors with a delta–delta shadow mask CRT. James D. Foley, Andries van Dam, Steven K. Feiner and John Hughes, *Computer Graphics: Principles and Practice,* Second Edition (pg. 159), ©1990 by Addison-Wesley Publishing Company, Inc. Reprinted by permission of the publisher.

The greater number of bits stored per pixel in the CRT, the more variations in the intensity of light per pixel can be processed in the CRT display. A standard way to maximize the variation of intensity per pixel is to connect the value stored in the frame buffer for a pixel to a color look-up table that contains a current value for each pixel during each scan cycle. The video controller uses the look-up table to determine the relative intensity of the red, blue, and green electron guns. See Figure 5.12. Instead of specifying different intensities of light per pixel in the frame buffer, the bitmap is used as an index pointer to a look-up table value. If the value of each entry in the look-up table is expanded to 24 bits, the number of colors available for display is increased dramatically.

An important specification item in the selection of a color monitor for publishing is dot pitch which is the distance expressed in millimeters between each group of red, green, and blue dots. A small dot pitch (26 mm or better) provides a sharp image. To create quality work in color, a monitor that can display 24 bit color graphics (16 million colors) when used with a 24 bit color processor board is invaluable.

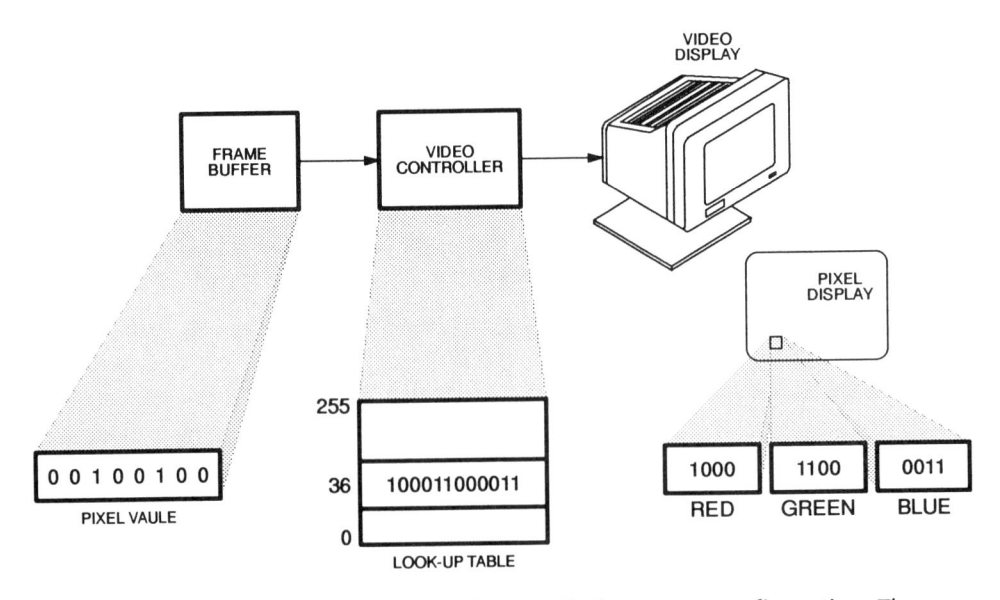

Figure 5.12. This diagram shows a partial raster display system configuration. The frame buffer stores the image to be displayed and contains a binary value for each pixel in system. In this case a pixel value of 36 is used as an index pointer to a video controller look-up table that contains a value for controlling the color of the CRT. The intensity of the red, blue, and green electronic guns are determined by percentage of strength indicated by the binary values in the look-up table.

COLOR MODELS

There are three main color models used by developers of color imaging, color display, graphic application software, and printing reproduction technologies. These are additive, subtractive, and perceptual models. Within these types there are variations that are not discussed here.

RGB

The Red Green Blue (RGB) model is used in all color television sets and most computer monitors. The RGB model of picture elements (or pixels) has numbers assigned (typically between 0 and 255) to a color lookup table in a video memory device. When a number is read by the DAC in the CRT, it produces an analog signal or voltage proportional to the number. The voltage activates the CRT's electron guns. The RGB model is an additive color model, where each primary color added to another yields a specific result.

CMYK

The Cyan Magenta Yellow Black (CMYK) color model is a subtractive model used in most color reproduction and printing systems. By combining percentages of these colors, an infinite variation in color can be obtained. The printing industry uses process inks to reduce loss of lightness and saturation in color reproduction.

CIE

The Comission Internationale De L'Eclairage (CIE) color standard is a leading example of a perceptual color model. This standard models the way in which humans perceive color. The CIE color model is gaining among desktop color technologies as color tool use moves from the exclusive province of specialists to the more general public. Adobe backs the CIEXYZ color model in its PostScript Level 2 color system.

Color Matching and Calibration

The challenge for color devices (color CRTs, scanners, printers, and image setters) is achieving some accuracy in the color from input to output because of the variations in color models used by different raster devices. There are color matching systems based upon printed samples or swatches of color. The PANTONE matching system is the most important. Color matching is difficult because at different stages of the process (input—display—output) there are different calibration techniques. The color perceived on the monitor will be different from the color on paper.

Fortunately many of the products work within different color modes so that the end user can have better control over color accuracy between the scan display and output processes. Vendors automating the calibration between color models by using menu driven setups to link one color model to another. A significant number of vendors are using the CIE model or variants of the color perception model because less experienced desktop users have a better chance of success.

REVIEWING GRAPHICS ON-LINE

Graphic systems are often purchased to speed up the process of production, especially in manufacturing and engineering environments. Often the process is delayed by the need to make intermediate paper copies of drawings for review, comments, and corrections. Alternative ways of making comments on the drawing are now electronically possible. Products such as InterCAP's Red Liner allow reviewers to make comments on the drawing without actually changing the original drawing. Red Liner creates a TIFF raster file that can be viewed by the responsible reviewer whose comments are placed in overlays to the attached drawing.

VISUAL DESIGN

Graphic images can convey information and help readers understand it. The cliche "a picture is worth a thousand words" has enduring validity. Some subordinate design considerations are important What message is the picture intended to communicate? Does the picture serve more than one purpose? Does the illustration conform to style criteria for the document as a whole? Does the file format of the electronic picture allow it to be easily incorporated into documents?

Three guiding principles for graphical presentation and design are consistency, clarity, and harmony. These criteria help avoid common mistakes associated with creating and editing pictures with computer-aided graphic tools.

Consistency

Drawings and pictures should make consistent use of visual elements. Establishing a consistent visual alphabet for elements (lines, text, shading, fills, and so forth) for certain classes of drawings appearing in publications requires a plan and a specification. Text labels, for example, should be consistent in size, weight, and style. Workgroups should be sensitive to the need for consistency throughout multiple sets of documents.

Clarity

The meaning of a picture is created by the sum of its parts. Visual information should reinforce the meaning of the data. Workgroups should coordinate the development of illustrations with the requirements of text files to ensure that clarity in communication is served.

Harmony

Effective use of space in graphic work is critical. The space limits imposed upon creators of graphic material arise from specific project constraints. Harmonizing visual elements in space (for paper or electronically distributed drawings) can be achieved by the application of balance and proportion. Balance calls for a symmetrical distribution of visual elements within a drawing. Proportion refers to the proper use of ratio and magnitude of elements. Rectangles within a line drawing, for example, should be sized proportionally with respect to one another. The rule of harmony extends beyond the requirements of a specific drawing. It also applies to the document layout in which a drawing appears.

INTERCHANGING GRAPHICAL INFORMATION

Graphic File Formats

We have discussed some methods for generating and using graphics in electronic publishing but we have not examined graphic file formats. Fortunately, there are standards and software tools available for making graphic files more portable. File formats are the conventional ways to organize data structures for processing. Most graphics packages use proprietary file formats to encode pictures in a manner that can only be used by the system which created the drawing. For example, a drawing created with MacDraw is encoded in a proprietary format. The picture can be stored in PICT format which many other drawing packages and publishing programs can interpret so the picture can be exchanged and reused. When we translate from one file format to another, the possibilities for editing the drawing depend upon several factors.

Graphics conversion tools are variously called filters or translators. They provide for the exchange to another system of a graphic made on a system using a different graphic editor. Some packages are more device independent than others. If we wish to import or export a graphic file and reuse a graphics illustration within a different electronic publishing program then the sending or receiving system must be able to translate that file. Figure 5.13 depicts the process of a graphical file conversion of a source drawing to an exchange format suitable for export to a target application program.

Graphic interchange formats include ANSI/ISO standards such as Computer Graphics Metafile (CGM) and Initial Graphics Exchange Specification (IGES), CCITT Group 4 (Consultative Committee on International Telegraphy and Telephony), and assorted industry standards such as Tag Image File Format (TIFF),

```
┌──────────┐   ┌──────────┐   ┌──────────┐   ┌──────────┐
│  SOURCE  │   │ CONVERT  │   │  EXPORT  │   │ CONVERT  │
│ GRAPHIC  │──▶│    TO    │──▶│CONVERSION│──▶│GRAPHIC TO│
│   FILE   │   │ PORTABLE │   │ TO TARGET│   │APPLICATION│
│  FORMAT  │   │  FORMAT  │   │  PROGRAM │   │  FORMAT  │
└──────────┘   └──────────┘   └──────────┘   └──────────┘
```

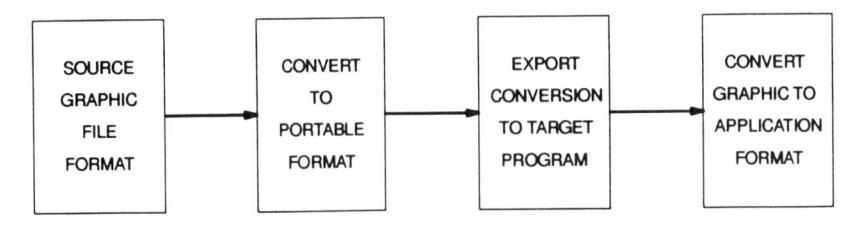

Figure 5.13. Simplified flow diagram of graphics file format translation and subsequent export to another program for reconversion.

Hewlett Packard Graphics Language, (HPGL), and Encapsulated PostScript (EPS). Application programs usually provide for conversion of one or more file formats for purposes of importing the data or for exporting it. There are some generic utility programs on the market which convert multiple file format inputs and outputs. Examples include HiJaak from Inset Systems, X-Change from InterCAP Systems, and CADLeaf from Carberry Technology. Figure 5.14 is a sample menu from CADLeaf listing some sample file formats from a directory that can be converted. Conversion program utilities such as CADLeaf provide for a range of graphic file

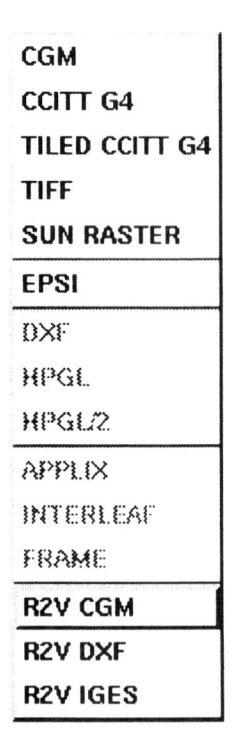

CGM
CCITT G4
TILED CCITT G4
TIFF
SUN RASTER
EPSI
DXF
HPGL
HPGL2
APPLIX
INTERLEAF
FRAME
R2V CGM
R2V DXF
R2V IGES

Figure 5.14. Sample drop down menu interface to CADLeaf, a graphic conversion utility program. (Courtesy of Carberry Technology, Inc.)

format conversions as well as graphic viewing tools to enable graphic browsing in hypermedia presentations. The DeBabelizer from Equilibrium Technologies can be used as file conversion utility and it also has a batch mode that helps users of large sets of images perform multiple functions such as scaling the size of color images in a computer batch mode. Since a batch program can run without operator intervention, it can reduce the time an operator would otherwise spend with repetitive tasks such as opening a series of graphic files to reduce the color scale from 24 to 8 bit color within an application.

HPGL

Figure 5.15 shows a diagram which was translated from an HPGL plot file into Interleaf graphic format. The source file used for input is shown next to the diagram. HPGL was designed to work with electromechanical output devices called pen plotters which draw lines upon computer command by moving pens across pages. Instead of being sent to a plotter, an HPGL file can be exported to a graphics editor which interprets the plotter commands and converts them into its own file format.

PICT 1 and 2

PICT is a file format used for many Macintosh graphic applications and is commonly used from one graphics program to another. PICT supports bitmapped and vector drawing formats. PICT2 has increased pixel depth and is especially useful for color applications.

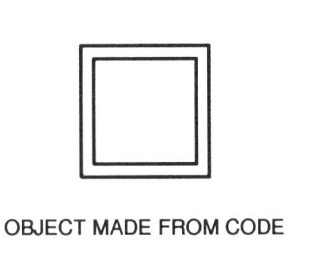

HPGL SOURCE CODE
(IN ASCII FORMAT)

IN;SP1;
PU0,0;
PD;PA200,0;
PD;PA200,200;
PD;PA0,200;
PD;PA0,0;
PU20,20;
PD;PA20,180;
PD;PA180,180;
PD;PA180,20;
PD;PA20,20;
PU0,0;
SP0;NR;

OBJECT MADE FROM CODE

Figure 5.15. HPGL plot file source code and processed image. The HPGL coded commands used—IN for initialize, PU for pen up, PD for pen down, PA for penabsolute, SP for starting point, and NR for not ready—reflect the pen plotter origins of the command language.

TIFF

Tagged Image File Format (TIFF) is an industry standard raster file format which resulted from a cooperative effort between Aldus, Microsoft, Hewlett Packard, among others, to establish a means for interchanging raster files. It is a widely supported raster file image format with capabilities for storing bitmapped data in monochrome, gray level, and full color RGB. Some publishing programs such as PageMaker accept TIFF files and use them as a convenient way to store scanned images. TIFF files have a specific structure which accommodates the identification of the major parts, data definition, and image storage organization (called tags) and the data itself.

GIF

The Graphic Interchange Format (GIF) is a raster file format developed by CompuServe for the PC. It is used extensively to support exchange of color graphic files.

EPS

An Encapsulated PostScript (EPS) file is another common file format used for graphic interchange. An EPS program is divided into two forms: ASCII EPS and Binary EPS (hexadecimal). ASCII EPS files include two versions of the graphic: a description of the PostScript output and a bitmapped preview image for display. The application program that receives the EPS file cannot edit the contents of the image. It can size, crop, or rotate the image but not alter it.

CGM

An ANSI/ISO 8632:1992 standard for vector/raster graphics file format interchange is Computer Graphics Metafile (CGM), a meta-language intended for picture capture, picture storage and retrieval, and picture transmission and interchange. Figure 5.19 shows a simple diagram of the structure of Version 2 CGM files.

As shown in Figure 5.16, CGM pictures consist mainly of a picture body that has control elements, primitive elements and attributes. The geometric elements include lines, rectangles, polygons, circular and elliptical arcs, and text. The attributes of lines for instance would include style, weight and color; font attributes would consist in font, character set, color, and so forth. Version 2 of CGM provides for picture segments. A picture segment is a group of primitives which is stored once and can be repeatedly used in a picture.

Version 3 capabilities of CGM expand graphical drawing elements and also provide for more efficient exchange of structured information related to graphics. One Version 3 capability defines external symbol libraries by referencing such libraries within the metafile.

DXF

The AutoCAD drawing interchange file (DXF) format is widely used as a standard in the CAD community. DXF files are ASCII files and as such can be easily exported to other CAD or drawing programs that, in turn, can interpret the DXF file structure.

IGES

The Initial Graphics Exchange Specification (IGES) is an international standard for interchange of CAD information for product manufacturing information. The complexities for exchange of complex geometry and related information are formidable. The IGES standard has been adopted by the Computer Aided Logistics Support (CALS) program of the Department of Defense as a means of interchanging product information from defense contractors to DoD agencies. A new standard called STEP is indebted to IGES for its origin and promises to be the future interchange of product information.

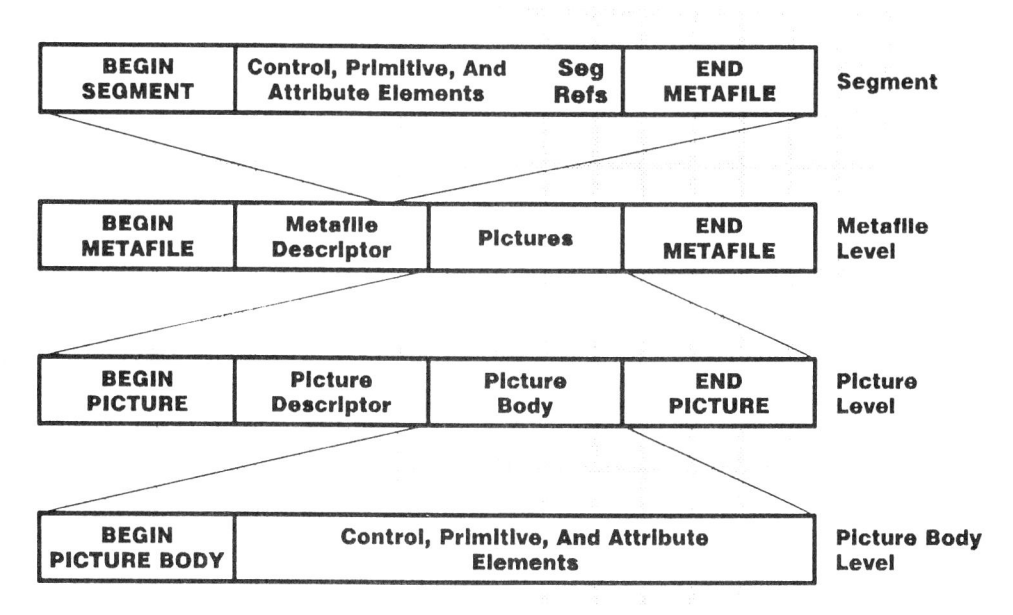

Figure 5.16. Structure of Version 2 CGM metafiles. An important feature of Version 2 metafiles is the introduction of the graphical segment which is a group of primitives that can be named and repeated in a picture for increased efficiency. Version 3 metafiles add 40 new elements to CGM exchange capability as the CGM standard expands its support to include raster images such as TIFF and external symbol libraries.

STEP

The Standard for the Exchange of Product data model (STEP) is not yet fully developed but it is an ambitious and evolutionary standard because current users of IGES will be able to migrate to STEP without losing their IGES capability. It will allow IGES users to evolve from their current level of data interchange to a much richer exchange including nongeometric information that is often lost in the interchange process.

Graphical interchange is far from perfect. When new capabilities within an existing graphics domain need support, such as the use of color, the software must also change for translating a picture from one file format to another. Users of translation software must follow the evolution of specific file formats. International graphic interchange standards such as CGM, IGES, and STEP hold great promise because they focus not only upon the geometry needed in the exchange but information associated with a graphic.

POSTSCRIPT: MEDIUM FOR GRAPHIC OUTPUT

PostScript is a computer page description language (PDL). As such it is the most widely used medium in the electronic publishing industry for interpreting output to a printed page. PostScript is supported by a wide assortment of output devices including laser printers, image setters, and typesetters from a variety of manufacturers. PostScript places or paints images on a page whether in the form of letters, lines, filled shapes, or halftone photographs. The paint may also be in black and white, gray scale, or color.

PostScript is device independent. If an application supports PostScript output, the document or graphic can be sent to any laser printer, color printer, or image setter which uses a PostScript interpreter. The resolution of the output will be as high as the device can accomplish. PostScript files can also be telecommunicated to another user and then printed by a PostScript compatible device.

PostScript is an interpretive language. It does not need a compiler as most high level programming languages do. One of the valuable features of the PostScript language is its ability to interpret every point of a page to the device. PostScript generates pictures on a page by tracing a current path and then painting that path to make it visible. The PostScript page model is two dimensional requiring two coordinates, x and y. All points on a PostScript page can be described in terms of these coordinates. The point of origin for a PostScript page is the bottom left hand corner or 0,0 point.

PostScript is also a rich graphics language. There are over two hundred commands in the PostScript language many of which directly relate to the creation of graphic objects. Figure 5.17 is a diagram of a graphic object (in this case a rectangle) and the PostScript code used to build it. The operators or commands used to build the PostScript are not that difficult to learn since they are English language expressions. In Figure 5.17, for example, the moveto, lineto, and closepath commands simulate the drawing of lines from one pair of coordinates to another in a logical fashion. The showpage command means print this image. Applications automate the interface to PostScript so the end user need not understand the working of PostScript in order to use it. A knowledge of PostScript can be very useful for electronic publishers who need to adapt it to special purposes.

GRAPHIC INFORMATION

Electronic publishers are increasingly able to afford products offering new capabilities and dimensions in graphics. The rapid evolution in computer graphics for the desktop is partly due to lower costs for computer hardware. Leading edge developments in graphics technology also come from the convergence of market interests in areas such as visual realism, numerical visualization, solid modeling, animation, and medical imaging, in turn stimulated by requirements in manufacturing, engineering, science, architecture, and the entertainment industries. Graphic material is part of an information base, and not merely an information embellishment, for example, as a drawing may derive from a larger database of which it is an integral part. A database may consist of financial, product, scientific, architectural, demographic, or other data that can be expressed in graphical form. If we can perceive pictures as intelligent objects that have connections to other objects (pictures of parts that make up an engine, for example), a new universe of information can be adapted to the way we work and learn.

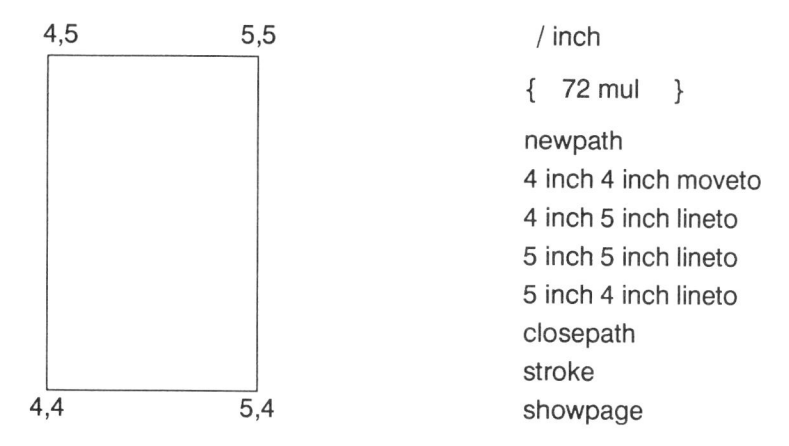

```
/ inch
{  72 mul  }
newpath
4 inch 4 inch moveto
4 inch 5 inch lineto
5 inch 5 inch lineto
5 inch 4 inch lineto
closepath
stroke
showpage
```

Figure 5.17. PostScript graphic sample with coding.

Intelligent Graphics

Still pictures and their parts can become intelligent objects by mapping the information stored with the drawings or pictures and making specific connections to other information. Examples of intelligent graphics include charts whose values are updated automatically by data from a program linked to it; graphics that have embedded links to related data for hypermedia applications; and multidimensional visualization graphs that use complex statistical data to make graphical representations.

An intelligent drawing application is shown in Figure 5.18. Here the drawings have been developed to support an interactive maintenance application. The product technology used is MetaLink Author and MetaLink RunTime from InterCAP Graphics Systems. A technician can use a terminal to lookup critical maintenance and repair information. The airplane shown in Figure 5.18 is not just another picture of an aircraft. It is a logical structure of objects including the engine and its sub objects: compressor, inlet assembly, and and turbine. By following easy to use menus, the technician can point to parts of the aircraft, click on an object that in turn displays another window with information about the object of choice. Tools such as MetaLink will eventually revolutionize the way groups plan, organize, and use graphical information to make work more efficient and less error prone. MetaLink is an application that is standards based. It uses native Computer Graphic Metafile (CGM) structures, so that the information embedded in the picture as well as the picture geometry can be exchanged.

Many disciplines can now correlate graphical representations with other computerized data. An architect may use an intelligent object library not only to describe the pictures of single family homes in a development but to link tables of cost data in a database that generate price estimates for model homes when features for various rooms are added or subtracted. Some drawing packages such as AutoCAD provide connections to a database program that stores information not only about the drawing's identity but all sorts of information related to cost.

Intelligent charts are another example of how computers connect data calculated on a spreadsheet program and translate it into visual form. Chart generating graphic packages are popular because the user can enter the data from easy to use menus. Charts add visual substance to reports and slide presentations. They can be especially helpful for visualization of statistical data where comparison of numbers is vital to the audience. Intelligent chart applications take advantage of the statistical power of spreadsheet programs to compute values that are transformed into bar charts, pie charts, or other two dimensional charting schemes.

Visualization

Visualization is a set of techniques using graphics to display complex numerical data relationships that can be used in any number of disciplines such as

Graphic Information **147**

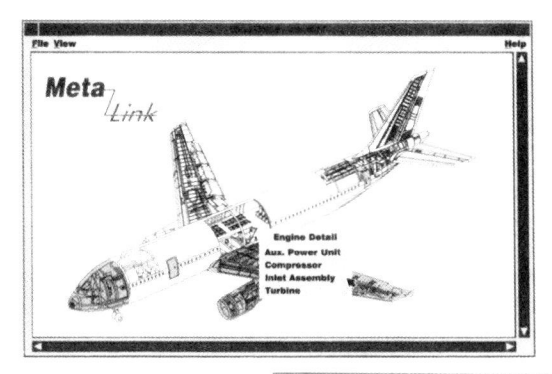

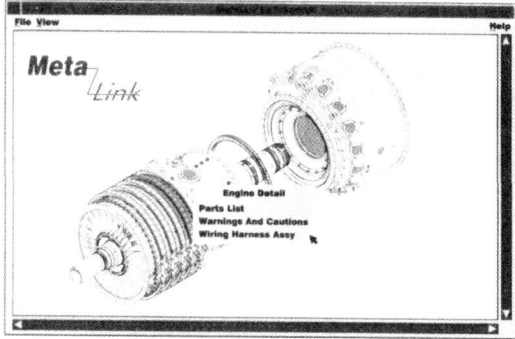

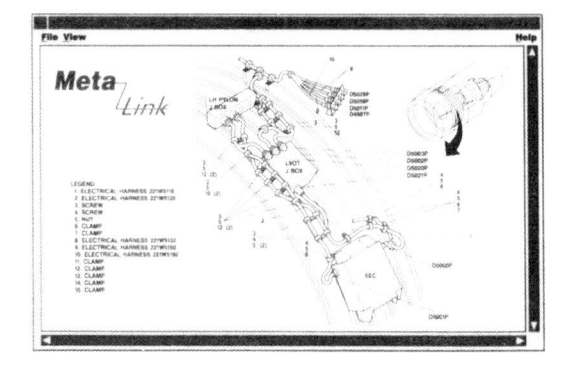

Figure 5.18. Shown above is a sequence of interconnected diagrams that illustrate an intelligent graphics application. An operator, in this case a maintenance technician or inventory specialist, uses a mouse and points to part of the aircraft. When the operator selects to view engine detail in the uppermost window and clicks on the mouse, a menu pops up guiding the operator to display an exploded view of engine subassemblies shown in the second window. Subsequent pointing to the wiring harness assembly generates a third display with view of the wiring harness with part lists. The linking of visual information about the aircraft to critical maintenance actions and parts inventory reduces the amount of time needed to diagnose problems and maintain aircraft efficiently. (Courtesy of InterCAP Graphics Systems.)

scientific research, engineering, financial data services, network management, social sciences, city planning and many more. Visualization programs make source numerical or statistical data visible. The challenge of visualization is to find meaningful ways to display complex patterns of statistical variables. Figure 5.19 is a sample visualization application showing a solid model of a hair dryer. The structural analysis software allows product designers to perform transient thermal analysis for heat flux and convection loads and create solid models of the hair dryer. The graphical models are also used to check the structural integrity of cross sectional properties. Visualization tools can be used as research and development productivity aids.

Another practical application is the display of real time measurement of critical data from sensors acquired for telemetry and supervisory control systems. The collection of measurements for a flight test application, for instance, may include such parameters as temperature, vibration, altitude, and air speed. Flight test engineers analyzing data from a test mission can quickly see whether certain patterns are within or outside certain measurement limits when the data is displayed visually. The behavior of certain measurements over time is sometimes best understood in visual displays showing multidimensional variations. Color can

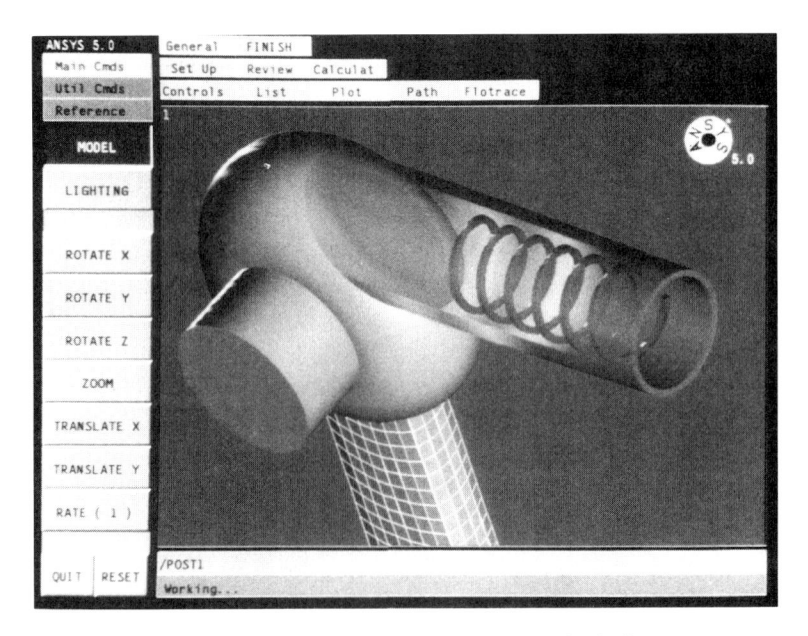

Figure 5.19. A sample visualization screen shot which shows a partially translucent shell, revealing the state of thermal value on the interior of a hair dryer model using the ANSYS (R) structural analysis program. (Courtesy of Swanson Analysis Systems, Inc.)

be used to show that certain measurements are out of threshold limits, supporting analysis of critical weaknesses in the aircraft. In many telemetry test environments, the summary analysis report of a test mission can be strengthened by the incorporation of visualization snapshots. Various diagrams can be captured and reused in the test reports to support test result findings and recommendations. The emerging industry use of electronic test reports is also noteworthy.

Visualization expresses the interconnectedness of information. There are many companies making affordable visualization tools suited to different application requirements. PCWave Point and Click from Visual Numerics, Data Visualizer from Wavefront Technologies, and Visualization Data Explorer from IBM are some examples of visualization software products.

Graphics and SGML

SGML authoring systems do not incorporate graphics directly in the text file. In SGML documents the graphic is stored in an external file, directory or database and referenced from the document instance. The document type definition contains an entity reference that specifies the external location. SGML authoring tools use graphic or figure entity dialog boxes to facilitate the indexing of illustrations. Each graphic entity reference has a notation which identifies the format of the file referred to from an SGML file. For instance, a notation can name a graphic format such as CGM or TIFF. The notations are defined in the DTD. Many SGML authoring systems allow users to launch an external application such as a graphics editor or viewing program directly from the SGML file they are authoring. In the SoftQuad Author/Editor system, for example, the user can specify a command line reference to an external application program such as a graphics editor. Refer to Figure 5.20. To launch the Paintbrush application shown in Figure 5.20, for example, the user might identify a command line from a Windows system as c:\windows\pbrush.exe%system in the Notation menu Action test box of the Author/Editor system.

A number of tools are available to users of SGML authoring systems to integrate drawings created in different graphic file formats into electronic books, multimedia collections, or printed applications. CADLeaf Batch, for example, systematically translates many drawing formats and converts the drawing into industry standard formats. These drawings can be automatically indexed and supported by an SGML based browsing system such as DynaText from Electronic Book Technologies.

Graphics Viewers and Databases

When creating graphics that may be reused or distributed to a number of users, it is important to identify and track the information and make it accessible for viewing, browsing, or updating. Some vendors have created iconic interfaces to

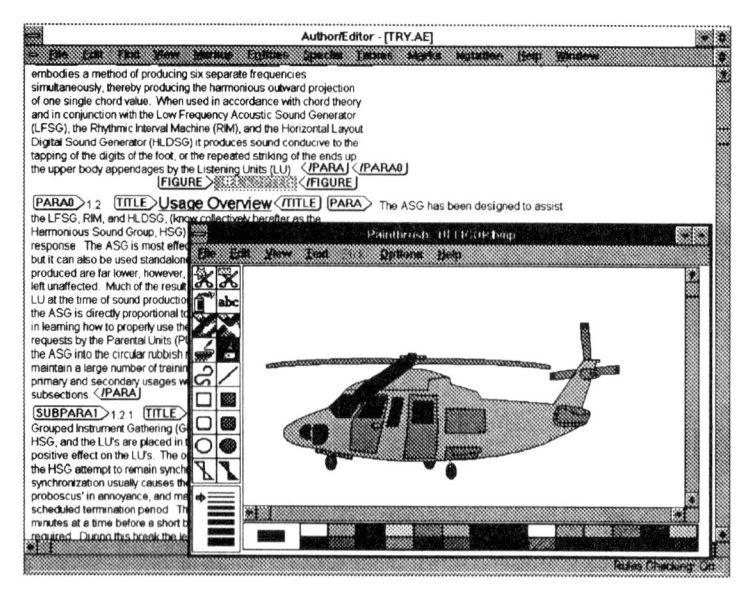

Figure 5.20. In SGML applications the actual graphic is not included in an SGML document instance but stored in an external file. An entity reference declared in the DTD and inserted in the SGML text file is used to define the location of a graphic. Some SGML authoring systems such as Author/Editor allow the graphic application that created the illustration to be launched directly from the SGML editing tool. (Courtesy of SoftQuad, Inc.)

pictures in a collection so that users can easily recognize them. HiJaak, for example, uses thumbnail icons of drawings in a collection for its graphic browsing tool.

Graphic designers and illustrators often reuse graphic objects for many applications. Building a library of objects can be a great efficiency enhancement. Developers and users of electronic graphic files can use graphic browsers to identify objects, portions of very large drawings or images, or the entire drawing. Products such as Kudo Image Browser make handy catalogs of image libraries.

As the number of graphics used in documents proliferates, users are turning to databases to track the graphic objects they have created or even store the objects. Databases can be used simply as a mechanism to locate the names and locations of graphic files. Some of these programs are used in conjunction with graphic viewers and browsers. CADleaf Viewer from Carberry Technology allows users to click on graphic files stored in a variety of file formats for display. ImageBASE from Visual Information, Inc., is frequently used for creating image catalogs on CD-ROM. It can batch process images, store image correction parameters and catalog the images.

CHAPTER 6

➤ *Database publishing*

➤ *Applications integration*

➤ *Exchanging objects*

➤ *Groupware and workgroup publishing*

➤ *Demand publishing model*

Dynamic Data and Smart Documents

*I*nformation is subject to change. Keeping document information up to date is a major headache. Many users of word processing and desktop publishing tools put information into documents via a keyboard, scanner, or some combination of file transfer or copy and pasting of data chunks from other sources. Once the data is inside a document container, the connection to other computerized information sources can be broken. The data within the files of the document will remain unaltered even though the source information generated with other computerized resources and applications changes.

It is never hard to find examples of difficulties encountered in keeping links in the chain of information between a document and its sources. Suppose a writer from a company that designs supervisory control systems is asked to write a proposal for using such a system for an offshore oil recovery platform. A specification for a similar system exists and is available for the proposal writer's use. The information in the specification, however, is in a state of flux. Since the specification is a detailed document, the proposal writer has difficulty determining the exact changes for the updates to the specification concurrently being made by a collaborative engineering team. The proposal writer does not have the luxury of waiting for all the changes to be stable, since the proposal must go out on a tight schedule. Efforts must be made to ensure that the latest information gets into the document, because the potential customer is interested in the many features reflected in the changes. Even though the proposal writer and the engineering group are use compatible word processing tools, they do not have an automated system to control the flow of data from one document source to another. There is a risk of making errors and there are many delays in incorporating changes accurately. Coping with changes can be problematic especially when there are inadequate means for updating information efficiently into affected documents.

One way workgroups can begin to accommodate dynamic data is to make their documents a little smarter. Users may be unaware that the data taken from another source (a database, for example) can reside within the document and still be linked to the originating program which can be used to generate further changes in data. Compound documents that include drawings, spreadsheets, and text and charts from different applications can become smart enough to link the intelligence of all the applications even when they reside on different desktops in a geographically distributed workgroup.

A smart document is a metaphor for the automatic or semiautomatic integration of computer files, objects, and database elements into a document. Smart documents are enabled by the set up of links, encoding of data attributes that tell computers something about the data stored in document databases and the rules that evaluate conditions for publishing certain sets of data. Smart documents, for example, can be capable of responding to dynamic data conditions. Once the source information is stored by a program, the intelligence within the data object created by that program can be reused in another program. By helping end-users cope with changes in information, smart document products can help organizations become more efficient in their document processes.

Making good use of smart documents depends upon a workgroup's mission, vision, and how it applies its knowledge to the tools. By taking advantage of converging applications, dynamic data linkage, and open information exchange, workgroups can rethink and retool ways of generating and updating documents. Some groups use intelligent document solutions to build a framework for publishing information tailored to special audiences on demand. The organization, contents, and assembly of the document are largely under computer control. The technology is used not only to gain efficiency in production, but to help specific audiences get customized sets of information in publishable form as needed.

Other key developments in dynamic document information integration include:

- Integration of spreadsheets, graphic tools, and databases to documents
- Conditional document assembly
- Database publishing
- Programming interfaces to publishing applications

- Groupware to pilot data integration
- Natural language translation

With new technical solutions comes a new set of challenges. Instead of a diet of data overload, groups now spend more time improving methods of communication and meeting requirements for targeting the information in documents to special audience needs.

Compound Documents: A Collection of Objects

Computer generated documents can be complex artifacts. Documents glue together text, numerical data, tabular listings, charts, illustrations, and photos, and for multimedia applications, video and animation as well. Part of the problem of redefining documents is that our frame of reference is based upon a paper model. In paper documents information is linearly presented and located in one place on a page. Electronic publishing gives us a way of building a computerized information base made up of many pieces of data that have their own identity. These pieces at once have boundaries and still blend together to make a whole. Ideally, groups needing access to data objects should be able to retrieve, distribute, manipulate these objects while working on different platforms and desktops.

Smart documents are made possible by advances in object oriented programming. The documents themselves are objects and so are the parts that make them. What is an object? An object is a unit of data. An object can pass messages to other objects. It can inherit characteristics from parent objects. The goal of many object oriented document applications is not only to exchange objects but to enable their reuse. The majority of the users of these programs do not have to learn anything about object oriented programming, because they are insulated from the coding process by user friendly graphical user interfaces and menus. Vendors are placing a high priority upon consistency of user interfaces to reduce relearning.

INTEGRATING INFORMATION AND APPLICATIONS

Electronic publishing cannot be separated from other information technologies used by workgroups and individuals across multiple desktops. Spreadsheets, charts, graphic presentation and engineering CAD programs, databases, and word processors, whether they are designed for the office, engineering and manufacturing, or other environments, have become indispensable tools for workgroups. When it comes to making documents that combine data from each application, groups often have limited means of putting the information together.

Spreadsheets are a case in point. As user defined formulas are applied, spreadsheet software computes numerical data for presentation in tables and or graphs.

Popular spreadsheet programs such as Lotus 1-2-3, Microsoft Excel, and QuattroPro use menus whereby characteristics are set up for data presentation as well as formulas for data calculation. Problems can occur, when transferring spreadsheet data from the spreadsheet application to a document. Until recently, users cut and pasted data via a clipboard and used some mechanism of filtering data between applications to help the importing application receive the data in manageable form.

This was arduous and slow and had the drawback that data had to be recopied from the originating spreadsheet each time it changed. To create a monthly financial report combining statistical charts and text, the users had to monitor data changes in the files of the spreadsheet program. Copying data from a spreadsheet program without a reliable data link or routine notification had been an error prone and inefficient process.

From Live Links to Application Suites

Methods for linking data such as Dynamic Data Exchange (DDE) from Microsoft help improve data integration between applications. DDE sets up a link between the originating application and the destination document. In the earlier example the user might choose a copy link command within Excel and paste in a document. A live link between application programs allows two documents to update each other in real time. For example, if we update a drawing with one application and that same drawing appears inside a text document, the drawing inside the document will update as well as the source document.

Sensing a sea change in workgroup demand for extensible tools, vendors have introduced products with built-in linkages to one another: spreadsheets, word processors, desktop publishing programs, databases, and graphic editors behave in such a way that the information created by one application can be reused in another with the advantage of using the strengths of each. For example, object linking allows users to place a spreadsheet object within the document and by double clicking on the table created from the spreadsheet, launch the spreadsheet program, update the spreadsheet using the menus from the spreadsheet program and still be at work within the document application.

As more applications conform to standards for interactive exchange of objects, documents will be created in a new way by combining objects from different applications to create a compound document. One industry standard is object linking and embedding (OLE) from Microsoft. Participating vendors create applications that conform to the OLE specification and users in turn benefit by being able to create compound documents based upon several applications linked together. The way such linking works can be illustrated by the numerical spreadsheet and a graphics application that follows OLE. OLE objects created in an originating application can be edited in that application. We can edit the object in place within the container document.

There are competing standards to OLE. One is OpenDoc, a compound document specification based upon ideas from a consortium of companies including Apple, Borland, IBM, Novell, and WordPerfect. OLE and OpenDoc are important initiatives for allowing developers of products from different companies to create applications that work together. Both the OLE and OpenDoc specifications view documents as critical repositories of information. Although these specifications have many differences, they each attempt further integration of vendor neutral applications and the open exchange of information.

Since OLE has been around for a while, there are more products developed by companies conforming to OLE than OpenDoc. Vendors such as Microsoft, Borland, and Lotus who make a variety of applications run on PCs have developed suites of applications that incorporate OLE and proprietary techniques to integrate word processing, spreadsheets, graphic editors, and databases. Mainly used in business document applications, the suites offer a common user interface and allow workgroups to share data among different applications. See Figure 6.1. Suites help workgroups reuse and integrate data while working interchangeably from one application to the other. They ensure data sharing across applications, apply interface consistency, establish a file revision level for group members, and easy access to any application from another. Suite applications are targeted to workgroups and offer special pieces of software to aid workgroup collaborators.

The PerfectOffice (formerly Borland Office for Windows) is an example of a workgroup integrated tool suite. Developed by WordPerfect Corp. (now called the Novell Applications Group), it allows users to exchange information objects among different applications and desktops. Objects can be shared across applications (including the document application WordPerfect, a spreadsheet, QuattroPro, and a database Paradox). Users work with common menus, icons, and tools while exchanging objects. Shared icons are used as tools throughout the suite. The Novell Applications Group has integrated ways for multiple workgroup users to share parts of spreadsheets (or other applications) throughout a network and identify those changes being forwarded.

Lotus offers a SmartSuite combination which includes a Working Together Bonus pack, a collection of tools for sharing data across applications and using functions from one application while having a session within another application. The suite includes Ami Pro, Lotus 1-2-3, Freelance Graphics, and Lotus Approach. The SmartSuite is the working together strategy of Lotus Development Corporation. As with the Novell Applications Group and Microsoft, Lotus intends that bundling these applications in a box will not only help sell more software but will offer something that works well to manage document information integration.

156 Dynamic Data and Smart Documents

Microsoft offers a suite (called Microsoft Office Professional) which includes Excel, Word for Windows, Power Point, Access, and Microsoft Mail. As with the other suites, the target of the Microsoft suite application is the workgroup. In this suite Microsoft offers enhanced versions of familiar applications such as Word for Windows (Version 6.0) and Excel (Version 5.0) and more recently developed tools including Power Point, a drawing tool, and Access, a database.

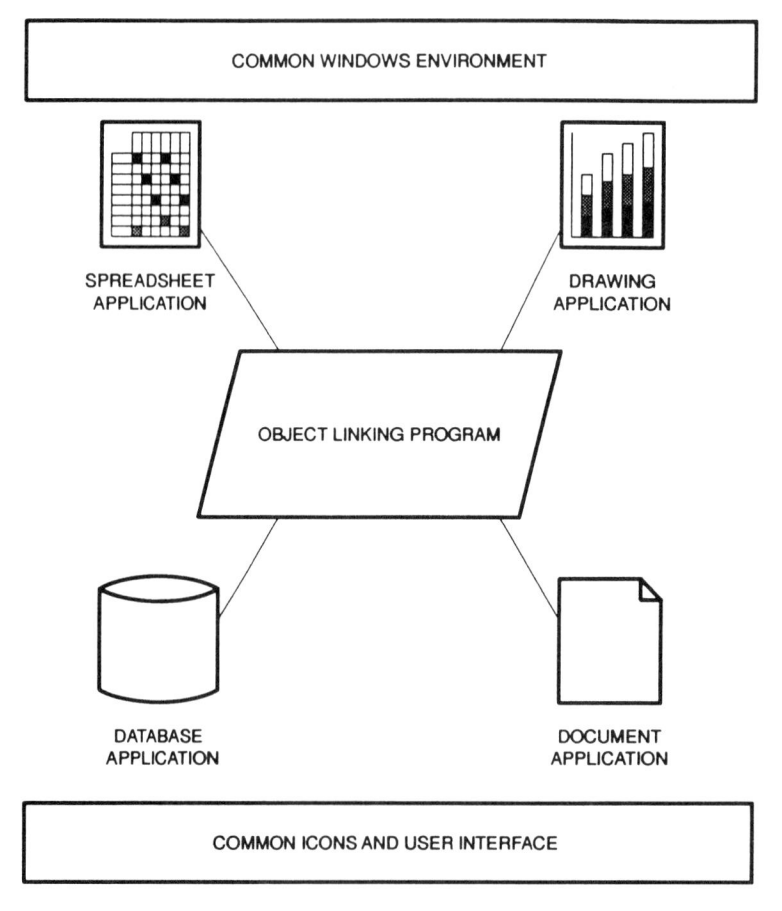

Figure 6.1. A key feature of object linking is the exchange of information among applications. Users gain immediate access to tools needed to modify objects created by any one of the applications. When a user modifies a table (originally created by spreadsheet) within a word processor, the menus and graphical user interface icons belonging to the spreadsheet are available along with those of the word processor.

Suites can be used by workgroups for any number of applications. To illustrate the role a suite can play, we consider the use for an international sporting goods retail company of the PerfectOffice in generating up-to-date product catalogs and price lists. Workgroups consisting of marketing managers, sales analysts, and staff writers, are responsible for communicating and updating sales information, as well as reusing some of the same information in other documents for marketing and sales. The price sheets and catalogs are updated according to price fluctuations for goods that change regularly. Workgroups located in geographically distributed locations depend upon accurate pricing information. With PerfectOffice, desktop users can publish information over a network and other users can subscribe to that information. The system integrates electronic mail between subscribers and publishers. At the headquarters of the sporting goods company, a sales analyst updates the price list and publishes the QuattroPro spreadsheets for the benefit of subscribers in regional offices. Slices of the updated spreadsheet data from QuattroPro and the Paradox database are loaded into WordPerfect documents by subscribers and distributed to customers. Users working within WordPerfect can negotiate menus from QuattroPro and Paradox while remaining within the WordPerfect application.

The sporting goods business is very competitive so accuracy of information exchanged among workgroup players is important, especially when the units are geographically distributed. Borland's workgroup desktop allows publishers and subscribers of QuattroPro spreadsheets and related data in the Paradox database to maintain version control tracking. This feature allows a number of published versions of spreadsheets related to the price sheets to be instantly available to anyone participating in the workgroup desktop.

One limitation of the application suites is that they do not support open information exchange. Another objection to the use of Mircrosoft's OLE specification is that the technology cannot support the transfer of large objects. Application suites are a giant step forward, however, because they fill the immediate need for better ways to make multiple applications work in building compound documents. A new generation of applications based on the OpenDoc standard for compound documents also continues the trend of increased interaction between applications, and intensify the objectives of vendor neutral cooperation.

GROUPWARE TO THE RESCUE

Workgroups are getting smarter about the way they use applications software. Instead of treating applications as standalone packages, they are making their desktops, applications, and data work together. The challenge for workgroups is to redefine how their documents are generated and to realign work processes for information exchange and integration. Linking data from different file sources into other documents requires changes to procedures and tools for integrating text, graphics, and other information sources. Making effective use of applications and data integration is a part of an organization's larger effort to implement groupware computing. Groupware encompasses both a technology and methodology to help workgroups collaborate on projects. Technologies include: document workflow routing, group calendaring, electronic mail, group authoring, and desktop integration.

As for methodology, the collaborating team must define its objectives and specify the workflow to simplify information sharing. In some cases, groups have to reengineer their work processes to make workflow more effective. Obvious prerequisites are a computer network and an understanding of how a team uses technology. (Groupware applications are meaningless in a standalone system used by only one person.)

Lotus Notes from Lotus Development Corporation is a leading edge groupware product. Users can not only integrate information across desktops but also set up and control the complex of workflow, communication, calendaring, and status reporting that help keep workgroup document and information objectives on track. Notes delivers the right information to the desktop by creating a networked based communications architecture that allows users to interoperate. Notes allows users who are running an editing application to exchange and information from one desktop to another. It currently uses the OLE specification to facilitate this. Other features of Notes include document management facilities for tracking document versions, powerful text search software, and workflow routing of jobs to users across a network. The key to workflow routing is a powerful messaging and electronic mail system based upon Vendor Independent Messaging (VIM) specifications. Notes tracks the routing of information among users collaborating on a project.

USING DATABASES AND DOCUMENTS PROFITABLY

Because data is a business asset, database publishing can be used profitably. It relies on methods and technologies used to retrieve information automatically from databases to build new documents or update existing documents. Data stored in a database is accessed, output to a target document, and formatted according to some preestablished template or style sheet. Subsets of the data can be retrieved on demand and put into a document for print or for electronic delivery.

From the outset database publishing forces users to consider the reuse of information. Figure 6.2 is a diagram of the database publishing process. Some of the advantages of database publishing are:

➤ Data in documents is kept up to date
➤ Less risk of error
➤ Avoids duplication of effort and associated costs of reentering data
➤ Centralization of document objects
➤ Reuse of source data for multiple outputs is controlled

There have been many evolutions in the use of documents in connection to databases. One classic database application involves the extraction of fixed length records for automatic assembly and formatting by a word processing or desktop publishing program. Many vendors offer off the shelf software applications that mediate between the database and publishing programs. Corel Ventura offers a database publishing interface that mediates between a database and publication system such as the Ventura Publisher or another system. STEP2 Software Inc. offers dbPublisher32 and other specific interfaces to desktop publishing packages including DataShaper Database Publisher for PageMaker that links to popular databases such as dBase, Paradox, and Fox Pro. The DataBase Publishing System, Inc., specializes in the linkage of relational databases (Oracle, Sybase, Informix) to Interleaf's publishing system. Some document management systems store information in records in the database and build a set of control records regarding documents in a library. In addition, there are systems that now store documents in a database.

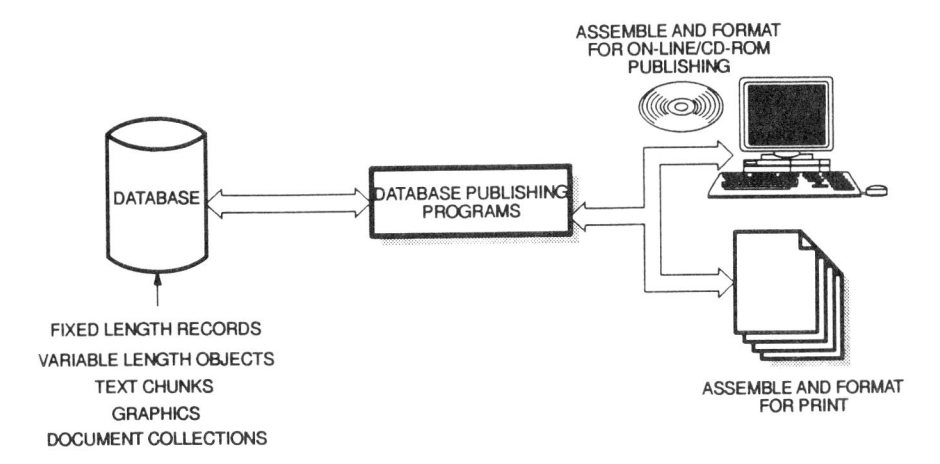

Figure 6.2. Simplified database publishing diagram that illustrates idea of extracting information from a database by the intermediacy of some program. The data then can be sent to a document formatting and assembly tool for output. Multiple reuses of the information can be exploited as well, including on-line and CD-ROM distribution.

To setup the first type of database publishing interface the user needs to follow certain steps. First, a style sheet or template must be defined for the document to be output. Second, the user must identify the records from the database that will be included in the document output. The user will also identify the order by which records will be sorted. Each record within a database can have many fields (for, example, the records kept for customers may include company names addresses, phone numbers, business contacts, and their names and addresses, and so forth). Once the database information to be targeted to documents have been identified, a control expression should be used from command menus supplied by the software to merge information into selected documents.

A company in the aviation business reduces in half the time it takes to produce product price lists and illustrated parts catalogs by adopting a database publishing approach. Before purchasing the database publishing solution, much of the data already in the database was rekeyed into the document application by another group responsible for a variety of publications. The company mails these documents to customers around the world, the information must be available in a timely manner. The company also publishes technical manuals that include parts lists and illustrated parts diagrams. Much of this same information exists in the database but the data is typically reentered into the publishing system application even though it already exists in a computerized database. Because the data in the parts database changes frequently, it is expensive and inefficient to maintain the modifications in two places.

Upon analysis by the aviation company, it became obvious that a high percentage of the information in the particular documents (product catalog, price list, illustrated parts document, specification sheets) appeared in tables. Tabular material, attractively formatted, can enhance both the appearance of a document as well as strengthen the communication process. One useful aspect of database publishing is the capability of building tables automatically in conjunction with word processing and desktop publishing systems.

Table generating software creates a grid of columns, rows, and cells upon command from a user menu. The typical table generator offers choices to design the size of the table, the number of columns and rows, cell text alignment, font selection, multiple page adjustable tabulation, table banner adjustment per page, and changes in height and width for cells columns and rows. This alleviates the tedious and costly task of formatting columns and rows manually. The problem is that tables often contain data that is subject to change or that the data that appears in the table already exists on another computer system. Database publishing systems work directly with document system table generator software to build the table based on information in a database which is the point of origin for changes to the system. In our sample application, the aerospace company set up a desired template for the table. Since the company uses Smartleaf from Database Publishing Software, Inc., the setup consists of indicating the place in an Interleaf document where various tables are built, creating one row of a table with the appropriate number of columns, and the database publishing application does the remainder of the table formatting.

The illustrated parts document presents a special challenge for the aerospace company because they include information that is formatted in tables and complex illustrations of parts that are referred to in the tables. The tables consist of 4 columns that include part name, part number, figure reference to the illustration, and a revision code column. Since this data is in the database, the company uses Smartleaf and the relational database to build the these tables and load the information into Interleaf document templates. The illustrations are also stored in the relational database. By using a product called Smartleaf/Librarian the company can connect the information in records related to the parts to the drawings. Any time a revision is made to the database, all of the revision coding is kept together, thus simplifying the updates of the complicated illustrated parts documents.

Database publishing not only merges data into documents upon computer command for report generation but some database applications also compare the contents of multiple versions of documents and immediately show detailed differences. The compare function might be used, for example, by two companies that have formed a business partnership. One company is designing and manufacturing the product; the other is responsible for marketing and sales. Both companies need access to data and documents that help the partnership work. They are already using database publishing to generate price lists, parts lists, and product catalogs. Product development and the communications work effectively. The company doing the design has developed various documents and drawings, product information for product specifications, and other documents. The marketing partner needs some of that same information. An accommodation is made and the development team sends its partner these documents so they can be used in proposals and marketing literature to launch the product into the marketplace. As time goes by the marketing company modifies the contents of its proposal files so that it no longer matches the contents of the original files of the developer. When the two companies compare the files they need to do a complicated manual comparison using a product such as Database Compare, the two versions can be examined automatically.

Conditional Assembly

Conditional document assembly, a feature of certain authoring systems, allows users to create versions of the same document with somewhat different content. For example, suppose we are creating a document that contains a generic description of three motor bikes, but the features listed for bike model 2000, 2050, and 2100 are slightly different. It is possible to contain those differences within the document but hide the characteristics that do not apply to bike types 2050 or 2100. Conditional assembly of a document accommodates the differences and will output specific versions upon computer command. The document is stored as a bundle, but parts of the document are given attributes or tags that condition those objects as distinct from other objects. The information common to all models of bicycles is left untagged.

To make the conditional assembly idea work, the user must identify certain information as conditional. Interleaf and Framemaker both provide features for users to build conditional documents. The user of the document can show or hide conditional text that applies and use markers to indicate where the conditional text is hidden. Conditional assembly works best where there are specific differences between the content of two or more versions. Both Interleaf and FrameMaker offer conditional text capability in their editing systems.

In the Interleaf software a control expression is applied to the document to make the right version of information appear. The document serves as a database in miniature. A different control expression will make another version of the document appear. See Figure 6.3.

Writing paragraphs that will embed three different versions of the information describing the bicycles, requires authors and editors to follow guidelines to make conditional assembly more effective. One helpful practice is to write the set of con-

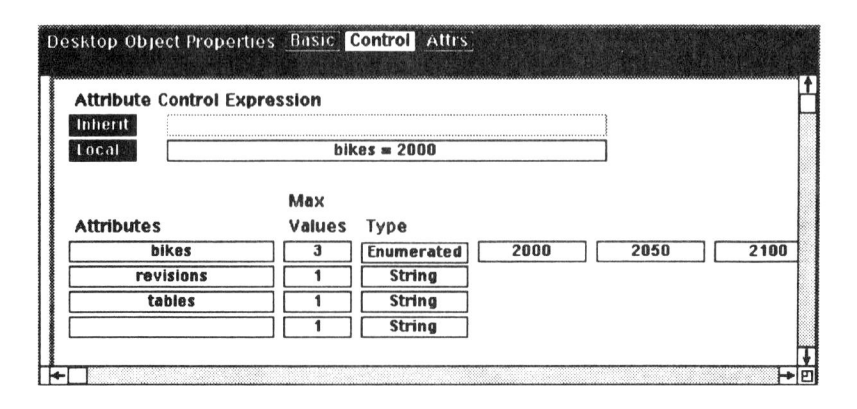

Figure 6.3. Conditional document information related to bike model 2000 will be shown in the document because the control expression *bikes=2000* has been applied. Information related to bike models 2050 and 2100 are also included in the document but hidden from display. (Courtesy of Interleaf, Inc.)

ditional text samples so they grammatically fit the context of the document to which they are attached. For example, the tagged information should include the appropriate punctuation and spacing so that it will not require editorial fine tuning in the document.

Storing Documents in Databases

In addition to drawing upon the resources of a database that has built-in tables of records that can be directly linked to documents, the process can be reversed. Documents and part of documents including graphics can be stored in databases. This information can be modified and reused to create new documents. (We discuss this as a critical aspect of a document management strategy for an organization in Chapter 10.) Storing documents or the objects that make them into databases helps document producers gain control of document files and the details inside those documents. To do this for large documents and information bases, the database technology must have the capacity to store binary large objects (BLOBs). These objects are variable length records that can represent different types of data formats.

Databases containing SGML documents or that build documents from SGML encoded information are special cases. In the first case, the database contains data encoded according to selected document type definitions (DTDs) and builds document instances based on those structural rules. By storing SGML tagged data in a database, document instances can be created from data that has been encoded according to the declarative markup required by a given DTD. Databases can help manage large sets of multiple DTDs and the elements and attributes stored with them. In the second case, SGML text documents are stored in the database. These documents are stored as records but maintain a relation to other information such as graphics, animation, and other video objects, associated with the document.

Document and information analysts build DTDs based upon their expert knowledge of the information that goes into publications. Once the information is categorized, a structure is defined for creating an indexed database. A database can define unique identifiers for all elements stored in it. The information stored in the database can then be reused by retrieving all the names and values of specific elements as defined by the DTD. Organizations that invest in a conversion to SGML can readily reuse the data because of the power of the database to sort and merge stored SGML tagged data into documents. Because SGML is platform independent, the data can be readily exchanged among different hardware software applications.

An example of a document database system is DynaBase from EBT Technologies which uses object oriented database technology. DynaBase allows users to check documents in and out and interact with an SGML editor such as the Adept editor series from ArborText. The system has a set of tools that allows collaborating authors and editors to change text stored in a database and comment on the work in progress. When the edits are finished the book can be published or "pressed" as an electronic document using the EBT's DynaText electronic book and browsing system. Collaborating authors can also view changes to versions of books that have been published as shown in Figure 6.4. One of the great advantages of storing documents in a database is that much tighter control can be applied over changes in the information.

Document Revision Control

Creators of documents typically wish to track document changes through the life cycle. Not all word processing and desktop publishing systems offer features for tracking changes. Most revision control software allows viewers to see changes that have been made to a document and conserves the changes over the project's life cycle. They can be visualized through a variety of mechanisms including strikethrough text, underlining, use of different colors to indicate revised information, and marginal indications such as change bars.

Adopting a document revision strategy presupposes some forethought about which information in the document changes regularly and which information persists with minimum changes. To resolve management of changes and revisions for an organization as a whole, it makes sense to investigate enterprise wide document management solutions.

Application Program Interfaces to Documents

Users who want to customize document publishing software, but whose off-the-shelf publishing technology does not meet such requirements, can invest in an application program interface (API). API's are offered with publishing applications so that end users can make better use of the power of off-the-shelf tools for their specific needs. APIs are usually implemented with a scripting tool, which is a software language utility that allows developers to write code that will instruct application programs how to behave under certain conditions.

What are APIs used for? They can be used to customize the integration of groupware software tools such as Lotus Notes. Users who have a proprietary database for which no standard off-the-shelf database interface exists may write an API script connecting the proprietary information in the database to the publishing application. APIs have been written to support application integration for better data sharing. Interleaf, Inc., pioneered a concept called active documents that relies on the use of an API. Active documents can access, evaluate, and act upon infor-

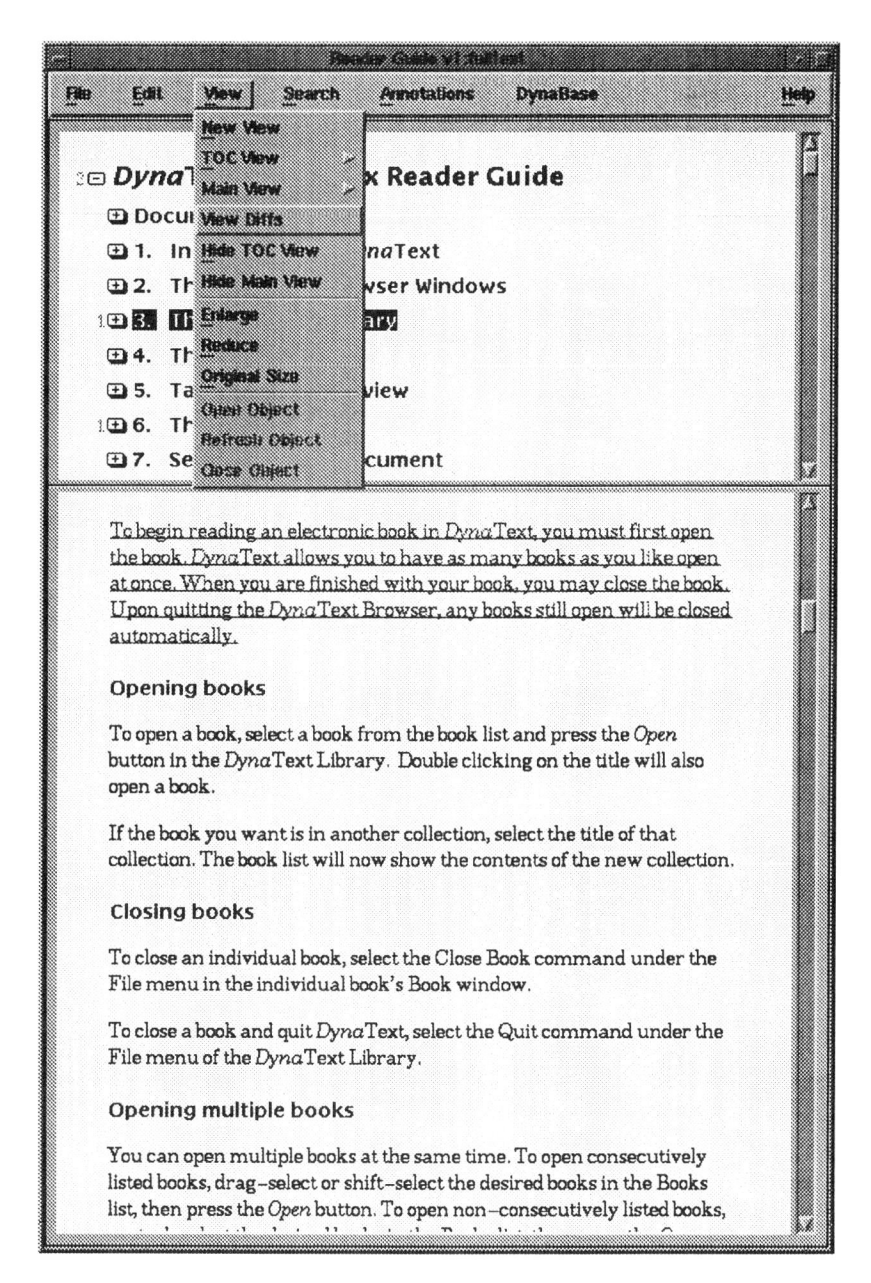

Figure 6.4. A new version of a DynaText electronic book can highlight changes between previous and current versions of documents within the DynaBase publishing environment. In this case the user has selected to view differences via a pulldown menu and the differences are underlined. (Courtesy of Electronic Book Technologies, Inc.)

mation from anywhere in the computing environment. Active documents are smart: they not only can get information from other documents but can evaluate attributes to decide, for example ,whether a given user should have access to a document. Active documents are enabled by scripts. Interleaf 6 allows users to write scripts using LISP, Visual Basic, or C++. Interleaf 5 offers a LISP scripting interface.

Active documents can have numerous uses. An active document can work in the background so that documents can be updated without being opened. An active document can be used to help customize parts of a training manual based upon the grade the trainee scored on previous sections. Users can invoke a process which routinely accesses parts of documents in a directory to build a status report. Active documents are useful for triggering related applications as a result of evaluating the information. For example, if an active document contains a table from a spreadsheet in which the numbers in a column exceed a certain threshold, the document can query another application for an explanation and create a special note.

Writers, educators, and others who are not programmers by trade will learn that an API does not require them to become sophisticated programmers. Bill Atkinson who created the HyperCard for Apple Computer had this need in mind when he created the HyperTalk scripting interface for HyperCard. The OpenDoc specification, which borrows heavily from Apple, also favors the use of an API designed for document users and not for programmers. The OpenDoc specification defines a scripting function called Open Scripting Architecture (OSA). Developers of applications following the OpenDoc OSA approach can offer very powerful scripting tools that allow nonprogrammers to manipulate customized applications for making and delivering compound documents.

In the absence of user-friendly scripting tools, organizations to use APIs for electronic publishing have at least three ways of approaching the development of special interfaces. The first is to hire a consultant for a specified contractual period from the vendor that offers the API or from a consulting firm with a specific API. The second is to hire a full time developer with significant programming experience. Finally, train members of the existing staff to learn the application, or borrow a programmer on loan if available. The decision of how to implement depends upon a development strategy.

Intelligent Document Translation

Computer assisted document translation is another example of intelligent document automation. Many companies today need to deliver documents and products with internationalized versions. Translating a document in a traditional manner is a labor intensive and time consuming process. Consequently, the costs associated with multilingual translation can be high. Machine translation has been attempted for many years but progress has been slow. The main difficulty for computers translating one natural language to another is the problem of ambiguity and complexity of languages. Progress is being made with the help of continuous experimentation and improvement in machine translation.

Early machine based language translation models were heavily dependent on data dictionaries that translated from one language to another on a word by word lookup basis. The problem is that individual words may have several different meanings. The context in which the words are used can radically change their meaning in a sentence. Intelligent machine translation technologies such as Multilingual Document Translation software from Logos Corporation have made great strides by concentrating upon the semantic structure of sentences rather than a word by word lexicography.

Computer assisted translation can also be aided by a database publishing methodology. After the initial translation, the documents that have been translated into various foreign languages can be stored in a database. The database library is used to control the use of the translated versions. The idea is to do the initial translation once and reuse the information. The Logos Intelligent Machine Translation System has utilities for updating the lexical database. The updating can be both for specific words and parts of speech and also for semantic and syntactic rules. Automatic translation technologies are designed to work with authoring technology systems. The Logos system, for example, works directly with a variety of specific formats for published output including Interleaf and WordPerfect.

On-Demand Publishing: Two Case Studies

The quantity, variety, stability, and reusability of data varies among organizations and workgroups. Each workgroup and each organization will need to reevaluate its requirements. But all organizations who put data into documents and use computers to generate documents can benefit from the on-demand publishing model. The model has three main parts: the first is information access; the second is sorting through the information base for data of interest to a specific audience; the third is automating the assembly of the particular information for specific distribution. The advantages of a system that can deliver publishing on demand are obvious. We will illustrate the concept by examples from two different worlds with separate sets of requirements.

Case One: Data Acquisition Reports

A company manufactures and develops real time data acquisition systems for aircraft and other test vehicles. Its customers take thousands of measurements of data from the vehicles during a real test and the acquisition system records the data on disk. Later these measurements are played back, compressed, and analyzed for the results of the test. The results are summarized and written in a report, which plays an important role in the customer's community because it sometimes determines whether the design of a vehicle is faulty or in need of improvement. The reports synthesize and summarize test results according to mission critical information requirements. Flight test critical information, for example, may include the state of measurement parameters such as temperature, air pressure, vibration, engine speed, altitude, and the like. Each parameter is associated with a range of values that represent boundaries or limits for normal operation. When something is out of range, the data acquisition system must check for whether the measurement is within limits.

To make the report, engineering analysts and their assistants at the test sites rekey much of the same information that exits in the system acquiring the data. The data acquisition system features a powerful relational database that contains information about parameters to be edited. But most of the report is generated in a labor intensive manner, and the delays in report delivery are directly attributable to the fragments of data that have to be pieced together and reorganized to make a coherent presentation. Data from different test mission printouts is often rekeyed into a series of small documents that are then cut and pasted together to make the basis for the text report. Although there is a powerful two dimensional graphics generation package that displays in critical measurements for the particular mission, these graphs are printed out and sometimes redrawn by another graphics editing system for inclusion in a report.

The supplier of the data acquisition introduced an automated publishing subsystem to its flagship data acquisition product that would simplify customer access to information at its source and offer value added services to its offering. The idea was to introduce a publishing subsystem tailored to the data acquisition system process. The publishing system interfaced directly to a relational database for on-demand subsets of information related to vehicles under test and the measurement parameters of special interest. A document information base also stored structured information organized under key topics of interest to engineering analysts and other subject matter experts. Special scripts were written to interface the publishing system to the database and other subsystems which are linked to the data acquisition process. Now parts of the report are automatically generated from records in the database. A special link to the graphic subsystem also provides for reuse of graphic displays related to specific sets of test measurements.

After successful introduction of the report generation system for paper output, the supplier of the data acquisition system decided to roll out an optional on-line reporting system taking advantage of advanced techniques in visualization and hypermedia presentation. To facilitate the multipurpose reuse of information for paper and on-line distribution, the report generation system was modified into a document database environment using SGML as convenient method for building an information design model. As real time data measurements are stored, channels of information can be accessed and graphically redisplayed using a combination of electronic document viewing and visualization software. The playback data is conjoined to text and animation data pinpointing problems related to the structural design of the vehicle under test. The statistical data is translated now into a visual experience linked to specific information. This hypermedia document can be delivered in conjunction with the report for analysis.

Case Two: Legal Documents

The art of automating technical reports may seem remote from automating a demand publishing application for legal publishers, but think again. A legal publisher customizes documents according to the interests of the special audiences in the legal community it serves. It helps lawyers find information tailored to topics of immediate interest. The research is accomplished by on-line access to information from Mead Data Central's LEXIS computerized legal data resources. Services like Mead Data's LEXIS put at the disposal of clients enormous volumes of legal data including new laws added each year. Quantitatively, the documentation associated with new laws added to the LEXIS database each year is staggering. In order to make the best use of on-line information sources, legal publisher needs to channel this information to specific audiences. The publisher realizes its customers do not want to wade through volumes of information to get what they want. They want special information on demand.

The solution connects a complex of tools including a relational database, a publishing program, special scripts that access information from the database and merge them into a document, and a demand printer. Information searches are aided by powerful intelligent text search software. Researchers sort through information downloaded from the LEXIS database and look up data across a large number of available documents under selected topics of interest to legal clients. Lawyers are tuned into vertical publications and specialized topics such as environmental law or patent law. Publishers who can serve specific client needs by sorting information according to topics can narrowcast or customize their documents. The system creates a table of contents based upon key topics. It selects the appropriate information from the database and assembles documents according to a template stored with the data.

Even though our demand publishing examples are drawn from two different worlds they have the common requirement of connecting a publishing system to computerized information sources and channeling that information selectively on demand into documents for printed copy or electronic document delivery. The documents derive information from the original sources and reuse information;

automate document format and assembly; and enhance delivery of specific information to customers. The ability of organizations to leverage information resources and make it accessible to individuals and workgroups is a vital part of modern communications. Nobel physicist Arno Penzias put it more succinctly:

> As work becomes increasingly information intensive, I see organizational success depending more and more on giving each individual contributor needed information at the right place, at the right time, and in the right form. The degree to which this requirement can be met depends crucially on the information architectures used, the organization's nerve system. (*Ideas and Information*, Simon & Schuster, New York, 1989, p.206)

Used properly, intelligent document applications can be a bold step toward delivering accurate information to appropriate desktops. The goal of capturing information on demand while making the documenting process more accurate and efficient is no longer unreachable.

CHAPTER 7

➤ *Workgroup interoperability requirements*

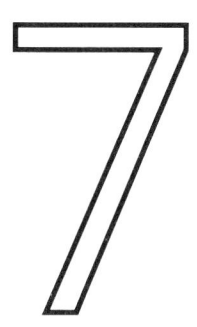

➤ *Document interchange standards*

➤ *Electronic reference documents*

➤ *On-line information services*

➤ *Document conversion*

Interoperability and Electronic Publishing

effective document computing for workgroups depends upon the deployment of networks, the exchange and reusability of document content and format, and the ease of accessing document information.

Networks provide a physical layer for high speed connectivity to services for accessing and distributing information from computers near and far away. Electronic reference documents (ERDs) and information bases are used in many organizations for viewing, retrieving, and distributing electronic document information. Conversion programs supporting standards for document interchange are commercially available. Exchange standards are also emerging so that document formats can be reused.

Interoperability has become the theme for organizations wanting to meld networks, exchange documents, and retrieve information, because networks and computers have been plagued by a plethora of disparate operating systems and communication protocols. In spite of the considerable progress in the development of technical solutions, document interchange also remains difficult. Proprietary word processing and desktop publishing programs use special markup instructions to encode the format and layout of the document. It is a major challenge to overcome the proprietary nature of formatting programs that has made information access and distribution difficult. Electronic document conversion programs, electronic document reference and display systems, and document management systems work around the obstacles imposed by file format incompatibilities.

Interoperability for workgroup publishing must allow:

- ➤ Neutral interchange of documents without dependence on specific hardware platforms or proprietary software
- ➤ Ease of access and reuse of information in documents
- ➤ Exchange of document format information

CASE HISTORY: FROM INFORMATION SEARCH TO DEADLINE

Successful workgroup collaboration requires the efficient transfer of document files from one computer to another. The transferred document should be computer readable and editable. The person receiving a document should be able to fully manipulate and change the information as required and to share information regarding the context and status of the document received. Can the recipient understand where the information fits within the document's structure? Can one discriminate the changes in content when the document is transmitted a second or third time?

For an example, let us consider that several departments in a corporation—marketing, engineering, graphics arts, and manufacturing—have a common deadline. A proposal must be delivered to a customer within short notice. All the contributors or authors want to use their desktop computers and authoring programs to generate the text and illustrations. Because they belong to different departments, they use a variety of computer systems as well as text formatting and graphics programs but for the duration of the project the proposal team is a collaborating workgroup. A collaborating consultant who lives hundreds of miles away intends to telecommunicate his portion of the proposal by dialup modem. Refer to Figure 7.1.

The contributors want to see their portion of a proposal file and those of other contributors as they work from different computers. This assumes a viable computer network and appropriate software to view an in-process document for comment. User-defined format conventions must be in place along with guidelines for review and production of the proposal.

There is another dimension to the problem. The company has amassed a wealth of legacy data that is not easy to reuse. It is stored electronically in a variety of file formats and it is difficult to find information related to topics stored in the documents. Much of this information would be useful in writing the proposal if it could be extracted simply and efficiently. Each proposal writer has only partial access to current information needed to answer questions posed by the procurement request.

From Information Search to Deadline **173**

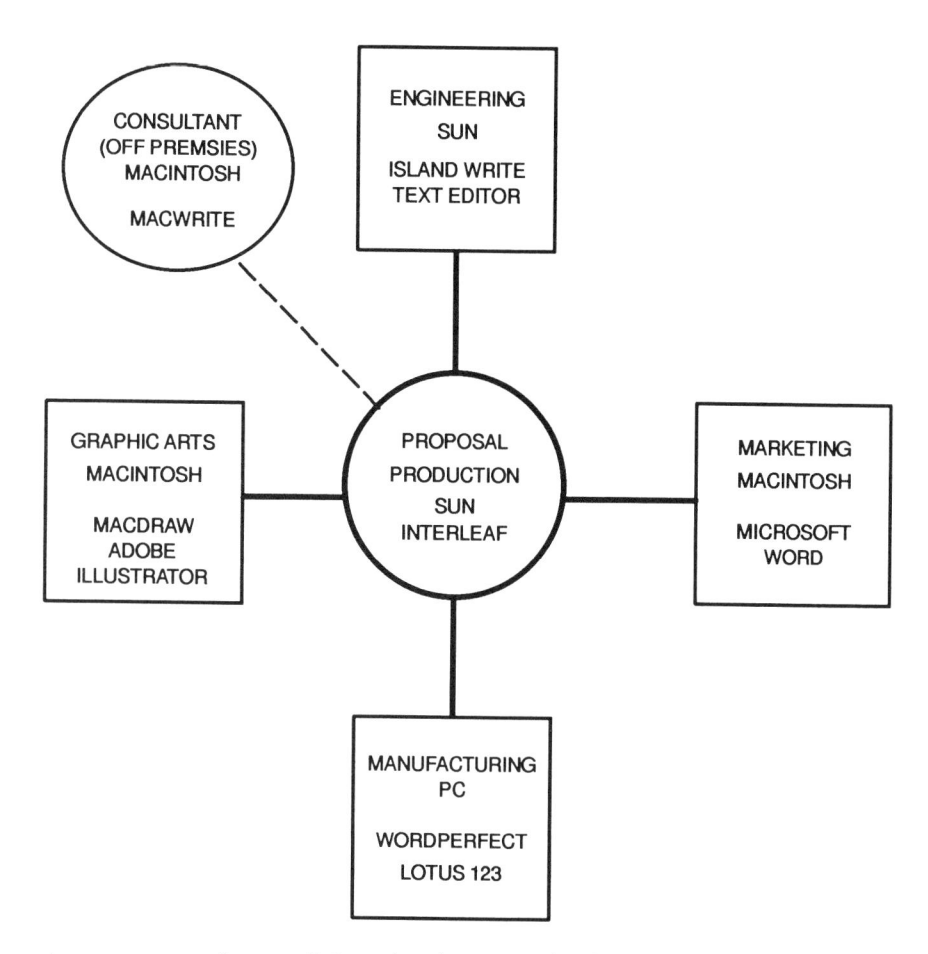

```
                    ┌─────────────┐
   ╭─────────╮      │ ENGINEERING │
   │CONSULTANT│     │    SUN      │
   │(OFF      │     │             │
   │ PREMSIES)│     │ ISLAND WRITE│
   │MACINTOSH │     │ TEXT EDITOR │
   │          │     └─────────────┘
   │ MACWRITE │
   ╰─────────╯
```

Figure 7.1. Creating a collaborative document (in this case, a proposal) involving heterogeneous computer platforms. Diverse application programs are also used by various departments so that collaborators face the difficult challenge of interchanging data.

As the deadline approaches, collaborating authors want to review the document they have drafted and make comments to the virtual document (that is, to the document in progress). To do this, the authors need an easy way of exchanging document data. They need a consistent approach to structure so the authors, editors, reviewers, and producers follow the same rules even with the differing computer systems and formatting programs They need a way of conveniently displaying and annotating the document. This requirement presents another key objective of interoperability which is bidirectional transfer of documents allowing authors to rewrite their portions of the proposal with the material in its most current state. In order for the system to know what the current state of the document is, special version control software is needed to track changes to the document as it is checked in and out of the system.

How well the collaboration proceeds depends upon several factors. First, there must be the appropriate physical and electronic means to support document transfers. We call this connectivity. The network must provide access among heterogeneous computer platforms. Second, the multiuser system we are describing in this case history involves more than one workgroup and presupposes planning, consensus, and collaboration. Each department represented in Figure 7.1 is a workgroup in itself tied electronically to its own Local Area Network (LAN). The workgroup needs a precise definition of workflow, a methodology for peer review, tracking of milestones, feedback on compliance with customer request, and status report on progress.

Technical solutions for this collaboration require suitable data communications and the introduction of electronic document reference and viewing software for authors, editors, and technical reviewers. Technologies supporting interchange standards such as Standard Generalized Markup Language (SGML) and Compound Document Architecture are applicable. In order to grasp the technical challenges posed by this example, let us examine the internetworking, document interchange, document viewing and distribution problems.

CONNECTIVITY IS KEY

Establishing a data communications infrastructure is indispensable for workgroup publishing. Data communications technologies range from low cost direct wire serial transfers or telecommunication modem links to the more sophisticated and expensive local area networks (LANs). These, in turn, can be connected to wide area networks. Hardwiring simply means connecting one computer to another computer (or other device) with wires and cable connectors. We distinguish between direct transfers using standard RS–232-C serial cables (which require an appropriate software driver or communications protocol) and Local Area Networks (LANs) which can be linked to form internetworks.

A standard interconnection between terminals and computers, or between microcomputers and other computers, still in use is RS–232–C developed by the Electronic Industries Association as a serial transmission protocol. (A protocol refers to a formal definition of message formats and rules two computers follow to exchange messages.)

When communication between computers is required by a direct serial link, an appropriate communication port must be set up to transfer files via an RS–232-

C cable. This includes the proper data rate. The setup is managed by a communications software handler that tells the computer what port is being used, what the data rate is, and what file is to be transferred. The software, which typically is not part of the computer's operating system software, also helps initiate and complete the transmission process. Each computer involved in the direct, serial, process needs to be setup for the transfer. There are several inexpensive software programs available for this purpose. Kermit is a "public domain" program originally provided by Columbia University. Laplink which runs on PCs is a very popular software program enabling serial communications between PCs and other computers.

LOCAL AREA NETWORKS: ETHERNET AND MORE

An extensively used type of hardwiring is the Local Area Network (LAN). (There are also wireless LANs using radio frequency transmission techniques which we will not discuss here.) A local area network is designed to join devices over short distances, typically within a building. This high-speed communication subsystem allows transmissions between computer systems. With a LAN, publishing users share resources (printers, scanners, and computers) more efficiently. Popular examples of LANs are Ethernet and Token Ring. Other familiar networks are Appletalk for Macintosh and Novell Netware for PC networks.

The transmission methods for local area networks include baseband and broadband networks. A baseband LAN transmits information at the same frequency over a single channel. Broadband is a communication channel with a large bandwidth and the ability to handle multiple high-speed transmissions. Many varieties of local area networks are available. Network configurations are called topologies. It is not possible to provide a detailed description of topologies in this chapter but we refer to specific examples showing how the LANs enable effective publishing solutions.

Figure 7.2 shows a publishing network linking together different subnetworks (Ethenet, Appletalk, and a PC network) computer systems and using a commonly accepted communications protocol called Transmission Control Protocol/Internet Protocol (TCP/IP). Included in the network is a file server with built-in Ethernet TCP/IP communication tools, a subnet of Macintosh computers using Appletalk but interfacing to the Ethernet via a gateway TCP/IP based product (Fastpath from Shiva Inc., for example) and a software terminal communications utility called Telnet. On one side of the Fastpath junction box are connectors to an Appletalk LAN and on the other side are connectors to 802.3 Ethernet. An IBM compatible personal computer can be linked to Ethernet using various packages (in this case Novell Netware running TCP/IP).

Figure 7.2 shows how organizations can use internetworking to meet specific communication objectives without sacrificing their investment in different computer hardware platforms. Interoperability standards allow the coexistence of the multiple subnetworks using different hardware.

Token Ring and Ethernet are well established Local Area Network (LAN) technologies. Ethernet access is rated at 10 million bits per second (Mb/s); Token Ring at 4 or 16 Mb/s. For very high speed LANs a technology called FDDI (Fiber Distributed Data Interface) provides a LAN that operates at 100 Mbps. FDDI can be employed in conjunction with 802.3 Ethernet or Token Ring systems.

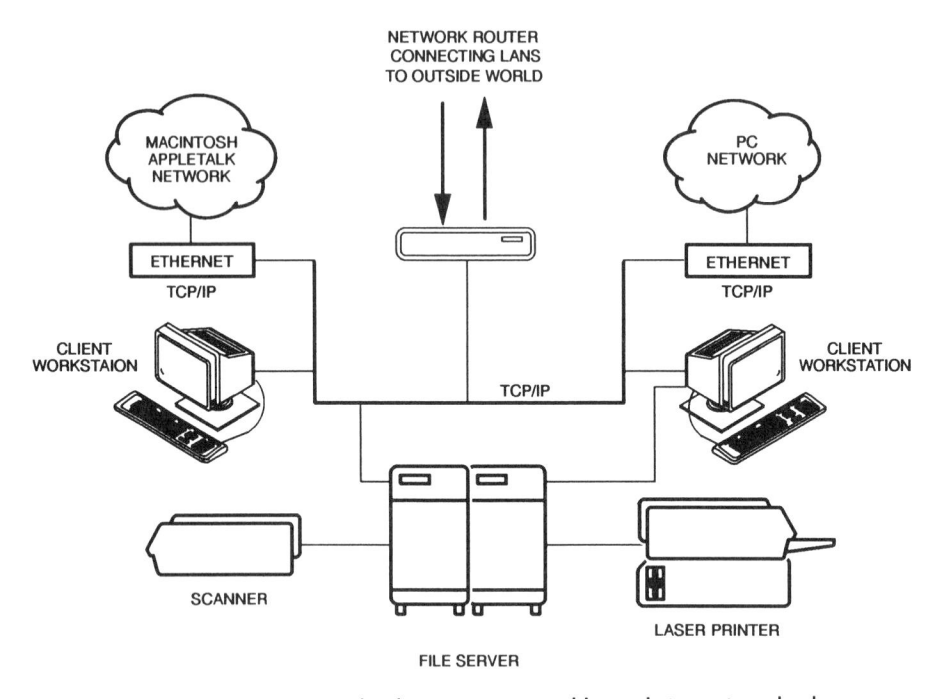

Figure 7.2. Local Area Networks shown connected in an internetworked electronic publishing system. The system not only includes different computer hardware and differing computer networks which have been linked by a common interface protocol called TCP/IP. Several different local area networks (Ethernet, Appletalk, and a PC Network using Netware from Novell) have been linked. Network terminology is somewhat arcane. In the diagram, TCP/IP stands for Transmission Control Protocol/Internet Protocol. A router is a dedicated hardware device used to route traffic on a network. In this case the router connects local area networks to telecommunicate with other computers outside the building or premises. A file server is a computer that provides services such as distributed file management over a local area network. A client workstation is an agent of a server that has access to shared files and distributed file management services over a local area network.

Workgroups readily benefit from LANs. In engineering and manufacturing environments multiple distributed computers linked by Ethernet combine resources from computer aided design systems with product information from text processing systems. LANs can provide the high speed access to graphics files where the volume of data to be transmitted and the time required for the transfer are cost related factors. They can readily help publishing specialists automate integration of subsets of information for assembly or viewing of documents.

Certain setup steps need to be executed to make the LAN recognize the devices on the network and help the communications process to work properly. TCP/IP is an industry standard adopted by the American National Standards Institute (ANSI) among others, and it is used in many establishments to connect computers as diverse as IBM, DEC, SUN, HP, Silicon Graphics, PCs, and MACs. Diverse network and computer technologies can be connected by using a common interface protocol.

Each network node in a TCP/IP network must be assigned an internet protocol (IP) address. This address contains four integer fields separated by periods. In Figure 7.3, the number 158.186.223.13 is an internet address. An internet address is a number assigned to identify a machine or node in the network. Network managers and system administrators add or delete addresses as they setup, or provision, the network.

Appropriate software must be installed to send and receive information across the LANs. One utility available with TCP/IP is the File Transfer Protocol (FTP) which allows users to transfer files with a minimum set of commands. For example, to initiate FTP simply type in the command ftp, followed by a sequence of commands such as "open," "get," or "send," to transmit or receive files. In Figure 7.3 using the get command followed by the file name, the user has elected to "get" a file called "features.doc."

With one of the many TCP/IP software packages installed in the PC, users can communicate across an Ethernet LAN to other PCs or other computers. PC users can exchange files rapidly and efficiently via 802.3 Ethernet running TCP/IP.

TELECOMMUNICATIONS AND ELECTRONIC PUBLISHING

To go beyond the immediate building or premises, telecommunications is a means of transmitting and receiving data over a wide area. These standards include traditional CCITT/ITU standards for communications via a modem or X.25 Packet Switch technologies, and more recent services such as Frame Relay, Switched Multi-megabit Data Service (SMDS), and Asynchronous Transfer Mode (ATM) based broadband data communications. The expected proliferation of ATM devices over

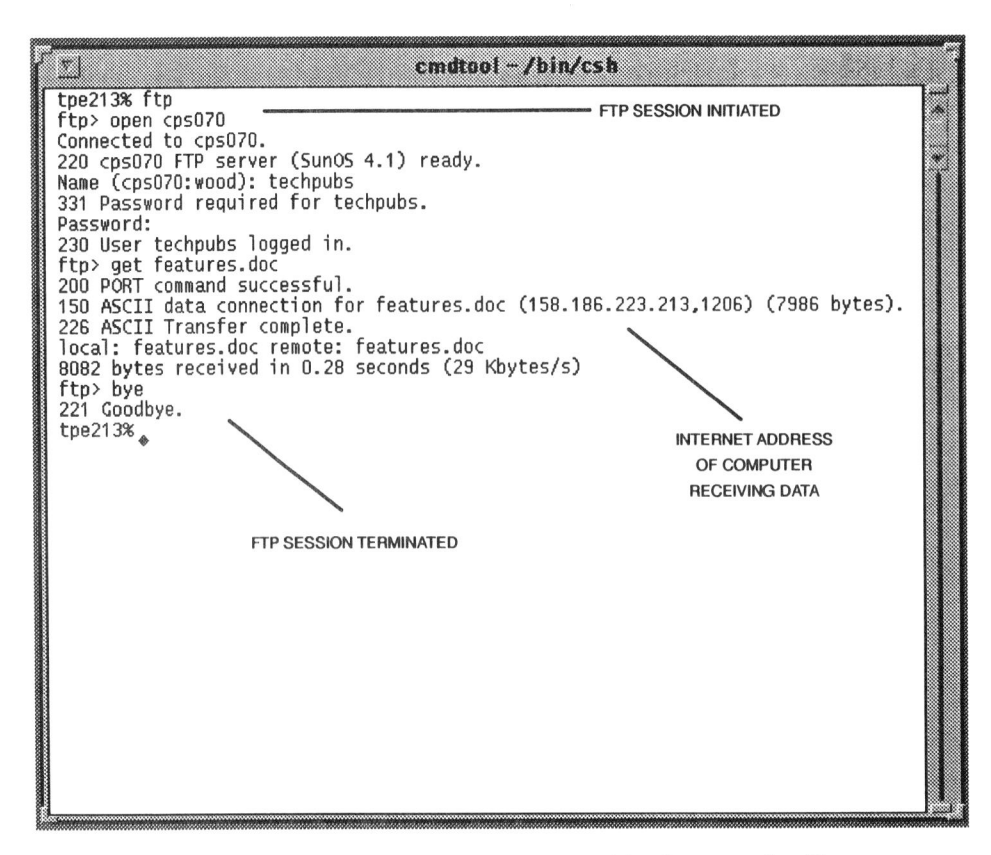

```
tpe213% ftp
ftp> open cps070                                      ─── FTP SESSION INITIATED
Connected to cps070.
220 cps070 FTP server (SunOS 4.1) ready.
Name (cps070:wood): techpubs
331 Password required for techpubs.
Password:
230 User techpubs logged in.
ftp> get features.doc
200 PORT command successful.
150 ASCII data connection for features.doc (158.186.223.213,1206) (7986 bytes).
226 ASCII Transfer complete.
local: features.doc remote: features.doc
8082 bytes received in 0.28 seconds (29 Kbytes/s)
ftp> bye
221 Goodbye.
tpe213%
                                                        INTERNET ADDRESS
                                                          OF COMPUTER
                                                         RECEIVING DATA

                  FTP SESSION TERMINATED
```

Figure 7.3. An example of using File Transfer Protocol (FTP) to transfer files over TCP/IP based network. A "get" command is used to transfer a document (features.doc) from a file server (cps070).

the next decade makes it the leading contender for unifying the technology of a data highway infrastructure. Among other applications, it supports interactive multimedia (text, voice, graphics, video) and very high speed data communications.

A modem is an inexpensive and popular desktop device for telecommunications. It changes electronic signals into audio signals to be sent over telephone lines. The term is short for modulator/demodulator. A modem converts digital information, that is, a pattern of ones and zeros from a computer, into an analog signal suitable for transmission over telephone lines. On the receiving end, another modem accepts the analog signal and converts it back into digital information for another computer.

The IEEE 802.3 Ethernet standard specifies data transmission rates up to 10 Mbps. A cost benefit of using file server technology with client seats distributed over a LAN is that network licenses of certain programs can be accessed by multiple occasional users. Small quantities of licenses that "float" to users over a LAN can be purchased rather than fixed licenses for every seat in the network.

Modems operate at different transmission speeds. These speeds are called the baud rate. The baud rate refers to the number of bits transmitted per second. Transmission is either simplex or duplex. In simplex transmission, the communication is always one way. Duplex transmission can be either full duplex or half duplex. If full duplex, two computers can communicate simultaneously; if half duplex two computers can communicate but only one way at a time.

There are different types of modems which can be classified by transmission type; that is, synchronous or asynchronous. An asynchronous modem connects different computers that do not share a common internal timing clock. With an asynchronous modem, the communication is independent of the internal timing of the different computers. Data is sent one bit at a time; however, the so-called start bit is fixed. Synchronous transmissions, by contrast, are clocked. The two computers operate at time sequences. Modem transmission speeds can be as low as 300 bits per second up to 28,800 bits per second.

The best modems for PCs are self adapting devices such as the Robotics Courier HST modem. Self adapting features include autodial capability, auto answer, and automatic tuning to the appropriate baud rate.

The rate at which data is transferred is an important consideration because document files can be exceptionally large. If a user needs large documents quickly, or has a frequent requirement to transfer sizable files, then an adequate transfer speed is essential. When uploading (sending) or downloading (receiving) files, the operational session includes some of the following steps:

- Turn on the modem (assuming it is connected; if not, connect it first)
- Startup telecommunications software
- Set modem speed
- Dial service and establish connection
- Verify communications and logoff

COMMUNICATIONS SERVICES AND THE INTERNET

Once tied into a telecommunications infrastructure, electronic publishers can avail themselves of connections to multiple computer resources. The development of on-line services is having a significant impact on electronic publishing. There are general on-line services that allow users to join discussion groups and exchange mail as well as services that allow electronic publishers to do research and gather up-to-the minute information. A variety of communication services are available as well as some services of interest to specialized users. The Internet is not a commercial service but a world wide collection of computers.

On-line Services

There are a growing number of on-line information services available to electronic and desktop publishers. These include America Online, CompuServe Information Service, Prodigy Interactive Personal Service and Dow Jones News/Retrieval. For a fee, users can access a wide set of computer information resources. Specialized services, such as LEXIS from Mead Data Central, provide on-line access to electronic law libraries for legal publishers and researchers. Others specialize in such services as distributing graphics or on-line fonts.

What are some of the main uses that general on-line services can be put to? The first is the ability to send mail and communicate with business partners or other professionals in the field. A second reason is to participate in forums such as the many desktop publishing forums available on CompuServe's Information Service. Users participating in on-line forums get answers to questions on such intricacies as those concerning the way a publishing package works or advice on equipment to use for a project. There are forums, for example, for Ventura, PageMaker, and Microsoft Word. Another use of on-line services is for research. Businesses needing immediate access to financial data can download financial reports from stock and bond markets, journalists can find up to the minute news information, and legal researchers can download the latest information from court cases around the country.

Tying Computers via the Internet

One of the great success stories of telecommunications networks is a world wide computer network called the Internet. Unlike CompuServe Information Service and other on-line services, the Internet is not a service but rather a unique network connecting millions of computers. Note that Internet is spelled with an uppercase I, not the lower case i for internet that represents a small network collection and the specific machine addresses nodes in the network. The Internet is a large collection of networks that use the same namespace and internetworking TCP/IP protocols. The Internet began as a government subsidized network. The Internet does not own the network pipes it uses. The success of the Internet owes much to the information resources it links together. It includes companies, universities, research foundations and individuals who participate in sending and receiving information. There are well over 15 million users of the Internet worldwide and the number is rapidly expanding. The information transferred over the

Internet may be electronic mail, electronic newsletters, publications, research data, or even multimedia information. The File Transfer Protocol (FTP) is still the primary method for transferring files over the Internet. The anonymous FTP service allows anyone in the world to access a restricted area of computer disk space to obtain information from the abundant computer resources of the Internet. Refer to Figure 7.4.

Forums and special interest groups share ideas and news. Electronic publishers can use the Internet to collaborate, exchange mail, and publish documents. Readers can access documents in a hypertext network called the World Wide Web (WWW) and browse through documents using special graphical browsers such as Mosaic or text browsers. Documents in the web use hypertext markup language (HTML) which is based upon SGML. (Refer to Chapter 8 for more information on the World Wide Web and the Mosaic interface.)

Within seconds, E-mail messages on Internet can be sent to desktops thousands of miles apart. Electronic journals are provided on Internet server computers

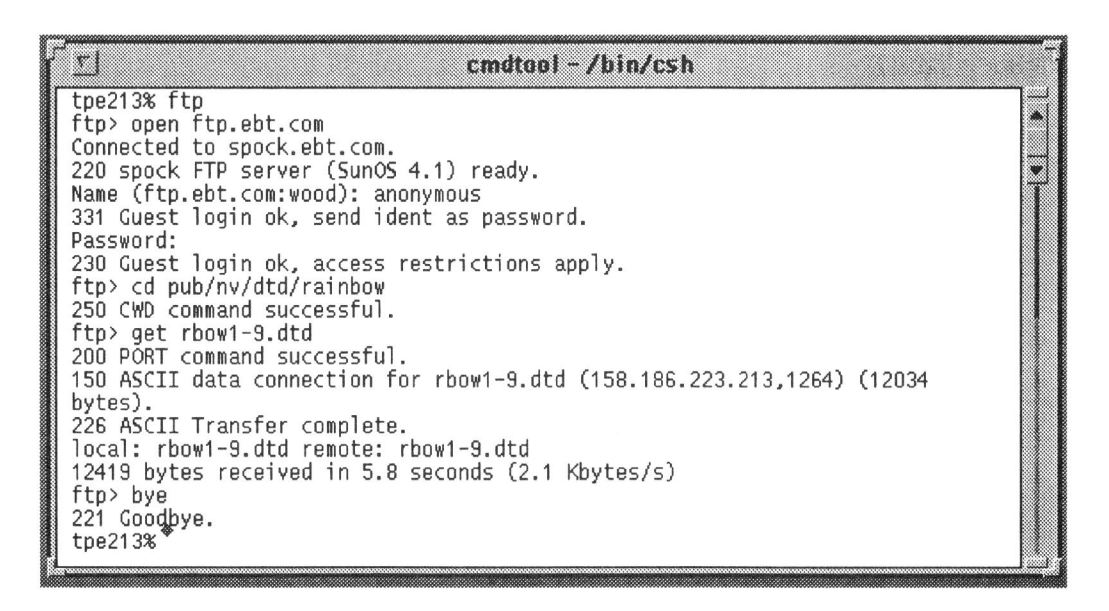

```
tpe213% ftp
ftp> open ftp.ebt.com
Connected to spock.ebt.com.
220 spock FTP server (SunOS 4.1) ready.
Name (ftp.ebt.com:wood): anonymous
331 Guest login ok, send ident as password.
Password:
230 Guest login ok, access restrictions apply.
ftp> cd pub/nv/dtd/rainbow
250 CWD command successful.
ftp> get rbow1-9.dtd
200 PORT command successful.
150 ASCII data connection for rbow1-9.dtd (158.186.223.213,1264) (12034 bytes).
226 ASCII Transfer complete.
local: rbow1-9.dtd remote: rbow1-9.dtd
12419 bytes received in 5.8 seconds (2.1 Kbytes/s)
ftp> bye
221 Goodbye.
tpe213%
```

Figure 7.4. An example of using an anonymous ftp login to a file server on the Internet. When the computer prompts the user for a login name, the user types in anonymous. This example has relevance for electronic publishers. By using anonymous ftp to log-on to an Internet server (called ftp.ebt.com) the user gets access to the Rainbow document type definition from Electronic Book Technologies, a public general purpose DTD (identified as rbow1-9.dtd) which is downloaded to the guest account. There are millions of computers tied to the Internet around the world. Users can do research, send and receive documents, and collaborate with partners on projects.

so that readers can log-on for reading. By far the most captivating and useful feature of the Internet that no existing commercial service can offer is that users can access information on millions of computers. Everything from government statistics on the economy, papers on population growth, and agricultural reports are available. Users can log-on to supercomputers for satellite and weather data, download scientific reports from hundreds of forums, as well and distribute comments around the world. Documents authored in Sydney, Australia, for example, can be transferred within minutes in PostScript format to New York or any Internet capable desktop and printed on a PostScript printer.

Electronic Publishing and the Information Superhighway

As a global network, the Internet is a partial model of what the information superhighway will become. Emerging standards for high speed packet switching services will radically improve transfer rates for telecommunicated data. The operational speeds for modem transfers and also for X.25 packet switch protocols (56,000 bps) are below the capabilities of the latest fast packet technologies: Frame Relay (between 1.54 megabits per second (Mbps) and 44.5 Mbps), Switched Multimegabit Data Service (SMDS-44.5 Mbps), and ATM (between 44.5 and 622 Mbps). Collectively these technologies and services will be integrated into a super set service known as Broadband Integrated Services Digital Network (B–ISDN). The basic unit of data communication for ATM and SMDS is a cell, a 53 byte message consisting of 5 bytes of header information that essentially identifies the type of message and the route or destination address of the cell. The remaining 48 bytes are the actual data content of the message. The great advantage of the cell is its fixed size which minimizes delays in network traffic and allows developers of ATM products to create very high speed devices. Cell data may consist of voice, text, video, music, graphics, or other data types. Frame Relay uses variable length packets which can be converted to cells over a B–ISDN network to enhance the efficiency and quality of service of wide area networking. Many local area networks are beginning to migrate to ATM cell technology so that performance of data communications in organizations will be simplified and enhanced. Developers of ATM data communication products and service providers (telephone companies and private network companies) are seeking to integrate existing data communications technology and services into evolving B–ISDN services. For example, the Internet Engineering Task Force (IETF) and the Internet Research Task Force are participating in forum discussions about how the Internet based TCP/IP protocol can coexist with the evolution of ATM cell networks.

Electronic publishers will benefit from this revolution in data communications. While much attention has been given to the interactive entertainment services (video and games delivered to one's residence on-demand) offered by the superhighway, less notice has been given to publishing applications that will flourish when the infrastructure of broadband technologies is fully in place. Private network companies, cable companies, and public telephone companies will roll out high speed data services to support interactive multimedia, telecommuting, electronic book interchange, and other electronic publishing applications. Figure 7.5 is a diagram of a wide area broadband network connecting LANs across a wide area network.

Organizations that subscribe to the data communications services will eventually hookup to publishing databases, electronic libraries, and multimedia databanks. Access to the data highway opens business opportunities for electronic publishers. The challenge for content providers and technical developers of electronic publishing tools is to create applications and services in step with the data highway evolution. Opportunities exist for companies seeking to partner with other groups in the distribution of multimedia and electronic books. Business alliances are already being formed for the superhighway prototype, the Internet. Publishers, printers, writers, graphic artists, journalists, and interactive video specialists can participate in new business opportunities.

To attract business, the telephone companies and other service providers will offer competitive qualities of service to subscribers including network management services. Subscribers will not have to manage the technical problems of getting the data from source to destination which is a significant cost when end users try to manage their own complex network. Users will be able to choose levels of service and share some cost for a large infrastructure when they partici-

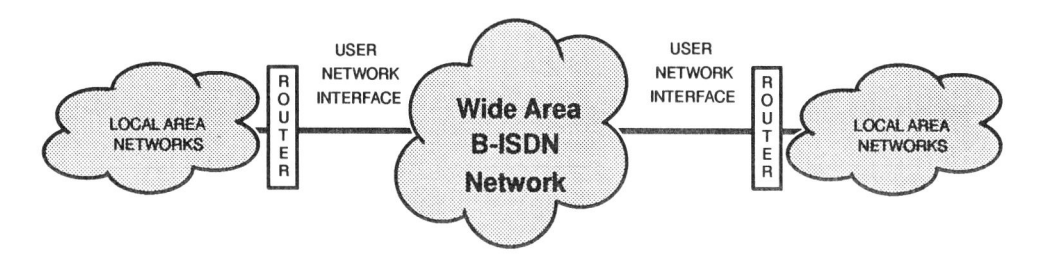

Figure 7.5. Broadband Integrated Services Digital Network (B–ISDN) shown connecting local area networks over wide area by way of a public telephone network. The telephone companies will use B–ISDN/ATM switches, much as they do voice traffic switches, to connect users over vast geographical areas. Electronic publishing and multimedia are envisioned as major applications for the electronic superhighway under construction. Other applications will include distance learning, document imaging, and digital libraries.

pate in worldwide connectivity. Service providers will also lease or sell appropriate devices (routers, set top converters) to hookup computers and display devices to the network.

DOCUMENT CONVERSION PROGRAMS

The more the possibilities of exchanging documents over networks are expanded, the more conscious we are of requirements for common file formats for document exchange. Vendors of electronic publishing systems have developed many special programs variably called conversion programs, translators, and filters. Text translators are software programs that read the specific markup or file format of a word processing or text editing program and convert it into another format acceptable for input to other document processing systems. The effectiveness of such translation depends upon several factors including the stability of the publishing software being translated, the usefulness of the object to be translated, and the long term benefits of using translators for certain applications.

One simple means of exchanging text is an ASCII text transfer. This method of transfer is reliable and easy to use. The disadvantage is that all format control will be lost because it purges the file format codes or instructions which word processing and electronic publishing programs use to instruct the computer. Much depends upon the need of the users. If the objective is to preserve the original format, this is not a desirable alternative. Flat ASCII also does not tell anything about the information inside a document but it is still a very useful, though limited, form of document interchange.

Conversion Programs at Work

Corporations, government agencies, service bureaus, and commercial printers have all struggled with the problem of document interchange. When a formatted document is built with one set of programs and format codes (called "markup" codes) incorporating that same information in another system with a different publishing program and markup requires an export or import filter as an intermediate translating tool.

The use of specialized software packages (translators, filters, or export/import devices) is necessary to preserve the integrity of the data transferred between different computer systems or systems with different electronic publishing packages. Publishing packages refer to these exchange capabilities as import and export features.

Formatting text editors, for example, use what is called specific "markup." The term markup derives from the traditional practice of typographers and copy editors who apply instructions to an author's manuscript regarding page layout, fonts, spacing, and so forth. Most word processing and desktop publishing programs contain such specific information intertwined within the document under creation. The fact that each vendor's specific markup is different from the next causes problems.

Import and export translators can play a useful role. Some suggestions for the selection, implementation, and use of translators are the following:

- Carefully evaluate the objectives to be reached before selecting a translator
- Test the translator to see that it works properly before deploying it for regular use
- Remember that translators must be maintained (or modified in time) as the publishing packages they relate to change version and release levels
- If the purpose of the translation is to preserve document format, be sure that the originator of the formatted document is working according to preestablished standards for document presentation established by the organization
- Determine whether the use of platform and format neutral SGML is a suitable solution

Good translators allow users to recover the original document or image. Import/export conversion programs are offered by almost every desktop publishing program and many word processing programs including Microsoft Word and WordPerfect. Some vendors such as Interleaf refer to these translation programs as filters. Most translation programs are unidirectional but some translators are bidirectional. For example, the user sends a file from System A, running Microsoft Word to System B, running Interleaf Version 5 or 6, from there an Interleaf file is converted to a Microsoft Word file ready for export to System A. Figure 7.6 diagrams both a unidirectional and bidirectional conversion model.

Document Interchange Standards

Conversion tools based on international standards offer a more universal approach to the document interchange problem. The objective is to create both platform and application independence for senders and receivers of documents. Neutrality means independence from the hardware system platforms which originally generated the text and graphic images. The standards have been developed by hardware and software vendors as well as those created by organized standard bodies such as ANSI and ISO. Leading document interchange standards include the Standard Generalized Markup Language (SGML), Open Document Architecture

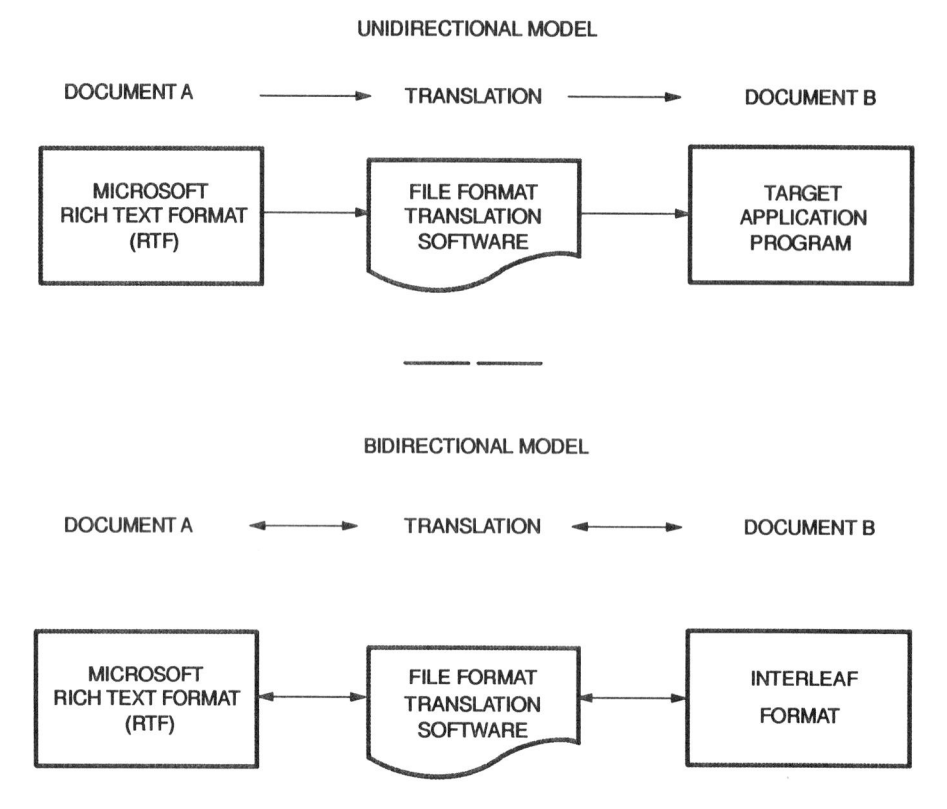

Figure 7.6. Unidirectional and bidirectional translation of document text data using Microsoft Rich Text Format (RTF) as the basic translation language. In the unidirectional case an application program such as a word processor can import RTF and translate the encoded RTF format into its own proprietary format. In the second case, the translation works both ways. The document can be imported into Interleaf, for example, and converted back into RTF for export.

(ODA), and the ODA derivative Compound Document Architecture (CDA) developed by Digital Equipment Corporation. The objective is to promote ground rules for independence from vendor proprietary hardware and software platforms to foster neutral document interchange.

SGML was adopted by the International Standards Organization (ISO) in 1986 as a system independent text interchange standard. Since then, SGML has gained wide acceptance as a publishing standard. A growing list of associations subscribe to SGML including: the Association of American Publishers, the American Library Association, the United States Department of Defense, the French Publisher's

Association, German Publisher's Association, the Japanese Electronic Publishing Association, the Modern Languages Association, the Telecommunications Industry Forum, the American National Standards Institute, and the Open System Foundation.

SGML solves many problems associated with document interchange while not requiring users to abandon the hardware or application programs they currently use. The main advantages of SGML for workgroups—and an organization—can be summarized as follows:

> ➤ SGML separates form and content
> ➤ SGML describes the structure and content of documents
> ➤ Since SGML uses generic descriptive markup as opposed to specific vendor–dependent markup, export and import translators do not have to be upgraded to meet document exchange requirements

The DTD gives a structural definition to information or content that can apply to several document instances. For example, the content of a proposal, specification, brochure, and user manual may come from a database of SGML encoded data. As discussed in Chapters 3 and 4, this data can be routed through style sheets and document formatters to create the specific formats required for those documents. In this chapter we are primarily concerned with SGML's role as a neutral interchange standard.

Since there is no universal DTD that defines the tags for all document instances, it is incumbent upon document analysts to select and design adequate DTDs. That is why planning is important. If the task of designing a DTD from scratch becomes too formidable, there are many public DTD's available that can save users time.

Conversion to SGML

The cost of conversion to SGML may or may not benefit the organization depending upon the specific scale of the conversion effort and the resulting return on investment in efficiencies, productivity, and quality. How does a company go about the data conversion process? What steps are involved? What tools are available to help organizations achieve such goals? Figure 7.7 diagrams the conversion process.

An SGML conversion tool maps the format (or appearance) of a document into a logical structure with SGML markup. Avalanche's FastTAG product uses artificial intelligence to look at a page and determine a structure from the format. The Avalanche Visual Recorder Engine (VRE) searches for visual formatting clues in the

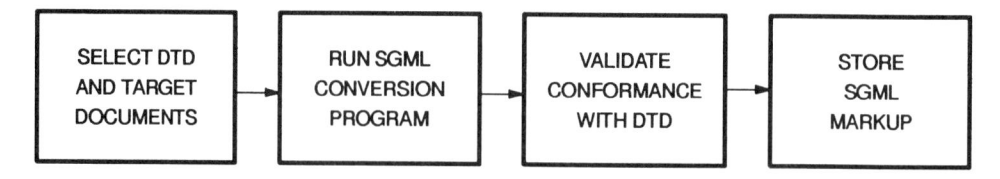

```
┌──────────────┐   ┌──────────────┐   ┌──────────────┐   ┌──────────────┐
│  SELECT DTD  │   │   RUN SGML   │   │   VALIDATE   │   │    STORE     │
│  AND TARGET  │──▶│  CONVERSION  │──▶│  CONFORMANCE │──▶│    SGML      │
│  DOCUMENTS   │   │    PROGRAM   │   │   WITH DTD   │   │    MARKUP    │
└──────────────┘   └──────────────┘   └──────────────┘   └──────────────┘
```

Figure 7.7. This diagram summarizes the generic conversion of proprietary format encoded documents to SGML markup by means of an automatic conversion program.

source document. Avalanche has a special programming language called Louise to aid in the conversion to SGML markup. FastTAG also offers utilities that convert specific file formats into SGML markup.

Before the computer conversion can proceed, the user group must create a DTD or select an available public DTD. Specific DTDs have been created for Department of Defense through the Computer-aided Acquisition and Logistics Support (CALS) initiative, the telecommunications industry by the Telecommunications Information Forum, and the Aviation Industry through the Air Transport Association. The ISO has also published DTDs for books, periodicals, and serials.

A general purpose DTD suitable for use in many SGML conversion projects is Rainbow from Electronic Book Technologies (EBT). Rainbow is a public DTD (available over the Internet) and has quickly become a practical point of departure for many organizations and users of popular programs such as FrameMaker, Interleaf, Microsoft Word, or Ventura Publisher. The DTD was specifically created to help users of proprietary formatting systems convert to SGML. In addition to the Rainbow DTD, EBT has developed proto models of "Rainbow Makers" for several file formats including RTF. The Rainbow Makers convert proprietary word processing formats into basic SGML. EBT has encouraged other companies to create Rainbow Makers and make them available to the public over the Internet. Once documents are converted to the Rainbow format, the SGML markup can be used for multiple purposes and can be converted or transformed into other industry standard DTDs. Products such as SGML Hammer from Avalanche or OmniMark from Exoterica can be used for this purpose.

After initial conversion, fine tuning may be required. The PowerPaste tool from ArborText can be used to transform data converted to Rainbow format and to verify that transformation from Rainbow to a destination Document Type Definition went properly. The operator can intervene and correct improper conversions.

SGML conversion tools can also be used to output SGML data to paper, databases, or CD-ROM. Organizations can retain and leverage existing investment in proprietary desktop publishing systems using them to format SGML encoded data. Conversion tools such as SGML Hammer, from Avalanche, or OmniMark can be used to map SGML markup into a proprietary format such as Ventura or Interleaf.

These same tools can be used to store SGML markup in a database or to load an on-line document display tool.

Document Format Interchange

SGML is a standard for encoding document structure and content. ISO standard 8879 does not support the interchange of document format, because SGML separates format from content. All the formatting and page layout magic performed by word processing and desktop publishing systems is done through proprietary software. Each proprietary system has its own method of setting up page layout and composition. The formatting features of publishing systems distinguish one from another. It is possible to exchange formatting information, if the the intent is to distribute the format information in final form. PostScript can be used. If we need to reuse and republish the information, there is an ISO standard for format processing called the Document Style Semantics and Specification Language (DSSSL) which is a language for processing and formatting an SGML document. It defines the presentation of the document in a vendor neutral way. The formats apply to print and/or on-line presentations.

An interim method of interchanging format information is a Format Output Specification Instance (FOSI). The so-called output specification (OS) was developed in conjunction with requirements for format interchange associated with the CALs initiative. Both Datalogics and Arbortext sell SGML authoring tools to support FOSIs.

Compound Document Architectures

In addition to tagging languages such as SGML, there are competing standards for interchange of documents including text as well as other objects. Open Document Architecture (ODA) is an ISO standard (ISO 8893). Compound Document Architecture (CDA) from Digital Equipment Corporation derives from ODA and is a platform neutral document interchange standard. These compound document methods use a document encoding scheme called aggregates. Aggregates can represent text, graphics, audio, and video content, as well as format. Aggregates are lists of entities linked as structures in computer memory.

Unlike SGML, compound document architectures attempt to encode both content and format. CDA uses encoding rules called Digital Document Interchange Format (DDIF). DDIF is an encoding language which is platform independent. It encodes all of a document's structural parts and stylistic presentation information in DDIF. End users are not responsible for this encoding mechanism which vendors provide in the background. Documents created with CDA's encoding conventions can be exchanged. CDA also provides a document viewing technology which allows compliant applications to display compound documents. At this time there is less commercial technology support available for compound document architectures than there is for SGML.

Acrobat

When we want to distribute documents to various platforms only for viewing, not editing, there are several possibilities. We can narrow the possibilities further if we want the viewer to work on all platforms, and we want to see the document as it has been prepared for print production. One possibility is Acrobat from Adobe Systems Inc., the creators of PostScript. Adobe's document interchange technology that incorporates PostScript is called Acrobat. It allows for the viewing of a document made from diverse applications on any platform (PC, MAC, and so forth). Acrobat uses Portable Document Format (PDF), which is a unique file format based upon PostScript. PDF files can be combined with structural elements of native file formats including SGML. A PDF file can store document appearance information and structure information in one file. PDF files can be ported across platforms for printing and viewing while preserving text, graphics, and images in a device-independent state.

Acrobat consists of several products including Acrobat Reader which allows users to view, navigate, and print documents. Acrobat Exchange includes Acrobat Reader but in addition to browsing, viewing, and printing, users can annotate documents and create and transmit PDF files. Acrobat Exchange also offers a live links feature. Acrobat does not give users the capability to modify or edit the document as does SGML but it does offer an electronic viewing ability on various platforms. Figure 7.8 is a diagram of the Acrobat user interface with a display example.

Adobe is not alone in building platform independent viewing applications. To support large document viewing, Interleaf's WorldView Press is a powerful technology that runs on PCs, MACs, and various workstations. WorldView supports color and SGML. WorldView can be used to make encyclopedic document collections for viewing.

PUTTING DIGITAL DOCUMENTS TO WORK

Evolutionary Strategy for Interchange

Many organizations faced with continuing deadlines and budget constraints are not yet ready to transform document practices and conversion processes to achieve interoperability. Some organizations are insulated from the problem because everyone uses the same word processor. Other organizations make modifications, or experiment, in departments or detached groups. Getting started, workgroups should build consensus within the organization about interoperability objectives. Some key questions organizations which should be asked before engaging in a conversion to a neutral document interchange standard such as SGML are:

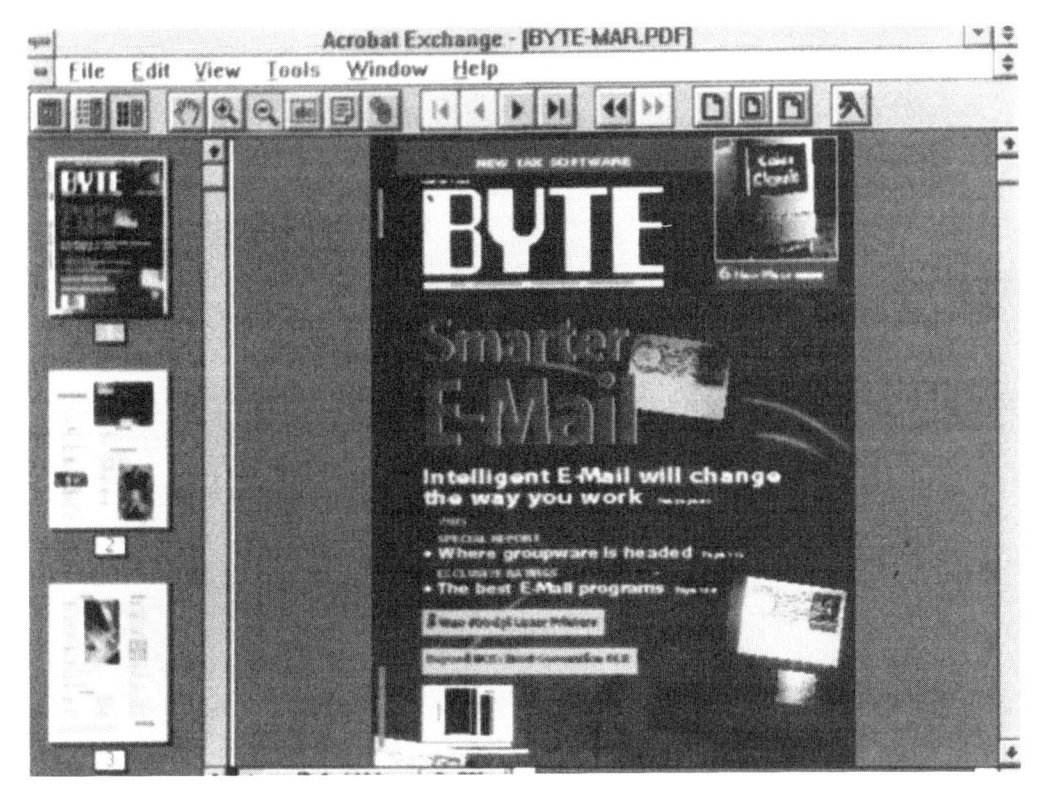

Figure 7.8. Acrobat Exchange sample showing display of Byte Magazine with thumbnails of pages from the magazine on the left. (Courtesy of Adobe Systems, Inc.)

- What conversion tools are used within the organization?
- How many documents are transferred from desktop to desktop in a week or a month? How often is the data reused?
- What is the average size of the documents transferred?
- What workgroups can or cannot access publishing system resources?
- Is there an objective or plan behind the introduction of new technologies?
- Does the plan take into account modifications to existing processes and special demands made upon user personnel?
- Is there a plan to migrate from paper to electronic document distribution? Are any document viewers or browsers used?

These questions can guide information managers and other responsible parties to make informed decisions for developing an interoperability strategy. One way to justify the cost of converting to SGML is to measure the time wasted on inefficient practices. Much of this type of cost goes undocumented such as reformatting data after it has been flattened to ASCII for reuse or searching through endless paper copies for data in order to rebuild documents reusing much of the same information. The true cost of conversion depends not only upon the volume of information that is being converted and the degree to which this information can be logically organized into standardized structures but also upon a collateral review of current practices for finding and reusing document information. Given the growth of information intensive industries throughout the world, it is no wonder that many organizations are starting to treat their legacy data with strategic interest.

SGML provides a solution for interchange of text documents but it does not cover the exchange of vector or bit mapped graphics. From the outset the file format used for graphical information should be decided. Organizations using graphics extensively should also establish practices for exchange of graphics information. (Refer to Chapter 5 for conversion tools). Interchange file formats such as computer graphics metafile (CGM) and Graphics Interchange Format (GIF) can be used. Users of SGML create entity references to graphics included in documents.

Building the Electronic Reference Document

Making documents electronic and interchangeable has its rewards. Organizations computerize documents to free the workforce from total dependence on paper. Many companies invest in document image processing systems and authoring systems to convert paper documents to soft or virtual copies. When exchanging that data among many players, however, it is important to have the data in a neutral format which can be piped to any platform. To make soft documents as useful as hardcopy, organizations are turning to electronic reference documents (ERDs). The electronic reference document displayed via a video terminal allows for viewing and quick access to document information. (We learn more about the nature of ERDs and their similarities and differences with multimedia documents in Chapter 8.)

To understand the value of an electronic reference document system for workgroups, consider again the task confronting multiple authors collaborating on a proposal. In addition to sending and receiving documents with specific file formats useful for editing, there are two other requirements that the collaborating group must confront. One is finding information rapidly so that background research can be done to answer questions for the proposal. The second is being able to view the proposal document in progress so that the collaborating team can see a digital version of the document in progress. The company has a large reservoir of document information on topics important to the collaborative proposal response but there is no easy way to get at the information without carrying volumes of paper documents around and searching tables of contents for answers to specific questions. Organizations who get caught in the syndrome of researching and building documents with paper only, probably spread paper faster than knowledge. Most ERD systems provide electronic text indexing and retrieval, allowing rapid searches and access of document information. Invaluable time is saved by looking up answers to questions in a document database. If the data is already encoded in a neutral format, it facilitates information searches. Authors can output information to multiple formats for paper or electronic distribution. Another value of an electronic reference document for the proposal collaborators is that the virtual document (that is the document of all contributors) can be displayed on their computer even though they may be working on different computer environments.

Document management system technology makes it possible to manage the workflow of proposals and other documents in revolutionary ways. A proposal group working on the network can follow the status of different parts of the proposal and peer review of the proposal on-line. Odesta Systems Corporation has introduced Proposal Works system for managing a multiauthored document with features that provide a view of the proposal at any point in its progress; assigns work orders to individual team members, supports dynamic peer review routing over a network, and allocates specific sections to writers for completion and auditing.

Organizations who maintain their data in a neutral format are well positioned to make collaborative projects work whether they be proposals, books, business plans, or reports. They can make electronic documents work for them instead of having proprietary format technologies. They can apply powerful resource tools such as electronic document reference and document management tools more effectively if the data is already in a neutral format. The theme of interoperability will continue to grow in importance as broader schemes for information sharing and distribution over wide area computer networks become prominent. By starting to meet interoperability objectives now, organizations will have a better chance of mastering document information resources.

CHAPTER 8

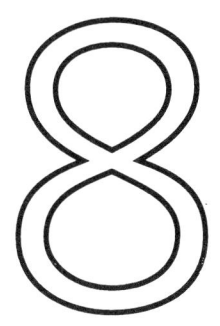

➤ *Electronic document viewing*

➤ *Hypertext and hypermedia*

➤ *Electronic reference documents*

➤ *Authoring and distribution*

➤ *Internet publishing*

Multimedia and Electronic Reference Documents

*h*ow do groups collaborate to create multimedia publications? How is multimedia being used in the workplace and in education? How do we organize the information for successful presentation and distribution? What are the similarities and differences between electronic reference documents (ERDs) and multimedia? What tools can be used to develop multimedia and ERDs on the desktop? What is the relationship of existing on-line information services and the future of multimedia? What technical problems must be overcome to make interactive multimedia accessible across networks?

Public interest in multimedia is growing rapidly. Multimedia is the use of a mix of text, graphs, photos, animation, voice, and sound to convey information. Electronic publishers are delivering interactive electronic books, hypermedia training programs, and multimedia reference works. Multimedia encyclopedias for CD-ROM from publishers such as Compton's NewMedia help audiences understand the usefulness and potential of the medium for the desktop. There have also been many notable desktop multimedia success stories within business, legal and medical services, the arts, education, and government. Commercial as well as in-house developers of interactive multimedia are exploring applications that depart from simple fascination with special effects and lead to rich sources of knowledge and information. Refer to Figure 8.1.

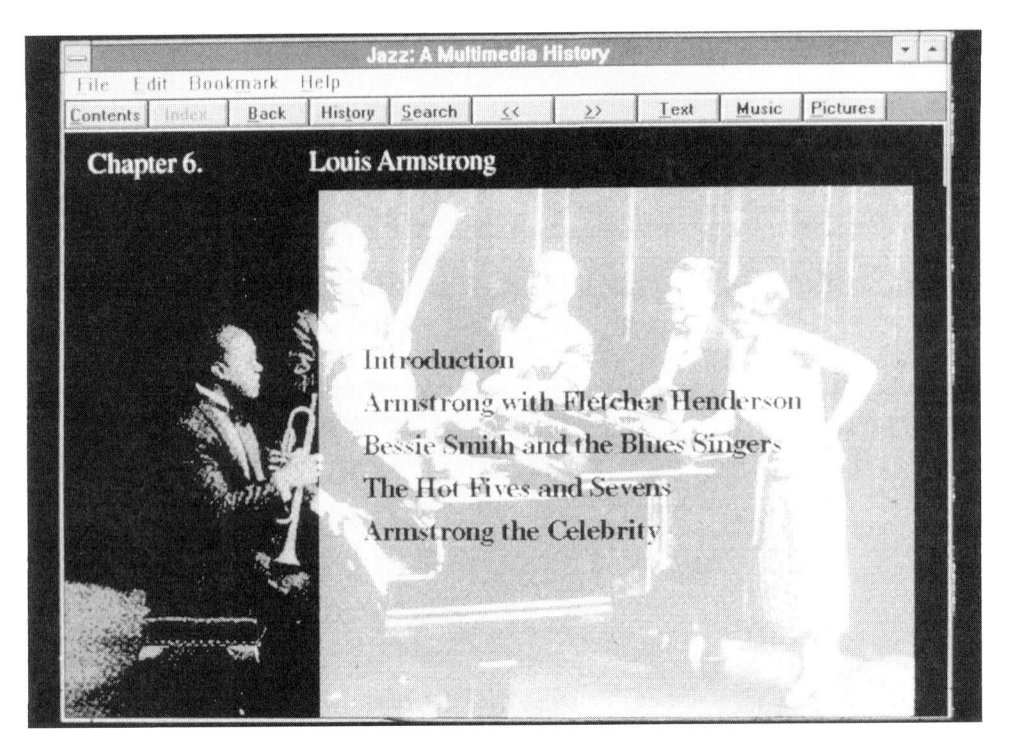

Figure 8.1. Screen shot from Compton's NewMedia Jazz: A Multimedia History. (Courtesy of Compton's NewMedia.)

ELECTRONIC DOCUMENT VIEWING

We commonly refer to the individuals who display electronic documents and multimedia collections as electronic document viewers. The viewer interacts with the system via a video display terminal and uses tools such as a mouse and keyboard to access information. There are important differences between the experience of reading printed literature and using interactive multimedia and electronic hypertext documents.

Beyond the Page

A printed document is a page sequential product. By accepted convention, authors, printers, publishers, and readers of printed material expect to find information organized within the serial boundaries of pages. The page has been a reliable form of communication for centuries, but it has inherent limits. Since printed pages are designed to be read mostly in a linear manner, they can restrict reader access to information. A page of paper is restricted to a two dimensional presentation of text and graphics. Multimedia is not limited to a linear model of presentation. Hypertext links text contents within or among electronic documents and files by embedded cross references. Hypermedia is an extension of hypertext and includes the linking of mixed content types (text, graphics, video, voice, and audio). The term multimedia is, with some exceptions, used interchangeably with hypermedia. Viewers, aided by hypermedia links, can branch, browse, and search in many directions for information. Viewers can access video, sound, graphics, voice, and animation in addition to text and graphics in multimedia collections. See Figure 8.2.

The printed page also constrains readers from accessing detailed levels of information. If we do a research project on the American Revolution and know the Declaration of Independence was signed on July 4, 1776, we have one piece of information. But students may want to know more about the signers of the Declaration and the events immediately preceding the actual break with the British Crown. Still others search for detailed information concerning the lives of average citizens in various colonies and towns of the period. A *properly organized* hypermedia data-

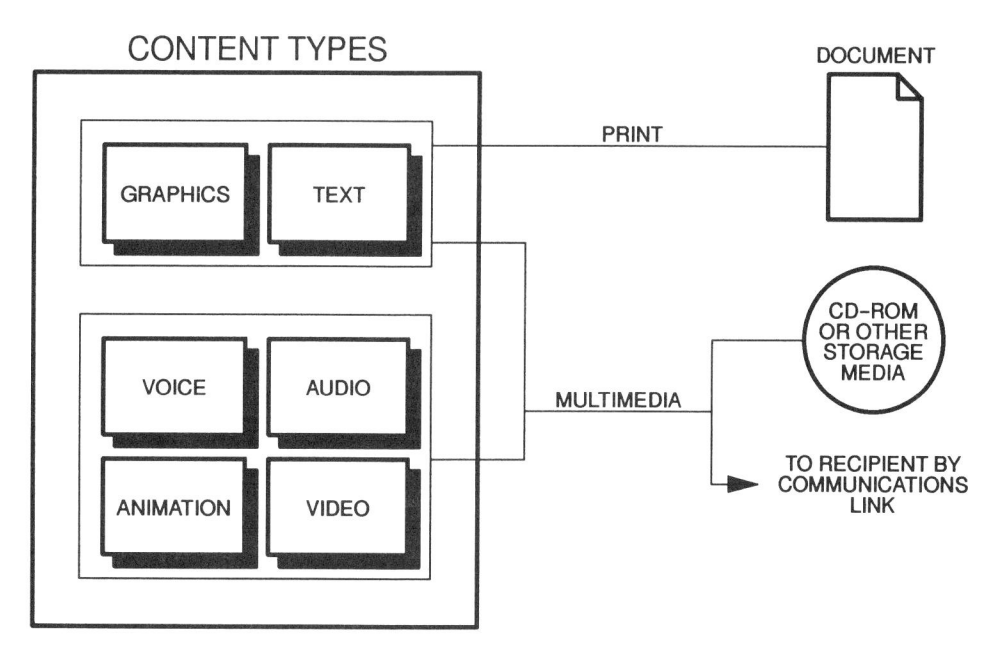

Figure 8.2. Contents of multimedia includes a mix of media types that cannot be included in a printed document.

base allows viewers to navigate through layers of information to find related topics, subtopics, and minor details.

Information in paper documents is frozen; hypermedia offers dynamic access to mixed information including video and animation. On the other hand, hypermedia can be mismanaged and there are many cases where print is the correct choice for the audience. Some prices have diminished for hardware and software products used to create and distribute multimedia publications. Many organizations straddle two worlds: the familiar universe of printed pages and the new found worlds of multimedia objects and on-line publishing. Managing a successful transition between the old and the new is a formidable challenge. As we learned in Chapter 4, workgroups and content providers who organize collections of information for multiple reuses have real opportunities for efficiency gains.

Hypertext and Navigation

Hypertext and hypermedia technologies accommodate the associative processes of human memory as well as structured cognitive behaviors. Interactive multimedia engages the associative and structured working of our minds. As hypermedia technology has evolved, a special vocabulary has grown with it that captures this multidimensional touring of the human mind. Three verbs that recur in hypertext discussions include link, browse, and navigate.

> ▶ Navigate—travelling through alternate paths or branches within the multimedia presentation package to find coverage of related material
> ▶ Browse—searching and displaying information among the multimedia collections on a semirandom basis
> ▶ Link—connecting pieces of information that are not presented in a linear progression

In addition to linking, browsing and navigating, hypertext jargon includes nodes and buttons. A node is the location or area where text or other media are located. The quantity of information in a node is variable. It may be a diagram, a page of text, a document, or a collection of documents. Buttons are visible marks embedded within an element that allow a user to branch or jump to another node usually after selecting the button with a pointing device. There are alternative methods for establishing user access to hyperlinks such as clicking on color highlighted or underlined text. Live tables of contents allow users to take a tour of documents by clicking on the title or section from the contents. See Figure 8.3.

Viewers can simultaneously display related information in computer windows with significant advantage. The viewer of a hypermedia book on architecture, for

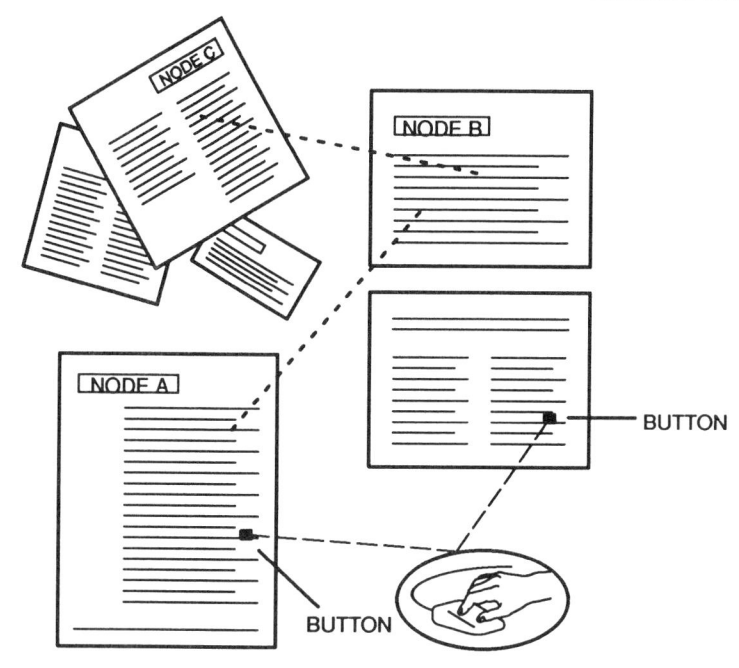

Figure 8.3. Hypertext linkage of topics with nodes and embedded buttons. There are many alternative models for linking information.

example, could be looking at a house floor plan in one computer window, an isometric view of the house exterior in another, an animated walk-through simulation in a third window, dimensioning and material information in a fourth, and pricing information in a fifth. The content of these windows can come from one or more nodes. Using a hyperlinking tool, the author and designer embed links and buttons connecting these nodes to assemble the desktop display work. Hypertext allows recipients of on-line documents to branch and navigate dynamically through topics by clicking on a mouse button to get to other collections of information.

Having been trained in a traditional orientation of creating and producing documents, there are several ways to view the context of reshaping documents to suit electronic hypertext and multimedia collections. Some possible alternatives are:

> ➤ Documents retain a linear structure but allow for jumps to other sections or information
>
> ➤ Documents are broken down into individuated chunks or cards
>
> ➤ Documents are compounded. The documents retain their individual

integrity but users create new documents based upon fragment showers from source documents

➤ A database of information using a hierarchy or structural model (such as SGML) can be used to represent the information in a collection from which multiple outputs are possible

Multimedia and Electronic Reference Document Applications

Multimedia is still in the process of inventing itself. Sometimes in the excitement of watching new technical developments emerge, developers and publishers become distracted from the basic message that multimedia and electronic reference documents are forms of communication. Before developing multimedia and electronic reference document collections, publishers need to take a look at how effective current forms of communication are. In-house publishers are learning that electronic reference documents can be practical and cost effective means of distributing knowledge to workers in an organization as well as to customers. Both multimedia and electronic reference documents can use mixed media, but multimedia has come to be identified with projects for computer based training, marketing presentations, and entertainment. Electronic reference documents and electronic information bases are primarily used for information searches to solve a problem quickly.

Why does our organization need multimedia or electronic reference documents? This is a healthy question. There are many reasons for considering such an investment including the ability to:

➤ Train employees

➤ Allow quick access to a legacy information base for customer support, product maintenance, and client training

➤ Streamline document updates and reduce cost of paper distribution

➤ Help manufacturing workers visualize what they are assembling

➤ Provide on-time information to workgroups—design, quality, and test engineers, for example—to accelerate product development

➤ Provide workers in government, banks, insurance companies, a means to search for answers to questions on-line rather than searching through voluminous documents

One way in-house managers and planners can begin to experiment with the tools and skills needed to make interactive multimedia work to an organization's advantage is to adapt current desktop information resources into a collaborative context. There are many uses of electronic documents, books, and databases that do not involve major production expense with video, animation, or audio. Electronic reference documents which feature interactive document viewing, hypertext, and intelligent indexing technology have become a preferred resource replacing paper documents in segments of many industries. Insurance professionals use electronic documents to process accident insurance claims more quickly, technicians in aerospace companies troubleshoot complex systems with by accessing a maintenance document database, corporate managers collaborate on business plans by distributing electronic documents, and physicians, nurses, and medical technicians query medical reference document information bases for diagnostic and other information. Electronic documents also reduce the cost of updating and reproducing paper documents.

Comprehending how electronic reference documents will improve knowledge distribution within an organization can clarify its usefulness. Product development is a one example of how multimedia may be introduced to improve organizational processes. By building an effective electronic document knowledge base, a company may profit from using multimedia and gain a competitive advantage. The idea is to use multimedia from product inception through the manufacturing, training, and support cycles. An initial cadre of product engineers and designers as well as manufacturing experts may use advanced CAD design, simulation, and product descriptive data in text and graphic formats to specify the design. Manufacturing engineers can benefit from recognizing how the development is progressing rather than being left out of the loop. The training group can begin to build an effective program from the use of preliminary product simulation and specifications. Customer support and help desk personnel can plan the organization of support information for in house and external functions. All players are allowed to access an electronic document database from their desktop or work areas. Critical to the whole process is the manner of managing data in the product information base. Any organization anticipating the use of hypermedia should examine its means of managing the workflow of information. A variation on the same information base can be distributed to customers for their use. See Figure 8.4.

Multimedia and electronic reference documents can help businesses and organizations of all kinds communicate and inform workers and improve performance of individuals and teams in manufacturing, engineering, commerce, and government. An organization's corporate policies, benefits, and safety information also can be distributed to the desktop for viewing. The user can browse through such information and search across many documents via full text searches or hypertext links.

Investment in multimedia and electronic reference documents can have a positive impact on the bottom line. The expense of developing an interactive multimedia training program, for example, may be offset by reducing travel to cus-

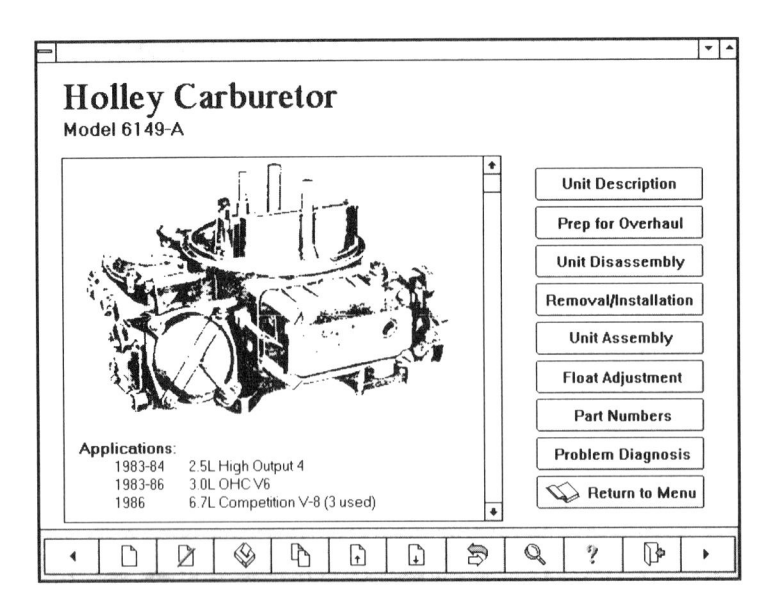

Figure 8.4. There are many applications of electronic documents and multimedia in the workplace. In many cases the same information base that will serve the customer can also help the in-house user needs as well. Product data that may be in service manuals as well as other documents can be distributed electronically within the company to reduce paper expenses and to allow customers and in-house users quick access to information. (Courtesy of InfoAccess, Inc.)

tomer training sites and eliminating some recurring costs related to course preparation and associated expenses for class materials. Proponents of electronic reference documents can demonstrate that on-line documents reduce paper expenses, streamline updates, and improve access to information critical in organizational efforts to develop products or deliver services.

There are different reasons and business purposes for which in-house publishers and commercial publishers develop multimedia and electronic reference documents. In-house publishers want to increase productivity, advance employee skill levels, and improve customer communications. Commercial electronic publishers are trying to make a profit on products created by electronic publishing and multimedia technology. They are concerned about production costs and the market size for investment in electronic books, magazines, reference tools, and entertainment packages. As the industry evolves distinctions are being drawn between content providers and multimedia title developers and producers. For example, a small scale content provider could specialize in multimedia textbooks for high school level students. As a publisher, this person sets the market objectives for selling titles to schools and school boards. The people on the staff help market and generate saleable textbook ideas. Another company may actually produce the multimedia titles. Authors, animators, and other specialists can be independently contracted for content creation. There is a growing market for electronic books and periodicals of all descriptions. Publishers can profit from reusing information for both print and on-line delivery applications if they have determined the appropriate markets for dual applications. Periodical publishers are already making their paper periodicals available for on-line viewing.

Commercial content providers and multimedia developer entrepreneurs are poised to take advantage of a large potential market in multimedia communications. Publishers of CD-ROM titles, many of whom also publish printed books, know that only ten to twenty percent of the population that own PCs have CD-ROM drives, and even a smaller percentage have videodiscs in their system. But with set top multimedia delivered to the home or the office not far away, many groups are gearing up to take advantage of new forms of electronic publishing and communication.

Both commercial and in-house developers of multimedia projects must weigh the technical limitations of technology available to them. For example, many real estate offices offer interactive access to property listings that show pictures of houses and neighborhoods as well as displaying text information details about price, availability, location, and so on. Some of these productions suffer from inadequate pixel depth processing in the graphic processing and screen monitor resolution in the realtor office. There are similar problems with the storage capacities for video on CD-ROM. Digital video can take up enormous storage space, so planning must account for how much video can be used and stored cost effectively.

Electronic Books and Documents for Education

Computer based training is not new, but the advent of interactive multimedia tools has made the applications of multimedia and training really take off. Some studies show that interactive instruction can help students increase information retention by as much as 50 percent as compared with traditional methods of training.

Examples of successful use of multimedia in education are not hard to find. Medical and biological instruction, for example, are already profiting from inclusion of multimedia in student instruction. The Animated Dissection of Anatomy for Medicine (A.D.A.M.) software allows desktop access to a database of graphic and text information related to the human body in windows at the click of a mouse. Developers of multimedia texts for human physiology can arrange for licensing access to the A.D.A.M graphical database for use in their own documents. Multimedia applications for every branch of learning are exploding. Hundreds of multimedia titles are being developed for schools around the world. Many of these use gamelike animations to engage younger students in learning while having fun. Electronic viewing tools available can bring classic texts to new life. Refer to Figure 8.5.

Interactive distance learning using multimedia will allow students to participate in educational programs remote to the service provider furnishing the instructional content. This differs from current televised learning that is broadcast unidirectionally and consists of playback video presentation of a lecture with sup-

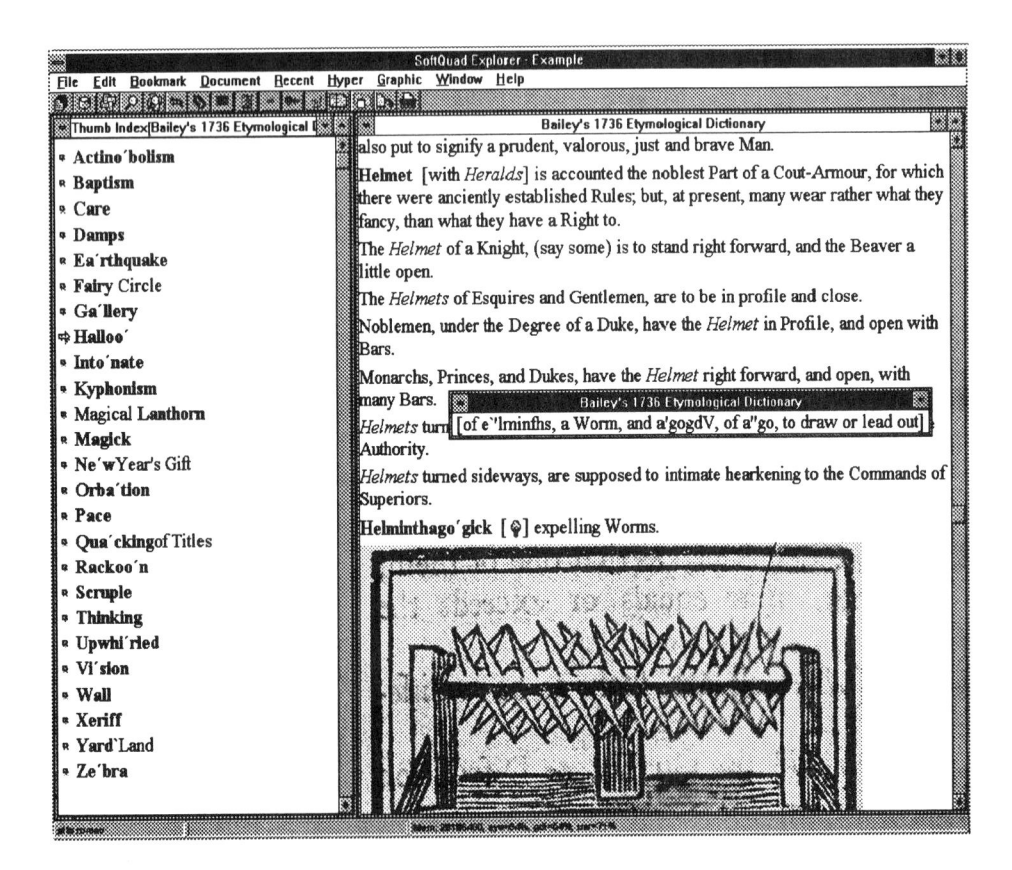

Figure 8.5. Use of on line viewing and indexing technology to enhance research of literary texts. In this case the SoftQuad Explorer browsing product is used to navigate Nathaniel Bailey's *Etymological Dictionary* first published in 1736. (Courtesy of SoftQuad, Inc.)

porting elements. Distance learning can help complement traditional methods of teaching and reduce rising costs for education including expenses related to physical plant and library facilities. The students must be able to access on-line libraries to do research and have access to quality instructional programming.

One of the challenges of using multimedia related to education is to help students adapt not only to doing research and learning according to multimedia collections presented to them, but also to be able to express themselves using multimedia just as students currently use writing as a means of expression in research projects. If multimedia is to become an effective means of communication and expression, then students ought to be able to use it. Being able to communicate with the medium means that we are able to study and learn because we are concentrating on what we have researched and what we are about to communicate. More time must be given to find ways to allow students at various levels to participate in projects that develop skills in communication and learning. With its conglomerate data types, multimedia offers a rich vocabulary for student expression.

Tools for Authoring and Interactive Viewing

Authoring tools for multimedia, hypermedia, and electronic reference document applications vary according to the approach taken to organize, link, and retrieve the information content of the collections. If we have already invested in tools to create text, drawings and images, these tools have a very important purpose in the development of a collection of information. Text and still pictures make up most of the content of current multimedia productions. Special tools (cameras, microphones, recording systems, and animation programs) are used for the creation of other multimedia content—video, audio, animation, and voice. Most multimedia authoring programs allow for integration and viewing of existing content types in a multimedia collection. The majority of programs offer a scripting tool to help developers customize interfaces to collections and build special displays.

There are two broad categories of authoring and viewing tools. The first category emphasizes the integration, synchronization, and presentation of mixed elements suitable for computer based training, kiosk applications, marketing, and entertainment productions. These tools allow users to rapidly organize video, audio, and animation elements in a collection. Methodologies for search, retrieval, and indexing of information are not stressed.

A key feature of this class of tools is the ability to create icons, buttons, menus, and dialog boxes that will provide reader/viewers of the multimedia collection easy access to the information. Icon Author from AimTech and Authorware Professional from Authorware Inc. both use a visual flowchart concept to organize the information. The organization will suit the way users will access information and how different content types are related to one another. An object oriented technique is used by the Aysemetrix multimedia toolbook. Objects are created or drawn and associated with a script that will cause a specific action when that object is selected. Buttons are created from a toolbox and assigned a specific name. If the button's script associates it with a particular selection of music or video, selecting the button will make that content run as programmed. The scripting language that empowers the object's functions is called OpenScript. Similar authoring systems attempt to integrate collections of information into a multimedia presentation on workstations.

The second category of authoring and viewing tools are alternatively referred to as electronic reference documents, hypertext and hypermedia document collections, and document information bases. One essential feature of these programs is the content indexing and retrieval software used for accessing and adapting text and other content objects from large information sets. When these viewing and navigation tools are used in conjunction with text, graphics, and other editing systems they become excellent vehicles for the delivery of electronic books and periodicals as well as being used for in-house on-line document distribution requirements. See Figure 8.6.

This second class of tools is more suited to document collections including substantial text content in the collection. The tools typically organize information created by a variety of text editors, imaging, and graphics programs as well as other content (video and animation for example). Some tool sets are standards-based so that the information content of the hypermedia collection remains in a neutral format. SGML editors can be used with complementary SGML viewers.

There are many SGML document display and navigation systems including: OLIAS from Hal Software Systems, DynaText from Electronic Book Technologies, Explorer from SoftQuad, and Guide Professional Publisher from InfoAccess Inc. These same tools are used in conjunction with SGML authoring products and they accept SGML and structural navigation as well as full text searches. FolioViews from Folio Corporation is both an authoring and presentation system in its own right. It is an excellent example of an electronic publishing system designed for workgroups.

What are the important criteria to look for when choosing an electronic document browsing system to distribute electronic reference and hypermedia documents? A robust indexing and searching system is indispensable. Some browsers have specialized searching and indexing capabilities that help the developer in organizing information collections and the end user to find and locate information on-line. One advantage of SGML based viewing systems is that users

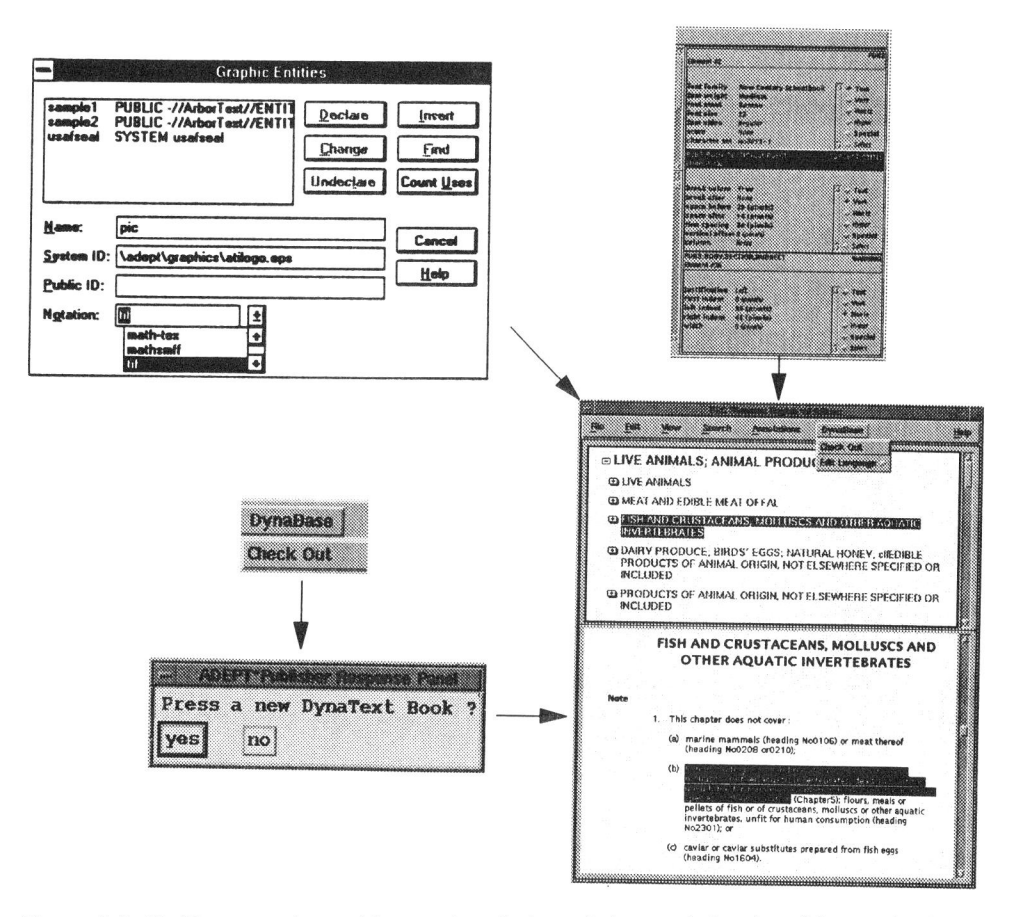

Figure 8.6. To illustrate the making and updating of electronic books with standards-based tools, this diagram shows screen shots that combine product offerings from two leading vendors in electronic publishing, ArborText and Electronic Book Technologies (EBT). Shown at the top left is a sample dialog menu from the ArborText Adept SGML authoring tool. Following the creation and parsing of an SGML encoded document and the suitable identification of graphs and other mixed content elements by use of entity notation, the data is readied for use in an electronic book using EBT's DynaText. A style editor from DynaText (shown at top right) is used to format the SGML structured data for presentation. When the book is completed, the electronic version is stored in EBT's object oriented document database called DynaBase. The book can be checked out for updates and directly edited with the Adept SGML authoring tool. When the editing is finished a new electronic book can be readied for press.

can search on structural tags. See Figure 8.7. Dynamic formatting is another useful feature. Text fills a window and upon command font changes and inline graphics are supported. Browsers that support annotations, bookmarks, highlighting, and hypertext linking, allow users to adapt information further. Platform independence is another useful feature for a browser/viewer. The viewing system of WorldView press for example is portable to different platforms and windowing systems.

Developers and designers of multimedia and electronic reference document collections should strive to:

> ➤ Work within the budgetary and planning guidelines for the project
> ➤ Achieve simplicity in presentation. This includes efforts to keep viewers from getting lost
> ➤ Use audio, full motion video, and animation for content effectiveness, not merely for decoration. A production does not need to have all media content types present to be successful
> ➤ Resist "forcing" use of hypertext transitions except where meaningful
> ➤ Plan the distribution system to end users carefully. End user comfort relies upon the developer's judgment of how the target audience will use the multimedia product

As the design and development of the multimedia effort proceeds, the development group needs to plan reviews of progress and, if necessary, take corrective action to get the project on track. The initial goal should be to prove the concept of the storyboard plan with a prototype model of the design. Developers must constantly place themselves in the position of the end users to judge the effectiveness of the presentation.

One collaborative technique for developing a multimedia presentation is storyboarding. This technique allows for the arrangement of topical ideas and design sketches on boards, pieces of paper, or computer terminals to be displayed on a wall for comment by the team—author, designer, animator, photographer, editor, and other participants. The team encourages mutual support within the framework of the development and production schedule and also in brainstorming sessions. If audio is to be used with animation and video, it is appropriate to begin correlation of sound to the visual sequencing of drawings and other elements and to be integrated into a whole. A storyboard consists of a set of visual elements designed to improve comprehension of the idea being presented. With team brainstorming, some ideas are eliminated. Ideas, images, and other information are salvaged, and the second stage of prototyping the design and content model are begun.

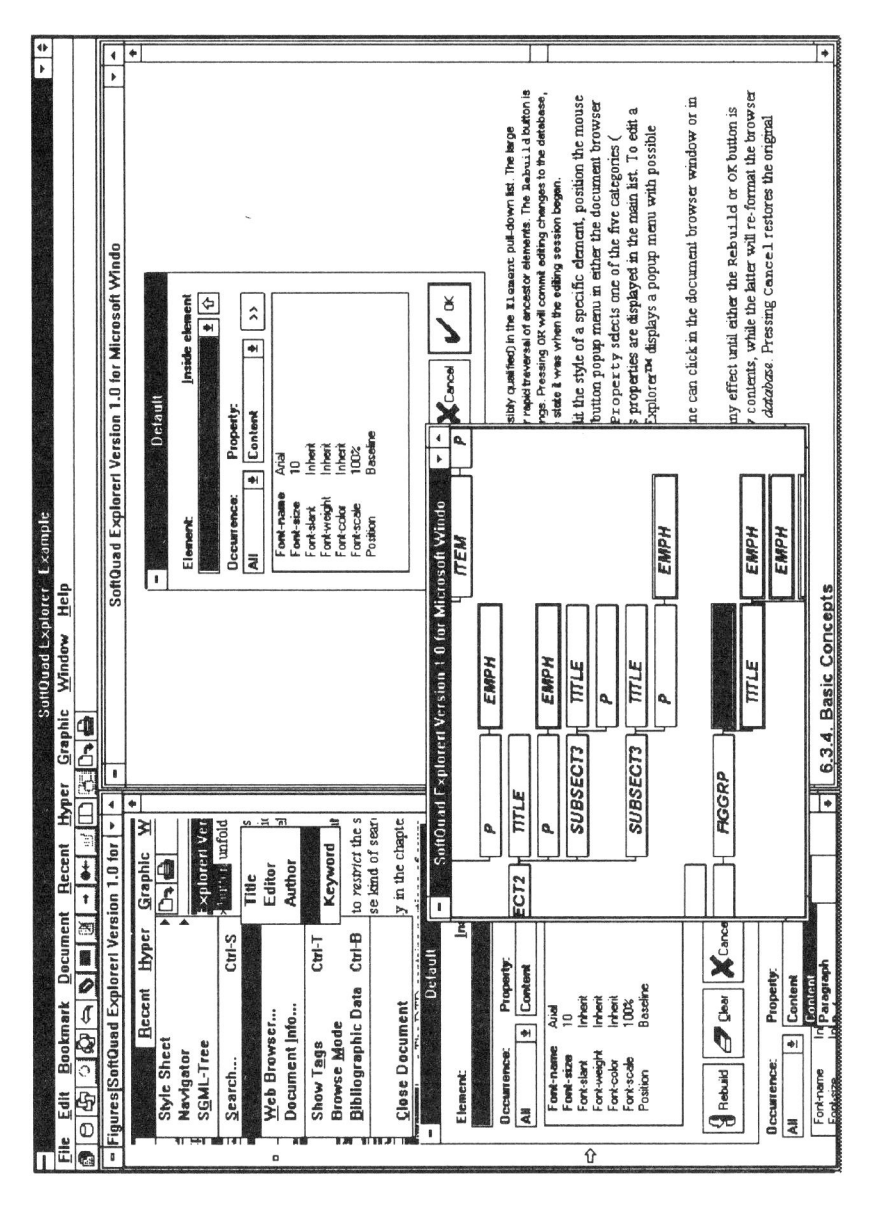

Figure 8.7. Sample screen of the Explorer, an electronic document viewing and navigation tool from SoftQuad. The advantage of an SGML based browsing technology is that it supports structural navigations as well as other searches such as full text queries. Readers can make annotations, bookmarks, and highlights for adaptation of on-line information. Graphics and audio are supported. (Courtesy of SoftQuad, Inc.)

209

Reader/Viewer Participation

Audiences should be invited to play an active role in the development of multimedia projects. The participation could be organized in several different ways. First, if we are developing a multimedia project for an in-house organization or for our outside customers, we should invite the end users into the project so they feel comfortable with the product. For example, if we are developing an on-line service manual that will be used by customer technicians, they should be allowed input to the planning and design of the project. If individuals are restricted from participating by travel constraints, they can still collaborate by telephone, FAX, or network communication. If the user population is broadbased, a sample population might be selected to provide feedback. Second, the developers need to determine if the information needs of the audience have been adequately met. Can the user easily access information? Finally, give the audience the opportunity to add something to the system. This may consist simply of being able to have some printed output from the system for a special purpose or the ability to share information with fellow users. Audiences should be viewed as collaborators in the multimedia development process. Are audiences ready to break away from the traditional model of linear paper publishing to accept multimedia on a large scale? The answer to this question, based upon the steady rise in multimedia usage, is yes. Audiences will be more enthusiastic if they are asked to be part of the process.

Multimedia developers should always keep their audience—the information consumers—in mind when they meld together the disparate content elements into a whole. This refers not only to the way we organize the information for access but also to how we predict the effects certain content types will have on the audience. Video, for example, is a time based medium. If the developers overdo the length of a particular video segment, viewers find it tedious. Inappropriate sound effects can overwhelm an audience. Planning the use of each content type must be carefully thought through.

CONTENT OBJECT ORGANIZATION AND SYNCHRONIZATION

The objects that make up a multimedia collection vary according to the project and presentation requirements, but the information in the presentation can be viewed as a set of objects that have a content file format (SGML, RTF, TIFF, JPEG, MPEG) and that may be linked to one another or to other hyperdocument collections. As collections grow it becomes problematic to index objects within collections for efficient retrieval. A content index of a multimedia and hypertext collections makes information more accessible. Indexing and retrieval systems for text have evolved steadily. Audio, graphics, and video clips are usually retrieved through keywords. There are efforts to establish graphic databases that can be queried by image content. For example, with IBM's Ultimedia Manager2, graphic content can be searched based on color, shape, and texture. Most mixed content models still work with words to retrieve, link, and interchange the collection types. There are also requirements for synchronizing time based content elements (video and audio, for example) and for compressing the size of large objects for storage.

Time Based Content

Among the technologies included in multimedia presentations, we give special attention to three content types that are ready to become part of the mainstream of desktop environments. These content types are desktop audio, animation, and video. Advances in the processing capabilities of desktop platforms along with favorable consumer pricing have attracted developers of tools which support desktop manipulation of these content types.

Multimedia is in its formative stages and consequently there are not firm standards regarding its uses or the hardware and software technology developed to support it. Depending upon the objectives of the multimedia application environment, the devices used to construct a multimedia platform vary. PCs, MACs, and workstation vendors are all in the process of developing configurations for a spectrum of uses. A consortium of companies led by Microsoft, has adopted the Multimedia PC (MPC) specification as a basis for configuring hardware and software applications. Apple has introduced two multimedia ready MAC platforms (Centris 660AV and Quadra 840 AV) that have built in voice, sound, analog and digital video and other interfaces. Silicon Graphics (the Indy) and other workstation vendors are doing the same. Packaging a multimedia ready hardware platform can reduce buyer anxiety about purchasing of special audio boards, microphones, speakers, video boards, communication chips, and storage devices such as CD-ROM and video disks.

Audio

The use of sound within electronic documents adds new dimensions to the communication experience. Sample applications include sound in marketing and training presentations, narrative voice overlays to appropriate animation and video clippings, and musical soundtracks as background to certain presentations.

The use of sound is based upon the conversion of audio signals from analog to digital form so that the information that has been converted into bits and bytes can be processed, edited and stored by computers. A digital to analog conversion (DAC) process allows us to replay the audio information via speakers. The quality of sound depends in large part on the circuitry used in the analog to digital (ADC) and the digital to analog conversion processes. The sampling rate and resolution of the ADC contributes to the quality. Quality here refers to the fidelity of the sound produced through the medium of the desktop computer. The quality of the reproduced sound also depends upon the end user's equipment, a factor that developers of multimedia using audio should not overlook.

There are four types of audio used in multimedia including: disk based digital audio, audio compact disks, interleaved media, and MIDI synthesis. In disk based recording configurations, the desktop computer uses a sound card to record the sound input to disk where it is stored for playback. Digital sound consumes large amounts of storage space, however, which limits the quantity of information to be stored. Interleaving sound with a video track is another technique for bringing it into the multimedia presentation. Special interleaving technology (such as Quicktime and Video for Windows) is used in the synchronization of audio and visual information in a video presentation. Using MIDI synthesis is another possibility for digital audio. Sound is created in real time by sequencing musical events that control a synthesizer. This approach takes little disk space. Finally, CD audio offers the possibility of using high fidelity audio for playback from a CD-ROM drive while the disk drive is used for other information in the multimedia collection, such as graphics, text, and animation. The fidelity is excellent, but it is unlikely that we will find one CD that has all the audio information. We can store different audio segments on high fidelity digital audio tape drive, then take the collection to a service bureau with a CD-recording system that can record the sound collection on CD disks.

Adding a soundtrack to multimedia collections is usually reserved for the final stages of the process. This approach has been adopted in the film industry and it has been imitated by multimedia developers who produce a script, shoot video, and generate appropriate still pictures and animation., and add additional narrative and a music sound track as the very last elements. Synchronization of audio and visual elements is a significant task. For example, putting musical segments together with sequences of visual frames requires precise timing and imagination to bring about the right dramatic effect.

Animation

Animation brings images to life by changing the position of objects in time (motion dynamics) and the structure, texture, and shape of objects, as well as changes in lighting and other techniques. Computer-based animation is used extensively in entertainment, education, and industry. For example, many training programs use animation to simulate skills required by pilots, industrial control system technicians, insurance teleservice agents, or surgeons. Animation is also playing a role in product planning, design, and simulation in architecture and industry. By using animation, architects can simulate the design of the building and allow customers to walk through the design and examine the exterior and interior space of a model in 3D. City planners and zoning specialists can view entire urban development projects and gauge the visual impact of planning decisions. Marketing specialists can use this protodesign information as a sales tool; mechanical engineers can visualize problems in a design concept before expensive prototypes are built; and reliability and quality engineers can analyze for the potential problems which otherwise might escape attention.

Until recently, animation has not been affordable on the desktop because the cost of hardware and software has been excessive. Animation software for the desktop is now flourishing but users in multimedia projects should coordinate with other contributors to ensure successful weaving of the animated material into the fabric of the production. Intensive storyboarding of the animation is required to sequence the visual changes. As with motion video, the timing of each element (lapse of time between frame changes) must synchronize with sound elements (narrator presentation and musical intervals, for instance) and the pacing must help viewers grasp the information intended. For example, if the viewer is being walked through a building the timing should not race from room to room before the eyes have time to adjust.

Interactive Video

Interactive video technology combines the use of video footage, nonlinear digital video editing, and hypermedia linking. The era of desktop video has begun. To develop digital video for the desktop it is necessary to know how the video information will be captured, stored, edited, integrated, and displayed.

Developers of desktop video will capture video using a camcorder video camera or playing pre-recorded material from a VCR or video disc. Prerecorded material includes commercially available video clippings that can be used in multimedia productions. For some systems such as the Silicon Graphics Indy or the Apple Macintosh AV, video capture is simple. The hardware to digitize the video is built into the platform, the user connects the camcorder or VCR into the video port and the video material is ready for editing. With nonvideo ready computers, a video board is used to convert an NSTC video signal into a digital format acceptable for the computer. The best video boards grab video frames in real time. If a camcorder is used for our source video, select one that has time code generation capability where the time code is linked to each frame in the footage. With the time stamp, the editing process and searching for specific frames is less difficult. Without the time code, the editing process can become labor intensive.

Once the video information is captured, it needs to be compressed so that the size of the video frames can be trimmed for storage, processing, and transmission. Developers of desktop video must reduce the size of the video information for storage on disk. One frame of digital video averages about one megabyte of information. There are compression algorithms available that help reduce video data appreciably. The Motion Picture Expert Group (MPEG) standard is the leading model for video compression. Many vendors design their products to use algorithms based upon MPEG.

Nonlinear digital editing of video depends in part upon the efficacy of digital compression schemes. Video editing programs with graphical user interfaces on the MAC, PC, and workstation, already exist for the desktop user to recall any frame of digital video, merge it with frames from other sequences, and create the appropriate footage. When this editing must be done on the outside, the service costs are expensive. Bringing this function under desktop control is a major breakthrough.

What is done with the film information after editing depends upon the overall objective. We may want to take a very small bit of computer video and send it electronically to other workgroup partners of electronic mail. We may include it in a multimedia production on CD-ROM or video disk depending upon circumstances and budget. We use an authoring program to identify content and manage hypermedia linkages within the collections of information in our multimedia database. Authoring programs will accept video stored in a variety of formats including Microsoft's Audio Visual Interleave (AVI) format and Apple's Quicktime. If we want a high quality master copy for full interactive video, we can use the nonlinear edit software to combine different frames so the end user can prepare an edit decision list which is ready for a quality film production on-line editing system. If we are settling for less quality, we can record to tape or CD-ROM directly from disk, and skip the mastering edit process and the data can be output to a VCR or CD-ROM.

Multimedia and Open Information

A model of open information based multimedia provides reusability and interchangeability of data among computer platforms. Such an approach allows for a consistent representation of the data including the links between documents to be processed by different applications. A common information base can be shared by independent applications processing the data for presentation.

Hypermedia Interchange Standard: HyTime

Many hypermedia and electronic reference document applications are platform dependent. Authoring and presentation programs can restrict the portability and reusability of information in multimedia collections. One proposed solution is the Hypermedia/Time-based Structuring Language (HyTime, ISO/IEC 10744), a standard for the neutral representation of hypermedia data. Its objective is to provide hyperdocument interchange between applications and preserve the links that are made between documents and document objects when the information is exchanged. HyTime, which is based upon SGML, does not try to account for all possible ways that the data can be processed and presented. HyTime standardizes the methods of addressing the parts of hyperdocuments and the multimedia objects that populate them by linking, alignment, and synchronization. In using SGML, the content model includes character data and entity references to graphics and other mixed content through notation declarations. HyTime uses the SGML entity manager to help locate information types in the collection.

An example of the successful implementation of HyTime is the Interactive Electronic Technical Manual (IETMs) model sponsored by the U.S. Department of Defense. The IETMs are used to help technicians maintain complicated aircraft, weapon systems, ships, and submarines. Studies show that it takes technicians less time to diagnose and repair complex equipment with the use of computer based documentation than with paper documents. Working with paper can be a hindrance for two reasons. First, the bulk of the technical documentation (sometimes multivolumes) makes searching for information awkward and difficult. The Navy, for example, has a special logistic problem with the sheer weight and size of documents required for maintenance of systems on the ship. By putting the information on-line, the Navy can free up space on ships. Second, a technician using paper documents must access the information on a page by page basis even though it may be helpful to branch across documents or chapters for simultaneous access or viewing of correlated information. A technical manual on a jet fighter may contain information on the operation and maintenance of many components in the aircraft including its instrument, flight control, and weapon systems. The operation and maintenance information related to such systems make up the content collections upon which the interactive manuals are based. Suppliers of equipment on new development programs for DoD are now required to deliver text documents in SGML, vector graphics in CGM or IGES, and bitmap graphics in CCITT-IV format.

The technicians using the IETMs need accurate and complete information to perform critical tasks in diagnosing and correcting problems promptly and efficiently. To help vendors of equipment deliver IETMs, the defense department has issued standards for the creation of these interactive electronic documents based upon HyTime and SGML. One of the standards, Mil-M-87268, defines content, style and presentation for IETMs. The second standard, Mil-D87269, addresses the architecture of revisable IETM source data.

Trouble analysis for complex systems requires a technician to follow a series of procedures in diagnosing problems related to equipment or system performance. The procedures cover a gamut of fault isolation, troubleshooting, and corrective maintenance. When a failure occurs, the technician will sequence through fault isolation procedures, and to other sub procedures and diagrams, to remove, replace, and/or repair a faulty part. The test procedure is presented in the traditional format of a troubleshooting tree.

With a paper representation of the troubleshooting tree, the technician normally has to turn to a variety of different pages scattered through the elaborate procedure. There are cross references to wiring diagrams and mechanical drawings that illustrate how to assemble and disassemble various parts of a system. These drawings may be scattered through other volumes of the technical manual that comprise the rigid page bound structure of its contents. The disadvantage to the technician is the effort that is necessary to search back and forth through various pages and volumes to find the cross referenced information.

An on-line version of the document, by contrast, has distinct advantages. The end user can look at a troubleshooting tree by clicking a synchronized table of contents, buttons, or graphic "hot" zones, instantly bringing onto the computer screen multiple windows of the diagrams, test procedures, mechanical assembly and disassembly drawings, and related parts information required to complete the specific troubleshooting procedures. A computer terminal with windows technology allows the technician to display and juxtapose information that would have to be found by turning pages back and forth in technical maintenance manuals. Figure 8.8 diagrams an interactive technical manual process.

Interactive Multimedia Association (IMA) On Compatibility

One of the problems of creating an international standard for multimedia is that it takes a very long time to generate and approve standards. The Interactive Multimedia Association (IMA) is a trade association that includes some of North America's most prestigious companies among its members. IMA and its members are trying to establish working standards in a compressed time frame. Various workgroups within the IMA are addressing problems related to compatibility, intellectual property, and technology convergence. The compatibility project addresses means for exchanging data across computer platforms. In a vote among the participating members two technologies: Open Media Framework Interface from Avid Technologies and Bento from Apple have been selected for data interchange and storage format. In another development, Hewlett Packard, IBM, and Sun Microsystems, Inc., have introduced a technology called multimedia services (MSS) that provides operating system level information to an application about the multimedia capabilities of a workstation.

DOCUMENT DELIVERY MECHANISMS

To be successful, multimedia applications must reach a target audience in a convenient and economical manner. How do the users receive the information? Developers and publishers of multimedia within organizations can choose from a variety of storage media or send the collections across a network. Hypermedia col-

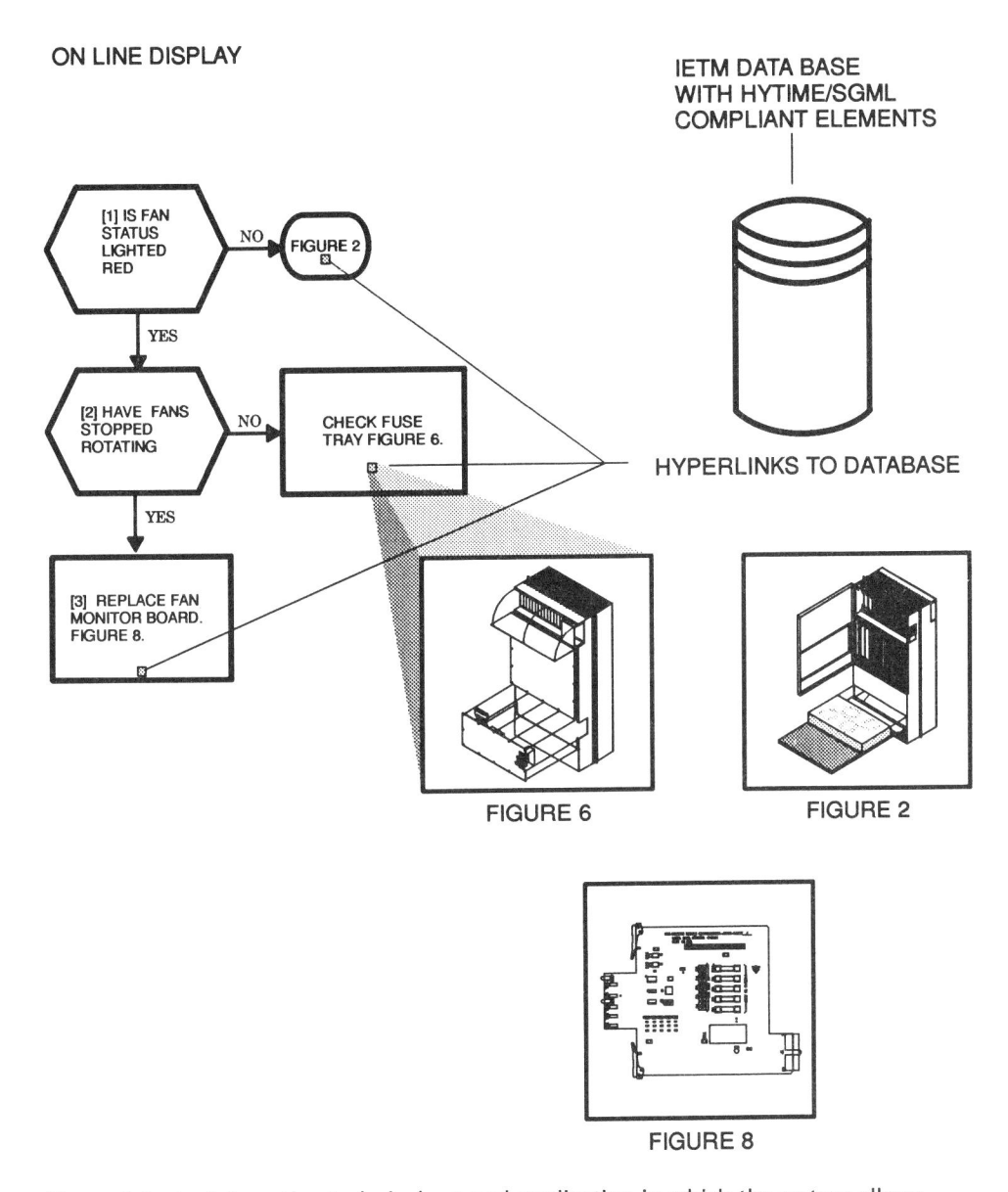

Figure 8.8. An interactive technical manual application in which the system allows non-linear branching to other parts of the interactive maintenance database depending on the context of the technician's work. When the technician uses a control pointer and clicks on a hyperlink button or graphics hot zone, the display screen opens a window that shows an illustration, table, video, or other relevant information that will solve the maintenance problem.

lections can now be economically recorded and distributed on various media. The choice of media for delivery of a multimedia application depends upon specific technical constraints of the developers and the targeted recipients of the information. The same applies to networked distribution.

CD-ROM Publishing

Delivering multimedia titles on optical media has become more affordable with the arrival of CD-Recordable (CD-R) drives for the desktop. Until recently, organizations wanting to record information on CD-ROM had to use a service company that had recording equipment. Organizations can now buy CD-Rs for under 10,000 dollars. The choice to buy a CD-R drive for in-house or to go outside to a service bureau depends upon several factors. First, the in house approach may be better if a low volume production and distribution of CD-ROM copies is desired. (The low cost CD-R drives typically create one copy at a time. The cost of blank CD disks is falling as demand rises).

The disks from the CD-R produce files in ISO 9660 standard format that normal CD-ROM players can read. The data is read form a hard disk and copied to a blank disk. Developers of multimedia titles can use CD-Rs for two purposes. First, they can generate premaster or beta versions of their work to test the timing and integration of elements. Once satisfied with the quality of draft developments, the producers can take their work to a service bureau for final production. Using CD-Rs to test integration and synchronization of elements can save time and money and eliminate extra handling costs which are charged by service bureaus to debug problems off site. The second use of CD-Rs is to produce quantities of CD-Rs for delivery to customers. Organizations and small publishers will be able to deliver customized sets of multimedia by pressing CD-ROMs rather than using a service bureau.

The advantage of CD-ROM disks is their large storage capacity (up to 700 Mb). Practical delivery of encyclopedic scale information would not be possible without optical disk technologies such as CD-ROM and video disks. Conventional CD-ROM systems provide read-only access to stored information. The advantage of read-only distribution to those who are furnishing the information is that the end users can not change the official record of the delivered documentation. There are many programs that offer the end user means to annotate collections of on-line documentation that they are reading.

Delivery of Multimedia over Networks

Many multimedia applications are designed for the single user desktop environment which limits the access of many players. There are ways that allow many users to access a multimedia program from a CD-ROM based server over a LAN. There are also ways to exchange multimedia objects across the Internet. Another step in multimedia for networks is underway in metropolitan pilot programs for interactive multimedia and video on-demand services. Through the telephone companies, cable companies, and computer vendors, the infrastructure of communications as we know it is being redefined. Interactive multimedia will become a key part of the service architecture of these networks.

On-line Hypermedia Authoring and Viewing on the Internet

As we saw in Chapter 7, the Internet is a world wide computer network. The Internet gives access to supercomputers with information as widely varied as weather satellite images of the earth and periodicals. Users share and exchange documents and participate in a great variety of news groups. The World Wide Web (WWW) started in 1989 in Bern, Switzerland as a hypertext system by which physicists could share information. A guiding principle behind the Web was the concept of universal readership. It is now the largest hypertext system in existence. As the Web evolved, a supercomputer center at the University of Illinois developed a browsing tool called Mosaic. Refer to Figure 8.9. This freeware tool allows users of different windowing systems (X-Windows, MS-Windows, and Macintosh) to explore documents available from different servers and supercomputers on the Internet. The Mosaic browser uses graphical user interface technology to provide information discovery and retrieval. Plain text, formatted text, hypertext, graphs, audio clips, video images, and documents can be displayed. Other browsers for the Internet include Cello and Chimera.

Meanwhile other companies such as SoftQuad have developed authoring tools for the Internet. HotMetal, the name of SoftQuad's Internet authoring product, can be used to create documents. SoftQuad has established an agreement with NCSA for integrating HotMetal with Mosaic. The Hypertext Markup Language (HTML) is used for authoring on the World Wide Web. HTML is an SGML Document Type Definition and the markup defined by the DTD can be used by authors on the web. A variety of commercial and scholarly publishers are making their publications available on the WWW. To provide information to the WWW, content providers set up servers that understand the HyperText Transfer Protocol (HTTP). Authors use an HMTL authoring tool such as HoTmetal from SoftQuad or convert documents to HTML with a conversion program. Documents are read by a browser like Mosaic and they are identified by Uniform Resource Locators (URLs). A URL identifies the location of objects including documents on the WWW.

In addition to specific developments on the Internet, new telecommunication technologies are emerging that support bandwidth hogging multimedia applications. The most promising of these technologies is ATM (previously described in Chapter 7). Since multimedia data collections can be quite large, sufficient bandwidth must be available and reliable data compression standards must be used to make wide area multimedia applications possible. Distance learners will take part

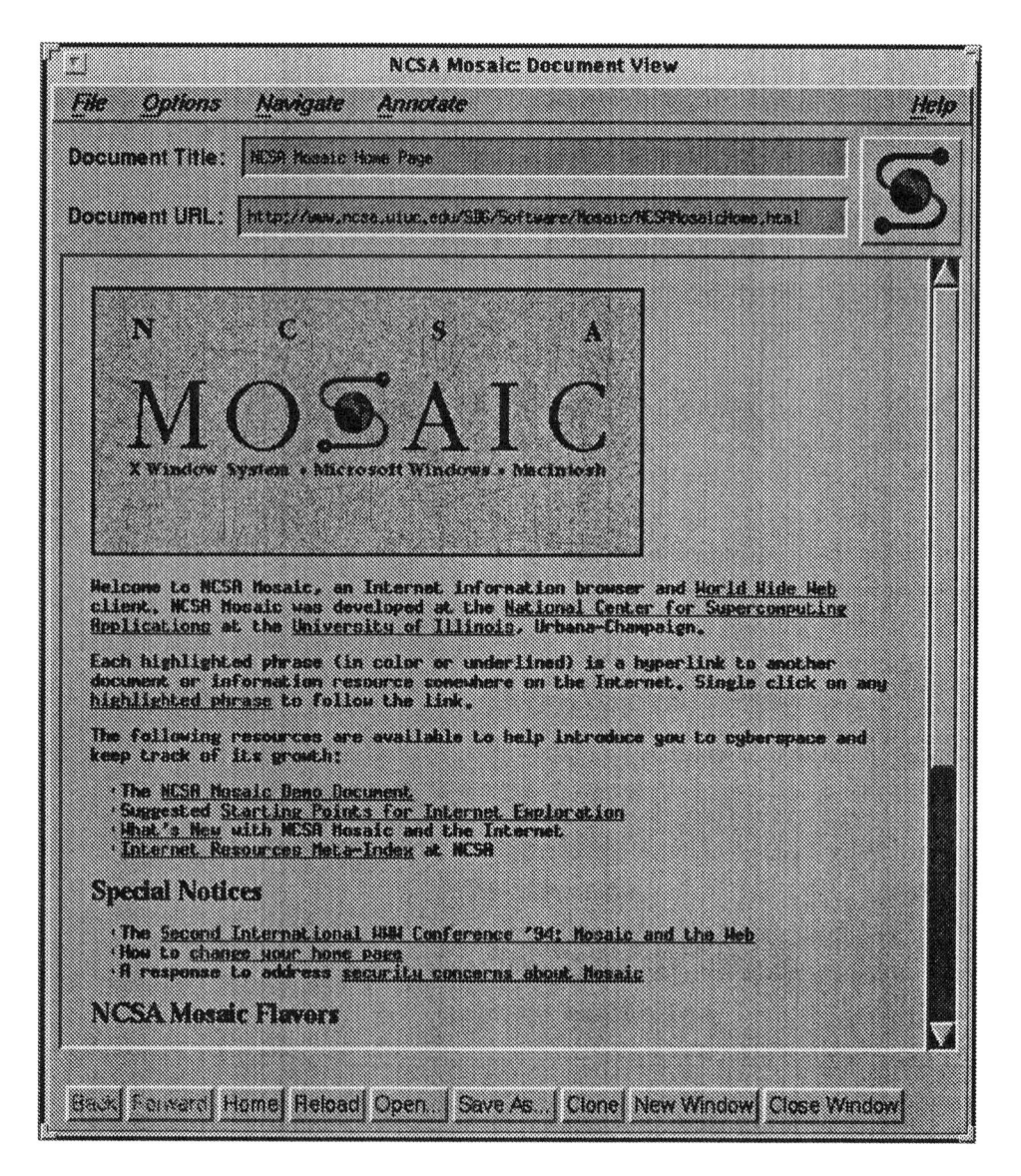

Figure 8.9. The home page of Mosaic, an information browser for the Internet, developed by the National Center for Supercomputing Applications (NCSA) at the University of Illinois. As a client of the World Wide Web, Mosaic is an example of how hypermedia can be used by collaborating groups to share information over wide area networks. Highlighted phrases (shown underlined in the screen shot) are hyperlinks to other documents or information resources. Documents are identified by title and a Uniform Resource Locator (URL) showing where the document can be accessed on the WWW.

in interactive classroom programming by connecting to large computers that provide expert instruction as well as coursework lookup; telecommuting workers will communicate with workgroups remotely from their homes as if they were at the office and; customers will shop through on-line services and multimedia yellow pages; and surgeons will advise colleagues long distance about complicated surgical procedures using visual and voice messages in real time. The distance between work, home, school, libraries, and entertainment centers will narrow.

Interactive multimedia on demand will popularize multimedia communication for a mass audience. End users will face information overload with the expansion of channels of information available to a mass audience. All multimedia users must plan for is the future to access, exchange, and organize information in a way that insulates participants from getting lost in the information surge. The Mosaic is a good beginning navigational tool that operates on a world wide network. Using HMTL is also a positive step in defining the importance of interoperability for a data highway. Document management and database technologies will furnish the means for organizing large scale multimedia libraries.

Developers of multimedia and organizations who plan to use the technology can learn from the way providers of on-line information services do business. Examples such as LEXIS-NEXIS from Mead Data Central represent a model for information service provision in specific fields of law and news. Although these services are mainly providing access to text, the evolution of on-line information service will include interactive video services for education, news, business, medicine and other fields. These services use intelligent search programs and document management strategies that help users access and retrieve needed information.

Ambitious models for on-line information services include digital libraries which are in their infancy. The fastest growing base in digital libraries of the future will be vast collections of multimedia objects. The challenge is to build an infrastructure which allows many players to enjoy service while protecting the interests of stakeholders who provide information in various collections. The electronic superhighway is part of that infrastructure. For companies seeing a need to provide or receive information on-line for various purposes, the time to plan the future is now.

INTELLECTUAL PROPERTY RIGHTS

There are two aspects to intellectual property worth noting. One issue relates to patents claimed by developers of multimedia technologies. The other intellectual property concern is tied to the ownership of the content base of the multimedia collection and the desire to copyright that information.

In November, 1993, Compton's NewMedia sent a bombshell through the multimedia development community by announcing its multimedia search patent No. 5,241,671 which treats searches for interrelated text and graphics information.

Reaction to the patent announcement has been largely negative. Developers are being asked either to enter into an agreement with Compton or pay them a royalty if they use certain techniques in their development. Whether or not Compton will take steps to enforce its patent claim is not clear, but there will be other problems with claims before the future of multimedia can be assured.

Intellectual property also extends to the content of the information distributed. Copyright as we know it applies mainly to the world of print. Intellectual property relates to ownership of pieces of paper. There are many law firms in the U.S. working on solutions to the intellectual property problem which relates not only to multimedia, but to electronic publishing as a whole and to digital library systems as well. Most observers point to precedents in the film and musical recording industries as models. Legal specialists may benefit from the current methods used to copyright musical recordings or video cassette reproductions. Much work remains to be done in this area. In any case, developers of multimedia productions must diligently seek permission to use content before production. To be on the safe side, be sure to consult your lawyer before plunging.

Opportunities for Entrepreneurs

Commercial publishers (books, newspapers, and periodicals) are exploring the market potential of electronic and multimedia publishing. Educational and entertainment publishing is rich with opportunities for content providers and multimedia producers. Reference works continue to be an attractive market for multimedia publishing. With more robust viewing and indexing tools available, such as those provided by DynaText and WorldView, commercial publishers can provide feature-rich resources for searching complex sets of information. Vertical markets in medical, legal, and financial publishing have real potential for growth. Multimedia narrowcasting for sports, political, and environmental journalism are excellent areas for commercial specialization.

There are also opportunities for printing companies and service bureaus who can capitalize on their knowledge of digital imaging technologies, photo processing, and electronic data conversion. Both can branch into services such as creating CD-ROM masters. New production businesses shaped around knowledge of audio, video, and animation are very promising. Consulting firms can engage corporate and government clients in advising

Commercial and in-house publishers need to evaluate costs not only of tools but of royalty arrangements charged by distributors of run time licenses of viewing and browsing technologies. Due care must also be spent in evaluating the right tools to do the job.

CHAPTER 9

➤ *Process reengineering*

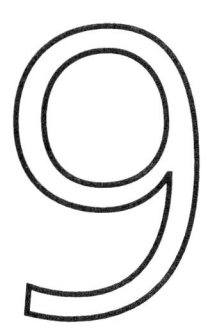

➤ *Benchmarking the process*

➤ *Workgroups and workflow*

➤ *Reengineering the information chain*

Reengineering the Document Process

Why should organizations examine processes as they introduce new technology? One reason is that the increased productivity expected with computer technology is often unrealized when organizations simply automate the existing processes instead of examining and changing them. In his original manifesto, Michael Hammer a chief exponent of reengineering explained why organizations should not continue to automate existing processes.

"It is time to stop paving the cow paths. Instead of embedding outdated processes in silicon and software, we should obliterate them and start over. We should "reengineer" our businesses: use the power of modern information technology to radically redesign our business processes in order to achieve dramatic improvements in their performance." (*Harvard Business Review*, July–August 1990, 104)

According to Hammer, the problem is not easy to fix because people in organizations often forget that processes even exist. They are preoccupied with organizational charts and the command and control management stereotype structures inherited from the industrial age. The information age requires a different approach. Real workflow in organizations, including those with sophisticated computers, frequently goes uncharted because it cuts across the boundaries of traditional departments.

What is a business process? As defined by Hammer, it is a set of activities that results in something of value for a customer. People don't think about processes that accomplish work in organizations because they have been conditioned to think and act within organizational structures and departments.

ELECTRONIC PUBLISHING: CATALYST FOR PROCESS CHANGE

Most people agree that electronic publishing is a revolutionary technology. Much attention has focused upon an assumption that word processing and desktop publishing technology reduces production costs related to making print documents. This has narrowed the focus of the process to creating and composing pages for print. Electronic publishing and document management technologies have radically expanded capabilities for producers and users to access and distribute information. The growth of networks and workgroup computing has combined individuals from different departments into nontraditional workgroups within organizations. But making process changes needed to get the full benefit of the technology is difficult for many companies to assess.

There is more to automation than speeding up an existing process. When faced with complex processes such as those associated with documentation in organizations, we need a fresh response to basic questions. What is our business purpose? Who are the customers? Does the customer need the documents we distribute? How does the customer use the information in the documents? How do our documents help the customer's organization achieve its business purpose? Does information in documents also help members of our company do their work better? How can that information distribution be accelerated or be kept up to date? What information in our documents is reused by others in the organization collaborating on related projects? How many departments are involved in the documentation process? Do individuals from different departments offer input to how the process works? What roadblocks prevent us from achieving our goals? These and many other questions should be considered in redesigning an organization's information workflow.

Power of Technology

Information technology dramatizes the shortcomings of existing methods in the workplace that lead to poor return on investment in this very technology. Economist Lester Thurow notes that the rate of return on investment for office automation has been well below that of equivalent investment for manufacturing processes. Process reengineering can help change that rate. It also lets us break old rules. By reengineering the processes related to documents, some organizations find they are not only improving productivity in functional publication areas but are bringing products to market on time and making government services more effective.

Power of Competition

Understanding the competitive uses of information technology makes organizations more productive and effective in a global marketplace. Reengineering can make an organization world class. When the use of electronic publishing tools is contemplated, consider how they will help provide innovative and effective use of information resources in a competitive market. A critical aspect of bringing products to market on time and delivering effective services is enabling group access to appropriate information.

Focus on Customers

It is essential that process reengineering focus on customer needs and what a customer wants from our documents. We must determine who the customers are including those within and those external to the organization. Information specialists and managers must rethink the process of information flow as it branches throughout an organization from points of origin to final encapsulation in various documents. Communication is what documents are all about and we need to be cognizant of how we communicate with customers.

REENGINEERING DOCUMENTS

The Quality Movement versus Reengineering

Because both quality and reengineering teams focus upon process, the objectives and methods should not be confused. Various types of continuous improvement and employee participation programs such as Quality Circles and Total Quality Management (TQM) are used to improve, enhance, or modify an organization's processes. Reengineering is more radical—looking at a process beginning with a blank slate. In some cases, the reengineering team may abolish an existing process and start over.

The quality movement in the U.S. can take credit for changing organizational attitudes about process and the importance of quality to customers. The quality movement has also helped organizations appreciate the value of groups communicating with one another in nonadversarial settings. Each employee contributes to the process. In cases where companies already have employee participation and quality programs, such forums can be used to analyze process problems related to documents.

Obstacles to Reengineering

The employees and managers of many organizations focus upon the narrow goals of a department as opposed to the business process as a whole. The industrial age command and control management model is intended to ensure that all the fragmented pieces of assembly line approach to production came together in a product. Management makes all the decisions regarding job structure and tasks. Each employee has a circumscribed set of tasks to perform. Without management control of fragmented processes, chaos would result. Bureaucracy justifies itself, because productivity ceases without it. Employees accept the legitimacy of the status quo and abandon new ideas and initiatives.

In a reengineered organization all employees must make decisions, not just the boss. Reinventing processes requires collaboration. Collaborative teams are encouraged to share information, ideas, and problem solving responsibility. The traditional paradigm for organizational departments is the vertical tree with departmental managers at the top of functional fiefdoms. By contrast, horizontally integrated organizations traverse functional boundaries, share and adapt information, and work in concert.

Organizations frequently misunderstand what documents do for a business and may think they have solved document problems by investing in word processing and desktop publishing technologies. In many cases these tools have streamlined one aspect of a publishing production process—document layout and print production. Many organizations, however, have missed the all important connection between critical information processes and documents. Learning to channel that information to desktops is a central theme of document reengineering schemes. A basis for reengineering documents is to foster productive knowledge sharing so that individuals can do many things more efficiently with collaborative technology.

Typically, the workflow of a publishing process does not coincide with the boundaries of individual departments. Successful workgroup publishing crosses the boundaries of traditional departments. Workgroups include members from many departments who contribute and access information with desktop tools. Michael Hammer uses the image of the business diamond to convey how the linkage works between process, jobs and structure, management, and cultural values. He notes that the structure of an organization should follow naturally from the processes or real workflow within an organization.

Cultural Values, Process Change, and Timing

Changing the culture of an organization means changing values. Consider what some of these value changes are—not treating business partners or customers as adversaries, accepting what the customer wants as a primary objective of work as opposed to the secondary objective of pleasing the boss, and recognizing that it is the customer who pays the salaries. Changes take time. It is difficult to alter values overnight. Employee roles change from controlled to empowered. Employees learn to work together for the good of the whole because they fail or succeed together.

It is possible is to initiate process change when a company is making new business plans to start a new research and development project or launch other new services. Another possibility is to reengineer processes when the opportunities arise to invest in new technologies.

Examining the Process

A guideline for examining the process of creating, using, and distributing documents is not a blueprint for all organizations. A team should be formed that can meet regularly and reengineer a process. A manageable team of between five and ten people should include participants from all groups that contribute to the publishing process and are the process "insiders." There should be representatives who are "outside" the process who may or may not work in the organization. A facilitator or captain is needed to move a group toward the objective. Start with a diagram of existing processes, looking for bottlenecks and problem areas. Critical factors to be examined include:

- ➤ Customer needs
- ➤ Defining accountability and process ownership
- ➤ Fragmentation in the process and division of labor
- ➤ Delays and use of tools
- ➤ Duplication of effort
- ➤ Related business processes
- ➤ Dramatic improvements

Reengineering the process often means scrapping the existing process altogether. Abandoning a dysfunctional process may be easier than fixing it. Begin by defining output (a specific document or class of documents). The value of a document type, for example, must be determined. How does it help the customer? What is its value relative to its cost? Does it need to be a certain length? Can the information be reused? Next, examine the information sources of the document type. Does the information originate with subject matter experts beyond the immediate departments producing the document? Who is responsible for generating this information? How often does the information change over time and how are the changes managed? If desktop technology is used, how does a document or slices of information that make a document get from one desktop to another? These are sample questions that can be asked.

Process reengineering of documents and related information processes can only be done in organizations that have a top down management backing for the idea. In information intensive industries, documents are inextricably bound with many processes. Selling the idea, making converts, and getting the word out takes diplomacy, dedication, commitment. Leaders need to obtain grass roots support for a reengineering initiative. Communication of reengineering goals is of utmost importance.

Reengineering documentation efforts go hand in hand with customer communication. Suppose the marketing, publication, marketing communications, and proposal writing departments of a company decide to reengineer related publishing processes. The long range goal is to improve the timeliness, usefulness, and cost of proposals, product literature, and assorted customer documents. The short term goal is to focus upon the proposal process and how it can be streamlined. By attacking this process first, the team hopes to learn more about tackling other documents related to customer communication. While brainstorming through the proposal process, a steady stream of good ideas, (not all of which are directly related to the proposal process), are recorded and reserved for later use on similar reengineering initiatives. Some of those reserve ideas can be reintroduced when those related processes are scrutinized.

DOCUMENT REENGINEERING OPPORTUNITIES

Watching the Paper Chase

A division of a major Fortune 500 company has a centralized reprographics center which leases two high-end large copiers ($48,000 per year). Distributed throughout the building are four high speed copiers ($6,000 per year), and eleven smaller copiers ($7,000 per year). The total lease cost for these copiers is $60,000 per year for five years excluding cost of paper and chemicals. Meanwhile the company has purchased thirty laser printers spread across the company ranging in value from $1,500 to $7,000 dollars apiece for a total cost of $98,000 dollars. What is the company getting for its business investment in copiers and laser printers? When workers wish to share information with their colleagues they march up to the nearest copier, make copies, and distribute them accordingly. The central copy center is used for large copy runs of proposals, manuals, test reports, and assorted other documents. The distributed copiers are used for local copying convenience.

Upon further analysis it appears that reliance on paper copies as a method of distributing information is symptomatic of a larger problem. The company is wasting more than paper. A reengineering work team is established to consider the cost and expense of updating and distributing paper documents in the company. They collect data related to the updating and distribution of specific documents: manufacturing test procedures, repair manuals, product specifications, and product data sheets. In one case they found that the company was distributing updated repair manuals for its aviation product line to customers around the world each year at a cost of 240,000 dollars. This figure included printing and associated material costs and not the additional expenses for updating the repair manuals.

Meanwhile, the company has research and development programs underway in five key businesses, but mainly uses paper to share information on many of those products. Although it has a first rate network infrastructure, computers on every desktop, and many word processing and desktop publishing packages, the company has not solved file format incompatibilities which stymie reuse of electronic document information.

The group analyzed various business processes related to the use of paper and information in the organization. They wanted to determine the value added to the process by conveying the information on paper. They even studied specific cases to determine how long it took participants to find documents and extract information after time elapsed from the paper copy transaction. The group accumulated sufficient evidence that confirmed excessive paper waste, misuse of copiers, and fragmented processes relying on information stored in miscellaneous electronic and paper file cabinets.

The reengineering team based the findings of its initial report on those documents and associated business processes which had been selected for analysis and review. Among other recommendations, the group suggested that the aviation publication department pursue delivery of electronic documents to its customers since the aviation industry has begun shifting its requirements from paper to electronic document distribution.

The reengineering group followed its initial investigations with a more thorough analysis of a trail of paper flow within one product line which makes intensive use of documents. After measuring the total internal paper distribution for a period of a month and examining related business processes, the group observed that critical document information is often hard to find. When critical information is needed, a searcher of the information must often use word of mouth to determine if relevant documents exist or not. In many cases the searcher will contact the author of a document to obtain a paper or electronic copy. The information in the paper document is sometimes out of sync with the paper document in a cabinet file folder. The electronic copy can be in a variety of file formats and may reside on many different computers which makes the document information inaccessible. The net result of inefficient use of processes and technology is the hidden cost of many overlapping business processes.

Process Recommendations

After a period of disentangling a web of process interrelationships, the reengineering group came up with its recommended process improvements:

- Establish a coherent process flow that accounts for the entire document life cycle
- Direct authors, editors, and others engaged in documents to standardize file formats to promote ease of document interchange. Investigate conversion to standard interchange models including SGML
- Index documents created by the company in a document library accessible by relevant workers
- Reconcile the electronic document versions with print versions
- Reengineer management information and reprographics centers around a concept of on-demand publishing; focus on retrieving information from a common document database

Potential Technology Improvements

Candidate technologies for improving many information processes at the company include:

- An electronic document viewing, indexing, and distribution system for use as a rapid information retrieval system by engineering, marketing, manufacturing, quality, and publishing personnel
- Document management and workflow management systems. These systems allow the control of workflow from desktop to desktop
- Demand printer that could be used to make high speed copies of proposals and other documents in the copy center. Demand printers can accept jobs across the network and eliminate difficult last minute collation of documents from a master. The large copier could be phased out as the evolutionary use of the demand printer proceeds. The reprographics center staff can be retrained to use the demand system facilitating user requests and turning more attention to the quality of the output

These technologies cannot correct process problems, but they can assist in handling the details of managing a large body of documents and the information they contain. Getting information to the right desktops on time becomes the principal guideline for technology acquisition. Applying appropriate workflow technologies can also assist managers and other players to streamline processes and improve communications across functional disciplines. Breaking dependency upon paper is difficult, but the reengineering team advocates training seminars and work shops to explain the concept of on-demand information and printing. Members of the reprographics center, the information services department, and other organizations will play a central role together in the reengineered process. Many of the players from these departments had never before worked together as a team, because of traditional barriers erected between departments.

Success Story: Mutual Fund Company

A mutual fund company has used process reengineering techniques to revamp its annual report generation and distribution process. According to Securities and Exchange Commission (SEC) regulations, the report must be delivered to subscribers at predetermined intervals. Although the company met its legal deadlines, it wanted to eliminate inefficiencies that added up to unnecessary costs in order to comply with the schedule. Symptoms of process problems included correcting data errors and controlling lead times for external typesetting. When the company finally put the shareholding reporting process under scrutiny, various inefficiencies became increasingly apparent such as:

- Delays in shareholder reporting
- Process fragmentation
- Multiple handoffs in workflow, delays, and errors
- External typesetting costs and lead times

Reengineering requires bold initiatives and the company began by hiring a process leader who had a background in process management. The process leader established a reengineering team. After analyzing the existing process, the team decided to reinvent it. The objective was to design a cost effective process that helped meet legal shareholder reporting deadlines without sacrificing quality. The team compared their shareholder reporting performance against competitors in terms of meeting shareholder report delivery schedules and overall report quality. To get an accurate picture of the scope of the report generation effort, the team measured its annual volume of documents produced, the page count of those documents, and the total volume of printing and mailing distribution. This data was used to give the team a way to measure unit costs for their current processes. These statistics offered an invaluable baseline to compare results of future innovations.

In designing a new process, the team focused on ways to:

- Reduce time of review and editing
- Establish ownership and accountability for the process
- Reorganize groups contributing to the process

The redesign of the process involved streamlining the use of technology. To eliminate handoffs, the reengineering team saw a need to reorganize the process, workflow, and the organization supporting the process. The team also found a key role for electronic publishing technology to reduce duplication of effort in report generation. It accepted the relatively new electronic publishing paradigm of separating document form and content. It so happened that much of the data or content that appeared in reports already existed on computers in accounting and other databases. In the existing process, there was a great deal of duplicate manual entry of data, that is, rekeying of identical information into different computers. This duplicate entry included the retyping of financial data into report documents by external typesetting operators. The reengineering team saw an opportunity to eliminate this redundant effort since most of the content in the report originated in accounting databases. Electronic publishing technologies linked numerical tables in the database to formatting templates in an electronic publishing system. This not only eliminated the costly reentry of the data but reduced the chance of errors of the duplicate entry. Since each time the data is rekeyed, another set of editing checks needs to be performed, the additional editing effort contributed to costly delays. With the new electronic publishing system, the format of the document is controlled by templates. A large portion of the document's content is automatically loaded into the template from the content database. The electronic publishing system with its special database publishing interface was purchased to streamline the reengineered process.

The reengineering effort resulted in substantial savings for the company. The company saved $800,000 per year by eliminating external typesetting costs. It has also decreased overall delivery time of shareholder reports. Perhaps most importantly, the company received positive feedback from its shareholders. The reengineering team continues its efforts to improve the process.

Reengineering Document Processes with Standards

An aerospace company found that reengineering documents around standards not only helped the company meet the demands of its customers but also helped save money in several critical business processes. By reengineering document and information processes together, as well as introducing concurrent engineering practices, the company's research and development and manufacturing teams began to bring projects to market on time along with the information to support those projects.

Sometimes the inspiration for change comes from unexpected places. We don't expect creative ideas and models to come from the federal government, but a Department of Defense (DoD) program called Computer Aided Acquisition and Logistics Support or CALS has sponsored a bevy of innovative approaches to connecting business process and information technology. One of the principal ideas in the CALS program has been to reduce the amount of paper flow between suppliers of documentation to the federal government. To standardize the electronic document information to be exchanged with the DoD on weapons programs, the CALS group pushed for standardized data transfer between defense contractors and government agencies. It has, for example, promulgated the use of electronic interchange and interoperability standards such as SGML, CGM, CCITT group 4, and IGES. Consequently, the CALS program launched the most advanced modeling of electronic publishing and information integration in the world. But the work of CALS did not stop with a definition of standards to be used and advancement of information technologies. CALS revolutionizes the way defense contractors and DoD agencies do business. The CALS message is that companies need to alter their own processes to support this new partnership.

When DoD contractors first learned of CALS there were two basic reactions. The first was from companies who claimed that they wanted a contract in hand that required them to comply with specific CALS requirements before they would buy into CALS. In effect, these companies saw nothing in CALS for themselves; it was mainly the government who benefited.

Other companies, like the aerospace company in our case study, saw an opportunity in CALS. Since this company listened to its main customer (the federal government) and studied the direction the customer was going, it learned enough from CALS to make a profit on it. The company concluded that the fundamental premise of CALS, more efficient life cycle management of information, made sense not only for its customer but for itself too. As the company thought through cost-effective ways of complying with CALS requirements, it saw opportunities for creating products, consulting services, and business partnerships. The company developed software programs that can help other organizations deliver information compliant with CALS standards such as the SGML based Interactive Electronic Technical Manual. A small consulting services group was spawned by the company to help other companies struggling to meet CALS requirements. The company began reselling the expertise it acquired in document and data interchange in CALS to companies in commercial nondefense markets. The aerospace company got on board with CALS to satisfy its major customer, but it reengineered its business by using process techniques such as concurrent engineering and electronic document interchange recommended under CALS. Even in an era of dwindling federal expenditures for new military systems, the company found it could compete better by having its own information base for engineering development, quality, manufacturing, logistics, data managment, and publications using open standards for information exchange. Use of paper for distribution within the company has been reduced dramatically.

With CALS, DoD defines a radically different working relationship between contractor and customer. Contractors who implement CALS will likely reengineer their business processes. To their credit, CALS planners saw the need to address problems of process change and use of standards as essential to the successful information integration within an enterprise. By advising and requiring companies to be more efficient in delivering electronic information, DoD is encouraging contractors to run their businesses more efficiently. Not a bad idea!

Tale of Two Companies

The following studies based on actual cases of two companies contrast their approaches to developing a document information base during a major product development cycle. Both companies design digital data communication products for the telecommunications industry. Identities have been kept confidential.

Company A has a management which views product documentation as an afterthought and a burden on the company's finances. Even though it has invested in technologies (workstations, networks, and desktop publishing) it has done so under the impression that such tools will increase productivity in the limited sense of helping the company with specific hurdles such as using a computer-aided design system to speed up the design process or a desktop publishing system to help produce proposals. This company is a newcomer to the data communications market. It has been a supplier of test systems to the defense industry, and it wishes to generate new commercial business in the post–cold war era. It is building a complex data communications product to be used by telephone companies and private network businesses—a highly competitive field. To get a jump start on the design of the product, Company A has hired a consulting team that helps them develop two documents: a business plan and a preliminary product definition. After the CEO of the corporation gives the green light to fund the project, a startup team is formed consisting primarily of engineers, managers, a small marketing group, and a few manufacturing experts. Conspicuously absent from the development effort are planning, quality, information, training, and publication specialists, key knowledge workers in the company. The company arbitrarily separates the product from information.

After a year of development, the engineering team grew to sixty-five people. Newcomers to the project consistently asked: "Where are the working documents (specifications, design documents, feature documents, and so forth) that one can read to understand the product?" The same question was asked by software, electronic, test, or mechanical engineers. The answer they got is: there are preliminary specifications and planning documents. In reality, these documents are fragments and they are not organized in any coherent product information base. Few knew whether the information in one document was more current than another document. No one could answer the following questions: Where are all the working documents in a document library? Is the information in one proposal the same as the information in five other proposals? What are the differences? Is the information in a generic specification consistent with the data in a detailed mechanical specification? As time went on, the information got further and further fragmented. To get up to date information, searchers had to interrupt various subject matter experts, or have meetings to verify the status of information. Workflow became more and more chaotic. Writers and publication specialists were frustrated by the disorganization. They were expected to produce documents with little source information and they are divorced from the development project proper. Schedule slippages became common because of the inefficiency of the process and the lack of reliable information. The schedule slippages for the product were costly, and the investment in a new business in jeopardy.

Company B takes product documentation and information seriously. It sees competition and time to market as the major factors for acquisition of a document management system to help in its development of its data communication products. It also understands the relationship between time to market and just-in-time information. Product documents deemed critical to the process include: marketing requirements, product specifications, computer-aided design drawings, proposals, design documents, white papers, product and feature descriptions, as well as user, training and maintenance documentation. All documents can be tracked, controlled and accessed by project team members, although different security permissions apply depending on the player's role. Subsets of the same information base are used by marketing in proposals, brochures, training guides, and customer support information. Accordingly, the information that goes in them is carefully scrutinized for the multiple purposes it may practically serve.

Company B is a new successful company that has been in the telecommunications business for ten years. Its aggressive stance in a competitive market stems in part from the confidence it has in its employees who are not only highly qualified, but well informed. Company B views product documentation as a mirror to its knowledge base, and as a distinct corporate asset. Since the company thinks of its investment as long term, it recognized a need to build a solid foundation for making and selling products as well as training and supporting a growing customer base. It involves knowledge experts from its publications, marketing communications, and design groups early along in the development process. These groups, in conjunction with network management and information systems groups, persuasively argued for a document management approach. The company invests seventy thousand dollars in an enterprise document management system which ties together the fragments of information to be molded into a coherent product information system.

This company used the development of its new data communication product as an opportunity for piloting the document management system, and for keeping the new product development/information costs under control by accelerating information access and management. The system will be used to establish a uniform electronic document library, to index critical data that will be reused in many documents, to synchronize changes throughout the document database, and to control workflow among team members assigned to various documents in the project. Document analysts and planners ensured that the interdependence of product development and information was coherent.

To accomplish this goal, the document analysts from company B focused upon an information model related to the design of the new product. They consulted industry standards for suppliers of network documentation and became knowledgeable in the requirements promulgated by Bellcore which is a research company serving client companies from the former Bell system. Bellcore advises suppliers of telecommunications products who wish to sell to Bell client companies about information to be delivered in assorted documents as part of the supplier's obligation to its customer. Accordingly, the document analysts outline and diagram an overall information hierarchy. This information profile also conforms to the latest requirements of the telecommunications industry for electronic document interchange. Company B has joined the Telecommunication Industry Information Forum (TCIF) and has followed developments of its Information Product Interchange (IPI) and EDI subcommittees. The IPI committee is defining the future of document information interchange between suppliers and customers (Bell Client Companies). They have adopted SGML as the key standard for interchange of data between the suppliers and end users to help reduce total dependence on paper as a means for exchanging information. Company B keeps in step with its customer base and its own internal direction.

One of the essential lessons to be drawn from these case studies is that attitude and understanding of document information in relation to product development and services can influence a company's decision about its future. Recognizing the value of documentation does not mean that we need more of it; it means that we must value the information that we know makes our business tick. Appropriately applied document management strategies help us make smart business decisions, bring products to market on time, and understand customer needs.

WORKFLOW AND ACCOUNTABILITY

Reengineering teams who examine and redesign processes have to focus on critical problems. There is no universal blueprint that fits all organizations. Successful reengineering of document processes requires a combination of patience, skill, and perseverance.

Overcoming Fragmentation with Document Workflow

Michael Hammer and James Champy see reengineering as a correction to Adam Smith's belief that division of labor always leads to greater productivity. Promulgated in his *Wealth of Nations*, Smith persuasively argued for minute division of labor to increase the production of goods. His philosophy has been applied successfully to the manufacture of everything from pins to automobiles. Breaking work down into small fragmented tasks, where one worker did only one task, Smith observed how productivity could increase geometrically.

Work in the information age can not be so easily broken down into fragmented tasks. What counts are the multi-dimensional aspects of work. If processes are too fragmented, workers are not concerned with the whole. There is the added problem that competing department managers and supervisors are concerned only with the tasks under their control. By contrast, reengineering advocates:

> ➤ Getting the job done once, not redoing it several times (such as entering data into a computer one time, not repeating that entry at various steps in a document cycle).
>
> ➤ Involving all people from all departments involved in the process to get on board.

When companies purchase advanced information technology such as electronic publishing, they may encounter divisions of labor across departments that serve as a handicap. Electronic publishing sometimes requires reengineering of work processes and job responsibilities to be effective. Electronic publishing tools, aided by local area networks, can increase productivity and bridge interdepartmental groups who work concurrently. But prevention of unnatural fragmentation in workflow is essential.

Accountability

The process should clearly define responsibilities of individuals and teams. Blurring areas of accountability with multiple handoffs does not get the job done properly. Traditional department models tend to blame the next or last department in the process for the problem. In a team environment, virtually everyone on the team is responsible and accountable for the project.

How does a workgroup ensure that value is added to the labor by workgroup members? By properly defining workflow and responsibilities for the process, each team member is expected to add the value of labor to that work. The team, however, must take responsibility for other team members when they ask for help or admit that they are asked to do too much. This is the real challenge of collaboration—the ability to share information and ideas and to motivate and support one another to success.

Reengineering the publishing process also means that we need to redefine the productivity of what we do as document collaborators. Workgroup publishing involves a complex of design and information requirements that begin with an understanding of what a customer needs. To meet such requirements and maximize quality and productivity goals, organizational workgroups should blend human skills and processes that lead to satisfied customers.

Benchmarking the Process

In Chapter 11, we will discuss a need to set goals, evaluate requirements and technologies, and, if feasible, benchmark candidate technologies. Benchmarking a process starts by looking at ourselves against the best in the class. What are the some of the ways we can benchmark the process? The first step is to agree on metrics that establish the criteria baseline for quantitative or qualitative measurements of a process. We can compare how long it takes to accomplish the needed outputs compared with the existing practices, assuming that the data for comparison is available. Benchmarking keeps us focused upon specific goals.

Managerial Leadership

The challenge for managers is to become less the full time decision makers and more like coaches helping players on the team get to their goal effectively. This means that managers must let team members make decisions without interference. Providing guidance, advice, and resources can be critical to the team's success.

Nothing of any lasting value happens without honest, open, and direct communication. If the CEO of an organization stands behind a reengineering effort, it gives the reengineered processes more chance of success. The CEO has to help communicate goals and objectives related to the reengineering effort. Workgroups can help define a collaborative method of information sharing. It can't really work well without encouragement from management. Management must learn how to be supportive and non-interfering in the process. Successful managers will want employees to satisfy customers not managers.

Using electronic publishing and document management technology to advantage requires not only an investment in technology, but a vision of how publishing and information services intertwine. By understanding how to open up the content of documents to users who need access to that content is a critical reengineering objective underway in many organizations. Misuse of publishing systems often comes about because processes interrelated to the main publishing process are left unaddressed. Matching tools to the isolated requirements of one functional area or process may speed up a process but ignore functional relationships to other group processes. By examining how workgroups use electronic publishing in relation to information resources, we can begin to understand why some of our document generating and consuming practices need to be reengineered.

CHAPTER

10

➤ *Risks of poor document management*

➤ *Information retrieval and knowledge*

➤ *Making documents secure*

➤ *Avoiding workflow bottlenecks*

➤ *Tracking changes*

➤ *Adding value to documents*

Document Management

*d*ocument information is a critical asset in any organization. To make informed decisions, bring products to market, or deliver services to customers on time, organizations need access to information on demand. Document management systems facilitate access, control, reassembly and distribution of information. In data intensive business processes, tools which control fragmented information resources can dramatically improve organizational performance.

WHY WE NEED DOCUMENT MANAGEMENT

Documents claim 40 to 60 percent of the average office worker's time, 20 to 25 percent of a company's labor cost, and 12 to 15 percent of corporate revenues. If these statistics are not startling enough, consider that 90 percent of the information related to an organization's business is contained within documents. Information stored in traditional centrally managed databases accounts for only 10 percent of an organization's total information. The rest is stored in documents in both paper and electronic form.

As organizations accelerate the creation of documents on multiple desktops, they learn that increasing productivity is not be measured solely by the number of new documents proauced. Gains in production can be offset by the labor intensive tasks of managing multiple versions of documents or finding and distributing information efficiently. Employees can average up to 200 hours per year simply looking for information in documents. The problem is compounded because retrieval of documents stored in a number of electronic formats can make information difficult to distribute and reuse. These hidden costs in information access adversely impact business critical processes in any organization.

The problems associated with document information retrieval and reuse are shared by many types of industries. Organizations turning to workgroup or enterprise wide document management technologies to solve the document information syndrome include:

- Legal firms who research large numbers of electronic documents and compile their own documents based on that research
- News organizations which capture, search, and verify information from news releases for purposes of classifying, generating, and editing other documents
- Engineering and manufacturing enterprises which create, update, and reuse complex documents to bring products to market on time
- Medical and health service industries which query electronic encyclopedias of medical information and process numerous medical documents
- Insurance companies whose workers access details from voluminous policy manuals to deliver client services
- Pharmaceutical companies who are required to generate information intensive documents for new drug application (NDA) processes
- Government agencies who use document management to maintain large document databases related to the maintenance of airplanes, environmental protection, health care, judicial cases, and legislative documents

It is not only document producers, librarians, and publishers who benefit from document management. Consumers who work outside the domain of document creation and production often require rapid access to information inside documents to perform a service, solve a problem, or build a product. Document management can streamline document production costs as well. Planned correctly, a document management system lets users retrieve and act upon information from electronic documents without infringing on data security or unauthorized access.

WHAT IT IS

Electronic document management includes the methodologies and technologies used to catalog, search, retrieve, assemble, distribute, and secure documents and document information. Document management systems perform many or some of these functions by integrating software products supplied by several vendors. A sample interface to a document management system that integrates many modular features is shown in Figure 10.1.

Convenient and powerful desktop tools—word processors, WYSIWYG desktop publishing systems, spreadsheets, graphic editors, databases, and imaging software—have allowed us to become proficient makers of documents. Groups who

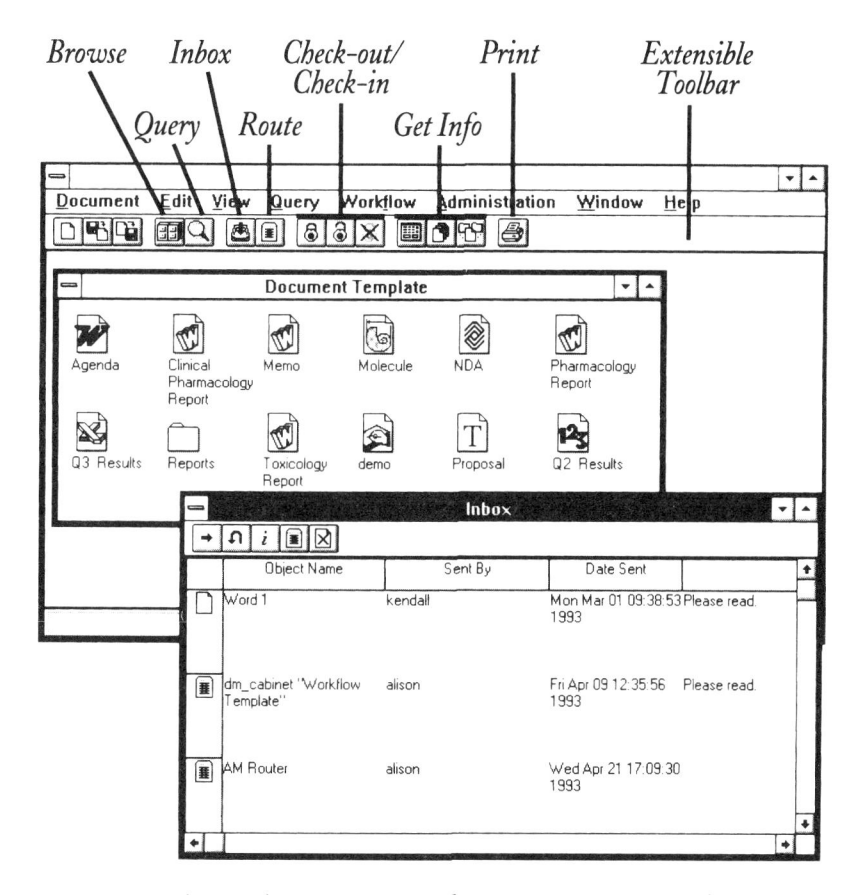

Figure 10.1. The Workspace user interface to Documentum's document management system illustrates some key features of a modular system approach from document check in and check out to workflow routing, document browsing, and distribution. Although users may access document management functions from their desktops, the main document management programs of most systems reside on a file server connecting many users and workgroups in a network. Multiple licensing arrangements enable concurrent usage and system access. (Courtesy of Documentum, Inc.)

are out of sync with each other when they attempt to share and distribute information can use document management systems to put an organizations's electronic document warehouse in order. By maintaining electronic document libraries, managing information workflow processes, and controlling document changes, document management software links the information chain that binds workgroup processes together. Some features common to document management systems include:

- Automatic cataloging of document libraries across networks
- Text search, indexing, and document retrieval
- Security management
- Automatic version and change control of documents
- Management of document workflow for groups

Document librarians and system administrators are not the only beneficiaries of document management systems. All users gain whether they help create documents or need to access information in documents. Those who have permission to access information can, in turn, create documents, or use that information to perform a work related task. Ultimately, the organization as a whole and its customers benefit from document management, because the people creating and using documents are more informed and efficient in their work.

Workgroups are increasingly tied together via networks. Users may be expert in the document subject matter, or information, but they often lack facilities for piecing together the fragmented source documents stored in many file formats on different computers. In addition, multiple versions of the same document with different dates may coexist in directories and documents which keep growing along with the paper versions stored in file cabinets. Workgroups need to manipulate data and system resources expeditiously as possible. Equally as important, they need to avoid redundancy and bottlenecks, pass parts of documents to other workers for review or search information from computer systems other than their own.

Document Life Cycles

Documents, especially those created by corporate and government organizations, can have long life cycles. A typical electronic document cycle is shown in Figure 10.2. The cycle involves the work of many individuals and one document may be an off-shoot of other documents. Document life cycles can be viewed as a circular process rather than a linear time line which implies a document has fixed beginning and ending boundaries. Sometimes documents result from collaboration between many groups who work with it at different stages of the life cycle. There

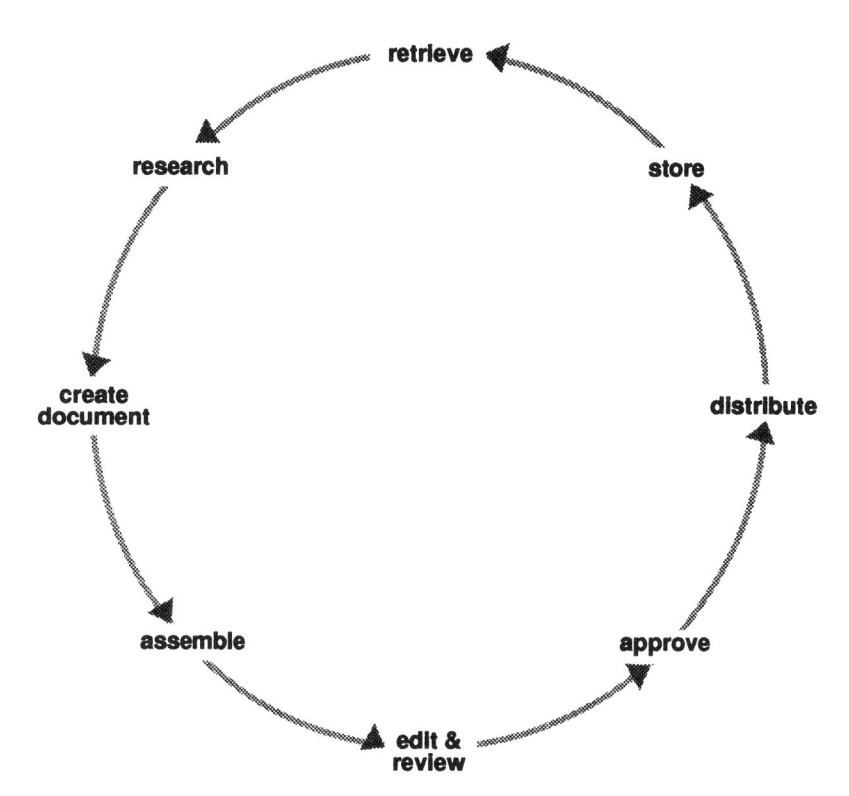

Figure 10.2. Electronic document life cycle workflow diagram. When documents are created electronically they become part of an electronic library. With proper planning, organizations can reuse information in documents efficiently. As multiple electronic publishing projects share common information over time, the data in one document can be recycled in other documents, or the original document itself may be updated periodically.

are some workgroups such as customer support and maintenance groups who may need to see many versions of documents relating to a product because the company is selling or maintaining a product that is evolving. Some users of documents are involved in the life cycle because they must review or edit what someone else has written. Authors stay involved in the life cycle because they update documents from time to time. Still others generate branch documents or create information that will be added to existing documents.

Since document life cycles involve multiple stakeholders, electronic document management tools must accommodate the needs of different user groups. The scalability feature of many document management tools can help collaborating groups in a company gradually increase the size of the system to suit the requirements of specific workgroups. Because the information in documents is vital to various groups, planning should involve the organization as a whole. Information officers and others responsible for evaluating document management systems should determine how varying systems can be scaled to meet the needs of the enterprise. In some cases, it may be necessary to integrate multiple document management systems supplied to workgroups in an organization. To avoid compatibility problems and to ensure that all document life cycle needs are met, the organization should carefully evaluate document life cycle requirements from the perspective of many groups and consider emerging standards for the interoperation of document management systems and the compatibility of these systems with existing user applications.

When planning the acquisition and deployment of a document management system, organizations should consider variables such as:

- How many groups or individuals need on-line access to document information
- Document workflow and the life cycle processes through document origin, approval, and retrieval
- Security requirements, including authorization to modify documents, restricted access to documents for viewing only, or no access privileges at all
- Frequency of document change and how it may affect other documents
- Quantity and types of critical enterprise documents

Document management systems can be tailored to the needs of specific workgroups. Some producer groups need the power of document management for the entire process. Other groups within an organization mainly benefit from text information retrieval. Planners of document management systems should define the different needs for groups and tailor the system accordingly.

TYPES OF DOCUMENT MANAGEMENT SYSTEMS

Document management systems are evolving rapidly and continually adding new features. Classifications of document management systems can be misleading because the rapid integration of technologies frequently blurs distinctions between classes of systems. There are three predominant types of systems supplying distinct markets for document management tools. These include text indexing and retrieval systems, document image management systems, and compound document management systems.

Text retrieval and indexing systems are based upon automatic indexing schemes providing accurate, fast, and flexible searches through large quantities of text data. These systems often feature powerful file format conversion utilities that enable searches through documents that are stored in proprietary formats. Used in conjunction with document viewing and multimedia technologies, text retrieval systems can index and elucidate information displayed.

Document image management systems use scanning technology for applications converting existing paper documents to electronic media. They capture an electronic image of the original paper document. The electronic documents, in turn, can be labeled, indexed, and stored on disk, tape, optical, or laser media. These systems provide the capabilities for scan image processing, document indexing, displays optical character recognition, and workflow management.

Compound document management systems incorporate modular tools to support library management, document viewing, workflow and revision control, text retrieval and document indexing, document conversion, and automatic document assembly. Compound document management systems are useful in information intensive industries (engineering, manufacturing, legal, medical, pharmaceutical) and where the reuse of information of different types is a critical factor in the documenting process. New documents can be created from a variety of existing information source systems. Compound document management systems can represent and manage mixed objects (text, graphics, audio and so forth) and serve the needs of a large variety of users.

Text Indexing, Search, and Retrieval

Based upon information given to the computer, document management systems can automate search, retrieval, and indexing of information from multiple documents. Guided by a graphical interface, a document database is queried for information related to a research topic or other information needed to complete a job task.

Text indexing and retrieval technology is now used extensively by corporations, government agencies, professionals in research as well as operational settings within government and industry. For example, the Canadian government's agricultural department inspectors use electronic text retrieval technology rather than paper documents to look up the regulations for legal import of agricultural products into Canada.

Insurance workers at Aetna Corporation use text retrieval systems to search electronic documents to find answers to questions regarding work procedures. Help desks and customer support departments in many companies now use text retrieval technology to answer questions about a product problem. An automotive marketing executive recalls that a consumer survey document completed in the past year describing consumer preferences for bucket seats was stored on some computer but since she had no immediate recollection of the title, author, or date, was unable to locate the document. By keying in the key words "bucket seat"a full text search and retrieval tool was able to find the document in seconds.

Text indexing and retrieval technology can even be the center piece of some information service businesses. For example, text indexing and retrieval systems have been used for many years in paralegal research and news services. Mead Data Central LEXIS-NEXIS research are highly successful information services with on-line legal information search (LEXIS) and news (NEXIS) for legal and journalistic professionals. The Mead Data does with its Lexis services is of critical importance to legal offices around the country. To help make the electronic law office a reality, the information service company adds 650,000 documents each week to its more than 188,000 million documents and makes money on the service.

One method used frequently by vendors of text retrieval is a full-text search system, which allows searches across multiple unstructured documents (no matter how large) to find specific answers to queries. Full-text search is based on the principle of inverted file indexing. All words in the text base are included in an alphabetically sorted list. In full-text systems, every word becomes a key word except for so-called "noise" words such as "the." Response time for searches is usually just seconds, even with large numbers of concurrent users searching within a document library. Industry analysts predict a major shift to text indexing technologies to help workgroups in corporations use document information rather than paper-based work instruction systems to do their jobs.

Some of the techniques used in text retrieval systems include phrase, Boolean, and proximity searches. Phrase searches refer to a search for an exact text phrase such as: "The president told reporters he had no new information on the terrorist attack." Searchers may want to use multiple search words in their query. Boolean logic applied to text searching means that Boolean operators (AND, OR, and NOT) can be used in the search query. A Boolean search for "rain" AND "snow" would find only documents that contained both words. Queries for "snow"NOT "rain" would find documents for snow, but not for rain. A search for rain or snow would yield all documents with either rain or snow in them. A proximity search supports retrieval of documents with two search terms occurring within a preestablished distance from each other.

Using Topic from Verity Corporation, a user can query a document database for articles on a topic such as automobiles. Figure 10.3 shows the results of such a synonym query. To assist the person making the query, the system offers the use of a thesaurus to help construct synonyms for the word manufacture. The general query also lists several auto makers as well. The system retrieves and highlights

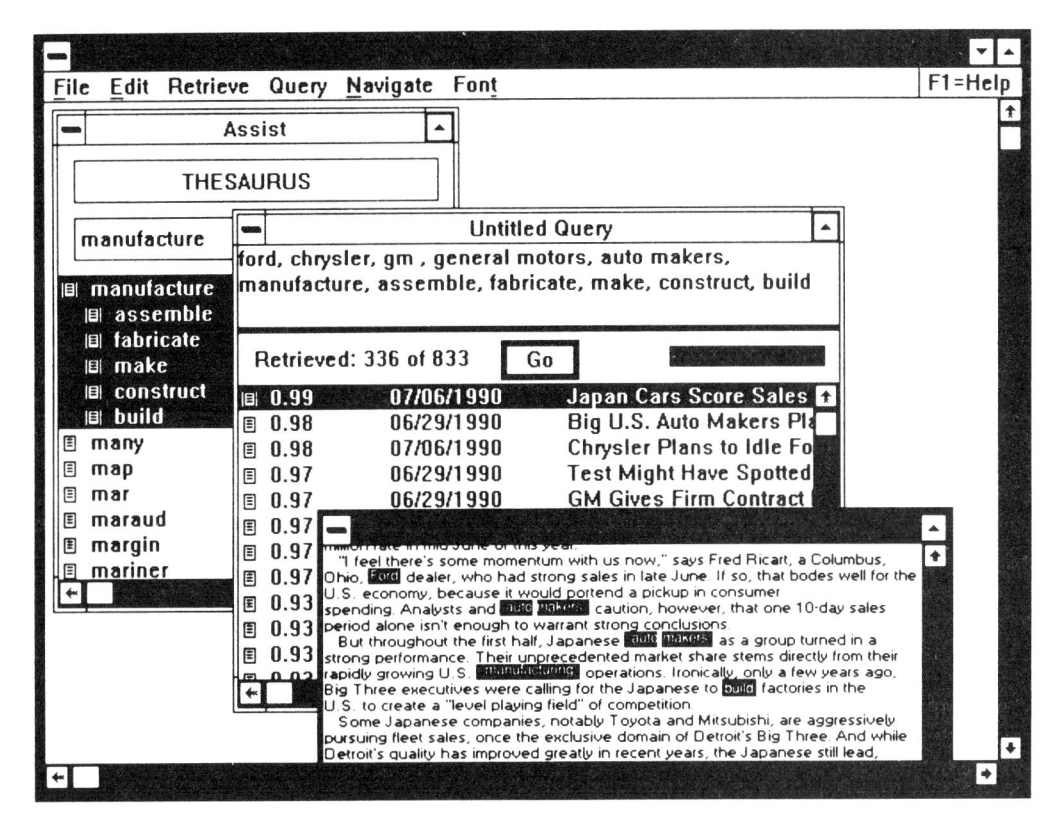

Figure 10.3. An example of a synonym query to a document database using the Assist tool to the Topic document retrieval product from Verity, Inc. The user builds a query to search for documents in a document library related to automobiles. The searcher is interested in auto makers and adds keywords related to manufacture. The system assists the user query by offering synonyms from a thesaurus. (Courtesy of Verity, Inc.)

the appropriate article(s) in a window. The searcher then clicks on that article which opens to video highlighted instances of the key words as requested.

Many vendors of text retrieval systems are adding SGML capabilities to their text retrieval engines to provide searches defined by structural criteria. Since SGML identifies and indexes the structure of text information, retrieval systems can be designed to search through structural indexes that help searchers find answers promptly and accurately. SGML offers a structural context for searches on tags declared in the DTD. For example, users could search on tags such as <procedure>, <warning>, <violation>, <risk>, <chapter>, assuming the tags are valid within the framework of a given DTD. Open Text, Alliance, Fulcrum, and Information

Dimensions, among other leading vendors of text retrieval systems, have incorporated SGML based searching capabilities in their products.

Document Image Management

Document image management systems provide on-line conversion, storage, and retrieval of documents and are sometimes used in conjunction with database technology for library and workflow management. Image processing systems can be used to convert paper records to electronic form. Document image management systems provide automatic identification of documents for retrieval. Scanners play a large role in image processing systems to make facsimile versions of paper documents. A paper document is passed through a scanner and the image is captured. The scanner creates a bitmapped image of the document. The main drawback of document image processing systems is that the electronic documents are image files and not computer readable text files. If optical character reader (OCR) software is used for electronic conversion of paper text data, the image processing system can pass the converted electronic text data to other sub-systems for reuse of the text data in other documents. The OCR software discriminates the alphabetic characters in the scanned image file and converts them to ASCII equivalents. This raw text data can be read by SGML converters or desktop publishing layout programs for formatting purposes. The ASCII data can also be processed by text search and retrieval software programs.

Specialized applications include conversions of technical drawings for manufacturing, engineering, or architecture into electronic form. Figure 10.4 is an example depicting a document image management system serving the Federal Aviation Administration (FAA) in the U.S. for retrieving documents related to aircraft and airmen. Drug enforcement officials at national, state, and local agencies are aided in identifying and retrieving information about aircraft and airmen listed on the registry. A primary system requirement is timely retrieval of the information. Key components of the system are the scanner that captures the paper document records, the workstations used to view, retrieve, and verify fidelity and accuracy of the scanned document, and the optical storage sub-system that stores massive amounts of documents.

Organizations as disparate as police departments, insurance companies, and manufacturing enterprises use image management technologies to store and retrieve information once printed on paper and stored in file cabinets.

Compound Document Management Systems

Compound document management systems integrate modular components to handle a variety of data types and processes and to support the entire document life

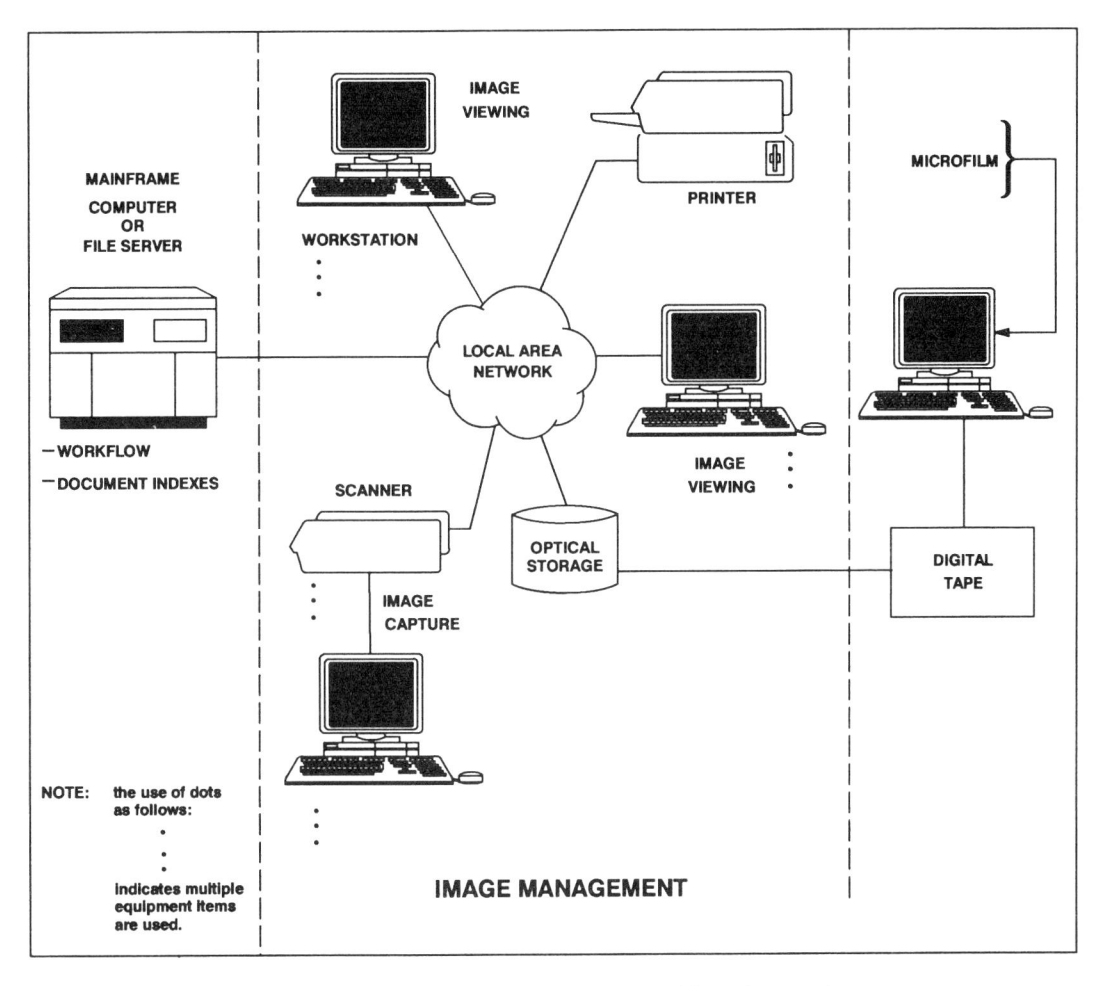

Figure 10.4. Document image management system used in a drug enforcement program. The system captures paper documents and converts them to digital form. Key aspects of the system are a document indexing and retrieval capability. Documents can be retrieved and viewed from workstations distributed over a local area network. (Courtesy of the FAA.)

cycle. They manage document libraries, track the interdependency of documents and the information inside documents, provide dynamic viewing over a network, allow for search and retrieval of information, and indicate the status of documents through the life cycle. A common feature is the capability to produce multiple document versions from a single database. For workgroups connected via a network the database may consist of SGML tagged text data, electronic drawings, and other components. These modular systems connect many pieces of the document process and offer a workflow subsystem to assure that review and approval cycles for document producers and reviewers are properly orchestrated. Most of these systems are scalable; they can be introduced to help several workgroups within an organization or the entire enterprise.

Leading vendors of compound document management systems include Interleaf, Workgroup Technologies, Xyvision, Odesta Systems, Documentum, X Soft, and Lotus Development, Inc. In addition to database tools, compound document management systems integrate technologies, such as text retrieval and search technologies. A diagram of a sample compound document management system is shown in Figure 10.5.

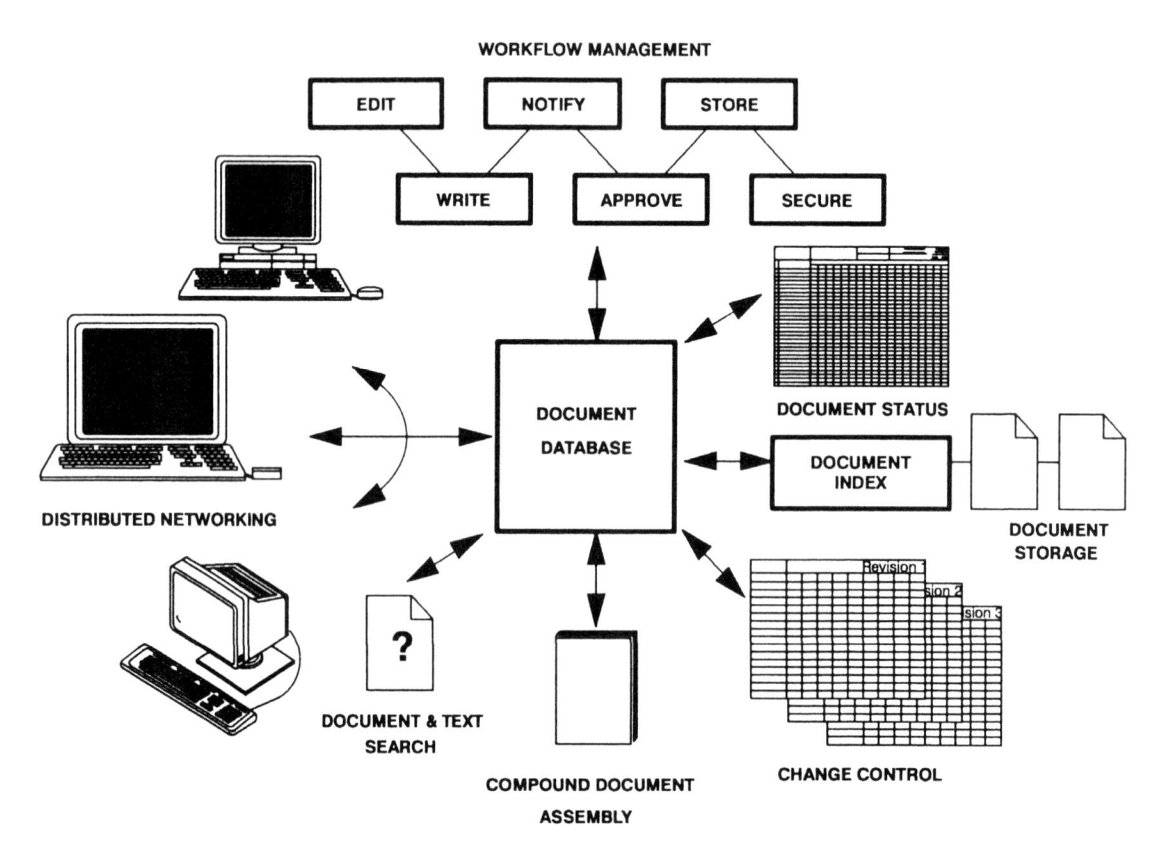

Figure 10.5. Modular compound document management system with distributed workflow management, automatic document assembly, library management, and indexing and retrieval capability. Such systems are often scalable to suit the needs of workgroups or an entire enterprise.

MAJOR DOCUMENT MANAGEMENT FUNCTIONS

Document management systems can be described as a set of interrelated subsystems. Because only a few vendors sell integrated systems that comprehend most of the possible functional areas, document management systems are sometimes sold as modular software components that can be installed separately or bundled together. The following list of major document management functions identifies capabilities attractive to a broad spectrum of workgroups.

Document file and library management is a core feature of many document management systems. Most document library management schemes use database technology to store information or records about documents that categorize and qualify the contents and location of the document. An electronic document library system catalogs, controls, stores, secures, and retrieves documents.

Change control management or version control is a systematic method for tracking changes in versions of documents and showing that status to the user. This is sometimes directly integrated with the library management check in and check out software. Change management can also incorporate on-line reviewing and editing tools so that authors, editors, and other commentators can annotate documents and make suggested changes for revision. Other versions of documents with changes highlighted can be displayed.

Workflow management automates the routing and tracking of information objects associated with digital documents. Workflow typically bundles several system functions together including document routing and event notification by electronic mail, as well as the annotation, distribution, and review of documents over a local or wide area network. To make document review and routing workable the document managment system needs some form of document viewing and distribution technology.

Automatic document assembly applies executable programs and scripts upon user command to extract contents of document objects, SGML encoded elements, and other indexed information bases to build a document for print or electronic distribution.

Library Management

Library management, a fundamental feature of document management systems, provides a catalog of documents and families of documents. Library managment logs all documents into a catalog system and also provides features for document security and archival. Sound practices for storing, retrieving, and managing document files have, up to now, allowed document administrators to manage directories and subdirectories for storing documents in an orderly manner. When it comes to indexing, archiving and securing document files, however, traditional file management approaches do not provide adequate facilities for interactive document administration and retrieval.

Document management systems allow database and document administrators to work in concert with authorized users to access a document or document objects through graphical user interface tools. A standard feature of a library management system is file locking for document check in and check out. When a document is checked out, the system makes sure that only one person at a time makes changes to documents.

Document Profiles

Document profiles are records containing elements such as author names, titles, dates, document specific codes, document issue numbers, revision levels, or other status information indispensable to the retrieval of documents. Effective document library management allows searchers to retrieve documents by reference to a controlled vocabulary used for a classification of documents. Workgroups can apply their knowledge of document types and related information by using consistent terms to describe documents. For example, Figure 10.6 is a sample document identification coding scheme used by one company to identify types of documents

| 0 | 1 | 1 | 0 | 0 | 0 | s | x | b | r | 0 | 1 | 1 |

Department   **Product Code**   **Type**   **Version**   **Issue**

Department   Product Code   Type

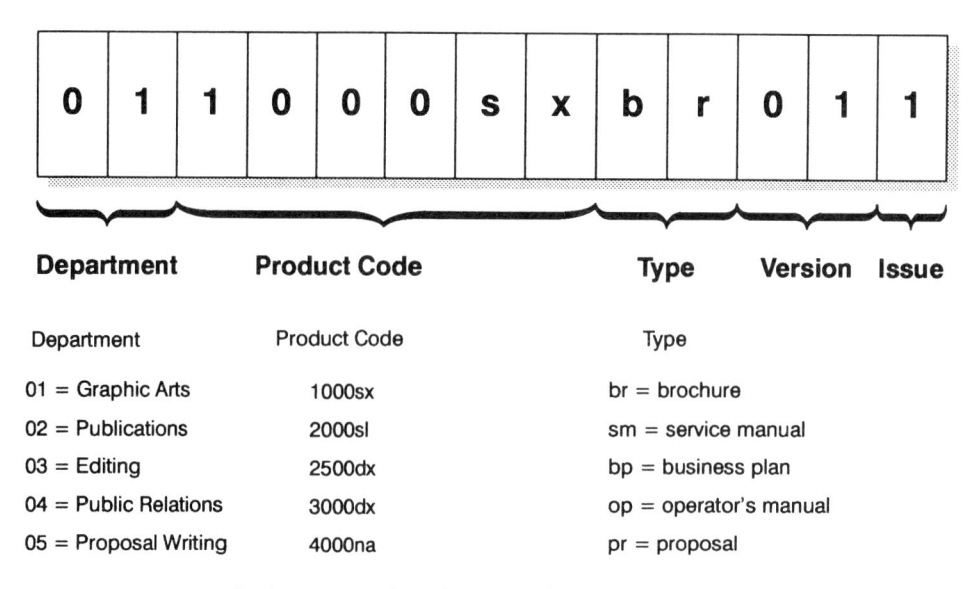

01 = Graphic Arts   1000sx   br = brochure
02 = Publications   2000sl   sm = service manual
03 = Editing   2500dx   bp = business plan
04 = Public Relations   3000dx   op = operator's manual
05 = Proposal Writing   4000na   pr = proposal

Figure 10.6. A sample document identification scheme used by publishing workgroups in identifying the types of documents, the related product codes, and departments responsible for document creation. The scheme is entirely arbitrary but it exemplifies how workgroups apply categorical knowledge so that document librarians and library systems can organize documents and objects in a meaningful collection.

for specific groups. It is a basis for categorizing information that can be indexed to expedite retrieval.

The identification scheme shown in Figure 10.6 includes a series of fields divided into groups, for example, the department field is coded as 01, a number preassigned to Graphic Arts. Other departments include Publications (02), Editing (03) and so on. Other fields indicate product codes and document types. Other fields deal with document versions and issue dates.

Figure 10.6 is an example of fixed field document identification. A field refers to a subset of sequentially positioned alphanumeric characters reserved for specific codes that represent preassigned patterns to identify information. In this case cooperating workgroups have created a table listing the code of each department, product, and document types, versions, and issues. This categorical profile or identification scheme allows users and document managers to store and retrieve information in an orderly and systematic fashion. Workgroups can also go a step further and subcategorize their knowledge of document topics into hierachies of documents and document objects. They can also indicate the relationships between documents and document objects. The document management system can then use this information to establish relationships between document families and the objects that exist within the document hierarchy.

Document Libraries: Document Objects with Properties

In a corporate or an organizational environment where a great number of documents are distributed over a network, database technologies play a significant role in keeping document records. As workgroups accumulate a store of knowledge concerning a family of documents relating to a given subject, they begin to organize that information into sets of related documents. Figure 10.7 is an example of a property sheet from the Interleaf RDM system. Some properties define the relationship of one object to another object. Certain objects may be described as parents to other objects that are children. If we make a change to a parent object, we may want the child to inherit that change. By using the power of object management technologies, a complex set of relationships between objects and groups of objects in the collection can be managed effectively.

Document Security

A security feature of document management systems is the control of system access. Document management systems provide some means for managing access to documents and notifying system users and administrators that documents are checked out. For example, a writer has the security privilege to access a document and modify it. A content expert has been assigned to review the document. This reviewer is allowed to make comments on the document using a technique called

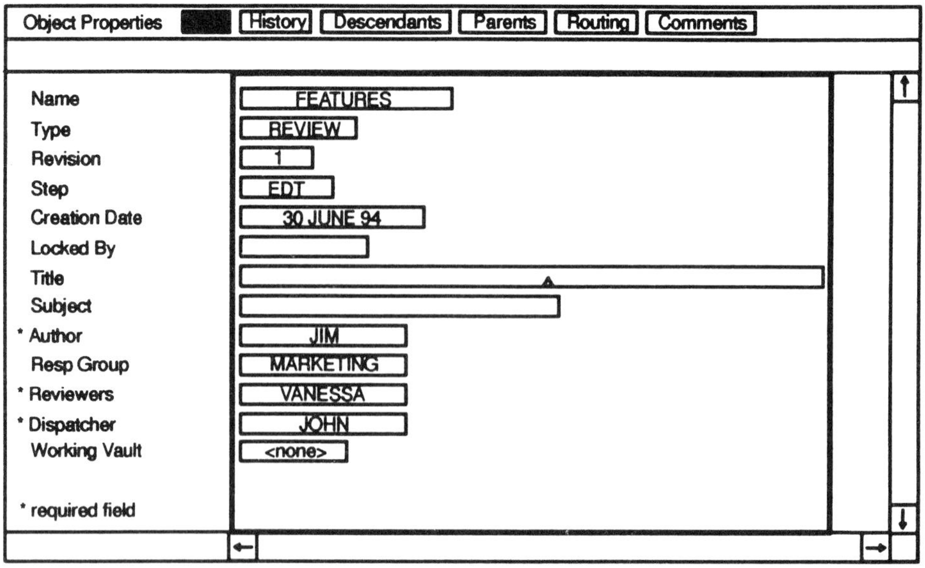

[Figure: Sample RDM object property sheet showing fields: Name: FEATURES, Type: REVIEW, Revision: 1, Step: EDT, Creation Date: 30 JUNE 94, Locked By: (blank), Title: (blank), Subject: (blank), Author: JIM, Resp Group: MARKETING, Reviewers: VANESSA, Dispatcher: JOHN, Working Vault: <none>. Tabs: Object Properties, History, Descendants, Parents, Routing, Comments. * required field]

Figure 10.7. Sample of an RDM object property sheet. The object properties sheet helps us identify information about the document. Attributes such as date, revision level, author, reviewer, and dispatcher are listed. The step field indicates the stage of the project within the review cycle. The reviewer will route the file to the dispatcher.

electronic red lining, but the document administrator does not give this person permission to modify the original document under review. Documents are secured by the system according to a preestablished plan for access and authorized use. When a document is checked out, the system prevents other users from editing it.

Document Archival

Taking documents off the system and storing them on some media (tape or disk) is commonly called archiving. Many systems use the concept of vault storage for files that are checked in and archived. When documents are checked in the system, the version level of the document can be automatically modified by the document management system or as per user requirements. Typically, documents are not checked in and released for archival until they are approved. Many document management systems offer automatic archival of a document based upon specified properties such as the date last accessed.

Version or Revision Control

Version control subsystems keep track of revisions in documents over time. For example, in manufacturing and engineering applications the ability to identify changes or modifications in a product information base requires a system for keeping track of documents that are updated. The documents in question may be technical manuals, specifications, parts catalogs, drawings, software programming instructions, or price lists. As modifications are made to products and their performance, the current literature should accurately reflect the change. For example, the aviation industry has found it is difficult to keep track of all the information and accurate procedures to maintain all of the parts and pieces that make up an aircraft. All users of documents in the information chain from quality and reliability to product support and training must be in sync regarding the changes. Many revision control systems will keep a complete change history on-line so that previous versions of a document can be accessed as needed.

The control technology can be applied to document changes in any discipline:commercial publishing and journalism as well as engineering, medical, legal, financial, pharmaceutical, insurance, and government documents. The costs associated with the management of changes to documents are very high. Having a system in place to control change can greatly reduce labor costs associated with tracking the changes.

Some version control systems store the exact changes to the original document without duplicating the data that has not been changed. If document A is out for revision and an author adds six paragraphs to a ten page document and deletes two other paragraphs, the document management change control system will store only those changes to the original document. Other systems use file compression techniques to improve the efficiency in storage of various versions. Version control systems that provide an accurate audit of changes which occur between revisions is helpful to managers, researchers, and document producers.

Workflow Management

Workflow is the process or sequence of activities performed by a workgroup as part of making, modifying, reviewing, accessing, releasing, securing, printing, viewing, or distributing documents. Workflow control systems allow workgroups and managers to orchestrate the life cycle of projects across networks and multiple desktops. Workflow systems coordinate the functions of people and projects.

Document workflow controls the management of documents from origin and creation through project completion. Workflow systems help project managers and players check the status of work being done on a group project in real time across the network. This feature connects the workflow system to an electronic viewing subsystem so that a document in progress can be viewed in its current state by any authorized member of the project. Workflow management systems notify project players of document status, or use electronic mail tools and other subsystems to communicate and instruct specific individuals in the group. Figure 10.8 is a diagram of the workflow cycle for the review of a particular document which may involve several departments and reviewers.

Event Management

Document event management is connected to workflow and electronic mail systems. When a document is ready for review, an electronic mail subsystem notifies the reviewer that it has been transmitted to his/her desktop. The electronic mail feature can be used with other aspects of the workflow cycle, such as notification of document completion, changes in a document status, or reminders about the interdependencies of documents managed by the system. Most workflow subsystems feature event management and electronic mail communication to various players in the workflow configuration.

Electronic viewing has become integrated as a standard feature of document workflow systems. Various members of a workgroup involved in the workflow process can view the document, make comments, or take action, without making direct changes to the document. Documents can be routed via networks to individuals for comment. Document viewing technology allows recipients to display and navigate through the document. The reviewer makes notes to a document, that can be dispatched to the author or editor making the changes according to established procedure. Adding electronic notes can take several shapes, one of which is electronic document red-lining. Using electronic color display to advantage, the comments appear in a color, such as red. An alternative technique, valuable when there is only a monochrome display, includes journal notes in windows attached to parts of the document under review.

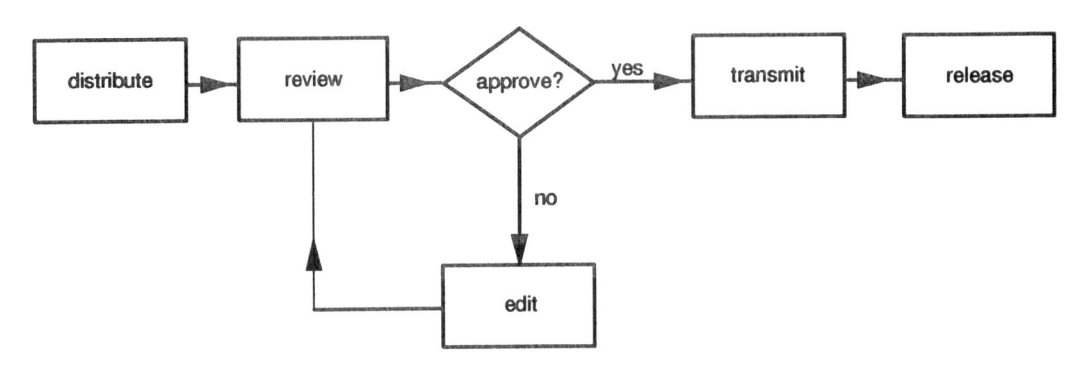

Figure 10.8. A workflow management model for document review.

Evolving Roles for Databases in Document Management

Databases play a key role in the evolution of document management technologies. One of the goals of document management systems is to raise user confidence in the reliability of information in documents to the same level that users have in the information found in database management systems used for finance, accounting and bills of material. To meet growing user expectations, developers of document management system technologies must keep up with the rapid change of pace in database technology itself. Both relational database management systems (RDBMS) and object oriented database systems (OODBS) are used extensively in document management technologies. The challenge is modifying database models to allow for easy incorporation of variable size data objects.

Some document management systems use documents as databases; while others try to store documents in databases. Full text indexing system document information bases are unstructured. As databases evolve document management systems will increasingly rely on them as a logical technology for controlled storage of information. One issue of paramount importance is the development of databases that are able to store SGML files or SGML encoded data as objects to maximize the reusability power of SGML data. Publishing system vendors are busily making alliances with database developers to enable advanced use of SGML and other objects from the database for automatic document assembly and the like. For example, the BASIS SGML Server from Information Dimensions, Inc. provides for component level retrieval, updating, and manipulation from SGML documents stored in the database. By enabling the retrieval of structured information at a component level, there is an increase in the precision of information searches. Concurrent users can access different parts of a document by checking out only those pieces that they want to modify. The BASIS SGML Server also has a built in parser that ensures that SGML documents checked in and out of the database conform to SGML requirements. DynaBase from Electronic Book Technologies, Parlance Document Manager from Xyvision, and SGML/DB from Berger Levrault of France are all examples of document management systems that use databases to support component level management of SGML.

Document Producers: Add Value to Information

With the many sophisticated features of document management at an organization's disposal, document producers may become complacent. They may forget that the ground work of document management largely depends upon how well individuals and groups apply their knowledge to enrich the information resources. In other words, the long term strategy is not to create an information mishmash that can be dramatically rescued by document management tools after the fact. A key part of a document management strategy is to improve and predispose information resources throughout the document life cycle process.

Christopher Locke describes how workgroups add value to document information resources.[1] By refining the treatment and organization of computerized information contained within documents, knowledge is acquired and shared. By adding value to information, workgroups pool their expertise to categorize, link, structure, compose, and assemble information. Document management includes the acquisition, sharing and distribution of knowledge in an organization. As creators of documents, authors and others can make a major contribution by building a foundation for document management.

Value is added to document information by categorizing it. Classifying and identifying document information at generic and more specific levels, begins the formation of document libraries. Libraries are organized collections of document information. A well organized electronic document library has an index specifying document classes, titles, attributes, and other characteristics that enable identification. The approach to indexing text information is important to retrieving sets of information from documents. (We have emphasized the importance of information in documents throughout our review and discuss specific information retrieval technologies in this chapter).

Value is added to information when it is structured so that it can be reused for multiple purposes. By creating electronic documents with an emphasis on structure such as afforded by SGML, workgroups can identify the structural elements defining the documents as well as the content of the information. These structural elements (as previously discussed) include those elements defined in a Document Type Definition (DTD). SGML facilitates the identification of document structures for indexing, exchange, and retrieval.

Relating information within documents leads to cross-referencing sets of data within a document or between documents. An electronic method for linking related information is called hypertext. Hypertext systems adapt audience requirements to the special capabilities of electronic document storage and technologies. It is best for workgroups to validate the criteria of information links.

When workgroups combine documents from existing documents to make new documents, they assemble the information according to specific audience information requirements. Procedural knowledge as applied to electronic publishing may use scripts or other software programs to automate the process of assembly.

Compositional knowledge requires techniques and expertise in visual presen-

---

1. Christopher Locke, "Foundations for Document and Information Management," Datapro Information Services Group: Reprinted from *Workgroup Computing Series: Strategies and LAN Services.* McGraw Hill, July 1992.

tation methods and design (such as page layout and use of type) to enhance the formatting of documents for paper or electronic presentation.

Judgmental knowledge recognizes semantic distinctions based upon conceptual content of documents that, by virtue of artificial intelligence, enables a computer to understand and interpret natural language. So-called expert systems are trying to remove people from decision making processes and supplant knowledge supplied by human readers who deal with text information. To date, advances in this field are limited. Humans add depth to knowledge and are at once imaginative and reliable interpreters of knowledge.

What Locke says about text resources also applies to graphical knowledge and the other objects included in document databases. When workgroups add specific value to information, they form a coherent basis for document management. Adding value means that workgroups define or redefine a knowledge base for their own organization.

Connection Between Documents and Knowledge

A document is the commonly accepted medium for distributing and acquiring information. Document readers assimilate information to acquire knowledge. This knowledge is applied to getting products to market, to managing information resources for research centers, to writing training guides on complex machinery, or to helping organizations comply with complex customer requirements. Knowledge is power. Enabling access to knowledge is critical to achieving organizational goals. It also empowers workers to do their jobs in a reengineered organization.

Those organizations that take documents for granted do not perceive the value of document management. It is a tool for controlling document libraries, indexing information, and managing changes of an interrelated electronic document repertoire. In an information age, document management can help an organization streamline processes, help workers acquire and use knowledge, and meet customer demands in a timely manner.

DOCUMENT MANAGEMENT AND STANDARDS

There are several emerging standards of document management users and developers. Document management standards are just beginning to be defined and products that support evolving specifications are still under development. The standards, sponsored by groups of vendors, address proposals such as the simplification of interfaces between application programs and document management systems or scaling document management services over networks. An existing standard that is proving highly effective in document management strategies is SGML. As a proven document interchange standard and as a vehicle to organize document content and structure in neutral form, SGML is playing a pivotal role in document management product development and in organizational strategies to build repositories of reusable legacy data available on demand.

How SGML Helps Manage Information Details

By managing the details of information within documents, SGML makes four major contributions to document management. First, SGML provides a dependable neutral method of document interchange which makes the management of document information more efficient. Second, SGML defines a document in terms of its structure. Documents are divided into sections, subsections, paragraphs, lists, footnotes, front matter, and so forth. By making documents conform to structural rules, SGML provides a logic and grammar to the search for document information. It is advantageous for organizations to develop a knowledge of structure in order to look up information based upon structured tags. Third, SGML can identify the content within the structure so that meaningful data elements and attributes can be indexed, retrieved, reused and managed efficiently across computer platforms. Fourth, SGML tagged data, as defined by a DTD, can be used for multiple outputs. For this reason SGML refers to a document as an instance of a document type. When the data changes, the information in the document need only change in one place. The information is managed more efficiently and the long range value of SGML is that it preserves the integrity of valuable information.

We have seen that text retrieval systems find specific text within documents. We have also noted that most text retrieval systems are using the structural identification properties of SGML to search for grains of sand in the document heap. Since SGML identifies the structure of information that makes a document instance, it is very helpful in document management systems.

Shamrock Coalition and Enterprise Document Management (EDM)

A coalition of vendors known as the Shamrock Document Management Coalition is defining issues related to interoperability between various document management systems. A partial list of coalition members include IBM, Saros Corporation, Adobe, Aetna, Andersen Consulting, Interleaf Inc., Hewlett Packard, Sybase and Wang Laboratories. The Shamrock group is concerned with the definition of application program interfaces (APIs) to enable enterprise library services and document communication methods over various computer architectures.

Open Document Management Architecture (ODMA)

New standards are also emerging for opening up interfaces to client applications running in conjunction with a document management system. Again the use of open APIs will play an important part in the development process. The objective of ODMA is to enable document management systems to integrate with desktop applications. The interaction takes place at the client level and enables easy integration of end user applications and document management systems. Several companies are working on the ODMA specification including: Adobe, Anderson Consulting, Cimage Corp., Electronic Book Technologies, Interleaf, Novell, New Science (Gartner Group), Oracle, PC Docs, SoftSolutions Technology, XSoft/Xerox, Watermark, WordPerfect, and others.

Document Enabled Networking (DEN)

The purpose of document enabled networking is to develop an open framework on which developers can build scalable document management services and applications. The services and applications will give users transparent, reliable and uniform access to information in electronic documents, regardless of where they are stored or in what form they exist. Some of the companies involved in making the DEN specification include XSoft/Xerox, Novell, SoftSolutions, and WordPerfect.

ORGANIZATIONAL RESPONSIBILITY

To ensure that document management systems serve the best interest of the organization as a whole, as well as specific workgroups, a forum should be provided for discussion and education of groups to make the best use of the system. Whether the Management Information Systems (MIS) group or other departments become responsible for the system, the objective should always be to maximize the availability of information for user groups. Since information system types are not always familiar with document processes and documenting groups are not always database literate, an educational dialog may be required to open communication between those who create, produce, and track documents, those who control the document management system, and other workgroups who need to access and use information from the system.

A fundamental consideration for any organization is the size and scale of the system. Small scale document management systems intended for a specific workgroup logically become the responsibility of a department or workgroup such as a publication group within a company. Enterprise wide document management systems are another matter. In one sense the system is for all players in the enterprise. Administration of the system may become the responsibility of an information systems group or related services. It is critical that underlying goals of the system (information access, for example) not be hampered by misplaced considerations of ownership.

APPLICATION SAMPLES

Managing Product Information

Managing product information is difficult and expensive. The information may be packaged in a variety of documents from bills of material, safety instructions and assembly procedures to customer support information. See Figure 10.9. The information is also used in many functional areas within an enterprise. If participants in the documenting process have done a thorough job, the information contained in the documents will be an accurate reflection of the product as it was built and shipped. (Unfortunately, this is not always the case.)

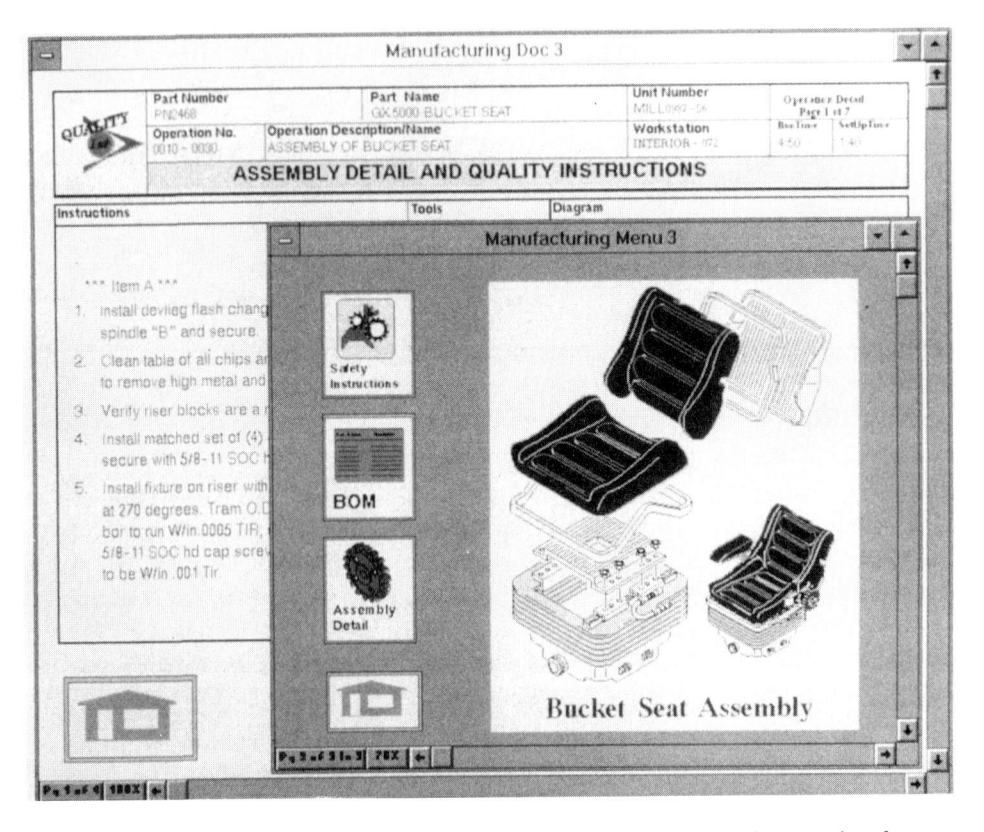

Figure 10.9. Product information access and development is a good example of document management technologies at work. In this screen shot from the Interleaf Intellecte compound document management system, the relationship of manufacturing documents and information to other documents underlines the interdependence of information among manufacturing, engineering, and customer support users of the product information base. (Courtesy of Interleaf, Inc.)

Product information is dynamic. It is difficult to synchronize changes of information that occur in any number of areas (for example, a request from marketing in response to specific customer requirements). Generated by many individuals from different departments, product information constantly changes through phases of design and development. All departments (such as marketing, engineering, manufacturing, test and quality, training, and customer support) depend on documents to design, build, test, sell, and maintain the product. All of these groups share an interest in product information, but such groups are not always aware that this common interest can be supported by a product document management system. Using workflow management to handle the web of information ties among documents can organize a complex information base for projects involving hundreds of employees, allowing all of them to be more informed and productive in the process.

Managing Government Information

Municipal, state, and federal government agencies and branches are acquiring document management systems to improve delivery of services and reduce costs. Various types of document management systems are used by government bodies to streamline operations. For example, the city of Cincinnati is using the BASISPlus text indexing and retrieval software so that city council members and other city employees can search for information rapidly on-line for answers to questions concerning proposed legislation, ordinances, and status of pending items awaiting decision by the city manager. The net result has been more effective flow of information between departments of the city government and less delay in solving municipal problems.

The Ontario legislative assembly staff is required to provide access to the daily legislative proceedings (the Hansard) and Precedents of the Proceedings. Using a document retrieval system furnished by the Open Text Corporation, legislative assistants can access and display information regarding dates, speakers, subjects, and text for all speeches made in the Assembly. A search on all the speeches delivered by a particular member on a topic over a given period, for example, is a common use of the system. The implementation of the document search and retrieval system has greatly reduced a labor intensive process.

The applications for document management in government from intelligence gathering and regulatory compliance to environmental research and judicial proceedings are growing all the time. One of the lessons learned in the use of document management systems in organizations is that the one size fits all does not necessarily apply to every aspect of the organization processes. The Wisconsin State Legislature, for example, is using a combination of tools to help lawmakers.

A document management system from Documentum provides database storage and access to legislative documents. When new legislative documents are created from parts of existing documents, the Smartleaf database publishing product is used in conjunction with Interleaf's publishing tool set to generate many of the documents automatically.

CHAPTER 11

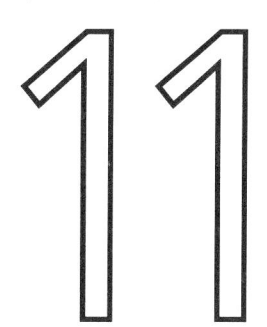

➤ *Analyzing requirements and goals*

➤ *Tips for planners*

➤ *Evaluating workgroup technologies*

➤ *Benchmarking and pilot projects*

➤ *Selected products and suppliers*

Workgroup and Enterprise Solutions

Over the past decade companies have made major investments in tools for worker desktops and have connected many desktops via networks. Most organizations, however, have not designed their systems around the concept of collaborating, retrieving, and reusing information stored in documents. Workgroups and organizations who want to make a transition to new methods of sharing, distributing, and reusing document information must rethink the use of existing and new technologies in the context of business purpose and long term goals.

As companies adopt a team approach to the needs of the organization, the window of opportunity widens to introduce workgroup publishing and document management technologies. Some companies have already adjusted their business processes and used new content based document information technology to compress time in achieving organizational objectives. Other companies have not yet reengineered their business processes but do want a better grasp of their electronic document and information resources. This chapter addresses issues related to planning integrated information/publishing systems for workgroups and the enterprise.

CREATING GROUP INVOLVEMENT: INVITING STAKEHOLDERS

Planning workgroup publishing and document management systems to improve information management and retrieval in an enterprise can be a large undertaking. Organizations that have already transformed themselves into team-based units will probably invite representative team members as well as managers, technical specialists and others to participate in planning an electronic publishing system. Commercial publishers are using business association forums as a means to discuss the market impact of electronic publishing.

There are several reasons for inviting system users and other affected groups to participate in the process. Users identify with the goals of the system. The process of system selection and design becomes less alien. Users and planners examine specific work problems and workflow methodologies before technology solutions are proposed. Users listen to views of other stakeholders which bolsters a collaborative framework for solving problems. Collaboration depends upon more than technology; it results from consultation and cooperation between group members.

Who are the stakeholders? Stakeholders include document users and producers. As document databases rapidly grow, in-house and commercial publishers are changing their focus from the format of documents to the structure and content of documents. The transition is associated with the growth of digital documents, the demand for sharing and distributing information between different computers, and requirements for reusing document information. Electronic publishers are becoming defacto information managers.

ANALYZING REQUIREMENTS

Making a profile of business, technical, and human requirements related to a workgroup or enterprise information/publishing system is a formidable task. We must combine a knowledge of how our business works with the role that publishing and document information plays within it. We must understand the dynamic interplay of business needs and document technologies connecting the work of individual groups and the enterprise as a whole. We must prepare people for change through participation, information sharing, and training. Underlining the need for participation through the requirements phase, will help individuals grow and will contribute to the process.

Focusing on human requirements will raise issues related to changing career roles and responsibilities, the need for safety related to computer use, and alternate possibilities for work such as telecommuting.

Business Model and Vision

Many corporations, government agencies, and other organizations who produce enormous numbers of documents are seemingly unaware that *they are in the information and publishing business.* The information in documents is very often vital to the organization's strategic interests. Whether documents are business plans, specifications, proposals, legal documents, training guides, or manuals, they contain the applied knowledge behind an corporation's products, a law firm's caseload and research, or a government's defense systems. Commercial publishers, who know they are in the publishing business, are looking at the phenomenon of electronic publishing as both a publishing and information service market opportunity.

We can define the technical requirements of the system when we know customer requirements, when we can specify the quantity, frequency, and potential growth of work; and when we have mapped the workgroup process used to create, produce, publish, distribute, and manage documents. To grasp the technical requirements, break down the functional requirements within the workflow such as document authoring, editing, review, and formatting. As the planning group models the resources required for each desktop, they should answer questions such as:

- How long are most of the documents published?
- What types of information are contained in our documents?
- Are the documents layout intensive?
- How do users currently extract information from documents?
- What is the production volume per month? Per Year?
- How often are documents electronically transmitted?
- Will the information in the documents be repeatedly used?
- How many workers are involved?
- What is the document workflow process?
- Do customers have an interest in obtaining our documents in digital form?
- Do we want a single access information retrieval type system for the enterprise?
- Do in-house customers need to view documents to perform work?

Answers to such questions should be based upon verifiable data. While looking at the work done in a publishing environment, we should accumulate workload data, and ask whether the processes themselves make sense for the work being accomplished. Matching tools to team needs and objectives is essential.

Workflow Requirements

Workflow connects the processes with the people. The workflow should be mapped to accomplish collaborative work efficiently. The essential processes are those that relate to information creation and dissemination. What is the nature of work performed by all players? How frequently is the work performed? Groups need to track processes such as the interrelation of the publication process and a document information retrieval process. The analysis of current workflow also provides clues as to the functional areas that may be bottlenecks in the current work process. Workflow technologies interact with other application technologies such as electronic mail, electronic document viewing and review subsystems, text indexing and retrieval, library management, scheduling, and assorted editing systems. Users and managers who need to check the status of work in progress on relevant desktops must clearly define a workflow model that enhances the cohesion of an organization's business and information goals.

Document Conversion Requirements

Documents often undergo several stages of conversion before an organization puts its digital documents in order. Initially, it might be necessary to convert paper documents to digital documents. This can be done by using scanning and optical character recognition software so that the data is transformed into machine readable text. Highly formatted documents (multiple column documents, for example) are difficult to process and there may be problems associated with the accuracy of the conversion.

There will be requirements related to storing electronic data in a consistent format so it can be reused, including conversion to a neutral structured format such as SGML. (Technologies used in SGML conversion are reviewed in Chapters 4 and 7.) Alternative formats may be used such as ASCII, DDIF, RTF, or Acrobat/PDF. Conversion to electronic format is indispensable for text search and retrieval.

Document Authoring Requirements

The use of specific authoring tools in the creation of documents contributes directly to document conversion requirements. Organizations must address electronic file formats used by authors if they want better access to their document information resources. Since authoring tools sometimes also determine how presentation formatting will be handled, decisions must be made on how to preserve the information while measuring productivity benefits and tradeoffs linked to separating formatting from the authoring process.

Another related authoring issue is the use of structured and unstructured methods. By pooling knowledge of document structure and content, a workgroup can establish an effective and organized basis for the storage and retrieval of information for multiple reuses. Finding new methods for measuring productivity based not specifically upon the number of formatted pages produced but on other criteria as well can be critical in the analysis process. Authoring and the various technologies available to support it must become part of an on-going educational process.

Information Retrieval Requirements

Companies need to break down barriers to information. The first step is to identify information that is of long term strategic interest. Much of this information will undoubtedly be in text format, so that it can be retrieved upon user query. It remains for organizations to determine how document information retrieval coheres with business objectives. Rapid information retrieval can improve the flow of information for product developers, narrow proposal and customer inquiry response times, aid legal and medical researchers, and offer government workers a means to streamline service applications.

A critical factor in planning information retrieval is the architecture of the document search and indexing system. Organizations will decide whether to create a single source information access concept or localize information searches to the needs of specific groups. Another architecture issue relates to whether the documents in information bases are structured or unstructured.

Closely associated with information retrieval requirements are growing applications for information integration between information systems, databases, and research and document databases. Information integration includes efforts to increase information accuracy by controlling it at its source as well as ensuring information reusability.

Document Distribution Requirements

The document distribution strategy ties together many threads of the electronic publishing system planning effort. Document delivery depends upon how we have captured, collected, and assembled it. If we have collected and assembled the data in ways to facilitate electronic as well as print distribution, we have anticipated the flexibility needed for various document production and distribution requirements.

There are two main reasons why workgroups use electronically distributed documents. It speeds up information access and it allows producers to update documents easily. To make digital documents work, producers need to know the requirements of those to whom the digital documents will be delivered. In many cases these same users may want both digital and printed documents.

Digital distribution requirements must be balanced with print needs. For producers, the ability to make multiple reuse of a single information source into both electronic and printed documents can be a significant cost benefit over the long term. The payoff for an investment in conversion to a neutral electronic format such as SGML becomes more apparent as one addresses document distribution requirements.

System Scalability Requirements

Many planners outline a full scale system implementation but begin with a pilot program to test out the system within the context of selected workgroups. Planners should examine the scalability features of the technology they are investigating. Scalability allows users to expand the configuration without incurring obsolescence or shortterm upgrade costs such as software licenses, platform investments (such as file server requirement) and other system growth/ capacity features. When modeling an application for a specific workgroup, remember that:

- The ability to upgrade and expand system hardware and the software on the platform is critical. It is important not to underestimate platform scalability and capacity
- Application software may be limited to certain operating systems and windowing products

Integration with Existing Systems

Most organizations do not build a system from scratch. They may have already invested in desktop hardware, word processing programs, desktop publishing and page layout software and other applications capable of driving laser printed output. The missing features are generally the absence of an overall information architecture and specific connectivity between applications handling publishing and formatting of documents, and those that relate to document content. The system technical requirements must elaborate the information architecture of the whole system and clearly identify the migration and evolution of existing sub-systems.

The definition of the system varies from one organization to another depending upon the type of publishing and information management, the size of workload, and specific customer requirements. This list of functions is merely suggestive.

- Text retrieval and indexing
- SGML authoring
- Document conversion
- Workflow management tools
- Document viewing
- Multimedia/hypermedia authoring
- Electronic document interchange and distribution
- Graphics and text translation
- Document management and text retrieval

Since the system may involve the use of multiple software, hardware, and network devices, the complexity of the integration may present unique integration challenges. Consider, for example, linking an existing computer system with a new publishing system. Applications as diverse as databases, spreadsheets, word processors, formatting translators, text retrieval and indexing tools, and document management tools need to be made into a coherent whole for user desktops. To get some applications to communicate with one another (for example, a database and an electronic publishing program) it may require writing code that will enable inputs and outputs from the combined programs to behave properly.

The challenge of system integration is not simply a platform and application issue. Existing publishing systems become more information oriented as users begin to learn more about the capabilities of information retrieval. The greatest challenge for information and publishing system planners is balancing the needs of producing deliverable documents (print and electronic) with the information needs in an organization's document database. The solution is to model publishing and information as on-demand activities and to design a system that meets the objective.

Ergonomic Requirements

With the increasing use of desktop technology in the workplace the incidence of repetitive stress injuries (RSI) is up. The growth of reported cases of RSI in the workplace is a serious concern for electronic publishers. So are the legal implications of RSI. Computer manufacturers and employers of workers who use computer devices for extensive periods at work can be liable for injuries related to RSI. What are some of the injuries associated with RSI? Musculoskeletal injuries are common, especially those related to the lower back. Carpal tunnel syndrome is caused by growth of tissue on the palmar side of the wrist that swells and puts pressure on the nerve that routes through the wrist. Other problems need to be addressed such as glare resulting from exposure to bright light sources. The sources may be a combination of light from video display terminals, florescent light, and other forms of office lighting, including natural light through windows.

To help prevent problems related to RSI, planners are turning to the field of ergonomics. This helps us provide an environment suitable for individuals to work comfortably and accomplish work tasks without undue stress to mind and body. Since electronic publishers work with tools that can lead to injury through overuse or improper training, it is important to design a system that addresses ergonomic concerns thoroughly and honestly. Some specific furnishings and tools that affect user comfort are:

> ➤ Furniture—adjustable height chair with back lumbar support; footrest; desk suited to support proper mounting of desktop devices, especially keyboard and video display

> Auxiliary devices, for example, ergonomic keyboards and pointing devices
> Anti-glare devices

The furniture for mounting various system devices and the lighting are important. The people operating the equipment should have a level of comfort that will help them use the system productively. There are three main elements to consider: the chair selected, the placement of the keyboard, and the distance of the user from the monitor. The chair must have sufficient back rest adjustment and support to minimize lower back ailments and the ability to adjust the height of the chair is critical. Individual users should be able to position their wrists properly in relation to the keyboard, so that they will not be raised upward to accommodate the height of the keyboard. (Some desks do provide pull out drawers on which a keyboard and sometimes computer mouse can be placed.) Proper lighting is important to control glare. If overhead fluorescent lighting is used, commercially available diffusers may soften harsh light that can cause eye strain. Glare reduction may require the installation of drapes or blinds to block out excess sun light.

Designing for injury prevention is a priority in the selection of desktop components as well as the workstation furnishings and lighting. Special components such as ergonomically designed keyboards and pointing devices are helpful. Not all injuries can be prevented by technology alone, users need training regarding ways to prevent injury. The good news is that the training costs very little.

Ergonomic design includes the space available for workstations and publishing equipment. These needs are complex and involve aesthetic, psychological, as well as physiological, aspects. New options will play a large role in the future design of the electronic publishing work environment. To control glare in the user work environment, bright light should not be in the user's field of vision. Tinting windows may be helpful and a terminal should always be placed perpendicular to light sources. Special anti-glare filters can be obtained to offset the problem.

Training Requirements

To use electronic publishing tools effectively, workgroups need an appropriate level of training. Training should not be limited to the specific use of an application program but should allow for continual strengthening of skills. The objective of the training program is to build the competency level of employees. One of the cost benefits of allowing employees to participate in the design of the system is that it can plant the seed for groups to share their knowledge with one another. Workshops allow small groups to swap information about system usage. This type of informal training should be fostered as a requirement. Training can provide a continuous redefinition of work processes made possible by technology.

TIPS FOR PLANNERS

Planners of workgroup-publishing and organization-wide document management solutions often face the complex task of disentangling and reintegrating several computer systems. The following tips are not meant to oversimplify the planning task, but to highlight themes to be addressed in the planning exercise.

Tip 1. No one technology will be the ultimate solution. The system may become a hybrid of SGML authoring, database publishing, document image and library management, text search and retrieval, workflow and change control. Multiple presentation and distribution types may also be supported.

Tip 2. Look at the existing system architecture which includes the network in place and other computer systems in the organization. Connecting desktops with computer networks makes new forms of electronic publishing possible. The underlying theme of connectivity design is open access and interoperability. This means sometimes interfacing with existing systems that were designed in a closed pre-open environment. Without connectivity computer collaboration becomes very limited. With it, we can share knowledge, design ideas, graphic images, video information, databases, text structured for smart interchange, and virtual libraries of information.

Tip 3. Storage space must be carefully analyzed for electronic publishing, document imaging, document management and text and indexing retrieval software.

Tip 4. Keep information in a neutral format to expedite information exchange and reuse. Application programs increasingly support international standards enabling end users to create and share data that is open and portable from system to system. (SGML and Computer Graphics Metafile (CGM), for example, are widely used open information standards.) Some customers require data interchange conforming to such standards and end users find that open information makes sense for the organization as well.

Designing for open information protects the investment in workgroup publishing in several ways. First, it allows us to contend with changes in new technological development. By designing information with an open structure, data can be ported to any future platform requirements. Second, an open information system ensures that other stakeholders, including customers and disparate organizational teams, can access information.

Tip 5. Account for the diverse needs of users, producers, managers, and administrators in the design of the system. Certain desktops, for example, those used by graphic artists, may need a larger size monitor than other system users or access to special photo imaging software and a color laser printer where others won't. Decisions are not made in terms of capability alone, but according to the work to be accomplished.

Tip 6. Measure return on investment (ROI) on a continuing basis. ROI is a standard for measuring productivity gain through the purchase of new tools. The cost benefits of the system must be analyzed by assessing efficiency and productivity gains. Simply put, the investor eventually saves enough money through a decrease in expenses, labor, and related overhead costs, to offset the technology investment.

As part of the business planning, estimate not only how much the system will cost but how much it will potentially save over time. Estimate the system costs by asking vendors for price quotations. To estimate the cost benefit, that is, how much the system will reduce costs some analysis is necessary. To predict a savings, there must be a basis for that estimate.

To measure ROI, sufficient data is needed to estimate the real cost of doing certain tasks without automated capabilities. Workgroups involved in a process should keep records regarding the time spent to complete specific tasks in order to make a meaningful analysis. The period of time to conduct the survey will vary. The sample data can then be compared to the time estimated to do the same tasks with the new technology.

EVALUATING TOOLS

An evaluation of available technology is an opportunity to test and verify the merits of hardware and software components. It is a way to simulate the operations of the system design prior to its implementation. Test and simulation help in selecting vendors and verifying the logic of the technology.

Several scenarios for test and evaluation are possible. Before beginning the evaluation, contact vendors whose products offer features that match the design of the system. Various journals, books, and organizations publish directories. The Datapro Information Services Group publishes reports on user ratings of workstations and similar topics. The Seybold Report is a useful guide for reviewing competitive offerings in electronic and desktop publishing and document management. Invite vendors whose products provide relevant capabilities to demonstrate their system approach. Some vendors will travel to demonstrate their products while others invite customers to a setting where the software will be shown. Others may send an evaluation copy of the software. Planners can collectively prepare for the evaluation by listing out features by product type. Specification and data sheets for products are available from vendors to help planners select those features most critical to improving business processes. Table 11.1 is a sample of a breakdown used in a planning analysis. After listing a feature related to a category, the planners can note whether the feature is required, and note the potential benefit of the feature to a group or the organization.

The screening of particular vendor products for inclusion in an evaluation process should be contingent on several factors. Some useful guidelines to follow in coordinating an evaluation include: 1) the availability of the products to be demonstrated on site or at a facility or within reasonable proximity to the client, 2) budgetary considerations, and 3) the compatibility of vendor products with existing platforms and windowing systems. Another way to narrow the field of vendor participation at the outset is to ask prospective vendors if they can meet user requirements as defined in the system specification. If the vendor system can support a majority of specified features, then the product can be included for consideration.

System Specification

An accurate system specification makes the process of system evaluation and selection more efficient. It will also prevent problems and surprises when the system is installed. A specification document can serve as a single source of information describing how system requirements will be met.

Experienced consultants can draft system specifications or the evaluation group can perform the task depending upon time constraints and other factors. Thoroughness is critical. The evaluators, vendors, and system users will all benefit from a clearly defined system. Misinterpretation of the specification and its purported objectives will be avoided if the information is subjected to rigorous peer review and if the communication process is opened for input from various user groups.

Rating the Products

A form should be designed for evaluating the performance of products that are demonstrated. Before scoring, the group should assign specific weights or values to each parameter to assess its relative significance. For example, applying a scale of 10, where 10 indicates the highest weight, a value of 2.5 means that the parameter is assigned a less significant weight. A sample form of weighted values per parameter is shown in Table 11.2.

When rating the products, the group applies a scoring methodology to show the degree to which it believes the product has the capability to meet the parameter or requirement. Using the weights of Table 11.2, if a score of 2 indicates compliance and the requirement is only partially met, the vendor system scores a 1 for that parameter. A 0 will indicate that the vendor did not satisfy the require-

Table 11.1. Sample Features/Benefit of Document Management

Application/Feature	Benefit
Library management	
File locking control	Prevents overwriting document updates
Automatic versioning of checked in documents	Keeps track of document changes
Managed access to multiple databases/platforms	Enables scalable service architecture
Document index and search	
Search multiple file formats	Reduces need for document conversion
Fuzzy searches	Search for wildcard near matches
Proximity searches	Narrows search to document position
Full text indexing	Assists unstructured document indexing
Search multiple databases	Queries multiple databases in search
Structural searches	Links index tables to structured data
Synonym searches	Includes thesaurus searching
Real time indexing	Shows search results and updates
Workflow Management	
Automatic routing of documents	Routes document to appropriate desktop
Status reporting	Creates router status directory
Electronic mail integration	Unix Mail, Microsoft Mail, cc:mail, etc.
Event notification	Flags events such as file check out
Compound Document Management	
Automatic document assembly	Creates mixed documents dynamically
Support for mixed media objects	Manages multimedia collections
Supports SGML objects	
Store SGML objects/documents in database	Controls component level SGML objects
Build new document instances from SGML objects	Repackages SGML documents on the fly

ment. The evaluation team then multiplies each score (0,1, or 2) by weight (2.5, 5, 7.5, 10) and adds all scores for each vendor.

Benchmarking

Once the system is specified, we can conduct a series of tests. Our selection of vendors and suppliers of tools can depend on these tests. The benchmark may cover both user judgment of certain products and specific product performance tests. To be most useful, the benchmark should simulate conditions of as many pieces of the system playing together as possible.

Two generic tests are operator judgment tests and time measurement tests. The tests indicate performance as well as a more subjective gauge of user comfort with system performance. A generic description of these tests is provided as a guideline. The tests can be modified to suit the specific needs of a user or organization. All tests should be kept as simple as possible, since the user will be relatively new to the system at the time of the test.

The **Operator Judgment** tests focus on how a product scores against a set of criteria or test parameters that affect the user interface to the system. Each

Table 11.2. Electronic Publishing System Sample Scoring

Measurement Parameters	Weight	Vendor X	Vendor Y
Document Search and Indexing			
Full text index	10	2	1
Fuzzy search	5	1	1
Multiple document base query	7.5	1	2
Search query log	5	2	2
Synonym searching	5	1	1
Proximity searching	7.5	1	1
Attach notes to text	5	2	2
User specified noise words	5	1	1
Structure searches	7.5	1	0
Search result sorting	7.5	1	2
Search multiple formats	10	1	2
Relevance ranking	5	2	0
Real time indexing	5	2	1
Total		**115**	**102.5**

specific parameter in this test involves a qualitative judgment that grades the performance of a system in a specific user operation. The operator performs certain operations and makes up a qualitative report on the system's capabilities. Criteria for the operator judgment tests include: 1) ease of learning the system, 2) breadth of features and functionality 3) ease of use, 4) appropriateness to user specified requirements.

The users are asked to rate a product's effectiveness within several categories. Each of these categories is worth n points. A perfect score for all categories would be 100 percent. The test evaluators are encouraged to enter comments to elaborate upon any qualitative issues that need clarification. Sample operator tests are summarized below.

Graphic format conversion

This test assesses the effectiveness of converting graphic files from one format to another. The operators test sample graphic files stored in different formats and convert them with the available product conversion software to determine the effectiveness of the conversion. The source files include graphics in vector and raster format. Some of the parameters used in the test include the amount of time needed to modify a file after conversion and the number of conversion filters available.

SGML/text conversion

The SGML/text conversion tests the efficacy of an SGML conversion tool. Each test poses a different conversion problem. The first test takes a digital document that has been freshly converted from a bitmap file and converted to digital (ASCII) format. The file is approximately 30 pages in length. An industry standard DTD is used as the target for encoding the source ASCII file. The second document will exercise a conversion from a word processing file format into the SGML Rainbow format. The test then transforms the Rainbow format into an SGML document conforming to a selected industry standard DTD.

Document indexing, search, and retrieval

This test evaluates document search and retrieval software capabilities. Multiple unstructured and structured documents stored in a variety of file formats are used in the test. In order to exercise the capabilities of a product thoroughly, the test steps through multiple searching and indexing strategies, including fuzzy, synonym, proximity, concept, and full text searches. The test provides for checking the product's capability to search and retrieve documents across multiple file servers and networks.

SGML authoring

This test measures the range of capabilities in an SGML authoring system. The test concentrates on several operational functions including ease of use and guidance provided by the editing tool. Among other parameters the test covers the context sensitive application of markup, automatic insertion of start tags and end tags, the ability to suppress markup, dynamic and partial validation, and structural navigation. Common source documents of variable length are used in the test.

Image editing

This measures the performance of the color photo image manipulation. Two color photos are scanned into the system. The test requires that the two photos are merged and edited for a series of enhancement effects including scaling, rotating, cloning, regional pixel coloring and editing, smoothing and color transformations, shadowing and pixel editing. The result is printed from a color printer for inspection.

Workflow

This test walks through a workflow product's ability to manage a sample document creation and review cycle. The test checks the software's capability for setting up a workflow process and the subsequent integration of event notification, electronic mail and routing tools to complete the workflow process cycle. Part of the test checks for ease of operator use in determining the status of the test document, the visibility of flagged events, and accessibility of the document and related objects to complete the task.

Document viewing and navigation

This test addresses a range of document viewing and navigation capabilities including support for linear and non-linear hypertext navigation, provision for user created annotations, acceptance of SGML or other standard formats, ability to render graphics inline and in other windows, and for dynamic changes of fonts and style according to window size.

The operator interface tests can be scored by individuals who have participated in special training sessions on the vendor systems. The same people should take part in scheduled practice sessions. After the round of practice sessions is completed, the operators can complete the operator judgment benchmark forms.

The **Time Measurement** tests are designed to assess: 1) the time required to perform discrete operations, and 2) the verification of functions specified by each vendor product. The time tests, like the operator tests, are modular. Each test measures the performance of specific software, not the system as a whole.

Automatic document assembly

This test can be applied to various software modules including database publishing programs and document management automatic assembly subsystems. The document assembly test is used in conjunction with a database publishing or word processing system. A template is defined for the word processing/desktop publishing program. The time measurement covers the time taken to extract data stored in databases or files for inclusion in an automatically formatted document.

OCR conversion

This test measures the time required to convert a 30 page clean and legible document into machine readable text as free from errors as possible. In addition to accounting for the time to set up the relevant OCR software, the test measures the time to edit the document after automatic conversion to make it error free.

Table creation using SGML tools

This test evaluates the automatic table generation capability of an SGML authoring tool. It measures the time to create a 3 page table with 4 columns and 25 rows per page, variable cell and column sizes on one page, and repeated table title and column heads.

Graphic conversion tests

This test measures the time for conversion from a series of vector file formats into others. It also measures any additional time to make the drawing acceptable, using a standard drawing editor, after the conversion.

Text search and retrieval tests

This test measures the time required to search through a large document database and with search and indexing retrieval software. Multiple documents and files are transferred to disk and used as test specimens. The documents collectively should be a minimum of 10 megabytes. A common hardware platform is used for the test. A variety of file formats are also used. The specific tests exercise a series of search and indexing options such as proximity search and multiple document base search.

Document on-demand printing

This test measures the time taken to perform the queuing, printing, and collating of multiple copies of a 100 page document from various platforms over a network. Several variations in the tests are performed to include back to back page printing, automatic stapling, and special cover/page insertions.

The design involves the selection of samples to be used as test documents which should include form and content suitable to the objectives of the plan. For consistency, the same operators should perform the time tests with all products and sub-systems. During the execution of each test, the test designer can serve as a witness to the test performance. This individual should record the time to complete a test operation, and other manipulations required to set up and execute a test function. Strict adherence to quantifiable criteria can make the time and verification measurement tests a reliable indicator of product performance.

Prototyping the System

A system should be introduced in a pilot fashion to meet the needs of selected workgroups before implementing an enterprise solution. In the planning phase, it is important to envision the system as a whole. In the implementation phase, it is best to work with a manageable scale. In practice, this means that the system is piloted on a small scale, then debugged and gradually expanded to other users. The initial pilot program may, for example, involve use of selected documents associated with a workgroup project.

Collaborative work depends on sharing information. It is important to make the system design flexible enough to meet new and unanticipated requirements. As the system grows, its overall effectiveness may well depend upon the efforts to continually improve the system and the processes related to its use.

WORKGROUP/ENTERPRISE PUBLISHING PRODUCTS

Because many products are new, it takes time to know the vendors and workgroup publishing/document management products. This section lists products and representative vendors of products and services. The list is not comprehensive, but it is representative of the products and companies supporting workgroup/enterprise publishing solutions. The products listed are divided by categories. No price information is included.

LIST OF PRODUCTS AND VENDORS[1]

Animation

Product/Service	Name of Company
Animator Pro/3D Studio	**Autodesk Inc.** 2320 Marinship Way Sausalito, CA 94965 415.491.2344
Composer	**Wavefront Technologies** 530 East Montecito Street Santa Barbara, CA 93103 805.962.8117
Macromedia Director	**Macromedia Inc.** 600 Townsend Street Suite 310 West San Francisco, CA 94103 415/252/2000

CD-ROM/CD-Rs

Product/Service	Name of Company
CDD 521 (CD-R)	**Philips Consumer Electronics** 1 Philips Drive PO Box 14810 Knoxville, TN 37914–1810 615.521.4316
CDU-561	**Sony Corporation of America** 1 Sony Drive Park Ridge, New Jersey 07656–8003 800.352.7669
InterSect CDR-74/84 (CD-ROM)	**NEC Technologies Inc.** 1414 Massachusetts Ave. Boxborough, MA 01719 800.388.8888

1. This list of products and vendors (by category) is not an all-inclusive list. An updated list will be available in future printings. The inclusion of a product does not represent an endorsement.

List of Products and Vendors **285**

Personal RomMaker (CD-R)　　**JVC Information Products Co.**
17811 Mitchell Avenue
Irvine, CA 92714
714.261.1292

435 Series (CD-ROM)　　**Chinon America, Inc.**
615 Hawaii Avenue
Torrance, CA 90503
800.441.0222

Color Image/Photo Editing

Product/Service　　*Name of Company*

Photoshop　　**Adobe Systems Inc.**
1585 Charleston Road
PO Box 7900
Mountain View, CA 94039–7900
415.961.4400

PixelFX　　**Mentalix**
1700 Alma Drive
Suite 110
Plano, Texas 75075
214.423.1145

Picture Publisher　　**Micrografx**
1303 East Arapaho Road
Richardson, Texas 75081
800.733.3729

Database Publishing

Product/Service　　*Name of Company*

Corel Ventura DataBase Publisher　　**Corel Corporation**
1600 Carling, Ave.
Ottawa, Ontario K!Z8R7
Canada
613.728.8200

dbPublisher	**STEP2 Software**
	1501 4th Ave
	Suite 2270.
	Seattle, WA
	800.527.2506
Info Publisher	**PageAhead Software Corporation**
	2125 Western Avenue, Suite 300
	Seatte, WA 98121
	206.441.0340
Smartleaf/Compare	**DataBase Publishing Software, Inc.**
	Suite 5300
	400 West Cummings Park
	Woburn, MA 01801
	617.938.0018
XData	**Exchange Software Inc.**
	724 Whalers Way
	Bldg. H, Suite 101
	Fort Collins, CO 80525
	800.788.7557

Desktop Publishing

Product/Service	*Name of Company*
Corel Ventura	**Corel Corporation**
	1600 Carling, Ave.
	Ottawa, ON K!Z8R7
	Canada
	613.728.8200
FrameMaker	**Frame Technology**
	333 West San Carlos Street
	San Jose, CA 95110
	408.975.6000
Interleaf 5/6	**Interleaf, Inc.**
	Prospect Place
	9 Hillside Ave.
	Waltham, MA 02154
	617.290.0710

PageMaker	**Aldus Corporation** 411 First Ave. South Seattle, WA 98104 206.622.5500
QuarkXPress	**Quark Inc.** 1800 Grant Street Denver, CO 80203 800.788.7835

Document Analysis

Product/Service	*Name of Company*
Near & Far	**Microstar Software, Ltd.** 34 Colonnade Rd. North Nepean, Ontario Canada, K2E7J6 613.727.5696
RulesBuilder	**SoftQuad, Inc.** 56 Aberfoyle Crescent Suite 810 Toronto, Ontario Canada, M8X2W4 416.239.4801

Document Image Management

Product/Service	*Name of Company*
AV Image	**Data General Corporation** 4400 Computer Drive Westborough, MA 508.366.8911
Lotus Notes: Document Imaging	**Lotus Development Corporation** 55 Cambridge Parkway Cambridge, MA 02142 800.346.1305

OmniDesk	**Sigma Imaging Systems** 622 3rd Avenue New York, NY 10017 212.476.3000
OpenImage	**Wang Laboratories, Inc.** One Industrial Avenue M/S 019-A90 Lowell, MA 01851 800.639.0828
Watermark	**Watermark Software, Inc.** 129 Middlesex Turnpike Burlington, MA 01803 617.229.2600

Document Management (SGML Database)

Product/Service	*Name of Company*
ActiveServer	**Active Systems** 8 West New England Park Burlington, MA 617.229.6668
BASISPlus SGML Server	**Information Dimensions Inc.** 5080 Tuttle Crossing Blvd. Dublin, Ohio 43017 1–800-DATA-MGT
DynaBase	**Electronic Book Technologies** One Richmond Square Providence, RI 02906 401.421.9551
ISYS	**Odyssey Development. Inc.** 8775 East Orchard Road Denver Technological Center, Suite 811 Denver, CO 80111 800.992.4797

InfoPak	**Mobius Management Systems Inc.** 1 Ramada Plaza New Rochelle, NY 10801 914.632.7960
OfficeSmith	**Office Smiths** Division of CTMG 11 Holland Ave. Suite 200 Ottawa, Ontario Canada 613.729.2043
Open Text/SGML	**Open Text Corporation** 180 King Street South Suite 550 Waterloo, Ontario, Canada N2J1P8
SGML Editorial System	**MID Information Logistics Group** Ringstrasse 19 D-69115 Heidelberg, Germany 49 6221 166091
SGML/Store	**Berger-Levrault AIS** 34 Avenue du Roule 92200 Neuilly sur Seine, France 33.1.46 40 10 60
PassagePro	**Passage Systems Inc.** 465 Fairchild Drive, Suite 201 Mountain View, CA 94043 415.390.0919
Parlance Document Manager	**Xyvision Inc.** PDM Marketing 101 Edgewater Drive Wakefield, MA 01880–1291 617.245.4100

Document Management (Workflow)

Product/Service	Name of Company
Analyst/Builder/Manager	**Action Technologies** 1301 Marina Village Parkway Suite 100 Alameda, CA 94501 510.521.6190
CMS/Workflow	**Workgroup Technology Corporation** 81 Hartwell Avenue Lexington, Ma 02173 617.674.2000
In Concert	**XSoft** A Division of Xerox 3400 Hillview Avenue Palo Alto, CA 415.424.0111
OPEN/Workflow	**Wang Laboratories, Inc.** One Industrial Avenue M/S 019-A90 Lowell, MA 01851 800.639.0828
WorkMan	**Reach Software** 872 Hermosa Drive Sunnyvale, CA 94086 408.733.8685

Document Management (Compound)

Product/Service	Name of Company
Documentum	**Documentum, Inc.** 4683 Chabot Drive Suite 102 Pleasanton, CA 94588–2748 510.463.6800

Intellecte	**Interleaf, Inc.** Prospect Place 9 Hillside Ave. Waltham, MA 02154 617.290.0710
Open ODMS	**Odesta Systems Corporation** 4084 Commercial Avenue Northbrook, IL 60062 708.498.5615
Parlance Document Manager	**Xyvision Inc.** PDM Marketing 101 Edgewater Drive Wakefield, MA 01880–1291 617.245.4100

Document Library Management/Middleware

Product/Service	*Name of Company*
Visual Recall	**XSoft** A Division of Xerox 3400 Hillview Avenue Palo Alto, California 94304 415.424.0111
PC Docs Open	**PC DOCS** 124 Marriott Drive Tallahassee, FL 32361 904.942.3627
Saros Document Manager/Mezzanine	**Saros Corporation** 700 Plaza Center 10900 N.E. 8th Street Bellevue, Washington 98004 206.462.0879
SoftSolutions	**SoftSolutions Technology Corp.** 1555 North Technology Way, Building H Orem, UT 84057 801.226.6000

OPEN/Profound

Wang Laboratories, Inc.
One Industrial Avenue
M/S 019-A90
Lowell, MA 01851
800.639.0828

Lotus Notes

Lotus Development Corporation
55 Cambridge Parkway
Cambridge, MA 02142
800.346.1305

Electronic Document Reference, Viewing, Hypertext, and Distribution

Product/Service

Name of Company

Adobe Acrobat

Adobe Systems, Inc.
1585 Charlestown Road
Mountain View, CA
415.961.4400

BookManager

IBM Corp.
4111 North Side Parkway
Atlanta, GA 30237
800.426.2255

Common Ground

No Hands Software
1301 Shoreway Road
Suite 220
Belmont, CA 94002
415.802.5800

KwAre/Omni Search

Knowledge Access
2685 Marine Way
Suite 1305
Mountain View, CA 94043
415.969.0606

Guide Viewer/Guide Reader

InfoAccess
2800 156 Ave. SE
Bellevue, WA 98007
206.747.3203

List of Products and Vendors

DynaText **Electronic Book Technologies**
One Richmond Square
Providence, RI 02906
401.421.9551

Explorer **SoftQuad, Inc.**
56 Aberfoyle Crescent
Suite 810
Toronto, Ontario
Canada, M8X2W4
416.239.4801

HyperCard **Apple Computer, Incorporated**
20525 Mariani Avenue
Cupertino, CA 95041
800.776.2333

Knowledge Retrieval System **Knowledge Set**
55 Ellis Street
Mountain View, CA
415.254.5400

OLIAS **Hal Software Systems**
3006A Longhorn Blvd., Suite 113
Austin, Texas 78578
512.834.9962

Pathways **Westinghouse Electric Company**
PO Box 746
Baltimore, MD 21298–6451
410.993.2214

xText **Flambeaux Software**
1147 East Broadway
Suite 56
Glendale, CA
818.500.0044

WorldView Press **Interleaf, Inc.**
Prospect Place
9 Hillside Ave.
Waltham, MA 02154
617.290.0710

Graphic Viewers and Linkers

Product/Service

MetaLink

CADleaf Viewer

Name of Company

InterCAP Graphics Systems
116 Defense Highway, 4th Floor
Annapolis, MD 21401
410.224.2926

Carberry Technology
600 Suffolk Street
Lowell, MA 01854
508.970.5358

Graphic Conversion Tools

Product/Service

HiJaak

X-Change

CADleaf Plus/CL Batch

DeBabelizer

Raster Master

Name of Company

Inset Systems
71 Commerce Drive
Brookfield, CT 06804–3405
203.775.5634

InterCAP Graphics Systems
116 Defense Highway, 4th Floor
Annapolis, MD 21401
410.224.2926

Carberry Technology
600 Suffolk Street
Lowell, MA 01854
508.970.5358

Equilibrium Technologies
475 Gate Five Rd., Suite 225
Sausilito, CA 95695
415.332.4343

Audre, Inc.
10915 Technology Place
San Diego, California 92127
619.451.2260

Graphics Drawing Software

Product/Service	Name of Company
Adobe Illustrator	**Adobe Systems Corp.** 15585 Charleston Road PO Box 7900 Mountain View, CA 94039 415.961.3769
Aldus FreeHand	**Aldus, Corporation** 411 First Ave. South Seattle, WA 98104 206.622.5500
Claris Draw	**Claris Corporation** 5201 Patrick Henry Drive Box 58168 Santa Clara, CA 408.987.7000
Corel Draw	**Corel Corporation** 1600 Carling Avenue Ottawa, ON Canada, K1Z 8R7 613.728.8200
Micrografx Designer	**Micrographx Inc.** 1303 Arapaho Road Richardson, TX 75081 800.733.3729

HyTime Tools

Product/Service	Name of Company
HyMinder	**TechnoTeacher Inc.** PO Box 3208 1810 Highland Road Tallahassee, FL 32303-4408 904.422.3574

Image Catalog/Browsers

Product/Service	Name of Company
ImageManager	**Electronic Imagery Inc.** 1100 Park Central Blvd. South, Ste. 3400 Pompano Beach, FL 33064 305.968.7100
ImageBASE	**Visual Information, Inc.** 600 17th St. Denver, CO 303.892.0304
Ultimedia Workplace/2	**IBM Corp.** 11475 Reeck Rd. Southgate, MI 800.UTS.7771
Kudo Image Browser	**Imspace Systems** 2665 Ariane Dr suite 207 San Diego, CA 92117 800.488.5386

Index, Search and Retrieval

Product/Service	Name of Company
askSam	**askSam Systems** P.O. Box 1428 Perry, FL 32347 800.800.1997
Ful/Text	**Fulcrum Technologies, Inc.** 785 Carling Ave. Ottawa, Ontario Canada K1S5H4 613.238.1761
Excalibur	**Excalibur Technologies Corp.** 9255 Towne Center Drive 9th Floor San Diego, CA 92121 619.625.7900

List of Products and Vendors   297

ISYS

Odyssey Development. Inc.
8775 East Orchard Road
Denver Technological Center
Suite 811
Denver, CO 80111
800.992.4797

Folio Views

Folio Corp.
2155 North Freedom Blvd.
Suite 1500
Provo, UT 84604
801.375.3700

On Location

On Technology, Inc.
155 Second St.
Cambridge, MA 02141
617.374.1400

Topic

Verity, Inc.
1550 Plymouth
Mountain View, CA 94043–1230
415.960.7600

ZyIndex

ZyLabs
1130 West Lake Cook Rd
Buffalo Grove, IL 60089
708.632.1100/800.544.6339

Internet Publishing

Product/Service

HotMetal Pro

Name of Company

SoftQuad, Inc.
56 Aberfoyle Crescent
Suite 810
Toronto, Ontario M8X2W4
416.239.4801

OLIAS

HAL Software Systems
3006 Longhorn Blvd., #113
Austin, Texas 78578
512.834.9962

Multimedia Authoring

Product/Service	Name of Company
Icon Author	AimTech, Corporation 20 Trafalgar Square, Suite 300 Nashua, NH 03063–1987 603.883.0220
Mediawrite	Paradise Software, Inc. 55 Princeton-Highstown Rd., Suite 109 Princeton Junction, NJ 08550 609.655.0016
Multimedia ToolBook	Asymetrix Corp. 110 110th Ave. NE #117 Bellevue, WA 98004 206.637.1500
Authorware Professional	Macromedia Inc 600 Townsend Street Suite 310 West San Francisco, CA 94103 415.252.2000

OCR Software

Product/Service	Name of Company
Genie	Solution Technology, Inc. 1101 S. Rogers Circle Boca Raton, FL 33487 407.241.3210
OmniPage Professional	Caere Corp. 100 Cooper St. Las Gatos, CA 408.395.7000
TypeReader	ExperVision 3590 North First Street San Jose, CA 95134 408.428.9988

Textpert	CTA, Inc. 747 3rd Ave., 3rd Flr. New York, NY 10017 212.935.2280

On-demand Printing

Product/Service	Name of Company
LionHeart	Eastman Kodak Company 343 State Street Rochester, NY 14650 716.724.4000
Xerox Docutech Network Publisher	Xerox Corporation Long Ridge Road Stamford, CT 06904 203.968.3000/800.DOCUTECH

On-line Information Services

Product/Service	Name of Company
America On-line	Quantum Computer Services, Inc. 8619 Westwood Center Drive Vienna, VA 22182 800.227.6364
CompuServe	CompuServe Information Services PO Box 20212 5000 Arlington Center Blvd. Columbus, Ohio 800.848.8199
Delphi	General Videotex Corporation 3 Blackstone Street Cambridge, MA 02139 617.491.3342
Dialog	Dialog Information Services, Inc. 3460 Hillview Avenue Palo Alto, CA 94304 415.858.2700

Dow Jones News/Retrieval

Dow Jones & Company
PO Box 300
Princeton, NJ 08543
609.520.4641

LEXIS-NEXIS Services

Mead Data Central
9393 Springboro Pike
Post Office Box 933
Dayton, OH 45401–0933
800.222.692

Prodigy Interactive Personal Services

Prodigy Services Company
445 Hamilton Avenue
White Plains, NY 10601
800.776.3449

Westlaw

West Publishing Company
620 Opperman Drive
Egan, MN 55123
612.687.7000

Scanners

Product/Service

Name of Company

PixelCraft

PixelCraft
130 Doolittle Drive
San Leandro, CA 94577
510.562.2480

IX-4015

Cannon Computer Systems, Inc.
2995 Redhill Ave.
Costa Mesa, CA 92626
714.438.3000

Scan Jet

Hewlett-Packard
3000 Hanover Street
Palo Alto, CA 94304
800-SCANJET, x 7802

Scanmaster scanners

Howtek Inc.
21 Park Ave.
Hudson, NH 03051
603.882.5200

JX 325/450/610	**Sharp Electronics Corporation** Sharp Plaza Mahwah, NJ 07430 201.529.9600
ScanVu	**Microtek Lab, Inc.** 3715 Doolittle Drive Radando Beach, CA 90278 310.297.5000

SGML Authoring Tools

Product/Service	*Name of Company*
Author/Editor	**SoftQuad, Inc.** 56 Aberfoyle Crescent, Suite 810 Toronto, Ontario Canada, M8X2W4 416.239.4801
ADEPT Editor	**ArborText Inc** 1000 Victors Way Ann Arbor, MI 48108 313.996.3566
InContext	**InContext Systems** 2 St. Clair Ave. West, Suite 1600 Toronto, Ontario Canada, M4V1I5 416.922.0087
Grif SGML Editor	**Grif S. A.** Immeuble "Le Florestan" 2, boulevard Vauban B.P. 266 St. Quentin en Yvelines 78053 Cedex, France 33 (1) 30 12 14 30
Intellitag	**WordPerfect Corp.** 1555 N Technology Way Orem, UT 84057 2300 801.225.5000

Interleaf SGML	**Interleaf Inc.** Prospect Place 9 Hillside Ave. Waltham, MA 02154 617.290.0710
SGML Smart Editor	**Auto-Graphics Inc.** 3201 Temple Avenue Pomona, CA 909.595.7294
WriteIt	**Sema Group** AG Building Place du Champ de Mars 5 Bte 40 B1050 Brussels, Belgium 32 25 08 53 23
WriterStation	**Datalogics** 441 W. Huron Chicago, Illinois 60610 312.266.3202

SGML Conversion Tools

Product/Service	Name of Company
Balise	**Berger-Levrault AIS** 34 Avenue du Roule 92200 Neuilly sur Seine, France 33.1.46 40 10 60
DynaTAG	**Electronic Book Technologies** One Richmond Square Providence, RI 02906 401.421.9551
FastTAG	**Avalanche Development, Co.** 947 Walnut Street Boulder, CO 303.449.5032

IBM SGML Translator	**IBM Corp.** 400 Columbus, Ave. Valhalla, NY 914.749.3409
OmniMark	**Exoterica, Corp.** 338 Parkdale Ave., Ste. 406 Ottawa, Ontario Canada 613.722.1700
PowerPaste	**ArborText** 1000 Victors Way Suite 400 Ann Arbor, MI 48108 313.996.3566
TagWrite	**Zandar Corp.** RR2 Box 962 (Hanley Lane) PO Box 467 Jericho, VT 05645 802.899.1058
TransSGML	**Xyvision Inc.** PDM Marketing 101 Edgewater Drive Wakefield, MA 01880–1291 617.245.410

SGML Parsers

Product/Service	*Name of Company*
Mark-it	**Sema Group** AG Building Place du Champ de Mars 5 Bte 40 B1050 Brussels, Belgium 32 25 08 53 23

SGML Kernel

Exoterica
1545 Carling Ave., Suite 404
Ottawa, Ontario Canada
613.722.1700

SGML Viewers

Product/Service	Name of Company
DynaText	**Electronic Book Technologies** One Richmond Square Providence, RI 02906 401.421.9551
Guide Viewer/Guide Reader	**InfoAccess** 2800 156 Ave. SE Bellevue, WA 98007 206.747.3203
OLIAS	**Hal Software Systems** 3006A Longhorn Blvd., Suite 113 Austin, Texas 78578 512.834.9962
WorldView Press	**Interleaf, Inc.** Prospect Place 9 Hillside Ave. Waltham, MA 02154 617.290.0710

Visualization

Product/Service	Name of Company
ANSYS	**Swanson Analysis Systems, Inc.** Johnson Road P.O. Box 65 Houston, PA 15342-0065 412.746.3304

PV Wave

Visual Numerics
777 29th Street, Ste. 302
Boulder, CO 80303
303.530.9000

Visualizer

Wavefront Technologies
530 East Montecito Street
Santa Barbara, CA 93103
805.962.8117

Workgroup Publishing & Application Suites

Product/Service

Name of Company

PerfectOffice

Novell Applications Group
1555 North Technology Way
Orem, UT 84057
801.222.4450

Interleaf 6

Interleaf, Inc.
Prospect Place
9 Hillside Ave.
Waltham, MA 02154
617.290.0710

Lotus Smart Suite for Windows

Lotus Development Corp.
55 Cambridge Parkway
Cambridge, MA 02142
800.343.5414

Microsoft Office Professional

Microsoft Corp.
One Microsoft Way
Redmond, WA 98052
206.882.8080

FrameMaker/FrameBuilder

Frame Technology Corporation
333 West San Carlos Street
San Jose, CA 95110
408.975.6000

Quark Dispatch   **Quark Inc.**
                                1800 Grant Street
                                Denver, Colorado 80203
                                800.788.7835

Technical Illustration Software

Product/Service   *Name of Company*

Illustrator   **InterCAP Graphic Systems, Inc**
                                116 Defense Highway 4th Floor
                                Annapolis, MD 21401
                                410.224.2926

Tech Illustrator   **Auto-trol Technology Corporation**
                                12500 N. Washington
                                Denver, CO 80241–2404
                                303.452.4919

CHAPTER 12

➤ *Opportunities*

➤ *Knowledge workers*

➤ *Learning organizations*

➤ *Teams and telework*

Electronic Publishing is Changing Careers

a knowledge of how to use and apply electronic publishing can lead to crossroads in career paths. Electronic publishing affects how individuals with traditional careers related to making documents as well as those who depend on document information do their job. It also links workgroup teams and allows them to redefine ways of making and distributing documents.

While electronic publishing was originally seen as a means to streamline existing paper document production processes, it has become a contributing factor to structural changes in the fields of communications and information science and has transformed methods of work. Pulling many technologies together, it connects people in novel ways of communicating, presenting, and managing information. Assembly workers in one corner of a company follow document based work instructions and drawings presented on a computer rather than paper, while in another area customer support personnel assist clients over the telephone with information retrieved from a document database. As individuals adapt to conditions and opportunities resulting from changing practices, they help define the requirements of the work place. Since electronic publishing will continue to impact how people work and what services and products their labor supports, we will examine some of the challenges, risks, and opportunities for managers and workers undergoing this technological revolution.

OPPORTUNITIES

Many positions are not new such as writers, editors, illustrators, and designers whose titles, among others, have not changed. But the skill requirements needed to obtain a traditional position have. Electronic publishing has irrevocably altered requirements for jobs that once had little to do with computer skills. New career titles such as computer animation specialist, document analyst, multimedia designer, or document database manager, require special expertise and computer training. Management titles may not have changed but managers are facing complex challenges not the least of which is to figure out what people do with electronic publishing tools.

Electronic publishing presents challenges to creative professionals with diverse backgrounds. It reaches beyond office workers to production specialists on the shop floor to maintenance technicians in the field to teachers in the classroom. This overview merely scratches the surface of jobs affected and opportunities for career development. Some of the categories derive from positions found within corporations and government agencies. There are positions within the companies that develop and sell electronic publishing products and systems and the many consulting services that help customers use electronic publishing effectively. Advertising firms, graphic art studios, and entertainment media companies are a growing source of opportunities for individuals gaining experience in computer aided graphics and photography as well as animation and multimedia. Publishers of electronic books delivered on CD-ROM are proliferating. Workers skilled with electronic publishing and related digital tools are needed in print shops, typesetting houses, and service bureaus. The world of broadcasting and print journalism are increasingly dependent upon electronic publishing technologies. Not surprisingly, electronic publishing is playing a growing role within institutions (universities, libraries, and research foundations), where qualified expertise is in demand.

Although human resource professionals try to follow trends in industry regarding job classifications and descriptions, organizations are slow to recognize structural changes in jobs that are in the process of reinventing themselves. Since an organization's own values and perception of the need for communication and information services color its judgment, it may lack the appropriate metric for observing and measuring changes in work performed.

Opportunities within Organizations

The effect of electronic publishing technology upon career roles has not yet been studied systematically. Official acceptance of new job titles takes time. The speed with which powerful tools and capabilities have been introduced into the workplace has outpaced efforts by management and human resource specialists to identify and codify evolving categories of work. Many organizations have not prepared for the organizational and process change required to accommodate technical advances. Some of the key factors affecting work performance associated with the introduction of electronic publishing in organizations are:

- Reduced time to create and produce documents
- New emphasis on visual forms of thinking
- Focus on information planning and retrieval
- Creation of new products (for example, multimedia documents)
- Expansion of work team beyond department boundary
- Development of process awareness

New Wave Opportunities

Career roles for individuals and groups are changing and will vary from one workplace to another. The variations relate to specific businesses and industries and to such factors as customer driven requirements that demand change from supplier businesses. Other variations are driven by market forces and competitive considerations.

Document Analyst

Document analysts are key players in the growth of electronic publishing applications and the transition from paper to electronic forms of document delivery. A document analyst examines categories of documents for structure and content. They study the requirements for structure and content as applied to a particular industry (aerospace, telecommunications, pharmaceutical, defense, finance, journalism, for example) and define that structure by referring to existing models for documents such as SGML document type definitions (DTDs). They also generate new document type definitions when existing DTDs do not suffice. The title of document analyst has taken on special meaning. With growing use of SGML as a document interchange tool, the need for document analysts will increase as more industries migrate to document interchange standards. Document analysts will be more in demand in organizations that recognize the importance of information as a critical part of the business.

Document analysts play a significant role in publication planning. One particular aspect is classifying information according its value over time (enduring or perishable). Document data with enduring value is called legacy data by SGML specialists. Legacy data is critical to long term business, research, or service and support processes. Document analysts help reuse document information intelligently, making content suitable for varied audiences and effective for print and electronic delivery applications. When the analysis function is done properly, the document analyst can map information to be authored and maintained in a database but used in multiple documents. The work performed by a document analyst is important to companies who value information and want to use and reuse it effectively. See Figure 12.1 for a position description of document analyst.

Electronic Document Designer

The electronic document designer combines knowledge of traditional typography with acquired skills in designing documents for electronic presentation and delivery. The role of the designer has much in common with the traditional designer of print media as both collaborate with other players in projects that have a certain scope, schedule, budget, audience, and skill requirement such as typography, graphic design, and visual imagination. See Figure 12.2 for the position description of the electronic document designer.

One critical difference in design work for the electronic document designer includes the concept of user navigation and random document access, better known as interactivity. Perhaps the most critical challenge for an electronic document designer is the task of simplification. The design must help the user understand the design of the document. Making information understandable for an electronic audience includes everything from IRS forms to pictures of complex machines.

The electronic document designer normally interacts with several players on a project. These players may include authors, editors, programmers, video specialists, and customers. Working in conjunction with such players, the document designer participates in the planning, storyboarding, development, proof of concept, and implementation phases of the project.

Publication Programmer

Publishing systems for workgroups can be enhanced by specialized expertise in the automation of tasks that integrate publishing applications with other computer software programs. The demand is growing for such expertise as more information is routinely distributed to more desktops, and more corporations are recognizing the need to integrate an information architecture that includes electronic publishing technologies.

A publication programmer works with application program interface (API) tools. Many vendors offer tool kits that enhance the functions of publishing software by writing programs to help customize the publishing environment. Interleaf, for instance, sells a tool kit that gives users access to what it calls active document technologies. An active document may consist of a financial report that

DOCUMENT ANALYST

POSITION DESCRIPTION

Analyzes requirements for classes of documents for different audiences. Researches information needs for those industries. Responsible for seeing how information may be used in multiple documents both within and outside the organization. Knowledgeable concerning standards for electronic document interchange including SGML.

ELECTRONIC PUBLISHING IMPACT

The document analysis role has expanded with the emergence of electronic interchange standards such as SGML. These analysts can play a significant part in the shift from paper to the paperless office. They can help assure that the information targeted for paper will also be available for electronic documents and that the quality of the information (accuracy and adequacy) is preserved over time.

QUALIFICATIONS

- Knowledge of document structures and types
- Familiarity with specific industry structure and information requirements (commercial book, periodical, and serial publications; defense, telecommunications, automotive, aviation)
- Experience with SGML authoring and document type definition (DTDs)
- Understanding of SGML conversion tools and applications
- Knowledge of print and electronic document distribution requirements

RELATED TRACKS

Document management

Information management

ORGANIZATIONS

Electronic Publishing Special Interest Group (EPSIG)

Figure 12.1. Document analyst position description.

ELECTRONIC DOCUMENT DESIGNER

POSITION DESCRIPTION

Designs presentation of electronic documents, books, hypermedia/multimedia projects for in-house production. Is familiar with windowing systems and interactive presentation for display terminals. Specifies project templates.

ELECTRONIC PUBLISHING IMPACT

Electronic document design has become an important field in its own right and more companies will focus on recruiting such expertise as they adopt electronic document delivery mechanisms.

QUALIFICATIONS

- Knowledge of digital type
- Experience with design for windowing systems
- Familiar with different demands of print and electronic presentation
- Experience with electronic layout tools
- Knowledge of digital color imaging

RELATED TRACKS

Multimedia design
Color imaging and prepress
Computer animation

Figure 12.2. Electronic document designer position description.

updates automatically when changes are made in a financial database. To use Interleaf's active documents effectively (or other vendor tool kits) requires a knowledge of programming. Interleaf offers LISP as its object programming tool; other vendors provide a C, C++, or another scripting tool as a programmable interface.

A publication programmer writes programs or scripts that enable special ways of sorting data, retrieving data, or manipulating documents. Whether to bring such a person on staff as a permanent position or contract consultants on an as-required basis depends upon long range planning. The programmer assists document managers, system administrators, and planning analysts in the selection and implementation of tools. For example, a publication programmer can:

- Automate connections of document workflow and viewing systems
- Use programmable tool kits to customize graphical user interfaces
- Write program scripts in support of database publishing initiatives
- Customize conversion or transformation of SGML data with aid of scripts
- Customize interfaces to other applications (spreadsheets, etc.)
- Convert graphic data from one file format to another
- Integrate a multimedia collection

There are numerous programming tasks that can help bridge documents and other information technologies for groups and organizations. A knowledge of programming in C, database query languages, and operating systems such as UNIX, is valuable to many organizations. See Figure 12.3 for a position description.

Document Management Specialists

A document management specialist is responsible for the planning and use of a document management system and related subsystems (database publishing, workflow management, and document retrieval and indexing). This includes document library management, document retrieval, compliance with electronic document interchange standards, updates and version control, workflow process planning, and automating assembly of compound documents. The individual should have a background in database management but also a critical sense of the structure of documents, the information that is in them, and how document management can facilitate information access. See Figure 12.4 for a detailed position description.

The document management specialist must collaborate with other stakeholders in the document process including writers, editors, and information consumers, if organizations want to manage information effectively. Document managers should advocate open information goals, while preserving system integrity and security. Corporations, medical and legal firms, and others seek the assistance of document managers to build specialized electronic libraries for intelligent information retrieval.

Document managers can modify the profile of the document management system to suit the needs of different user groups. Since various workgroups within an organization can access a document management system, it is important to profile the information needs of authorized groups who may not originate the

PUBLICATION PROGRAMMER

POSITION DESCRIPTION

Responsible for analyzing technical requirements for electronic publishing tools and for implementing specialized tool kits as well as script programs for automating special publication requirements. Responsible for the evaluation, selection, and implementation of application program interface (API) tools.

ELECTRONIC PUBLISHING IMPACT

Many publishing programs provide an application program interface so that users can automate various aspects of the document creation and delivery cycle. Since these capabilities add important benefits to users both in terms of productivity or enhancing products to be delivered to customers, it has opened up many programming opportunities for qualified individuals.

QUALIFICATIONS

- A degree in computer science, knowledge of object oriented programming
- Broad-based knowledge of publishing system technologies
- Experience with scripting programs to automate special publishing objectives
- Understanding of text and graphic file format structures
- Capable of writing and maintaining programs to supplement electronic publishing effort or integrate systems
- Capable of testing and evaluating system performance
- Knowledge of database publishing

RELATED TRACKS

Publishing system analysis
Database publishing
Multimedia programming

Figure 12.3. Publishing systems analyst position description.

DOCUMENT MANAGEMENT SPECIALIST

POSITION DESCRIPTION

Serves as document database and workflow system administrator within corporations, government, and institutions such as libraries.

ELECTRONIC PUBLISHING IMPACT

The use of document database tools is growing in conjunction with tasks such as managing document libraries and deploying document workflow systems on the desktop. Document management specialists should understand the value of information and promote open information access.

QUALIFICATIONS

- Computer science or library science background
- Familiarity with document retrieval systems
- Experience with relational databases
- Knowledge of documentation standards
- Understanding of document version control automation
- Familiarity with document workflow systems

RELATED TRACKS

Database administration
Image management
Data management
System administration

PROFESSIONAL ORGANIZATIONS

Association for Information and Image Management

Figure 12.4. Document management specialist position description.

information in certain documents but who need access to it to accomplish their work. A marketing and sales group may want to check documents in and out to the system to read the current product catalog and proposal data. Another group may want to check the same documents out to update them. Managers may need a profile of the current document workflow while others search for specific information in documents, and still others use the routing and review features of the system to streamline a process. One of the main goals of an enterprise document management system is to increase the productivity of all users. Document managers must aid individuals and groups collectively meet the overall goals of an organization.

Multimedia Specialists

Multimedia specialists are redefining the conventions for communications related to training, entertainment, marketing, manufacturing, customer services, and research. This specialist develops various aspects of authoring, integration, and production of multimedia projects. The technologies used include software programs that organize collections of information such as film, music, print, and voice, and hardware devices that support the development, production, and distribution of multimedia. Multimedia specialists collaborate to link a variety of media into a collection that can be interactively retrieved on computers.

The potential applications for multimedia are many and varied and the list will expand when interactive multimedia via the electronic superhighway is available in the home. Consumers will demand a mixture of entertainment, information, and training, from the increased number of channels. Qualified individuals are needed to support the production of new multimedia titles. Within corporations as well, there will be a major need for multimedia specialists. Commercial applications include everything from real estate sales to the presentation packages of corporate vice presidents. Kiosks at museums and trade shows use interactive multimedia presentations for visitors to follow events or information related to programs or current shows. Similar needs exist within corporations to help employees and customers learn about products and services. Multimedia advocates also have professional opportunities in mass communications, journalism, education, and free lance consulting. See Figure 12.5 for the position description.

Multimedia productions generally result from collaborative efforts and in many ways resemble movie productions. Multimedia projects involve storyboarding and scripting, and the integration of audio, still pictures, animation, video, and voice. The multimedia project director is analogous to the film director but there are two main differences: multimedia allows the audience to interact with the medium through the computer and movies are dominated by the medium of film which is not the case with multimedia. Multimedia makes specific demands on

MULTIMEDIA SPECIALIST

Assist in the development of marketing, training, medical, engineering, and commercial applications generally. Work on a contract basis or in corporate/small business enterprise with a variety of tools for marketing communications, training, manufacturing support, or digital library reference. Specific positions will be available for designers, writers, editors, animators, video specialists, and managers.

POSITION DESCRIPTION

The category of multimedia specialist includes various subclasses of work such as interactive video, computer animation, digital photography and imaging, and multimedia authoring.

ELECTRONIC PUBLISHING IMPACT

The category of multimedia specialist includes various subclasses of work such as interactive video, computer animation, digital photography and imaging, and multimedia authoring.

QUALIFICATIONS

- ➤ Computer science, broadcasting, graphic arts, interactive video/film specialization
- ➤ Familiar with hypermedia mapping strategies
- ➤ Experience with film scripting is a plus
- ➤ Knowledge of marketing presentation multimedia
- ➤ Knowledge of electronic audio technology
- ➤ Coordinate use of scanning technologies for photo inputs

RELATED TRACKS

Interactive video

Electronic document design

Audio specialists

Electronic reference document specialist

Figure 12.5. Multimedia specialist position description.

authors, designers, and risk takers (publishers, managers, producers). Two multimedia subspecialities are computer animation and interactive video. Organizations will need such expertise in house as requirements grow to support new forms of training, marketing, and delivery of information to meet customer requirements.

Interactive Video Specialist

An interactive video specialist arranges computer related video productions in concert with other specialists such as writers, graphic designers. Although some training in narrative video (movies, documentary, television scripting) is appropriate, the computer use of film will require thoughtful use for display within the limits of computer windows. Knowledge of compression techniques for desktop video is essential as well as a comprehension of digital video editing, mixing, and recording tools.

Computer Animation Specialist

There are certain advantages for using animation in the electronic information age and computer animation is hot. Animators with training in computer assisted animation software programs can obtain jobs in such arenas as the design of video games, advertising, marketing communications, and training projects. Animators can adapt to the size constraints of video display terminals and younger computer users, weaned on computer games, are primed for animation presentations. Developers of educational and otherwise "serious" projects should remember the success of the playful (never forget that Sesame Street puppets were designed for the television screen). Television commercials can teach us volumes about effective mixing of image, voice, and sound, in a tightly edited 30-second commercial.

Electronic Publishing for Knowledge Workers

What is the connection between knowledge and documents? Documents are a repository of information. Information, properly channeled, can become a source of knowledge for individuals whose work depends upon access to up to date information. A knowledge worker is a trendy term to denote individuals who depend on access to information to do a job. Knowledge workers may be customer support help desk specialists in telecommunications, pharmaceuticals, manufacturing, or many other fields. They may be researchers in law offices, news service analysts, health care specialists, financial analysts, city planners, or intelligence analysts. They also include library professionals, test technicians, and environmental engineers. These workers need information that is traditionally found in paper documents and libraries to help them do their work effectively. Knowledge workers who have depended upon paper documents to do their job now have on-line access to information from electronic document databases.

To be effective, knowledge workers must access information within critical time frames. These workers require better ways of sorting through document information bases to solve problems. Knowledge makes work effective; it builds businesses, it sells products by discriminating one company's products from the competition, and it gives employees skills to become effective in various roles.

Customer Support Help Desk Specialist

The help desk specialist, another trendy title, retrieves information with the benefit of automated indexing and retrieval systems. The help desk specialist may be occupied in a wide spectrum of corporate contexts. Refer to Figure 12.6 for the position description. One familiar context is customer support via telephone to diagnose problems. The customer support help desk specialist can sort through volumes of technical documentation using automated text search, indexing, and retrieval software.

Another help desk function is general information specialist within a company so that everyone (from executives to sales specialists) can use that person to search for information related to competition, product, pricing strategies, and company policies and practices. The rising demand for help desk specialists result from the need to react in a timely manner within a competitive marketplace and to supply potential and existing customers with supporting information and services on demand.

Information Research Specialist

Corporations are beginning to recognize the need for research specialists who can find valuable information and retrieve it for specific disciplines such as legal and financial research as well as governmental research in environmental or health related matters. Legal research assistants can make use of on-line legal information sources such as Mead Data Central's Lexis services to gather information on relevant cases to help lawyers prepare briefs. Secondarily uploading the researched information into a template for printing documents for specific audiences is a valuable function performed by the research specialist.

Traditional Roles Redefined

Editor

There are editors for all seasons. We glue adjectives to the noun to differentiate the breed: managing editors, technical editors, copy editors, line or substance editors, senior editors and assistant editors. In what ever way we modify them,

HELP DESK SPECIALIST

POSITION DESCRIPTION

Assist in-house personnel, partner companies, or customers in finding information related to products, systems, or related services by accessing an on-line document database. Help desk specialist may have some knowledge of a given field (manufacturing, maintenance, marketing, finance, health, or product) but skills in research and communication are most important.

ELECTRONIC PUBLISHING IMPACT

Electronic publishing is at the center of information repository and retrieval. Because volumes of information can be accessed and retrieved quickly and efficiently, there will be a growing tendency to use help desks both in the context of customer support and internal corporate communications.

QUALIFICATIONS

- ➤ Training in library science or information management
- ➤ Familiarity with on-line text retrieval systems
- ➤ Effective communication skills
- ➤ Knowledge of customer requirements (both internal and external)
- ➤ Aptitude for sharing information

RELATED TRACKS

Information resource specialist

Information broker

Customer support hotline specialist

Figure 12.6. Help desk specialist position description.

however, editors are stakeholders in the publication process. They are to documents what quality control experts are to manufactured products.

How have the roles of the editor changed with the advent of electronic publishing? There are special electronic publishing tools available to an editor for automating certain editorial tasks. Spell checkers, indexing tools, and automated retrieval related text topics and front matter are critical assets to the editor's desktop. An auxiliary feature to spell checking is the ability to add words to spell checker dictionary allowing the editor to maintain a custom file of acronyms or special phrases, that are unique to a corporation, scientific discipline or industry. From basic word processing features such as the search and replace word string to more complex algorithms for checking the length of sentences to compiling a keyword index in a desired format, the tools editors can apply to their craft continue to appear. On-line editing tools include the ability to add comments either in marginal notes, or strikethroughs, and to maintain changes to manuscript versions over time. Even the use of color display monitors for editors can make a difference. When the manuscript is reviewed by an editor on-line, the editorial comments can be made in a different color than the manuscript. On-line review technologies such as Electronic Review form ArborText add dimensions to an editor's tool kit. Other editing tools include grammar and writing style checkers. Proof Positive from Avalanche Development Company is a combined grammar and style checker. It offers readability and document statistics concerning sentence word length.

Editors can derive major benefits from learning structured authoring systems especially those based upon the Standard Generalized Markup Language (SGML). Exposure to SGML and its multiple uses provides a solid grounding for grasping forms of document organization such as hypertext as well as indexing and retrieval technologies. Most editors have traditional training in document structure that follows classic guidelines for linear, rhetorical presentation. Editors should help redefine criteria for measuring the effectiveness of new forms of communication. Hypertext systems are often used in conjunction with indexing and retrieval capabilities. Editors must consult with authors and document analysts to understand the information design that organizes a hypertext collection. Editors, working in conjunction with authors, are ideally suited to the task of building organized collections of linked and indexed information. It complements the training and orientation of editors who traditionally sort out relationships in sequential documents through the editing process. See Figure 12.7.

In the age of information glut, editors can lead the assault on language abuse. By insisting on economy and clarity of language, editors perform a service that artificial intelligence cannot duplicate. They can also assist in opening the information

EDITOR

POSITION DESCRIPTION

Responsible for substantive copy editing of articles, brochures, books, reports, manuals, advertisements, and proposals. Work with on-line editing tools in workgroup setting. Capable of working under stress. Ability to organize and map linking of key structures in documents for aiding in on-line documentation. Superior language skills and ability to write clearly. Able to advise publishers on worthiness of manuscript for publication.

ELECTRONIC PUBLISHING IMPACT

The growth of documents created on computers poses new challenges for editors. How do editors preserve quality in an era of information explosion? By insisting on economy of language and clarity of expression editors can always make a lasting contribution. Electronic tools for editors are available; editors will do well to learn document workflow systems that allow for on-line review and comment of documents over networks.

QUALIFICATIONS

- ➤ Knowledge of text editing systems
- ➤ Familiarity with publication process cycle
- ➤ Experience with on-line editing systems
- ➤ Knowledge of automated indexing systems
- ➤ Excellent communication skills
- ➤ Exposure to hypermedia linking techniques
- ➤ Well organized, attentive to detail, practitioner of clear and concise writing

RELATED TRACKS

Document analyst

Figure 12.7. Generic editor position description.

in document databases by using electronic markup pertinent to document type definitions for sets of documents, or redefining electronic document structures.

Editors are sometimes classified in a dual role as writer/editor. Although this split role may be best avoided by better resource planning, the writer/editor should be in a favorable position to argue for the need of computer assisted technology to perform dual roles. Writer/editors should be educators for members of other workgroups in an organization that may need to use desktop authoring and editing tools effectively.

Writer

Electronic publishing has found new audiences for writers. From hyperfiction to multimedia authoring, electronic publishing has changed the mode of communication between writer and audience. In this brave new world, writers can be at the center of a universe whose boundaries are expanding and the potential of reaching new audiences is enormous. Some of the critical factors shaping the writer's mission in a world attuned to the electronic word include: connectivity through wide area networks and computer connected desktops links writers to information sources and readers world wide; research and data gathering can be conducted electronically; markets are expanded by virtue of global connectivity; writers can still reach audiences through the printed word and remind electronic readerships where to find special printed material; an electronic audience can respond to the writer creating new forms of dialog; the writer can be a special broker in organizing information elements in a multimedia project. Writers can begin to retool by using the computer as more than a word processor or electronic typewriter. By learning structured authoring techniques and new modes of nonsequential forms of presentation, writers can explore multiple uses of information for themselves and their readers. See Figure 12.8.

Many pundits expect the development of interactive multimedia delivered to homes will make a mass consumer market conscious of the power of electronic publishing. Writers will help fill the content void of new information channels. The demand for writers to help create scripts for new media applications (interactive video, animation) will be on the rise. Opportunities abound for writers to extend the limits of their imaginations and forge new forms of communication.

Through the written word, writers have always been able to extend the power of the human voice to many audiences. With electronic publishing and multimedia, writers can reach larger audiences and reawaken the primal power of the voice as a part of a document collection. Since other media may be mixed with the written word, the writer must consider how the electronic word reverberates with other media.

WRITER

POSITION DESCRIPTION

Responsible for work in one of the following activities: journalism, book and periodical publishing, marketing communications, technical communications, business and proposal writing, script writing and multimedia training projects.

ELECTRONIC PUBLISHING IMPACT

Writers not only use tools such as word processors and SGML editors to create documents, they also use computers to do research, share data, and collaborate with other members of a workgroup.

QUALIFICATIONS

- Writing experience and writing portfolio
- Good research and communication skills
- Knowledge of audience needs
- Experience with word processing and desktop publishing
- Familiarity with hypertext and document retrieval technology
- Knowledge of structured authoring

RELATED TRACKS

Marketing communications
Journalism
Technical communications
Proposal writing

Figure 12.8. Writer position description.

Graphic Artists and Illustrators

Whether making 2D or 3D drawings, manipulating digital images, merging color photographs, or creating special fonts, computer graphics is a pervasive presence on the desktop. Few graphic artists have resisted computers and the proliferation of software packages that offer powerful features to create graphic images and objects. While there is a wide difference in the quality of the graphic capabilities among systems and graphic software, more programs are available offering quality features at lower prices. It may be necessary to use several software packages to achieve specific results. See Figure 12.9.

Graphic artists are challenged to maintain high standards for their profession as well as the corporations and agencies they represent. Graphic artists must keep current with the pace of digital technology and the software and hardware tools that create, capture, and mix text, drawings, images, and photos. As with other professions that have had to cope with the introduction of computer aided technology, graphic artists need to maintain standards and prove to clients and organizations that quality as well as productivity counts.

Technical illustration is a specialized field within graphic arts. Like other disciplines, computer-assisted tools are changing the lives of these career specialists. Technical illustrators work within industries for electronics, aviation, aerospace, shipbuilding, computer technology, architecture, and variety of other disciplines. See Figure 12.10 for a description of a technical illustrator position.

Experience with computer aided systems becomes mandatory for the illustrator just as experience with computer assisted design and drafting tools is for the draftsman.

- Knowledge of intelligent graphics
- 3D applications
- Visualization technology
- Preparation of art for on-line and multimedia presentations

Technical illustration is a good example of an effective tool to aid manufacturing. Using pictures of complex objects via computer terminals on an assembly line, manufacturing personnel are able to see better how pieces fit together than by looking at two dimensional pictures on paper. The same base drawing can be used in the field to help a technician repair the unit. Delivery of on-line graphics to customers requires knowing how customers will use graphics that have intelligent components. Intelligent graphics allow the customer to interact with a drawing or

GRAPHIC ARTIST

POSITION DESCRIPTION

Designs layouts for documents and other media as required. Selects and implements design concepts with responsible author, editors, and marketing communications specialists. Uses electronic publishing tools where feasible for productivity and other gains.

ELECTRONIC PUBLISHING IMPACT

From 2D and 3D drawing editors, to scientific visualization, to color imaging tools, to virtual reality, the graphic artist is surrounded by different possibilities for the creation and fusion of media. Digital imaging tools for photo styling and image editing are revolutionizing the profession. Computer-based animation is a field with enormous potential. Design for multimedia applications requires the integration of several areas of graphic arts expertise.

QUALIFICATIONS

- Knowledge of graphic editing systems
- Experience in typography
- Portfolio of layout and design achievements
- Proven versatility in illustration
- Aptitude for training in use of new technologies
- Experience with photography

RELATED TRACKS

Animation
Technical illustration
Virtual reality simulation

Figure 12.9. Graphic artist position description.

image when using a pointing device to select a designated part of the graphic object.

Graphic artists and illustrators need to be able to retrieve graphic information. Each drawing must be properly catalogued and identified because without careful codification, illustration groups could find themselves buried under a mass of irre-

TECHNICAL ILLUSTRATOR

POSITION DESCRIPTION

Creates technical illustrations for reports, manuals, proposals, electronic reference documents, and other publications as required. Has experience with graphic editing tools for illustrators.

ELECTRONIC PUBLISHING IMPACT

Technical illustration packages are available that assist illustrators in the creation and production of complex objects. The illustrations can be used in support of aerospace, medical, automotive, computer, architecture, and other industries needing technical graphics.

QUALIFICATIONS

- Knowledge of graphic illustrator or computer assisted design systems
- Experience in mechanical illustration
- Portfolio of technical illustrations
- Ability to execute isometric, 3D, and trimetric drawings
- Knowledge of electronic typography
- Ability to translate drawings from other electronic file formats

RELATED TRACKS

Computer assisted design and drafting (CADD)
Multimedia design

Figure 12.10. Technical illustrator position description.

trievable information. Objects within drawings that can be reused in other drawings need special attention. The codification scheme must include an indication of the revision level of the drawing or illustration in the catalog. Illustrators should work carefully with document management specialists to codify information for timely reuse. Graphic artists and technical illustrators should also explore other areas of design that require interdisciplinary understanding of the content that informs the image as in solid modeling and visualization technology.

Publishing System Administrator

Who is the first person you run to when you have a problem? Who worries about system security and updates passwords? Who periodically checks to make sure that the files are in order and that there is enough available disk space on the system? Who conducts periodic backups? If the system is small and the application is strictly personal publishing then it is likely that the system administrator wears several hats for an all-in-one business. But in a larger setting—a corporation with in-house publishing capabilities or a manufacturing/engineering enterprise with large publication data banks—it is the system administrator that is indispensable.

The duties of the system administrator in an electronic publishing system are complex.

- Backing up the system and verifying that system backups occur correctly
- Setting up and maintaining security for passwords and permission schemes to access certain files
- Taking direct action for bringing system up or shutting system down
- Local Area Network administration including the setup of addresses
- First level diagnosis of system problems

The system administrator must know both the application side of electronic publishing as well as the main tools of the operating system. The individual may be responsible for contact with the vendor of the equipment for coordination of technical assistance. The administrator plays a key role in monitoring the health of the system. The system administrator performs classic functions such as checking for disk utilization, archiving old files, and cleaning unwanted information from the system. These tasks require a calendar and regular procedures. The system administrator is responsible for the calendar of events handled on the system: backups, upgrades, or diagnostic interventions. Effective backups to publishing files are indispensable. Casual administration can result in unnecessary and costly mistakes. To be effective, however, the system administrator needs full support from related workgroups. See Figure 12.11 for the position description.

The system administrator is also usually responsible for local area network administration and coordination of file management, transfer, storage, and retrieval. Some tasks resemble those of system librarians generally, but more specific publication related skills are emerging. The system administrator must be familiar with the conventions of book layout and appearance and be ready to control the final production of a manuscript. A system administrator should understand and enforce system security which means preventing unwanted access, using passwords for access to key system accounts, and understanding the system of safe storage of tapes, CD-ROM, and other media used for the permanent storage.

PUBLISHING SYSTEM ADMINISTRATOR

POSITION DESCRIPTION

Responsible for the routine care of the system as well as being the first person to consult in event of a system problem. Duties include system backup, software installation, disk storage bank management, interface to network services, and coordination with document management specialists.

ELECTRONIC PUBLISHING IMPACT

The growing size and complexity of systems using publishing applications and efforts to integrate publishing applications with other systems and computers requires concentration and focus. Special requirements in system administration derive from expansion of local area networks, database integration, and disk capacity management needs.

QUALIFICATIONS

- A degree in computer science or specific training in system/network administration
- A thorough grounding in computer operating systems
- Administrative experience in computer file security
- Awareness of standards related to publishing
- An understanding of distributed workgroup publishing
- Experience with backup, archival, and retrieval of files

RELATED TRACKS

Document and workflow management

Figure 12.11. System administrator position description.

Technical Writers

For years technical writers lacked tools for their difficult job; namely, communicating how medical equipment, automobiles, airplanes, missiles, bicycles, computers and other devices can be installed, operated, and maintained. Word processing and desktop publishing tools have streamlined the production headaches associated with laying out documents with pages of integrated text and graphics. More recently, tools for the delivery of electronic documents and hypermedia collections have appeared on technical writer desktops. Requirements for electronic document delivery pose new challenges for technical writers to concentrate on document structure and organization. This includes requirements for information design. Technical writers should think of their craft more in terms as cultivators of information and less as formatters of information. When technical writers use tools, they need to control the process of gathering and organizing the eclectic information that builds a reusable information base. They achieve that control primarily by having the access to data on their desktop that they previously struggled to obtain. Even in the past when they did receive the data, it would inevitably be paper copies of text and illustrated material. This limited technical writers in information gathering and production, whereas now much of the technical data (specifications, mechanical drawings, technical diagrams, part listings) can be directly transferred to the writer's desktop. Writers can be responsible for the production of a manuscript but if they get their data in a more timely fashion and use structured methods to organize it, they can use the presentation and conversion templates to maximize production efficiency. See Figure 12.12 for a description of a technical writer position.

Knowledge of electronic publishing and related tools is a necessary component of a technical writer's career. A technical writer must learn how source data on other systems can be imported and how the data created electronically for a technical publication may be used in production. Many technical writers are now learning how structured authoring systems work as the focus has shifted from the production of paper products to the preparation of information for on-line delivery. This means the role of the writer is shifting to gatherer and filterer of information for different audiences. Technical communicators must learn the process of adding value to information.

Word Processing Specialists

In the beginning there were secretary typists, then word processing specialists, and more recently, electronic publishing/typesetting operators. What's next? The answer is not altogether clear, nor are all the current results encouraging from a career perspective. If we look back at the evolution of the deployment of word processors and desktop publishing tools in organizations, the first transition of importance was making a secretary typist into a word processing specialist. Secretaries had performed many more duties than merely typing: they were assistant administrators to managers. They knew a lot about running organizations and communications because of their connections to managers and supervisors. Many companies, however, reorganized their secretarial help and assigned some of them to centralized word processing organizations. Although these operators received

TECHNICAL WRITER

POSITION DESCRIPTION

Writes technical manuals, reports, marketing brochures, and other documents for various industries including: aviation, defense, pharmaceutical, petrochemical, computer, and medical. Works directly with text editing and graphic editing tools in authoring phases. Participates in decisions related to the authoring of documents for electronic delivery.

ELECTRONIC PUBLISHING IMPACT

Technical writers have been in the forefront of technology change for over a decade. That status is not likely to let up as more and more requirements for delivery of electronic documents evolve. Technical writers need to assert themselves as information specialists and communicators who can help with product information planning including products of the future that will obey human voice commands.

QUALIFICATIONS

- ➤ Degree in technical writing, journalism, English, or equivalent experience
- ➤ Ability to research, collect data, establish audience and purpose
- ➤ Write technical manuals, reports, and related documents in clear simple prose
- ➤ Ability to work with other individuals on project (editors, coauthors, and technical staff, engineers, researchers, and lab assistants)
- ➤ Some technical background or experience in at least one field relevant to technical literature (for example, computer science or chemistry)
- ➤ Experience with text editing, word processing, or other systems
- ➤ On-line documentation experience

PROFESSIONAL ORGANIZATIONS

Society for Technical Communication (STC)

Figure 12.12. Technical writer position description.

training in word processing technology, they lost some ground in learning other aspects of the business. In addition not all aspects of the role of the word processing specialist have been clearly defined. The word processing specialist paradox is that job deskilling and upskilling happen concurrently.

Another phenomenon affecting the work performed by word processing specialists is that other individuals within companies have access to word processing software and keyboard their own material. Word processing specialists cannot always depend upon the keyboard as a means of survival, because there are also health hazards associated with the overuse of such equipment as the computer keyboard. Word processing specialists are taking on additional duties which depend upon the operator's access to certain publishing functions such as template setup for various documents. If properly trained and if the level of responsibility is well defined, such specialists may, for instance, assume a role in the implementation of a typographical design. See Figure 12.13 for the position description.

Journalists

Broadcast and print journalism has been widely affected by developments in electronic publishing. The growth of newswire services, special on-line news and retrieval services from information service providers (such as Mead Data Central's Nexis research or Dialog Inc. news services) means that on-line information distribution and retrieval is used by an increasing number of subscribers. We cannot hope to explore all the impacts electronic publishing has in the world of journalism but only some of the significant trends resulting in new directions and opportunities for journalists.

Electronic newspapers have just begun. One of the disadvantages of newspapers as we know them is that they are a mass produced as a "one size fits all" product. Most subscribers read only 10 percent of the information in a newspaper. It is another limitation of newspapers that once read they are discarded. Retrieving information from paper journals is cumbersome and time consuming.

Now most newspapers consider themselves to be in the publishing business. Electronic newspapers will shift the focus to the information business. There are three obstacles to why electronic newspapers are not a reality to date: management uneasiness with how to conduct the new business, investments in expensive capital equipment, and potential loss in revenue from advertising income.

High tech layout and print production devices for newspapers and magazines continually evolve toward high speed, digital, electronic publishing solutions. Graphic artists for newspapers use specialized graphics software accommodating layout of advertisements.

One form of periodical publishing, printed newsletters for small businesses

WORD PROCESSING SPECIALIST

POSITION DESCRIPTION

Use word processing, scanning, and other technologies to enter and manipulate text and graphics information for the building of proposals, reports, and other documents required in a corporate setting.

ELECTRONIC PUBLISHING IMPACT

The proliferation of word processing tools to desktops in all corporations has diminished to some extent the need for dedicated keyboarding specialists.

QUALIFICATIONS

➤ Expert at text editing and word processing manipulations
➤ Able to work under pressure with team members
➤ Has familiarity with computer communications
➤ Knowledge of publishing templates
➤ Sensitive to document security issues

RELATED TRACKS

Data management
Document management assistant
Electronic document conversion specialist

Figure 12.13. Word processing specialist position description.

and free-lance journalism have been a desktop publishing success story. There are numerous packages available for PCs and Macs that have enabled newsletters of all descriptions to flourish. In addition to printed newsletters, electronic newsletters are thriving on the Internet. These newsletters can be a vital asset to existing businesses (law firms, corporations, and health care providers, etc.) or a means for entrepreneurs (including journalists) to establish a market.

Journalist authors and researchers are engaged in an industry committed to perishable information or "news." Paradoxically, one of the obvious advantages of electronic publishing is the ability to store and preserve words, articles, and even "news." The Los Angeles Times has installed an electronic document retrieval system that is saving the company hundreds of thousands of dollars per year. There is enormous opportunity for journalists to enjoy greater access to information through electronic research. Journalists can train and prepare themselves for use of appropriate technologies to retrieve information to access data banks and resources through international networks to digital libraries. Such data banks and networks will be evolving and maturing over the next decade.

The journalism-multimedia connection cannot be overlooked. Audience accessibility to world and local events will continue to be revolutionized by options for participants reading electronic sources in conjunction with televised reports displayed by window selection. In one window, audiences will capture a conventional filmed report. In other windows, the audience can look at text reports on the same events or tune in to a variety of audio reports. Interactive video and broadcast technology is an important aspect of the changing directions in journalism.

Many large newspaper organizations have a staff of individuals whose main role is to build files of headlines which are then stored and used as pointers for the retrieval of information. Automated information retrieval is critical for research. By using electronic markup such as SGML that identifies key elements of news headlines and other structural elements for retrieval, the task is automated at the point of origin.

So-called narrowcasting has been a godsend to magazine publishers. Periodicals in computers, travel, politics, sports, real estate, finance, and health (to name a few) have flourished by tending to specialized audiences. This trend will continue with electronically distributed journals over many network channels.

The role of education journalism is obviously important. The National Broadcasters Educational Association publishes guidelines for use of technologies in electronic journalism. The Association for Education in Journalism and Mass Media also tracks trends in technologies for education in traditional print journalism.

Management: Opportunities for Coaches and Consultants

Management models in the United States are gradually shifting away from the stereotype of managers as iconic partitions in a vertical command and control power pyramid to other symbolic roles. One new image is the manager as coach of workgroups within flat organizations. In practical terms this signifies that managers can entrust more responsibilities to teams for making decisions which is counter to the traditional premise that permission is granted through a chain of command. Coaches still make decisions but they entrust members of the team to share that burden based upon the player's competence and ability. Coaches underline the importance of teamwork. They do not divide the group into favorite and unfavored players. Coaches are primarily motivators of their teams. They prepare the team for change (new game plans for new opponents, new audiences in new environments, and new challenges). Coaches instill a positive winning attitude. There are limits to the coaching analogy: work may lack the glamour and glory of sport, but the symbolic connection to the coach is meaningful to managers in search of a workgroup leadership model.

The role model of manager as consultant adds intellectual texture to the spirit building idealism of the coach. The consultant model, especially useful for managers who are hired from the outside, may be asked to analyze requirements, to address process problems, and to construct a plan and vision with the team. Consultants behave with a certain detachment, a quality that has always served managers well. The roles of consultant and coach need not be mutually exclusive. Both roles can be employed to serve the needs of managers coping with changes related to "disruptive" technologies such as electronic publishing.

Managers who inherit responsibilities related to electronic publishing can:

- Help teams to create goals and a vision for the future
- Allow employees to participate in technology evaluation and use
- Listen carefully to all inputs regarding the use of technology
- Refrain from pigeon-holing the roles people need to play when the technology is implemented
- Discuss openly changes in employee job roles
- Involve the team in considering advantages and disadvantages of technology choices
- Encourage employees to express ideas and seek innovation
- Help employees connect electronically and functionally
- Design and articulate a plan for change

Management opportunities related to electronic publishing cut across several disciplines. These categories involve skills ranging from business planning and budgetary expertise, technical equipment planning and acquisition, to publication production management. Managers should acquire some expertise in electronic publishing as it applies to the discipline and business requirements. For example in a publication department in a corporation, the supervisor of production with certain skill level knowledge of typography and graphic art, should update his professional qualifications in the future to include some familiarity with the field of electronic publishing. This knowledge is not obtained only while observing productivity gains and losses but by coaching and motivating employees to learn and grow with the challenges that the new technology offers.

Graphic Arts Manager

Graphic arts managers are at the eye of the digital technology storm. A graphic arts manager needs to stay abreast of changes in digital technology in imaging, monitors, color printing, and photography, that are revolutionizing the manner of doing work in studios, corporations, and service bureaus. The graphics arts manager must be able to think through electronic-multimedia as well as print media requirements. See Figure 12.14 for the position description of graphics arts manager.

Responsible for a department whose role is the design and production coordination of a catalog, a magazine, a corporate annual report, or a brochure, the graphics arts manager should be able to define requirements for delivery of electronic graphics for various customers. In addition to visual creativity, knowledge of the craft, and supervisory skills the graphics arts manager must know how electronic tools can improve the quality and productivity of the graphics designers, artists, and other specialists involved in the business. These tools include:

- Graphic editing systems
- Computer-aided animation software
- Clip art library
- Photo and color imaging
- Color printing
- Image setters and film recorders
- Font technologies
- Desktop video

Sometimes the graphics arts manager will have to straddle two worlds: one tied to traditional processes, work habits, and expectations and the other moving inexorably toward digital encapsulation of photographs, images, typography, color, and output. Both graphic arts and print production managers in corporations must stay abreast of developments within service companies that provide contracting work for printing, design, and data conversion. Advertising agencies, other special agencies that support corporate marketing communications, printers, and service bureaus that do business with corporations have to stay on top of developments within client companies in order to offer competitive services and present intelligent alternatives to companies doing work in-house.

Print Production Manager

The print production manager must combine those unusual talents of exacting organizational skills, superior business acumen, excellent motivational abilities, with a solid foundation in publishing or printing. The production manager must

GRAPHIC ARTS MANAGER

POSITION DESCRIPTION

Directs graphic artists, designers, illustrators for creation of advertisements, brochures, reports, manuals, and other media projects. Responsible for the evaluation of electronic publishing tools for graphic artists.

ELECTRONIC PUBLISHING IMPACT

Computerized graphic applications of all descriptions are multiplying from design to technical illustration to animation. The manager must assume the challenge of staying abreast of technological developments. Graphic arts managers will be leading the way for change to new technologies including virtual reality simulation and visualization.

QUALIFICATIONS

- ➤ Degree in graphic arts design or management or equivalent training
- ➤ Knowledge of design and digital pre-press systems
- ➤ Proven aptitude for group leadership
- ➤ Understanding of graphic format exchange standards
- ➤ Comprehension of color imaging and display technology

RELATED TRACKS

Mulimedia design management

Figure 12.14. Graphic arts manager position description.

know the cost of all the elements that go into making the product such as paper, typesetting, electronic tools, photography, presses, and binding. Decisions must be made about whether to do the work in-house or on the outside for selected functions. Accordingly, the production manager must be thoroughly versed in the technologies that are reshaping print and production tasks. Investments in digital desktop imaging and printing technologies such as laser printers, color scanners, color printers, image setters, and other devices must be examined. The cost of purchasing such technologies should be weighed against contracting to the outside for special services. See Figure 12.15 for a position description of the print production manager.

The activity of the production manager depends upon the kind and number of publications generated. The product, the market, and the size of the operation also determine the kind of budget a production manager has for the activity. The manager in conjunction with other responsible parties and subordinates must weigh the advantages and disadvantages of investment in electronic publishing technologies. Print production managers must be knowledgeable about managing digital information which means that many elements of the process can be recomposed and recycled and some information can be directed to electronic displays.

Reprographics Manager

In many corporations the reprographics manager has the responsibility of redesigning in-house printing services. This includes shifting from total reliance upon paper resources and increasing support for network interchange of electronic documents and on-demand printing. Paper is not going away overnight but greater emphasis will be placed upon the control of paper printing and streamlining the process. Among the challenges confronting reprographics managers is the retraining of employees through programs that result in better management of network printing resources, focusing on improving the quality and limiting the quantity of printed products. This conversion makes the reprographics center an adjunct of the information and document management process. Reprographics managers and supporting staff must find creative ways to make transitions to a paperless office that preserves the quality of printing without the waste.

Technical Publications Manager

Many electronic publishing products are targeted for the technical publications market. The stuff of technical publications—user and repair manuals, proposals, training and reference guides, and the like—are laden with graphic illustrations, tables, and extensive text. Technical publications are expensive to produce and revise. Word processing and desktop publishing tools have helped publication groups overcome manual production nightmares with long lead times, expensive layout and pasteup chores. Routine updating of technical documents to keep them current with changes in products or systems can be managed with revision control software that keeps an historical log of changes to document versions. With proper planning the technical publications manager can buy electronic publishing systems that can save the company money.

The experimental work for technical publications has not stopped with the automation of production tasks for paper documents. Technical publications are in the forefront of applications for electronically delivered documents including interactive electronic technical manuals and embedded product user manuals.

PRINT PRODUCTION MANAGER

POSITION DESCRIPTION

Directs print production group in corporate magazine or commercial printing houses. Hires, trains, and assigns personnel for duties in pre-press operations and production processes. Where necessary coordinates with outside services for printing and production.

ELECTRONIC PUBLISHING IMPACT

The revolution in digital imaging is changing the business of print production throughout the spectrum of processes from capture of photographs to the use of 32-bit color for desktop manipulation for output to color printers, image setters and other devices. What are the quality tradeoffs in digital desktop technologies? Print production managers must come up with the answers.

QUALIFICATIONS

- In depth understanding of digital imaging (scanner, display, and output devices)
- Complete familiarity with color laser printing
- Knowledge of binding technologies
- Understanding the options for out-sourcing work
- Familiarity with the business aspects of printing

PROFESSIONAL ORGANIZATIONS

The National Association of Printers and Lithographers
Printing Industries of America

Figure 12.15. Print production manager position description.

Technical publication managers have justified the investment in electronic publishing because it was going to streamline the production of paper documentations. In the shift to demand to on-line documents, managers must guide the group and the company through a period of transition. This means reeducating various levels of management and redirecting the focus of technical documentation from a publishing service to an information service.

TECHNICAL PUBLICATIONS MANAGER

POSITION DESCRIPTION

Directs technical writers, editors, and production support in a variety of publication projects including manuals and catalogs. Coordinates project schedules and responsibilities with graphic arts manager and related workgroups. Hires, trains, and assigns writers and editors for publication projects. Aware of publication costs. Responsible for analysis of electronic publishing tools to be used by writers and editors. Participates in evaluating processes affected by the use of electronic publishing tools.

ELECTRONIC PUBLISHING IMPACT

Technical publications have been a test bed for electronic publishing for the last ten years. Some managers have seized the opportunity to acquire desktop publishing to improve productivity of paper based documentation. More recent developments encourage the use of electronic forms of document distribution.

QUALIFICATIONS

- Grasp of processes that make a technical publication
- Experience in technical writing in relevant subject areas
- Command of text editing and authoring systems used in technical writing projects
- Knowledge of all elements that contribute to publication costs
- Familiarity with on-line documentation technologies
- Ability to assess information needs of company and customers.

PROFESSIONAL ORGANIZATIONS

Society for Technical Communications

Figure 12.16. Technical publications manager qualifications.

All levels of publishing system managers must recognize the critical need to integrate the system with other applications via networks. Managers must spend time communicating with other departments and groups that contribute to the publishing system and find ways to open new paths for information sharing.

Electronic Publishing and the Learning Organization

How do we motivate employees to collaborate as a group but allow them at the same time to grow as individuals? The answer lies in an idea called the learning organization. The concept has been translated into practice in some major U.S. corporations with remarkable success. Organizational learning involves sharing of knowledge and insight. Businesses have knowledge banks stored in the heads of individual employees. Managers who encourage the collaborative sharing of knowledge can be rewarded. Electronic publishing fosters access to open information through the use of document management and electronic search and retrieval systems over networks.

The learning organization is one which cares more for fostering competence in its employees and less for perpetuating a bureaucratic management concerned with rules and directives. Learning organizations make learning a priority and are prepared to translate this concept into budgetary goals and long term planning commitments.

Telecommuting

Economic and social forces are making telecommuting an attractive alternative. The cost of commuting long distances in crowded urban areas; environmental regulations in states such as California relating to congestion and pollution; expenses related to creating and maintaining office space for employees; and parental concern over child care and proximity to young children are critical factors in building the case for telecommuting. With the advent of an electronic communication infrastructure, the necessary tools are in place to make telecommuting practical on a large scale. Many corporations have run pilot programs with telecommuting and have had success within the experimental boundaries of such programs. One concern with telecommuting has been the managerial perception of employees at a distance. These concerns are likely to diminish as managers understand that electronic mail and workflow control over networks are effective tools. As wide area networks mature there will be a boom in telecommuting. Specific electronic publishing developments such as document management and workflow technology and electronic document interchange and distribution will make the retrieval control and flow of information easier to manage. Managers will warm up to the idea of telecommuting as soon as they understand how to monitor the activities of geographically distributed employees.

Vendor Generated Opportunities

In addition to opportunities within organizations, the vendors who supply electronic publishing products have expanded their workforce to meet growing demands for various applications. Marketing or selling electronic publishing is a challenging career. The people who sell a product or system have to stay abreast of technological developments because they are the communicators between the worlds of the engineers and designers, on the one hand, and the customers, on the other. To be successful they must correctly read customer requirements. The technical qualifications for this role vary but, in an era of open systems and open information, marketing specialists must look beyond immediate solutions to understand the full picture of customer needs.

The market explosion of electronic publishing related packages on the market has left many without adequate preparation for using these tools effectively. In fact, vendors do not always have resources to offer training on all of the products they offer. The demand for training will rise in years to come especially with respect to how layered applications in graphics, databases, publishing layout tools, indexing and retrieval tools play together. Training opportunities may exist with the company which developed the product, with a consulting group, or with an authorized third party group such as computer dealerships.

To be a successful trainer, one must have better than average communication skills, a solid foundation in the tools being taught, and a proper understanding of customer requirements. Trainers sometimes work in conjunction with marketers and consultants to demonstrate the features of products and systems for potential customers. Trainers are a resource for recording and communicating customer satisfaction and dissatisfaction with products. A trainer must learn how to help customers overcome misconceptions regarding product functions or performance.

There are also many career opportunities for professionals in the technical support or field service sectors of the business. Electronic publishing must help others meet immediate and long term goals. Customer support personnel who can isolate problems and solve them are are always in demand when problems occur. An aptitude for isolating problems, for thinking logically, and for working under pressure are essential. In many cases customer support personnel must be prepared to travel to field locations where they will be challenged to apply expertise in hardware and software to disentangle problems. Having experience and training in electronics and computer science is especially helpful, as well as an understanding of publishing and related applications. Many companies provide telephone service support as the first line of problem assessment and diagnosis. Field personnel as well as hotline telephone support specialists may use interactive technical manual retrieval technologies to solve problems.

Opportunities for Entrepreneurs

Less conventional but potentially profitable career paths for enterprising individuals are the marketing and implementation of electronic publishing services. Service businesses in electronic publishing are booming. Some examples include:

- A multimedia publisher concentrating on marketing multimedia titles to high schools and middle schools
- A consulting firm specializing in solutions for electronic publishing including training, publication programming, and SGML conversion. Consultants provide integrated publishing solutions for companies who do not have in-house expertise
- A technical publication service group that produces interactive technical manuals as well as conventional print versions of technical documents as required by corporate and government customers
- A service bureau that uses electronic printing technologies (demand printer, color printer, and other laser printers) with appropriate network technologies to interface on-line to client companies wishing to print documents off-premises for cost efficiency
- An electronic journalism publisher who steers his enterprise toward providing selective information on-line for different audiences
- A business that uses the Internet network as a basis for marketing communications

Our discussion here does not provide business planning guidelines. Risk takers will do well to use their imaginations and not rely on preconceived notions about markets and the future. Many new markets can be opened by linking information and publishing services. Planners of new businesses should keep these linkages in mind.

Consulting Careers in Electronic Publishing

Companies often lack sufficient expertise to address all aspects of electronic publishing planning and implementation. Reputable consultants have an important role to play in assisting corporations and other organizations through periods of transition. Consulting for publishing environments where there is an effort to integrate and manage information and publishing systems over networks might include:

- Planning the electronic publishing system
- Integrating publishing and information systems
- Guiding workgroups in the creation of on-line document delivery and database publishing systems
- Writing specific programs to help organizations link electronic publishing software to other software applications (such as databases) to achieve special objectives
- Planning system upgrades and training

This list merely scratches the surface of possible opportunities for consultants. Some consulting groups are licensed distributors of equipment and product services. Consulting is a very challenging field and where electronic publishing is concerned, both a breadth and depth of technical expertise is necessary. A good consultant must also recognize that organizations have various stakeholders who must be treated with respect when solving real solutions to problems. Bringing those stakeholders together and listening to their requirements are essential to the process.

Is This a Cottage Industry Renaissance?

If telecommuters can work at home for corporations, individuals can use the home to open businesses. Freelance work in almost every conceivable aspect of electronic publishing is expected to flourish over the next decade. One cottage industry worth watching is workgroup collaboration that extends with partners over a network such as the Internet. Being able to exchange information over a network allows collaborating partners to share resources and expenses, meet deadlines, and control costs related to renting offices. Partnerships may include collaboration between writers, editors, designers, video and sound experts, printers, or others as needed.

ACADEMIC PUBLISHING AND DIGITAL LIBRARIES

Electronic publishing is beginning to change the way the academic community publishes research and the role perceived for libraries as electronic research evolves. The disadvantage of current periodical publications for academic research is that the hard copy publications are costly to produce and there are often long delays between exchange of information among contributors. Academics have begun to form special interest groups who exchange information on-line across a wide variety of disciplines. There are now electronic exchanges developing for Chaucer and Shakespeare studies as well as biochemistry and nuclear physics.

As scholars and other researchers begin to regularize the exchange of information electronically what role will libraries play? For that matter what about the idea of digital libraries and the future of the virtual library of interconnected networks? Libraries as we know them are expensive to maintain and the information that libraries hope to keep up with continues at an exponential growth rate. Trade-offs can be made between the costs of expanding space in libraries to keep pace with the growth of information and the investments in computer and network infrastructures that enable the access to electronic versions of books and articles. Copyright issues have to be addressed and precedents for copyrights in the film and audio recording industries are already being cited by legal experts who track intellectual property issues.

Library schools throughout the United States are preparing for the eventuality of digital libraries. Graduate and undergraduate programs now focus on electronic card catalogs, electronic search and retrieval systems, and electronic books. As for a vision of the future, there are great expectations for the growth of digital electronic libraries. Classes include mandatory orientation in computer science, collaborative courses in hypermedia, and electronic search and retrieval systems.

Careers for graduates of library science programs in fields related to information research (customer help desks, information broker, document management) are on the rise. Many will find positions as text retrieval specialists within corporations or government where expertise in the application of electronic search technologies applies. Electronic news retrieval services in journalism, law, and medicine will continue to proliferate.

Education—Academic

The academic world's response to electronic publishing will have a decided impact upon career developments. Predictably enough, the academic world has experienced some technology shock as it confronts the usefulness of automation and its relevance to professional training. Many professional disciplines (graphic arts, journalism, library science, computer science, and arts and sciences) taught at colleges and universities now use electronic publishing tools in some form as a basis of support instruction in labs or the classroom. Even though the automated software programs and tools are sold to universities at significant discounts,, colleges and universities often have limited funds to spread computerized tools around the campus. Often the main focus goes to the computer science department with a sprinkling of resources given to other disciplines. One solution is the consortium or multi-department sharing of limited resources for collaborative goals.

Multidisciplinary Approach

Adopting a multidisciplinary approach to the use of computer resources for electronic publishing and related applications in graphics and industrial design is a solution with a wide range of educational objectives. An example of this approach at work is Mississippi State University's Design Works program. Partially funded by the National Science Foundation (NSF), Design Works combines six components: graphic design presentation, animation, architectural design, interactive dataware, scientific visualization, and virtual environment simulation as a way of meeting a broad range of needs. The funding includes support for fifty Silicon Graphics workstations and advanced applications in animation, technical illustration, SGML text authoring, computer-aided design, and many other applications. What makes the program most attractive is that students from various disciplines:

computer science, graphic arts, liberal arts, architecture, and science are learning and sharing notes in a collaborative environment. By sharing resources within a multidisciplinary model, universities will enrich the work force of the future in ways that go beyond the technology itself and address head-on the real issues of knowledge sharing.

The multidisciplinary approach to electronic publishing technologies also helps instructors spread the knowledge burden intramurally so no one department is left to explain all concepts in related technologies, for example, platforms, user interfaces, programmable setups, and strategies related to electronic publishing, design graphics, and scientific visualization. These obstacles can be formidable if the instructors and administrators from various disciplines do not think through the long range goals and the deployment of evolving technology for study, use, and analysis. It serves to overcome an instructor's objection to teaching fundamentals of computer technology while shortchanging a curriculum in the "prime" discipline of graphic arts, journalism, communications and the rest. Institutions of higher learning, technical schools, vocational schools, and even secondary educators should seek multidisciplinary approaches to the teaching of evolving technologies. If the focus upon the technological capabilities is too narrow (only seen from the eyes of a graphic artist, for example) then the students will not grasp the potential application of such tools.

Learning More about Developments

To learn more about developments in the field it is useful to read publications, attend trade shows, join special interest groups, and make use of on-line resources in job hunting. All of these resources help to keep abreast of technological developments.

The periodicals can be divided into two categories: generic trade journals in computers, networking, and information management and more specific periodicals in electronic publishing, multimedia, and graphic arts. Some periodicals listed can be found in book stores and news stands, but others are available by subscription only.

Generic trade journals include:

- ➤ Byte Magazine
  One Phoenix Mill Lane
  Peterborough, New Hampshire 03458
  603.924.9281

- ➤ Beyond Computing
  590 Madison Avenue
  32nd Floor
  New York, NY 10022
  212.745.6326

- The Internet Business Journal
  Strangelove Internet Enterprises
  208-A Somerset St. E.
  Ottawa, Ontario, K1N 6V2
  Canada
  613.565.6641
- Open Systems Today
  600 Community Drive
  Manhassett, NY 11030
  516.562.5222
- PC Magazine
  One Park Avenue
  New York, NY 10016
  212.503.5255

Specific trade journals related to computer assisted publishing include:

- PC Graphics and Video
  859 Willamette Street
  Eugene, OR 97401-6806
  503.343.1200
- The Seybold Reports
  428 E. Baltimore Pike
  PO Box 976
  Media, PA 19063
  215.565.6864
- New Media Magazine
  901 Mariner's Island Boulevard
  Suite 365
  San Mateo, CA 94404
  415.573.5131
- Publish
  PO Box 5039
  Brentwood, TN 37024-9816
  800.685.3435
- Graphic Arts Monthly
  PO Box 17533
  Denver, CO 80217-0533
  800.637.6089
- Communication Arts
  PO Box 10300
  Palo Alto CA 94303-9979
  800.258.9111

- SGML Newswire
  (available on the Internet)
  sgmlinfo@avalanche.com
  Avalanche Development Company
  947 Walnut Street
  Boulder, CO 80302

- Imaging Magazine
  1265 Industrial Highway
  Southhampton, PA 18966-9839
  800.677.3435

- The Gilbane Report
  Publishing Technology Management, Inc.
  University Place
  124 Mt. Auburn Street, Suite 200N
  Cambridge, MA 02138
  617.576.5700

- High Color
  21 Elm Street
  PO Box 1347
  Camden, ME 04843
  207.236.6267

- Electronic Publishing & Printing
  29 N. Wacker Dr.
  Chicago, IL 60606
  312.726.2802

In addition to periodicals there are many trade shows and other user group conferences. Of special interest are the Seybold, Online Publishing, Documation, and the Association of Information and Image Management (AIIM) conferences. The Seybold conferences are held in three geographic locations (San Francisco, Boston, and Paris) each year and each conference features a variety of electronic publishing and desktop publishing products in its expositions, as well as offering educational seminars and programs for attendees. The AIIM conference concentrates on exhibiting products in document image management. AIIM has consistently underlined the importance of workgroup collaboration in document management. The Documation conference focuses on document management technologies and standards related to document management. The Online Publishing conference specializes in developments related to electronic books and periodicals for commercial and in-house publishers. More information about schedules and logistics of these conferences can be obtained by contacting:

> ➤ The Association of Information and Image Management
> 1100 Wayne Avenue
> Suite 1100
> Silver Spring, MD 20910-5699
> 800.477.2446
>
> ➤ Documation Conference
> Graphic Communications Association
> 100 Daingerfield Road
> Alexandria, VA 22314
> 703.519.8160
>
> ➤ Seybold Conference
> ZD Expos
> PO Box 5855
> San Mateo, CA 94402
> 800.433.5200
>
> ➤ Online Publishing Conference
> Graphic Communications Association
> 100 Daingerfield Road
> Alexandria, VA 22314
> 703.519.8160

Electronic publishers can stay abreast of developments in standards by joining the Electronic Publishing Special Interest Group (EPSIG). In addition to publishing the EPSIG *News*, the EPSIG organization sponsors many training seminars and lecture series related to SGML for commercial, scholarly, and technical publishing. The SGML SIGhyper: SGML Users' Group Special Interest Group on Hypertext and Multimedia is a valuable resource for developments in standards for hypermedia. For more information contact:

> ➤ EPSIG
> PO Box 25707
> Alexandria, VA 22313-5707
> 703.519.8184
>
> ➤ SGML SIGhyper
> TechnoTeacher, Inc.
> 1810 High Road
> Tallahassee, FL 32303-4408
> 904.386.2562

PUTTING DESKTOP MAGIC TO WORK FOR YOU

Tips for career growth and change are not easy to summarize but, at the risk of oversimplifying the obvious, what follows is an attempt to highlight ideas that may have some enduring significance.

First of all, try to think through objectives and set specific career goals. How are selected professions being affected by technical developments in electronic publishing? Focus on performance standards for work in your chosen profession. The technology should help you to achieve the highest level of performance possible. Don't settle for the lowest common denominator of practice. If professionalism has meaning, it can be held up to standards espoused by professional associations, universities, as well as corporate and government norms.

Second, get training where you can and put the training into practice. Magic cannot work without discipline. Become as knowledgeable as possible in a specific technology important to your field. If you cannot afford to subscribe to trade magazines or attend trade shows, use local libraries as a resource and write to vendors of products to supply you with information that can bring you up to date with technical developments. If you are trying to acquire more knowledge about a particular software program, seek out knowledgeable specialists who may work near you. Consider joining user groups who share ideas about dimensions of a product you may be starting to use. Apply the knowledge you acquire and do not hesitate to share the knowledge with fellow workers. Fostering the learning organization in small ways contributes to a better workplace.

Third, if you don't have access to a computer at work, save money to purchase one. If you cannot afford a new computer, shop around for a used one. There are plenty of attractive deals around. As soon as you can afford it, invest in selected programs in a field of interest. Get your hands dirty by learning how to use the programs and evaluate their importance to your career objectives.

Fourth, if you are seeking a new job, take advantage of on-line job announcements. There are on-line jobs posted on the Internet by various groups, and many of them relate to professional careers in fields deeply affected by electronic publishing. For example, the Internet has many News Groups that post jobs such as the misc.jobs.offered News Group. There are, of course, many off-line listings of jobs available. Make good use of information resources in universities, colleges, business and trade schools.

Finally, all workers who expect career changes as a result of acquired skills need to exercise patience. Even though the trade journals hype up the pace of rapid technical changes, official job titles change slowly. Don't expect every corporate, government, or academic institution to embrace the message of change or even understand why change is necessary. The evolution of career change is uneven, because patterns of work relating to the creation, distribution, and management emerge slowly. Some changes give individuals the opportunity for new careers which may be a surprise to readers who assume that automation axiomatically eliminates jobs. New technology in and of itself is not responsible for job displacement, although some job deskilling and displacement does occur based upon business decisions. Changes in work patterns (including job displacement) are social and economical, not technical, decisions.

Unfortunately, we cannot explore critical issues such as compensation for value added to labor in this work. It is also difficult to be enthusiastic in periods of corporate downsizing and short term thinking. If we are looking for light on the shores of darkness, try to envision the opportunities afforded by electronic publishing as an invitation to a renaissance of creative exploration. Navigating new worlds and uncharted territories is as close as our desktop. The magnitude of change in communications owing to electronic publishing can be as significant as the invention and spread of the printing press. In time, there will be many social, economic, and political changes that will evolve with new communication technologies. If we care about communication and the dignity of labor that nourishes it, we can foster creative and practical uses of electronic publishing technology as we work, educate, create, and publish.

Bibliography

Ahearn, Hally. "SGML and the New Yorker Magazine," *Journal of the Society for Technical Communication* (Second Quarter—May 1993): 210–218.
Barrett, Edward ed., *Text, ConText, and HyperText, Writing with and for the Computer.* Cambridge, MA: MIT Press, 1988.
Benzon, William and Friedhoff, Richard. *Visualization: the Second Computer Revolution.* New York: Abrams, 1989.
Blair, David C. *Language and Representation in Information Retrieval.* New York: Elsevier Press, 1990.
Brandon, Joel and Morris, Daniel. *Re-engineering Your Business.* New York: McGraw Hill, 1993.
Brandell, William "SGML Keeps the Flow in Workflow." *LAN Times* (February 22, 1993): 1; 86.
Bryan, Martin. *SGML: An Author's Guide.* Reading, MA: Addison-Wesley, 1988.
Comer, Douglas E. *Internetworking with TCP/IP: Principles, Protocol, and Architecture.* Englewood Cliffs, NJ: Prentice Hall, 1991.
Cote, Raymond and Diehl, Stanford. "Searching for Common Threads." *Byte* (June 1992): 290–305
Crane, Gregory. "Hypermedia and the Study of Ancient Culture." *IEEE Computer Graphics and Applications* (July 1991): 45–50.
Cronin, Mary J. *Doing Business on the Internet: How the Electronic Highway is Transforming American Business.* NewYork: Van Nostrand Reinhold, 1994.

Cronk, Randall. "Unlocking Data's Content." *Byte* (September 1993): 111–120.

Csenger, Michael C. "Electronic Document Management: The 21st Century Mail Sorter." *Information Week* (June 21, 1993): 58–60.

Davidow, William and Malone, Michael, *The Virtual Corporation.* New York: Harper Collins Publishers, 1992.

Davidson, W.J. "SGML Authoring Tools for Technical Communication." *Journal of the Society for Technical Communication* (Third Quarter—August 1993): 403–409.

Foley, James, Van Dam, Andries, Feiner, Steven, and Hughes, John. *Computer Graphics: Principles and Practice,* Reading, MA: Addison Wesley, 1991.

Gebhardt, John and Henderson, Lofton. "The New Computer Graphics Metafile Computer Standard." *CALS Journal* (Fall 1993): 43–63.

Gerwirtz, David. *Lotus Notes Revealed!*. Rucklin, CA: Prima Publishing, 1994.

Goldfarb, Charles F. *The SGML Handbook.* Oxford: Oxford University Press, 1990.

Goldfarb, Charles F. "HyTime: A Standard for Structured Hypermedia Interchange." *CALS Journal* (Summer 1992): 49–54.

Goodman, Danny. *The Complete HyperCard Handbook.* New York: Bantam Computer Books, 1988.

Grantham, Charles E and Nichols, Larry D. *The Digital Workplace: Designing Groupware Platforms.* New York: Van Nostrand Reinhold, 1993.

Hammer, Michael. "Reengineering Work: Don't Automate, Obliterate." *Harvard Business Review* (July-August 1990): 104–109.

Hammer, Michael & Champy, James. *Reengineering the Corporation.* New York: Harper, 1993.

Hansen, Rebecca. "Document Management and Databases—What's the Relationship?" *The Gilbane Report on Open Information and Document Systems* (July 1993): 2–16.

Hayes, Frank "SGML Comes of Age." *UnixWorld* (November 1992): 99–100.

Heim, Michael. *Electric Language: A Philosophical Study of Word Processing.* New Haven: Yale University Press, 1987.

Henderson, Lofton and Mumford, A.M. *The CGM Handbook.* Academic Press, June 1993.

Herwijnen, Eric van. *Practical SGML.* Norwell, MA: Kluwer Academic Publishers, 1990.

Holzgang, David A. *Understanding PostScript Programming.* San Francisco: SYBEX, 1988.

Horn, Robert. *Mapping Hypertext.* Waltham, MA: The Lexington Institute, 1991.

Horton, William. K. *Designing and Writing On-Line Documentation.* New York: John Wiley and Sons, 1991.

Hsu, Meichun and Howard, Mike. "Work-Flow and Legacy Systems."*Byte* (July 1994): 109–116.

Hunt, Craig. *TCP/IP Network Administration.* Sebastopol, CA: O'Reilly & Associates, Inc. 1992.

Karney, James. "SGML: the Quiet Revolution." *PC Magazine* (February 9, 1993): 246.

Kieran, Michael. *Desktop Publishing in Color.* New York: Bantam, 1991.

Kiesler, Sara and Sproul Lee. *Connections: New Ways of Working in the Networked Organization.* Cambridge, MA: MIT Press, 1991.

Koulopoulos, Thomas M. "Coping with Transformation in the Age of Empowerment." *Modern Office Technology,* (April 1993): 15–23.

Krol, Ed. *The Whole Internet User's Guide & Catalog.* Sebastapol, CA: O'Reilly & Associates, Inc. 1992.

Lanham, Richard A. *The Electronic Word: Democracy, Technology, and the Arts.* Chicago: University of Chicago Press, 1993.

Lipton, Russell. *Multimedia Toolkit.* New York: Random House, 1992.

Locke, Christopher. "The Dark Side of Document Image Processing." *Byte* (April 1991): 193–204.

Locke, Christopher. "Making Knowledge Pay." *Byte* (June 1992): 245–252.

Locke, Christopher. "Foundations for Document and Information Management." *Datapro Workgroup Computing Series:Strategies & LAN Services* (July 1992): 1–12.

Lu, Cary. "Publish it Electronically." *Byte* (September 1993): 94–109.

Malamud, Carl. *Stacks, Interoperability in Today's Computer Networks.* Englewood Cliffs, NJ: Prentice Hall, 1992.

May, Thornton A. "Know Your Work-Flow Tools." *Byte* (July 1994): 103–108.

Mitchell, William J. Liggett, Robin, and Kvan, Thomas. *The Art of Computer Graphics Programming: A Structured Introduction for Architects and Designers.* New York: Van Nostrand Reinhold, 1987.

Murray, Philip. *From Ventura to Hypertext.* Knowledge Management Associates, 1991.

Nelson, T. *Literary Machines.* Swarthmore, PA: Nelson, 1991.

Nielson, M. Gregory, Voegle, Keith, and Collins, Brian. "Introduction to 'An Annotated and Keyworded Bibliography for Scientific Visualization.'" *IEEE Computer Graphics and Applications* (July 1992): 23–24.

Opper, Susanna and Weiss, Henry Fersko. *Technology for Teams, Enhancing Productivity in Networked Organizations,* New York: Van Nostrand Reinhold, 1992.

Partridge, Craig. *Gigabit Networking.* Reading, MA: Addison Wesley Professional Computing Series, 1993.

Pea, Roy. "Learning through Multimedia." *IEEE Computer Graphics and Applications* (July 1991): 58–66.

Penzias, Arno. *Ideas and Information.* New York: Simon and Schuster, 1989.

Piersol, Kurt. "A Close-Up of OpenDoc." *Byte* (March 1994): 183–188.

Reinhardt, Andy. "Building the Data Highway." *Byte* (March 1994): 46–74.

Reinhardt, Andy. "Managing the New Document." *Byte* (August 1994): 91–104.

Reynolds, Louis and DeRose, Steven."Electronic Books." *Byte* (June 1992): 263–268.

Ribarsky, William. "Navigating the Data Flood." *Byte* (April 1993): 129–135.

Rose, Marshall T. *The Simple Book: An Introduction to Management of TCP/IP-base internets.* Englewood Cliffs: NJ: Prentice Hall, 1991.

Schrage, Michael. *Shared Minds: the New Technologies of Collaboration.* New York: Random House, 1990.

Schriver, Karen A. "Quality in Document Design: Issues and Controversies." *Journal for the Society of Technical Communication* (Second Quarter—May 1993): 239–258.

Schwartz, M. F., and Tsirigotis, P.G., "Experience with a Semantically Cognizant Internet White Pages Directory Tool." *Journal of Internetworking: Research and Experience* (March 1991): 23–50.

Shushan, Ronnie, Wright, Don, and Birmele, Ricardo. *Desktop Publishing by Design.* Seattle: Microsoft Press, 1990.

Smith, Joan. *The Standard Generalized Markup Language.* London: British National Bibliography Research Fund; Dover, NH: Longwood Publishing Group, 1986.

Sosinsky, Barry. *Beyond the Desktop.* New York: Bantam ITC Series, 1991.

Stein, Richard Marlon. "Browsing Through Terabytes." *Byte* (May 1991): 157–164.

Stockford, James ed. *Desktop Publishing Bible.* Indianapolis, IN: Howard W Sams & Company, 1990.

Stone, Summer. *On Stone: The Art and Use of Typography on the Personal Computer.* San Francisco: Chronicle Books, 1992.

Templeton, Brad. "The Newspaper of the Future." *The Internet Business Journal* (November 1993): 6–7.

Thurow, Lester. *Head To Head: The Coming Battle with Japan, Europe, and America.* New York: William Murrow, 1992.

Tolhurst, William A., Pike, Mary Ann, Blanton, Keith A., Harris, John R. *Using the Internet.* Indianapolis, IN: Que, 1994.

Udell, Jon. "Start the Presses." *Byte* (February 1993): 116–134.

Vaskevitch, David. *Client Server Strategies.* San Mateo, CA: IDG Books, 1993.

Whitehead, Nigel. *Hypertext and Hypermedia, Theory and Applications.* Reading, MA: Addison-Wesley, 1991.

Weber, Jack. "Visualization: Seeing is Believing." *Byte* (April 1993): 121–128.

Wright, Haviland. "SGML Frees Information." *Byte* (June 1992): 279–284.

Glossary

Access Management A document management function normally associated with file locking mechanisms for document check-in and check-out.

API (Application Program Interface) A programming or scripting language used with an application to satisfy specific user requirements.

Application Program A computer program that allows users to perform tasks such as word processing or image editing.

ASCII (American Standard Code for Information Interchange) A baseline standard (ANSI X3.4 – 1977) for computer data interchange. ASCII provides a scheme for computer encoding of characters in seven bits with an extra bit used for parity check.

ATM (Asynchronous Transfer Mode) A data communications technology based upon the dynamic allocation and transfer of information organized into 53-byte structures called cells.

Attribute An SGML (Standard Generalized Markup Language) markup qualifier indicating a property or condition of a textual element such as confidentiality or reference identification.

Benchmark Testing The use of specific tests to measure the performance of a product against a pre-defined set of criteria.

Bento Format A compound document storage format developed by Apple. Used in conjunction with the OpenDoc standard.

Binary A coding method that uses zeros and ones as the basis of computer hardware/software communication.

Binary Large OBject (BLOB) Text or other data objects stored in mixed media databases.

Bit The smallest unit of information (a one or a zero) in a binary system. Eight bits comprise a byte.

Bitmap A non-vector representation of picture elements on a video screen.

Browser A user interface tool to aid the search for information through hypertext, hypermedia, and multimedia documents.

Byte The standard unit of computer communication. One byte is comprised of eight bits, a combination of zeros and ones.

CCITT Group 4 A standard raster graphic fax format also used for the neutral exchange of images.

Cell A 53-byte structure consisting of 5 bytes of header information, including an addres, and 48 bytes of data.

CDA (Compound Document Architecture) A compound document scheme developed by Digital Equipment Corporation (DEC) for the neutral exchange of document information including form and content.

CD-R (Compact Disk Recorder) Drive An optical device used to record information on blank compact disks.

CD-ROM An acronym for Compact Disk, Read Only Memory. CD-ROMs are optical data storage media for computers, comparable to audio CDs, and can hold an average of 550 – 650 Megabytes of data.

CD-ROM Drive A device used to read and replay computer information from pre-recorded CD-ROM disks.

Cello A browser for the Internet and client of the World Wide Web (WWW) created by the Cornell Legal Research Institute. Cello can be used to navigate documents composed in hypertext markup language (HTML).

CGM (Computer Graphics Metafile) An ISO standard (8632) graphic file format for picture capture, storage, retrieval, transmission, and interchange.

Client A software application module or object that uses the services of another module. In distributed computing, client workstations use the services of file servers, communication servers, print servers, etc.

Compound Documents A document that combines different data types (text, graphics, sound, video, animation) into a single file.

Computer Aided Publishing The use of compatible computer hardware and software tools to create documents with computers.

Conversion software A program for converting a file from one storage format to another.

Database Publishing The process of extracting and formatting information stored in databases via software programs.

Data Exchange Format (DXF) A file format supported by the AutoCAD computer aided design program and used for the conversion and interchange of graphic information.

Demand Printer A network printer that collates and reproduces multiple copies of a document at very high speeds upon user command.

DDIF (Digital Document Interchange Format) A platform independent encoding language that can account for a document's structural parts and stylistic presentation information.

Desktop A metaphor for the organization of space on a computer video display terminal.

Desktop Publishing A set of software programs and editors that enable the composition, layout, formatting, and printing of documents from a desktop microcomputer (hence the name).

Document Analysis The process of breaking down a document's structure and content.

Document Image Management A system that digitizes indexes, sorts, routes, stores, retrieves, and displays documents, including pictorial material.

Document Management A set of tools and software modules for administering, assembling, storing, retrieving, indexing, revising, and reusing document information.

DPI (Dots Per Inch) Base unit of measure of the resolution or density of an image calculated according to the number of micro dots clustered to form an impression of a letter or picture.

DSSSL (Document Style Semantics and Specification Language) An ISO standard for vendor neutral document layout and format processing that applies toboth printed and electronic documents.

DTD (Document Type Definition) The definition of markup rules for a class of SGML documents.

Electronic Libraries Large scale digital document repositories with automated facilities for resource discovery and distribution of documents over networks to end users.

Electronic Publishing A generic term for computer-generated documents that can be distributed to computer displays, retrieved through an on-line service, stored in a database, recorded on optical media, or printed via compatible hardcopy devices.

Elements A logical or structural unit of a document such as a paragraph, section, or chapter.

Entity A unit of information that may be referred to by a symbol to identify special characters sets and data or externally stored files including references to graphics and other data types.

ERDs (Electronic Reference Documents) A synonym for hypertext and hypermedia documents.

Ethernet A high speed data link protocol used extensively in Local Area Networks (LANs).

File Compression A process of mathematical algorithms in the form of a computer program used to reduce file size and manage file storage and transmission. Typically used to archive large images or for transportation of data via floppy disks or modem.

File Formats The various results of encoding text, graphics, or other data in computer applications. Some typical file formats include TIFF, GIF, DOC (a word processing document format) and ASCII.

Font A complete assortment of one type and size of a typeface.

Format The design of a document for print or video display viewing, often a pattern to be used repeatedly.

FTP (File Transfer Protocol) An Internet protocol for transferring files from one computer to another.

Full Text Index A system for sorting and indexing every word in documents excluding "noise" words such as "the" and "an."

Fuzzy Search An automated means of finding near matches for search terms.

Groupware A software system for workgroups allowing them to communicate and manage information more effectively.

GUI (Graphical User Interface) The deployment of bitmapped graphics and window management to enable human dialog and interaction with computer operating systems and application programs.

Halftone The screened, converted result of a continuous-tone photo into equally-spaced dots of varying sizes used for print reproduction.

HPGL (Hewlett Packard Graphics Language) A vector-based graphics language used primarily for Computer-Aided Design, or Drafting (CAD) and Computer-Aided Manufacturing (CAM) plotters. Also used as a file format when storing graphics.

Hypermedia A linked set of data types including text, graphics, video or other information that can be accessed in a non-linear progression.

Hypertext Text linked to other text or other text documents for viewing and authoring via a computer display.

Hypertext Markup Language (HTML) A language closely related to SGML that is used for markup of documents that can be viewed via World Wide Web (WWW) clients such as Mosaic and Cello.

HTTP (Hypertext Transfer Protocol) A protocol used by the Internet's World Wide Web (WWW) servers enabling information providers to distribute HTML documents.

HyTime (Hypermedia/Time-based Structuring Language) An ISO standard language for the structured representation of hypermedia information.

Icon A small, usually static, pictorial representation of a computer function, application, or command on a display screen.

Imagesetter A device that records high resolution type and graphic information on photographic film or resin-coated paper.

IGES (International Graphics Exchange Specification) A standard file format for computer aided design (CAD) and computer aided engineering (CAE) drawings.

Interoperability The technical solutions that allow disparate computing devices, networks, and applications to work together. Associated with open system computing.

Internet A worldwide network of computer systems.

JPEG (Joint Photographic Experts Group) A still picture file format and compression standard. The JPEG algorithm can reduce the size of graphic images by 25:1.

Kerning The typographical control of spacing for any given letter pair used to make the letters within typeset words fit together better.

LAN (Local Area Network) A high speed data transfer network connecting computers and peripherals over relatively short distances.

Macro A compiled set of instructions, data, or symbols that helps eliminate the need to rewrite the instructions everytime a user executes that same set of instructions.

Markup Markup can be specific or descriptive. Specific markup contains instructions related to a document's appearance. Descriptive or general markup indicates the logical contents of documents such as title, heading, paragraph, list, table, and the like.

Memory A temporary storage area for computer information; normally associated with Random Access Memory (RAM).

Middleware A multiservice resource for user administration, messaging, and database replication for enterprise or workgroup computing applications including document management.

Mouse A small hand-held device electronically represented by an on-screen pointer, used to select and manipulate objects in a graphical user interface or windowing system.

MPEG (Motion Picture Expert Group) A compression standard for motion video images.

Mosaic A browser developed by the National Center for Computer Applications (NCSA) used for discovery and retrieval of information on the Internet's World Wide Web (WWW).

Multimedia The use of mixed media (text, graphics, film, animation, and audio) in an interactive computer presentation.

Navigation A metaphor for information discovery in hypertext and hypermedia systems. The process of using paths, links, and assorted visual and structural cues in viewing electronic reference, hypermedia, or hypertext documents.

Object Oriented Programming A software technique based upon a theory of reusable data and code. A means of activating data (a) by situating programming procedures (called objects) within the data itself; (b) by telling objects to act when messages are sent from other objects; and (c) supporting reuse of code by allowing objects to inherit properties of related objects.

Object Oriented Database A uniform method of representing all parts of a data collection as objects and storing those objects, each of which contains information about itself, in a controlled base.

ODA (Open Document Architecture) An ISO standard (8613) for document interchange that includes a provision for the exchange of formatting information.

OLE (Object-Linking and Embedding) A compound document technology developed by Microsoft that allows users to work within a single document while manipulating data from several executing applications or editing systems.

On-line Services Commercial information services such as CompuServe or Prodigy Interactive Personal Service that offer subscribers access to information resources, interest group forums, and information sharing opportunities.

OpenDoc A vendor-neutral compound document standard that allows for the use of multiple editing systems and the embedding of different content types in a single file.

Open System Any of the various solutions proposed by consortia and standards associations to introduce interoperability in heterogeneous computer systems and networks.

Operating System The software that manages overall computer input, output, security, user administration, file storage, and utility services.

Optical Character Recognition (OCR) A process embedded in a software program, which recognizes alphanumeric characters in a graphic format and converts the characters into editable text.

Page Description Language The codes, usually built into a program or hardware device, that allows an output device to render on-screen information into hardcopy on pages.

Page Layout Programs Software that helps automate the design and format of typeset pages.

Parser A program used to determine whether a document's markup and structure conform to the rules of a DTD.

Pica A typographical unit of measurement. One pica equals twelve points. Six picas approximately make one inch.

Pixel Short for picture element. A pixel is the smallest unit of information of an input device (scanner) or output device (laser printer or display monitor).

Point The smallest unit of measure of type. There are approximately 72 points to the inch.

Popup Menu A graphical menu that appears suddenly (or "pops up") usually when a button is pressed on a pointing device while using an application program.

PostScript A page description language created by Adobe Systems, Inc. PostScript has become the standard language used by laser printers and imagesetters in connection with desktop publishing.

Program A combination of instructions that direct computer actions.

Proximity Search A technique used to find terms relative to their position in a document.

Relational Database A database with a tabular structure of rows and columns and data values featuring virtual views of data relations. A query language is used to access information from the database.

Revision Control Software A system for tracking document changes and updates.

ROI (Return on Investment) In electronic publishing, the rate at which the cost of technology is offset by productivity enhancements in the workplace.

Scanner An optical device that reads visual information and converts it into a digital format for use in various software applications, such as image editing or OCR.

Server A computer program or device that provides services to workstations. There are variety of servers for files, communications, electronic mail, the World Wide Web and so forth.

SGML (Standard Generalized Markup Language) An international standard (ISO 8879) for the neutral markup of document structure and content.

Software A set of programs used to direct computer actions.

SPDL (Standard Page Description Language) An ISO standard for representation of pages to output devices.

Structure Search The use of document structure and structural markup to find information.

Synonym Search A technique in document search and retrieval of using a list of synonyms to locate documents.

System Administrator A person responsible for overseeing the well-being of a computer system.

Table Generator A program that automatically generates tables with adjustable columns, rows and cells for inclusion in documents.

TCP/IP (Transmission Control Protocol/Internet Protocol) A suite of communication protocols providing transport and network services.

TELNET A protocol providing terminal services in the Internet suite of protocols.

Template A reusable set of predefined options encompassing the overall format or structure of a document.

TIFF (Tag Image File Format) A raster file format developed by a consortium of companies and frequently used as a means of interchange of images from one system to another.

Typeface A group of characters set apart by a particular design, such as Helvetica.

Type Size The specification that allows a designer or typographer to indicate how large or small type on a page should be. Type is usually measured in points. See also "point".

Type Slant A type description that indicates the optical direction of type. A typeface can have either an italic font or oblique font, both of which slant to the right. Type almost never slants to the left.

Type Weight The optical heaviness of type; a "book" or "normal" weight is used for standard body text. "Bold" is a thicker body weight and is darker in appearance. Other weights include "thin," "semibold," "medium," and "ultra".

Typography The practice of selecting, setting, arranging, and printing type.

URL (Uniform Resource Locator) An emerging standard for specifying objects on the Internet including files and newsgroups.

Versioning A technique for automating the control of document updates in document management systems.

Visualization The use of computer graphics to clarify patterns of information.

WAIS (Wide Area Information Servers) A combined user interface and information protocol that allows a user's workstation to act as a librarian and collection agent.

WAN (Wide Area Network) Data communication supported by various technologies over a geographical distance.

Window A bitmapped work area on a computer display screen.

Workgroup Publishing The use of computer assisted publishing in a networked, multi-user environment. A subset of workgroup computing. Concerned with the collaboration of authors, editors, designers, subject matter experts, document analysts, and others who collaborate via computers for the creation and distribution of documents.

Workflow Management The automation of distributed work processes to be performed by members of a team using desktop tools. As it applies to documents and document management, the automation of processes for the creation, editing, review, and approval of documents.

World Wide Web (WWW) A world wide distributed hypertext/hypermedia system available on the Internet. The system was conceived by the European Institute for Particle Physics (CERN) in Switzerland as a means to distribute and share information.

WYSIWYG An acronym that stands for "What you see is what you get." A type of graphical user interface in which the display representation is a reasonable facsimile of what the output would be from a hardcopy device, such as a laser printer.

Index

A
Acrobat, 80, 100, 190, 270
A.D.A.M., *Animated Dissection of Anatomy for Medicine*, 203
Aliasing, 121
Animation, 75, 211, 284
Animation specialist, 318
API, application program interface, 27, 164, 262
ArborText, 28, 67, 91, 164, 321
Archival, 256
ASCII, American National Standard Code for Information Interchange, 50, 52, 105, 141, 184, 250, 270
ATM, Asynchronous Transfer Mode, 23, 177, 219
Authorware Professional, 205
AutoCAD, 143, 146

B
Bezier curves, 122
B-ISDN, Broadband Integrated Service Data Network, 23, 182
Bitmapped, 120, 141, 215, 250
BLOBS, binary large objects, 163
Boolean search, 248
Browse, 198, 220
Buttons, 198, 205

C
C and C++ language, 26, 312
CAD, computer aided design, 119, 153, 201
CADLeaf Batch, 149
CALS, Computer aided Acquisition and Logistics program, 58, 143, 189, 232
CCITT, Consultative Committee on International Telegraphy and Telephony, 139, 215, 233
CDA, Compound Document Architecture, 186, 189
CD-ROM, Compact Disk—Read Only Memory, 12, 19, 68, 102, 159, 188, 195, 203, 218, 284
CGM, Computer Graphics Metafile, 31, 138, 142, 156, 149, 215, 233, 275
Clip art, 130
Collaboration, 101, 200, 208, 226, 238, 245, 267
Color imaging, 285
Color models—RGB, CMYK, CIE, 137
Compound document, 153, 189, 246, 252, 290
Compression (lossless and lossy), 133, 211, 214, 257
Copyright, 130, 216, 221, 344

366 Index

CorelDraw, 32, 120
CRT (cathode ray tube) monitors, 21, 133

D
Databases, 158, 188, 217, 221, 249, 259
Database publishing, 32, 161, 285
Datalogics, 67, 91
DDE, Dynamic Data Exchange, 154
DDIF, Digital Document Interchange Format, 189, 270
DeBabelizer, 141
Default, 83
Demand printer, 23, 60
DEN, document enabled networking, 263
Design, 63, 72, 81, 83, 99, 213, 310
Desktop publishing, 286
Desktop tools, 243
Dialog box, 47, 205
Digital video, 203, 211
Document analyst, 287, 309
Document image processing, 33, 246, 250, 287
Document instance, 111
Document interchange standards, 30, 185, 189
Document management, 53, 241, 288, 290, 313
DTD, document type definition, 29, 51, 68, 103, 149, 163, 157, 219, 249
DynaBase, 79, 163, 165
DynaText, 58, 78, 149, 165, 206
DXF, drawing interchange file, 143

E
Editor, 319
Electronic document, 292
Electronic document designer, 310
Electronic publishing, 7, 51, 74, 99, 182, 203, 260, 268, 307
E-mail, 158, 181, 214, 253, 258
EPS, Encapsulated PostScript, 31, 140, 142
Erasable optical drives, 20
ERD, electronic reference documents, 171, 192, 195
Ergonomics, 273
Ehternet, 22, 175

F
FastTAG, 32, 91, 187
Fidelity Investments, 53, 231

file format, 49
FileVision, 150
Financial reports, 52, 231
FolioViews, 78
FORTRAN language, 26
FOSI, Formatting Output Specification Instance, 91, 97, 189
FrameMaker, 30, 47, 86, 89, 120, 162

FTP, File Transfer Protocol, 177, 181

G
GIF, Graphic Interchange Format, 142
Graphic artist, 325
Graphics software, 295
Graphic primitives, 122
Groupware, 157
Grids, 81, 124
GUI, Graphical User Interface, 26, 43
Guide Viewert, 36

H
Help desk specialist, 201, 247, 319
HiJaak, 140
HTML, Hypertext Markup Language, 181
HPGL, Hewlett Packard Graphics Language, 31, 140
Hypercard, 166
Hyperlink buttons, 76, 119, 217
Hypermedia, 29, 57, 141, 195, 213
Hypertext, 197, 219, 260, 292

I
Icons, 122, 205
IconAuthor, 29, 205
IETM, Interactive Electronic Technical Manual, 57, 29, 215
IGES, Initial Graphics Exchange Specification, 139, 143, 215
IMA, Interactive Multimedia Association, 216
Indexing, 201, 210, 222, 244, 247, 296
InfoAccess, 78, 206
Information research specialist, 319
Information superhighway, 182, 221
InStEd, Interactive Style Sheet Editor, 80
Interactive display, 76, 195
Interactive video specialist, 218

I

Interfaces, 44
Interleaf publishing program, 30, 49, 53, 65, 67, 78, 85, 97, 120, 159, 162, 166, 185, 255, 310
Internet, 22, 179, 219, 297, 333, 350
Interoperability, 171, 193
Interpress, 35
IRV, International Reference Version, Standard 646, 50
ISO, International Organization for Standardization, 50, 185

J

Journalists, 332

K

Knowledge workers, 318

L

LANs, Local Area Networks, 22, 174, 183, 219, 253
Laser printer, 23, 58
LEXIS, (NEXIS), 169, 180, 221, 248, 319, 332
Libraries, 150, 221, 242, 250, 291, 344
Linking, 198, 208, 213
LISP language, 27, 166, 312
Logitech, 19
Logos Intelligent Machine Translation System, 167
Lotus Notes, 34, 67, 158, 164

M

MacDraw, 139
Macintosh windowing system, 45
Mac operating system, 26
MacPaint, 120
Marquandt Corp., 18
Markup, 108, 111
Mentalix, 132
Menus, 47, 205
Metafile, 142
Meta-language, 142
MetaLink, from InterCAP Graphics Systems, 146
Microsoft Windows, 15, 44
Microsoft Word, 49, 67, 84, 126, 180, 185, 188
MIDI, Musical Instrument Digital Interface, 25, 212
MIS, Management Information Systems, 53, 263

Modem, 172, 178
Modular systems, 252
Motif windowing system, 45, 58, 65
Motion video interface, 25
MPEG, Motion Picture Expert Group, 214
MS-DOS, Microsoft Disk Operating System, 14, 26
MS-Windows, *see* Microsoft Windows, 45
Multilingual document translation software, 35, 167
Multimedia, 29, 195, 216, 298, 316, 334

N

Navigation, 198, 221
Networks, 175, 201, 218, 244, 251
Nodes, 198
NTSC, National Television Standard Committee, 25

O

OBEX, Object Exchange, 155
OCR, Optical Character Reader, 250, 298
ODMA, Open Document Management Architecture, 185, 262
OLE, Object Linking and Embedding, 154
OmniMark, 111
On-line services, 180
OODBSm, Object Oriented Database Systems, 259
OpenDoc, 155, 166
Open Look windowing system, 45, 49
OSA, Open Scripting Architecture, 166, 206
OSF, Open Systems Foundation, 46

P

PageMaker publishing program, 30, 81, 85, 120, 142, 159, 180
Paintbrush, 120
PAL signal, 25
Parsing, 207, 259
PASCAL language, 26
PCDATA, Parsed Character Data, 105, 109
PCL, Page Control Language, 35
PDF, Portable Document Format, 190
PDL, Page Description Language, 34, 100, 144
Perseus Project, 56, 57
Periodicals, 346

Index

PICT, 139
Pixels, 120, 132, 141, 203
PostScript, 34, 80, 144
Printers, 58, 60
Print production manager, 336
Publication programmer, 310
Publishing system administrator, 328

Q
Quark, 91
Quattropro, 154

R
Rainbow DDT, 103, 109, 188
RAM, Random Access Memory, 13
Raster image, 120, 134, 142
RDBMS, Relational Database Management Systems, 259
Reengineering, 223, 234, 261
Retrieval, 296
Reusable information, 107, 214, 229, 242, 310
RTF, Rich Text Format, 31, 270

S
Scalability, 272
Scanners, 18, 58, 131, 250, 300
Screen capture, 129
Security, 255
SGML, Standard Generalized Markup Language, 29, 32, 50, 67, 79, 91, 97, 100, 149, 163, 181, 185, 187, 206, 233, 249, 259, 262, 270, 275, 288, 301, 309, 349
Shamrock Coalition, 262
Silicon Graphics INDY workstation, 16, 27
Sonart document, 152
Smartleaf, 161
Snapshot, 129
Softquad, 67, 69, 78, 91, 109, 149, 206
Standards, 261
STEP, Standard for the Exchange of Product data, 143, 144, 159
Sun Microsystems, 46
System administrator, 328

T
Tag, 68, 105, 189, 208, 249
Tape drives, 20

TCIF, Telecommunication Industry Information Forum, 236
Technical illustration software, 306
Technical writers, 329
Telecommuting, 341
Template, 83, 91, 103
Text search, 37, 248, 262
Text retrieval, 247, 262
TIFF, Tag Image File Format, 31, 138, 142, 149

U
UNIX operating system, 26, 46, 313
U.S. Department of Defense Mil Sld 28001, 104

V
Vector graphics, 120, 215
Vendors, 284
Ventura Publisher, 84, 159, 180, 188
Version control, 253, 256
Videodisk, 21, 203, 213, 218
Visualization software, 146, 149, 304

W
WANs, Wide Area Networks, 22, 253
Word processing specialists, 330
WordPerfect publishing program, 30, 31, 47, 67, 155, 185
Word processing tools, 28
Workflow, 113, 201, 223, 244, 250, 253, 257, 265, 269, 290
Workgroups, 9, 40, 71, 113, 157, 206, 226, 238, 244, 260, 267
Workgroup suites, 156, 305
Workstation computers, 12, 15
Worldview Press, 97, 100, 190, 206
WORM, Write Once/Read Many, 20
Writer, 323
WWW, World Wide Web, 181, 219

X
Xerox Corporation, 14, 60, 67
X-Window system, 46

Z
Zoom in, 127

DATE DUE

AUG 28 1996			
SEP 2 2 1996			
AUG 27 1998			
SEP 1 1 1998			
MAY 3 1 2001			
JAN 2 9 2001			

DESKTOP MAGIC